Spatial Processes and Form

Social Areas in Cities

Volume I
Spatial Processes and Form

Edited by

D. T. HERBERT

Senior Lecturer in Geography,
University College of Swansea

and

R. J. JOHNSTON

Professor of Geography,
University of Sheffield

JOHN WILEY & SONS

London · New York · Sydney · Toronto

Library of Congress catalog card number 75-30943
ISBN 0 471 99417 0

Photosetting by Thomson Press (India) Limited, New Delhi
Produced by offset lithography by Unwin Brothers Limited
The Gresham Press, Old Woking, Surrey
A member of the Staples Printing Group

To

Our Parents and Families

Preface

Urban studies have become extremely popular in the last two decades and a number of important books have been produced on topics such as those dealt with here. Indeed, the social geography of the city is almost an overpopulated field and some brief justification for yet another book might be valuable. Our view is that no book to date has provided an overall synopsis at a high level. Introductory texts give brief mention to many, if not all, of the topics covered here, but most take a fairly narrow viewpoint, based often on only one of the social sciences whose methods and findings are relevant to work on social areas—sociology, economics, psychology and political economy. Hence, we have attempted to cover the whole field of urban studies as they refer to social areas and decided that the best way to face this daunting task was to commission a series of chapters by experts on particular aspects of the field, who would be able to approach their particular topic within a wider view of the whole. Each author is, of course, responsible for his own view; our responsibility was for the structure, for the selection of authors to provide chapters for the various slots and for the final production.

The book was conceived as a whole but for practical reasons is published in two separate volumes. This procedure has not presented any problems of substance as the structure was already organized into distinctive parts. In this first volume the aim is to comprehend those processes at work within society which are related to social stratification and to demonstrate their expression as residential differentiation. As divisions exist within society, so they are mirrored in urban residential patterns and the links between social space and social geographical space are provided by the mechanisms of the housing market and the process of residential mobility. This detailed view of the patterns and their underlying processes provides the basis from which behaviour and life styles can be examined in the second volume. Urban residential pattern is then regarded as the environmental stimulus which in its turn underlies many social problems in the city and has prompted policy reactions. In their individual parts, the two volumes stand as detailed examinations of distinctive approaches to city structure; in combination they comprise a comprehensive urban social geography.

In assisting us with this task, we are grateful to the contributors for agreeing to participate, for their acceptance of our idiosyncrasies and for their good-natured reaction to our badgering. To our publishers, who launched us on the project and guided us through it, we are grateful for all their help: and the final product would never have emerged without the work of a number of secretaries and technical staff, notably at the Universities of Canterbury and Sheffield for Ron Johnston and at the University College of Swansea for David Herbert, but also at all of the institutions at which our contributors are or were based. Preparation of the index and assistance with proof reading has been by Ann Barham, to whom we owe a great debt.

D. T. HERBERT
R. J. JOHNSTON

Summary of Contents of Volume II

Spatial Perspectives on Problems and Policies

1 Sociospatial Differentiation and the Use of Services
C. J. Thomas

2 Political Behaviour and the Residential Mosaic
R. J. Johnston

3 Social Deviance in the City: A Spatial Perspective
D. T. Herbert

4 Urban Education: Problems and Policies
D. T. Herbert

5 Cities in the Mind
T. R. Lee

6 Community, Communion, Class and Community Action: The Social Sources of the New Urban Politics
Colin Bell and Howard Newby

7 Deprived Areas and Social Planning
Elizabeth Gittus

List of Contributors

DR D. T. HERBERT	*University College of Swansea*
PROFESSOR R. J. JOHNSTON	*University of Sheffield*
PROFESSOR J. S. ADAMS	*University of Minnesota*
DR F. W. BOAL	*Queen's University, Belfast*
PROFESSOR L. S. BOURNE	*University of Toronto*
KATHLEEN A. GILDER	*University of Minnesota*
PROFESSOR R. A. MURDIE	*York University, Ontario*
PROFESSOR D. W. G. TIMMS	*University of Stirling*
PROFESSOR J. E. VANCE, JR.	*University of California, Berkeley*

Contents

Preface vii

General Introduction: Social Areas in Cities 1
D. T. Herbert and R. J. Johnston

VOLUME I

An Introduction: Spatial Processes and Form 5
R. J. Johnston and D. T. Herbert

1 Social Bases to Social Areas 19
D. W. G. Timms

2 Ethnic Residential Segregation 41
F. W. Boal

3 Institutional Forces that Shape the City 81
J. E. Vance, Jr.

4 Housing Supply and Housing Market Behaviour in Residential Development 111
L. S. Bourne

5 Household Location and Intra-urban Migration 159
John S. Adams and Kathleen A. Gilder

6 Residential Area Characteristics: Research Methods for Identifying Urban Sub-areas—Social Area Analysis and Factorial Ecology 193
R. J. Johnston

7 Spatial Form in the Residential Mosaic 237
R. A. Murdie

Index 273

General Introduction: Social Areas in Cities

D. T. Herbert and R. J. Johnston

A feature of current industrial-urban societies is their awareness of, and wish to remove, many of the social and economic problems with which they are beset. This is not to say either that the current problems are necessarily worse or more widespread than they have been in previous decades or that there have not been major efforts in the past to rectify perceived social ills. But there can be little doubt that societies as a whole, through their democratic institutions, have only recently accepted major responsibility for ensuring individual well-being and adequate living standards for all citizens. Many factors have undoubtedly contributed to the production of this welfare orientation, among them the effects of major industrial recessions, notably that of the 1930s, and the increasing concentration of populations into large urban areas, which has made the problems readily apparent to most citizens. Furthermore, these societies have largely succeeded in creating economic systems which can produce sufficient wealth for their needs—though not necessarily at the right time, so that economies move through booms and slumps—thus making it possible to direct attention towards the problems of ensuring a reasonably equitable distribution of this wealth.

The present book is mostly concerned with those countries usually considered as being in the 'advanced industrial' stage of economic development—in Daniel Bell's (1974) term, they have post-industrial societies. And these countries, notably those of the 'English-speaking world', also have among the highest levels of urbanization in the world. Their social problems are very apparent, therefore; they are widely publicized and, increasingly, pressure groups are developing the strength to force recognition of the need for immediate solutions. Such problems cover a wide range, including environmental pollution and dereliction, the difficulties of relocating large numbers of people and a variety of social ills, most of them related to some form of economic and social deprivation.

Because most of the population in the relevant countries live in cities and towns, these problems appears as urban problems. It is necessary, however, to distinguish between two types of problem, which can briefly be called those in the city and those of the city. The former are general problems, which appear to be urban simply because of the population concentration; presumably they would continue to exist even if the population distribution were markedly altered. Problems of the city, on the other hand, are those which are created by the pattern of population concentration. Identification of the types of problem being approached is important, of course, since the nature of their origin will strongly influence the effectiveness of various programmes proposed for their solution. For example, air pollution from motor cars will continue whether or not the population of London and New York is scattered through their relevant hinterlands, assuming constant rates of car use. But a dispersed population distribution will probably not cause localized, very dangerous high pollution levels, like those currently experienced in Tokyo. Thus, the correct policy to be pursued depends on whether all pollution is to be removed (presumably by improved engine design), which is the solution to the problem in the city, or whether only the peak pollution areas are to be countered, which is the problem of the city (that presumably can be tackled by settlement pattern strategies).

This separation of problems in and of the city is important to the purpose of the present book. Poverty, for example, is apparent in many cities, but is probably largely a problem in the city. It may be concentrated there, to a greater extent than is the total population, because un- and underemployed people are attracted to the potential urban opportunities, but the existence of the urban places does not create un- and underemployment. Tackling the cause of that problem, and several others, requires attention to the economic structuring of the society rather than to its spatial structuring; indeed, population concentration may partially alleviate it because it is more easily perceived and serviced in large cities.

There are many social problems which it is believed, at least by some persons, are of the city. Again, two different types are identified. The first are those which are a function of urban size and, often by implication, the consequent high population densities which accompany large size. There is a large literature associating social problems to these factors. Much of it has been at least partially discredited. Numerous scholars writing earlier in this century, for example, contrasted the 'romantically-idealized' community life of small settlements to the impersonality, competitiveness and anomie of towns and cities (Wirth, 1938, summarizes much of this), but later writers have shown this notion of a rural-urban continuum to be false, suggesting few real differences between settlements of different size along these lines. Nevertheless, many problems are still related to city size, although associations may often be interpreted as causal inferences. (There is, for example, considerable evidence that larger cities have higher crime rates, but are the latter a product of city size or merely a reflection of the greater attractions of large cities for potential criminals?) As a consequence, there is a considerable literature on the question of optimum city sizes, much of it related to economic issues but some to matters of social concern (Richardson, 1973).

The second type of social problem of the city comprises those which are brought about, it is believed, by the internal spatial structure of the urban place. Within cities, the major spatial characteristic is separation of land uses.

Arguments relating to economic efficiency are often advanced to account for this separation; its continuance is ensured in most places since it is a major canon of town planning practice. In most cities, the main land use consists of residences and associated open spaces. Within this, too, there is spatial separation of different population groups, according to a number of criteria, such as age, social class and race.

To many people, this spatial separation of population groups is a cause of, or at least it exacerbates, a number of social problems. Certain districts housing a particular type of family, for example, might be seen as 'breeding places' for crime and delinquency or other social diseases; the segregation of children of different social classes, both at local play and in the neighbourhood school, is thought to be not in the best interests of the development of social and academic skills; and there are many claims that some groups are able to obtain better public facilities and services for their areas than are others. To counter these perceived problems, there is a similarly large literature proposing the solution of social problems through alterations to the spatial structure, notably by the production of 'socially-mixed, balanced neighbourhoods' (Etherington, 1974).

Evaluation of such a policy, and of others which involve manipulation of the spatial structure of residential areas, such as the building of facilities to foster a 'community spirit', requires understanding of the present situation. This involves several stages. The first demands comprehension of the social and economic processes which have produced, which maintain and, at times, which alter the residential mosaic. This social patterning of the city, with the separation of various land uses and population groups, comprises an integration of many overlapping and interdependent forces, so that although the general morphology of a city may be almost immediately decipherable the details are complex and require much unravelling. Secondly, it is necessary to understand the interactions between an individual and his or her environment, so that the role of the social milieu as an influence on behaviour can be identified. Again, this is not a simple task, for the environment may reinforce a person's predispositions or it may counter them; the latter is the most interesting from our point of view, and so information on predispositions and on the relative strength of environmental forces in different conditions is required. All of this is very demanding on data and on technical expertise; it may involve working with a few individuals at depth or it may, as in the scale of analysis focused on in this book, involve analysis and interpretation of data referring to large population aggregates. The last stage involves appreciation of the probable effects of various planning schemes and of the side-effects which will almost certainly ensue. These must be assessed against the overall goals of social planning to see whether the ends justify the means and whether the ends are desirable in themselves.

The structure of these books of essays follows the sequence just outlined. In volume one, we focus on the social map of the city, how it comes about, how we can identify it and what shape it has. Attention is largely directed at generalities relevant to those countries that form what we have already termed the 'English-speaking, advanced industrial world', notably Australia, Canada, Great Britain, New Zealand and the United States, although some mention is made of France, Germany and Sweden also. In volume two, the focus swings to the other two stages, with chapters on the role of the sociospatial environment as a structural effect on behaviour and on some of the possible programmes which emphasize social change through spatial change. No firm conclusions are drawn. Whether the end is desirable and justifies the means is in large part a function of personal ideology, although academic work can, and must, attempt to inform and then to participate in the decision-making about desirable ends.

REFERENCES

Bell, D. (1974). *The Coming of Post-Industrial Society*, Heinemann, London.

Etherington, W. (1974). *The Idea of Social Mix: A Critical Biography*, Research Paper no. 7, Centre of Environmental Studies, London.

Richardson, H. W. (1973). *The Economics of Urban Size*, Saxon House, New York.

Wirth, L. (1938). 'Urbanisation as a way of life'. *American Journal of Sociology*, **44**, 1–24.

An Introduction: Spatial Processes and Form

R. J. Johnston and D. T. Herbert

A visitor to any city in the 'English-speaking world' will soon discover, as he moves through its streets, that its residential districts vary in their character. Some of the differences will be very obvious, such as the type of housing and its density, and the upkeep of homes, gardens and public spaces. Others will be apparent from the number, distribution and types of shops in the area (Johnston, 1966a; Pred, 1963), or the stripped cars at the kerbside (Cybriwsky and Ley, 1974a) and the graffiti on available walls (Cybriwsky and Ley, 1974b). And the inhabitants themselves may give some further clues to district character, not only by their language or accent but also by whether children play on the street, for example, or whether mothers walk or drive to the neighbourhood shops. From such observations, the visitor may be able to compile a social map of the city. He may attempt to analyse it, noting perhaps that the 'better class', clearly more expensive housing areas are on the higher land, upwind of the city's noxious industries. And if he has strolled around enough cities, he may make comparisons, leading perhaps to generalizations about urban residential structure.

Why do all these differences, and many others, exist? Why does San Francisco have a Chinatown and a Nob Hill, London a Hampstead and a Bethnal Green, Toronto a Kensington and a Rosedale, and Sydney a Paddington and a Vaucluse? (Even tiny Temuka, in New Zealand, has a Sodtown!) In more general terms, why do urban populations get sifted out according to such apparent criteria as social class, to produce ghettos and middle-class suburbia, slums and exclusive, high status areas? The first volume of this book is designed to answer these questions, providing accounts of the various social and economic mechanisms which produce a mosaic of districts of different character and of the spatial form which these districts take.

SOCIAL CONFLICT AND SOCIAL AREAS

The basic answer to all of these questions is that the urban landscape is a mirror reflecting the society which maintains it. Within the countries with which this book is mainly concerned—Australia, Canada, Great Britain, New Zealand and the United States—the capitalist ethic is strong. Competition is a major feature of social and economic life; the strongest prosper, but the majority achieve reasonable levels of social well-being and paternalistic humanitarianism provides for many of those who suffer various deprivations. The result is a complex system of social inequalities: the many-faceted division of labour, which accompanies and promotes industrialization and the consequent urbanization, creates groups which differ not only in their role within the economic system but also in wealth, in status and in power, the three rewards for success in the competition. Many groups with different amounts of these three rewards (and also aspirations for further rewards) can be identified. The most commonly recognized are those usually called the social classes, whose number varies, according to problem and analyst, from two upwards.

Social classes are continually in conflict over the rewards of the urban-industrial economic system. Those who have high levels of status, wealth and power aim to maintain their relative position—perhaps even to improve it—and to ensure that their next generation enjoy similar privileges. Others, with lower levels, may similarly aspire to more, for themselves and for their successors. Given that the amount available for all is limited, then competition for as large a portion as before is ensured. In the ultimate analysis, each individual (or individual household) will be fighting for himself, but the weight of numbers induces him to compromise by joining a group which participates in collective bargaining. The conflict is then between two or more groups, usually for either wealth (as with trade unions and employers) or power (between political parties, for example).

Conflict between groups for the rewards which society produces spills over into competition, and occasionally conflict, for places in which to live. The basic need is for a dwelling, but of considerable importance to many households is the location of that dwelling within the city. Their concern may be with access, with obtaining a home whose location minimizes the financial and mental costs of journeying to work and to shop, to school and to leisure. But it is more likely that their concern will be with the character of the neighbourhood, the people who live in it and the social milieu which they create. People thus compete to live in various social environments, as part of the more general conflict between social groups, and, once they have obtained a home in the environment of their choice, they will act to maintain its character, to protect their investment. This conflict is for 'goods' which they themselves do not produce, though they will produce them for others; such 'goods' are generally termed externalities (Cox, Reynolds and Rokkan, 1974; Mishan, 1967). Positive externalities are benefits produced by the actions of others, in this case others living or owning property nearby. An example would be the property value appreciation resulting from the rezoning of adjacent land from rural to residential use. Negative externalities are the opposite—costs or disadvantages induced by the actions of others. Pollution from an incinerator or a reduction in the area's status by the sale of a home to a lower-class family than is presently typical there are examples of these.

In the conflict over externalities, people may have greater freedom to act as individuals in the choice of where to live than they have in, say, wage bargaining, but they are probably much better able to assess the general character of a neighbourhood's population before they move in to it than they are that of particular households. In this way, social groups are important in the residential location decision. These groups are competing for three types of positive externality and thus, by implication, to avoid the contradictory negative externalities (Cox, 1974; Downs, 1970). The first is that the public behaviour of their neighbours should be consonant with their own, thereby assisting the household in maintaining its social position. As Duncan Timms points out in the first chapter of this volume, this neighbourhood consonance is frequently viewed as particularly important in the socialization process for children, who are generally restricted in their spatial range to the immediate environs of the home. Their models of behaviour are provided by their immediate family, by their school and by others they meet. The first are under parental control; the second and third are provided by the local area, in that most children attend one of the nearest schools to their home. Other behaviour models, for all household members, may also be provided by the neighbourhood—these form a focus of the second volume of this book—and belief in their existence may play a part in determining where people choose to live.

The second externality for which people compete is status and social advancement, which can be obtained through interaction with people who can assist, perhaps unknowingly, in the achievement of social aspirations. Many parents, for example, hope that their children will 'improve' their status by marrying into what they perceive as a more desirable social group, and they may believe that by living among such a group they give their children a greater chance for such advancement (Beshers, 1962). Such a belief is based on an assumption that social networks are spatially defined, that social contact is a function of spatial propinquity. This assumption has been widely debated and tested in the sociological and geographical literature. There is evidence, for example, that brides and grooms are likely to live near to each other before their marriage (Peach, 1974; Ramsøy, 1966), that people have more to do with their near-neighbours than with those who live only a few dwellings away (Johnston, 1974) and that many suburbs comprise a large number of local informal groupings (e.g. Whyte, 1960). In discussion of such findings, however, others claim that the major determinant is not spatial distance but social distance (e.g. Gans, 1972; note that many of the studies, such as that by Ramsøy already quoted, held social distance constant in order to demonstrate a spatial influence), while a further group argue that the city is one large social network in which, because of ease of movement and communications, distance is irrelevant (Craven and Wellman, 1974; Webber, 1964). The validity of this claim may depend on the social group to which it refers (as Pahl, 1970a, points out).

As Timms emphasizes (chapter 1), however, perhaps the important point with regard to the development of social areas is not whether propinquity does influence contact patterns but that people apparently believe that it does. The current debate in many of the social sciences between the positivist viewpoint which uses 'objective facts' to reveal social reality as the basis of theory and the phenomenologist/idealist approach which emphasizes that the important theory is that of the actor not that of the observer is clearly illustrated here. Timms points out (as also does Terence Lee in a chapter in volume two of this book) that a city's residents have their own 'mental map' of their home area on which they base their actions. A considerable amount of research has been conducted into the nature of these maps in recent years (Downs and Stea, 1974). Within cities, it seems that residents have their own representations of the social pattern (Johnston, 1971b), which probably are not stored in the traditional map form. Furthermore, there tends to be considerable agreement, not only among residents but also between residents' maps and those produced by positivist investigations (Johnston, 1973a), which suggests that research can proceed with some certainty that the analyst's description of the social map of the city is somewhat akin to the resident's own impression of it.

The final positive externality for which households compete concerns property values. In a capitalist society, which permits and indeed often encourages property dealing, the status of an area is invariably reflected in the value of its homes and its land. The higher the price of a home in a certain area, the more socially exclusive that area can be, given that wealth and status rewards are distributed together. But, furthermore, properties are frequently viewed not only as homes but also as investments, especially when there is little confidence in other forms of investment—such as industrial shares. Land and property become major speculative investments, and their owners (often their occupiers also) will act to protect their capital by fighting for positive externalities—those which will enhance values and increase price inflation—and against negative externalities (see Harvey, 1973).

In the conflict for these externalities, the competitors do not begin on an equal footing. Those with wealth and power are better able to manipulate the socioeconomic and political systems which distribute—sometimes unintentionally—the externalities. New intra-urban motorways, for example, tend to depress property values in their path and environs, so 'threatened' groups fight against such potential negative externalities, with different levels of success (see Seeley and Wolpert, 1974; Wolpert, Mumphrey and Seeley, 1973). Indeed, the techniques of cost-benefit analysis, as applied in the Fourth London Airport site investigations, for example, tend to favour those who have most to lose in absolute rather than relative terms (Adams, 1970).

As a consequence of this unequal competition, those with most wealth and power are able to dictate the form of the urban residential mosaic, allocating other groups to areas outside that which their 'social and economic superiors' normally visit. Thus, it is the rich and the powerful who can command the most desirable building sites (see Mann, 1965). The residential pattern of the city is only one, albeit the major, example of this; holiday resorts, commuter villages, second-home settlements, and even rural recreational areas, are all socially segregated. As Duncan Timms makes clear in his chapter, there is a number of different ways of studying these patterns and their attendant social processes, with the choice between them largely one of scale of analysis.

Territories and minority groups

The patterns and processes discussed in the previous section can be considered as a particular case of the operation of territoriality. This concept has recently been introduced to the study of human behaviour by ethologists such as Ardrey (1966, 1970) and Morris (1967). In brief, the ethologist's argument is that a genetic trait in all birds and animals (including man) produces a need to define a 'home area' or territory, the defence of which is the 'territorial imperative'. In the large city, privately owned housing clearly represents such territory and its defence through rights to repel trespassers is widely applied. This, however, is but one example of territory at the human scale. Social groups, it is suggested, also define their own territories, to which they retreat in order to form their own 'social world' which excludes individuals and groups with whom they wish no contact. Sennett (1973) suggests that people choose to live among others whose behaviour is conformal to their own rather than face the uncertainties of living among different groups in *terra incognita*. Thus, cities comprise a whole host of overlapping territories, many of them actively defended (Suttles, 1968).

Within urban societies, it is the minority groups—often recent immigrants—which most commonly operate a territorial system, sometimes in concert with similar acts by their so-called 'host' society, but often even where the latter does not exist. As Fred Boal makes extremely clear in chapter 2, such territorial behaviour can be a consequence of segregation to fulfil one or more of a number of functions, such as group defence, intergroup avoidance and cultural protection. Each of these processes may produce a similar spatial pattern. To uncover the pattern involves investigation at the correct scale, which may involve the plotting of individual residences (e.g. Scott, 1955) rather than the rapid mapping of ward or census tract data. Boal differentiates, in their formative processes, between colonies, enclaves and ghettos, but points out that no study of pattern alone can distinguish between the last two.

The spatial segregation of minority groups presents perhaps the most extreme example of the operation of social separateness mechanisms within urban areas, resulting in a pattern which is often akin to the caste system of certain pre-industrial societies. Using the terminology previously employed, undoubtedly the main reason for this is that many groups within an urban society perceive greater potential negative externalities from spatial mixing with members of ethnic minority groups than from a similar degree of mixing with other socioeconomic status groups. Thus potential 'invasions' by, for example, Negroes into presently white residential areas in American cities may create much more reaction from the incumbents than a similar 'invasion' by other groups. The reaction may vary from retreat (Rose, 1970) to avoid conflict, through accommodation (Molotch, 1969), to conflict by defence of the status quo. (Orbell and Uno, 1972, have recently adopted Hirschmann's (1970) theory of exit, loyalty and voice to model such a situation.)

Nevertheless, it may be that in all cases the resulting segregation is greater than the actors desire. In a recent ingenious simulation game, Schelling (1974, p. 53) has demonstrated that 'a moderate urge to avoid small-minority status may cause a nearly integrated pattern to unravel and highly segregated neighbourhoods to form'. An individual living in a grid-plan estate may require that: if he has one neighbour he must be of the same social group as himself; if he has two, one must be of his group; if he has three, four or five, two must share his group membership; and if six, seven or eight, three similar neighbours are needed. An initial random distribution will probably be integrated. A few will not have sufficient neighbours of the right group and so they will move; after the moves segregation will almost certainly be the norm, with most people having more neighbours of the relevant group than are needed to keep them content. Thus, segregation is an accentuation of social needs, given spatial constraints; to what extent it fuels social conflict, as propounded in Sennett's (1973) theory, is an interesting topic for further study.

HOUSING MARKETS

The discussion so far in this introduction has largely concerned the social bases for residential location choice, although, as pointed out in the discussion of property values, these social criteria involve economic considerations also. Focus on these social processes alone presents a distorted picture of the operations which produce the urban residential mosaic, however. It assumes that individual households and social groups are the only actors involved in the drama, when in fact there are also many stage managers and directors involved: indeed, many of the actors—individual households—may have little choice at all in where to live. This point was made several years ago by Form (1964), but has only recently been taken up to any extent, notably by Harvey (1973, 1974). Apart from the households, operation of the land and property markets involves such others as the estate agents who arrange transactions, the banks and mortgage agencies which finance them and the governments which legislate for them and then raise taxes (rates, stamp duty, etc.) on their value. The households may be primarily interested in a home as a place to live in and only slightly in its value as an investment, but to the other actors it is the latter function only which is important—except for some governments which see housing programmes as a major component of social policy.

Examples of the role of these various institutional groups in the housing market are manifold; in most of them, it is clear that they often determine spatial patterns that best meet their own ends rather than responding to the latent demands of their customers. Thus, it is in estate agents' interest to ensure that property values in various parts of the city are maintained, and if possible increased, since they are paid a commission which is a fixed percentage of the selling price. To do this, American estate agents, most of whom personally conduct would-be buyers around potential purchases, have clearly-defined spatial sub-markets within their home cities and direct different types of client to areas which provide a social match to the customer's characteristics (Palm and Caruso, 1974). They may act to change the social milieu of an area, however, if this is likely to be to their advantage. The 'gentrification' process—the upgrading of lower status, inner city areas—now operating in many large cities (Hamnett, 1973) is an example of estate agents and financial institutions, notably building societies, operating in this way for their own gain (Williams, 1975).

National governments are often very powerful influences on urban residential structure. Their policies towards protection of tenants, for example, may have an important effect on the number of furnished rooms available, and therefore on their rents and their standards. In Britain, successive governments in the present century have encouraged, to a greater or lesser extent, the provision of public housing for rent (Robson, 1975), whereas in other countries, owner-occupation through purchase in the 'free market' has been preferred. In New Zealand, for example, very cheap loans are available for a wide spectrum of income-earners and public housing forms a very small proportion of the total (Johnston, 1972, 1976).

The growth of large cities, with their complex division of labour and over-lapping social and economic networks, has led to a rapid movement away from the paternalistic rural and small-town societies in which it was incumbent on an employer to provide housing for his workers. The free market system which replaced this workplace–residence link created vast inequalities, however, so that governments have had to move in to regulate the activities of financial institutions. In a wide-ranging survey of this government–institutional interaction Jay Vance outlines (chapter 3) how different societies on opposite sides of the North Atlantic have fashioned different accommodations. He illustrates the continuing interplay of three crucial factors in determining the consequent housing market pattern:—those of land availability, the development of transport technology, and ideology.

Although it is usually national governments which fashion the ideology, local governments are often involved in putting it into practice. Town planning legislation, involving not only the determination of available space (Hall and coauthors, 1974) but also the particular spatial configuration of land uses, is almost invariably operated by local governments, as is the public housing policy. The latter, in particular, can vary considerably in its intensity and effects between administrations (Boaden, 1971; Dye, 1966; Harloe, Issacharoff and Minns, 1974). Redevelopment of obsolete residential areas, too, may be largely financed by national funds, but its implementation, and hence the groups and areas it affects, is a local function (Duncan, 1974; Hamnett, 1973).

Unravelling the social mosaic of the city involves an understanding of the housing markets and the mosaic of areas which they comprise (Harvey, 1974). Following on from Jay Vance's general survey, therefore, Larry Bourne presents in chapter 4 a detailed assessment of housing market operations in contemporary cities. He shows that these have been studied in a variety of ways: micro-economic models to account for general spatial patterns (see also chapter 7), urban development models which operationalize certain simple assumptions to predict future patterns and behavioural models focusing on the various decision-makers—a sequence which follows the general trends within social sciences in the last two decades. The results, as Bourne indicates, often lead to market failures, to mis-matches between what are supplied and demanded, which again is likely to be a generator of social, and thus spatial, conflict.

THE CHANGING CITY

A major feature of the urban residential pattern of most cities is its constancy, once established, as studies of high status suburbs have shown (Johnston, 1966b, 1969). Despite major changes in the individual occupants, the characteristics of areas tend to remain (Johnston, 1973b; Tryon, 1967), which is a reflection on the efficacy of the market operations. Within this general state of dynamic equilibrium there is change, however, as new housing is added to the stock, obsolete housing is removed and other housing is passed from one social group to another. The nature of such changes is outlined in Larry Bourne's chapter, and some of its implications are discussed in the succeeding one on migration (chapter 5).

One of the major features of the general dynamic equilibrium is that it continues, despite massive population mobility. The extent of such movement is unknown, since fully updated population registers recording all changes of address are rare, and estimates must be made from occasional sample surveys and censuses. Results from the latter are probably conservative estimates of mobility rates, because the questions asked refer to place of residence at two dates rather than all moves in between. Figures usually quoted suggest that about 15–20 per cent. of the population move annually (Simmons, 1968), although some move every year so that a complete turnover every six or seven years is very unlikely (Morrison, 1967).

Migration of this magnitude, within so compressed a space, must be orderly if chaos is not to emerge. The extent of orderliness is captured by the simple question which is the major building block of the chapter by John Adams and Kathleen Gilder (chapter 5): 'Can the migration behaviour of households that move be predicted from information about their origins?'. In answering this, they focus—both in a detailed literature review and in a discussion of a data set recently collected for Minneapolis—on social and spatial constraints, on movement which follows the changes in the housing market, outlined by Bourne, and on imperfections in the adjustment processes of migration. The social and economic constraints are those which require a particular neighbourhood type for movers, allowing them to meet the needs of their move—probably related to space requirements—within an acceptable price range and an accepted social milieu. In a large city, however, a wide range of viable alternatives is usually available to many potential movers, but the number and location of those investigated is constrained by spatial factors. Adams and Gilder point out that most urban residents are able to assess the neighbourhoods in part of the city only—their home sector—and this restricted mental map means that their search space, and hence their move, will probably be over a short distance and oriented along their particular sector (Donaldson, 1973; Poulsen, 1973).

Mobility is great in industrialized societies, not only within their cities but also between them. Until recent decades, most movement was rural to urban, towards the 'streets paved with gold', and our models of urban residential patterns are based on this migration, usually of relatively low status persons (Johnston, 1971a). More recently, however, this stream has been outnumbered by an urban–urban flow, usually of relatively high status persons (hence the term 'the intermetropolitan circulation of elites') whose information spaces for jobs are national, if not international, in scope (Keown, 1971). As Adams and Gilder point out, this pattern has led to the development of new institutions, such as the multi-city estate agent and the 'all-in package move' (see also Packard, 1973). If such a migration stream becomes more dominant, it could lead to a restructuring of the urban system, with each city containing both a mechanism allocating 'locals' to housing and part of a national mechanism allocating the 'spiralist cosmopolitans' to 'organization men suburbs' (Whyte, 1960) in whichever city they are posted to that year.

THE SPATIAL FORM

The city, then, comprises a complex mosaic of residential areas, characterized by both stability and flux. A wide range of processes produces and maintains this mosaic, many of them overlapping so that the areas themselves often gradually merge into each other rather than occupy discrete spatial units. How then can this mosaic be unravelled to provide descriptive information on the urban structure—itself perhaps generative of hypotheses concerning its origins—and inputs for analytical work on the role of the sociospatial environment or other social processes, such as those discussed in volume two of this book? Answers to this question are invariably located in a pragmatic research world, using data matrices compiled for other purposes, because of the immense resources needed to collect all the needed information from primary sources—notably households—in a large city. Such data are usually provided by census authorities and reflect their constraints and conceptions; they often provide only surrogate variables to describe the social and economic processes that produce spatial separation, from which any classifications of social areas are best estimates only.

Two methodologies—social area analysis and factorial ecology—have been developed to manipulate census data for intra-urban small areas, of which the latter, an inductive approach, is now by far the most popular. Both approaches —their methods, their findings and their disadvantages—are discussed in Ron Johnston's chapter (chapter 6). In the general context of social area formation and maintenance, several drawbacks of these approaches must be noted.

Firstly, they deal with population aggregates (usually several hundred households) and thus interpretation faces the issue of the ecological fallacy (Alker, 1969; Robinson, 1950) of making inferences about individuals from data on groups. Yeates (1972) has reported on some useful tests of the validity of making such inferences, with encouraging findings concerning the consonance of individual and area characteristics. Secondly, it must be reiterated that the data used almost invariably refer to 'objective facts' about individuals and households; their occupations and ages are recorded, as are their dwelling types and tenures, but not their social attitudes and aspirations, their social contacts and life styles. Analyses have been made which relate these social attributes of areas to the land uses of various districts (Bourne and Murdie, 1972). In general, however, factorial ecologies focus overwhelmingly on the social and demographic aspects of residential patterning, which undoubtedly accounts for the relative paucity of literature on spatial patterns in housing markets.

Finally, it must again be stressed that the real units employed in such analyses are arbitrarily defined, usually for logistical purposes in census-taking. The social areas defined from them are not communities, therefore, or even neighbourhoods as that term is often used, because of both the absence of any data on social networks and the social irrelevance of many of the boundaries. Recent work has inquired into the relationship between 'real' community boundaries and those imposed in factorial ecologies (Palm, 1973a, 1973b; Stutz, 1974), with disappointing results for those who would interpret the defined social areas in terms of social networks. Of course, many writers on the contemporary city deny the existence of strong local communities (however, see Suttles, 1972), except perhaps in particular areas such as those occupied by minority groups. It may be, therefore, that factorial ecologies index the consequences of particular social processes—notably the relative separation of different social groups to obtain externalities in, for example, status, protection of property values and socialization of children—but do not provide a framework within which social life is necessarily constrained.

All of the discussions so far have been devoid of any mention of spatial scale. Notions of territoriality among social groups and of perceptions of area differences by institutions involved in the housing market suggest reasons for the spatial separation of groups, but make no direct statements about either the size of social areas or their relative location within the city. Where, for example, do the high socioeconomic status households live—in small, exclusive clusters located at random through the city or in one large block at the edge of the built-up area? This general topic has been intensively researched for more than half a century, with much of the work based on the contributions of a distinguished group of Chicago sociologists. Bob Murdie (chapter 7) reviews the three major models of the spatial form of urban residential patterns which this work has produced and evaluates the empirical evidence pro and con in terms of the question: 'What proportion of the variation in social area characteristics can be attributed to each model?'.

CONCLUSIONS

The residential mosaic of the city is brought about by the intersection of a large number of vested interests, most of them selfish and to do with the social and economic welfare of the individual, as he perceives it, rather than the overall welfare of society. The operation of social processes produces social classes. Representation of these as groups along a unidimensional continuum is usually facile, for there are many criteria—wealth, status, power, life style, attitudes, etc.—which can define class membership and many people are members of more than one class. Many of these groups, it seems, aspire to live apart from members of other groups, producing a demand for social areas. This is met by a second set of forces, mostly economic, which creates housing markets that also are spatially segregated, reflecting the economic and social desires of a minority in the population. Meshing the social classes with the housing markets produces a set of housing classes (Pahl, 1970b; Rex and Moore, 1967), comprising groups with different levels of access to the variety of dwellings (by type, tenure and quality) and social areas within the city. A major feature of the housing provision is its longevity, relative to that of its occupants (Jones, 1969), so that often the matching of social classes into housing classes is far from perfect. The consequence of this is that areas of housing stress are created, with the greatest stress being for those social groups with least wealth and power in society: the operation of spatially circumscribed housing markets is a frequent contributor to social inequalities.

The seven chapters in volume one of this book discuss in depth the major social and economic processes that produce housing classes and the spatial form of the city which is the result. Most of the discussion is at the level of general statements with wide applicability, rather than a focus on particular cases and instances of idiographic mechanisms and patterns. There are cross-cultural differences, of course. Several authors (e.g. Gittus, 1964; Robson, 1969) have argued that the importance of public sector housing in British cities so distorts the 'free market' that the Chicago-based models discussed in chapter 7 are irrelevant there (a conclusion which is hard to justify from Robson's own empirical work on Sunderland). This public sector housing may also be a major constraint on the operation of the migration models discussed by Adams and Gilder, but council tenants do move (either by officially organized transfers or personally arranged 'swaps') and the patterns of who applies to move, from where and to what, may well be very similar to those identified in the private housing market. Understanding the city requires general theories, however, which can be applied to and modified in particular situations; the contributions here are chapters pointed towards such general theories.

REFERENCES

Adams, J. (1970). 'Westminster: the fourth London Airport?'. *Area*, **2** (2), 1–9.

Alker, H. R. (1969). 'A typology of ecological fallacies'. In M. Dogan and S. Rokkan

(Eds.), *Quantitative Ecological Analysis in the Social Sciences*, The M.I.T. Press, Cambridge, Massachusetts. pp. 69–86.

Ardrey, R. (1966). *The Territorial Imperative*, Atheneum Press, New York.

Ardrey, R. (1970). *The Social Contract*, Delta Books, New York.

Beshers, J. M. (1962). *Urban Social Structure*, The Free Press, New York.

Boaden, N. (1971). *Urban Policy-making: Influences on County Boroughs in England and Wales*, Cambridge University Press, Cambridge.

Bourne, L. S., and Murdie, R. A. (1972). 'Interrelationships of social and physical space in the city'. *Canadian Geographer*, **16**, 211–229.

Cox, K. R. (1972). *Conflict, Power and Politics in the City*, McGraw-Hill, New York.

Cox, K. R. (1974). 'Territorial organization, optimal scale and conflict'. In K. R. Cox, D. R. Reynolds and S. Rokkan (Eds.), *Locational Approaches to Power and Conflict*, Halsted Press, New York. pp. 109–140.

Cox, K. R., Reynolds, D. R., and Rokkan, S. (1974). *Locational Approaches to Power and Conflict*, Halsted Press, New York.

Craven, P., and Wellman, B. (1974). 'The network city'. In M. P. Effrat (Ed.), *The Community: Approaches and Applications*, The Free Press, New York. pp. 57–88.

Cybriwsky, R., and Ley, D. (1974a). 'The spatial ecology of stripped cars', *Environment and Behavior*, **6**, 53–68.

Cybriwsky, R., and Ley, D. (1974b). 'Urban graffiti as territorial markers'. *Annals, Association of American Geographers*, **64**, 491–505.

Donaldson, B. (1973). 'An empirical investigation into the concept of sectoral bias in the mental maps, search spaces, and migration patterns of intra-urban migrants'. *Geografiska Annaler*, **55B**, 13–33.

Downs, A. (1970). *Residential Segregation by Income and Race*. Hearings before the Select Committee on Equal Educational Opportunity of the United States Senate, 91st Congress, 2nd Session. pp. 2966–2980.

Downs, R., and Stea, D. (Eds.) (1974). *Image and Environment*, Edward Arnold, London.

Duncan, S. S. (1974). 'Cosmetic planning or social engineering?'. *Area*, **6**, 259–270.

Dye, T. R. (1966). *Politics, Economics and the Public*, Rand McNally, Chicago.

Form, W. H. (1954). 'The place of social structure in the determination of land use: some implications for a theory of urban ecology'. *Social Forces*, **32**, 317–323.

Gans, H. J. (1972). *People and Plans*, Basic Books, New York.

Gittus, E. (1964). 'The structure of urban areas'. *Town Planning Review*, **35**, 5–20.

Hall, P., Thomas, R., Gracey, H., and Drewett, J. R. (1974). *The Containment of Metropolitan England*, George Allen and Unwin, London.

Hamnett, C. (1973). 'Improvement Grants as an Indicator of Gentrification in Inner London'. *Area*, **5**, 252–261.

Harloe, M., Ischaroff, R., and Minns, R. (1974). *The Organization of Housing*, Heinemann, London.

Harvey, D. (1973). *Social Justice and the City*, Edward Arnold, London.

Harvey, D. (1974). 'Class-monopoly rent, finance capital and the urban revolution'. *Regional Studies*, **8**, 239–255.

Hirschmann, A. O. (1970). *Exit, Loyalty and Voice*, Harvard University Press, Cambridge, Massachusetts.

Johnston, R. J. (1966a). 'The distribution of an intra-metropolitan central place hierarchy'. *Australian Geographical Studies*, **4**, 19–33.

Johnston, R. J. (1966b). 'The location of high status residential areas'. *Geografiska Annaler*, **48B**, 23–35.

Johnston, R. J. (1969). 'Processes of change in the high status residential areas of Christchurch, 1951–1964'. *New Zealand Geographer*, **25**, 1–15.

Johnston, R. J. (1971a). *Urban Residential Patterns*, G. Bell, London.

Johnston, R. J. (1971b). 'Mental maps of the city: suburban preference patterns'. *Environment and Planning*, **3**, 63–71.

Johnston, R. J. (1972). 'Towards a general model of intra-urban residential patterns: some cross-cultural observations'. *Progress in Geography*, **4**, 83–124.
Johnston, R. J. (1973a). 'Spatial patterns of suburban evaluations'. *Environment and Planning*, **5**, 385–395.
Johnston, R. J. (1973b). 'Social area change in Melbourne, 1961–1966: a sample exploration'. *Australian Geographical Studies*, **11**, 79–98.
Johnston, R. J. (1974). 'Social distance, proximity and social contact'. *Geografiska Annaler*, **56B**, 57–67.
Johnston, R. J. (1976). *The New Zealanders*, David and Charles, Newton Abbott.
Jones, E. (1969). 'Resources and environmental constraints'. *Urban Studies*, **6**, 335–346.
Keown, P. A. (1971). 'The career cycle and the stepwise migration process'. *New Zealand Geographer*, **27**, 175–184.
Mann, P. H. (1965). *An Approach to Urban Sociology*, Routledge and Kegan Paul, London.
Mishan, E. J. (1967). *The Costs of Economic Growth*, Staples Press, London.
Molotch, H. (1969). 'Racial change in a stable community'. *American Journal of Sociology*, **75**, 226–238.
Morris, D. (1967). *The Naked Ape*, McGraw-Hill, New York.
Morrison, P. A. (1967). 'Duration of residence and prospective migration'. *Demography*, **4**, 553–561.
Orbell, J. M., and Uno, T. (1972). 'A theory of neighborhood problem solving: political action versus residential mobility'. *American Political Science Review*, **66**, 471–489.
Packard, V. (1973). *A Nation of Strangers*, Longman, London.
Pahl, R. E. (1970a). *Whose City?*, Longman, London.
Pahl, R. E. (1970b). *Patterns of Urban Life*, Longman, London.
Palm, R. (1973a). 'Factorial ecology and the community of outlook'. *Annals, Association of American Geographers*, **63**, 341–346.
Palm, R. (1973b). 'The telephone and the organization of urban space'. *Proceedings, Association of American Geographers*, **5**, 207–210.
Palm, R., and Caruso, D. (1974). *The Real Estate Industry, Housing Market and Home Search*. Paper to the Association of American Geographers' Conference, Seattle, April 1974.
Peach, G. C. K. (1974). 'Homogamy, propinquity, and segregation'. *American Sociological Review*, **39**, 636–641.
Poulsen, M. F. (1973). 'Intra-urban migration and the measurement of sectoral movement'. *Proceedings, Seventh New Zealand Geography Conference*, 91–99.
Pred, A. R. (1963). 'Business thoroughfares as expressions of urban Negro culture'. *Economic Geography*, **39**, 217–233.
Ramsøy, N. R. (1966). 'Assortative mating and the structure of cities'. *American Sociological Review*, **31**, 773–786.
Rex, J. A., and Moore, R. (1967). *Race, Community and Conflict*, Oxford University Press, Oxford.
Robinson, W. S. (1950). 'Ecological correlations and the behavior of individuals'. *American Sociological Review*, **15**, 351–357.
Robson, B. T. (1969). *Urban Analysis*, Cambridge University Press, Cambridge.
Robson, B. T. (1975). *Urban Social Areas*, Oxford University Press, Oxford.
Rose, H. M. (1970). 'The development of an urban subsystem: the case of the Negro ghetto'. *Annals, Association of American Geographers*, **60**, 1–17.
Schelling, T. (1974). 'On the ecology of micro-motives'. In R. Marris (Ed.), *The Corporate Society*, Macmillan, London. pp. 19–64.
Scott, P. (1955). 'Cape Town: a multi-racial city'. *Geographical Journal*, **121**, 149–157.
Seeley, J., and Wolpert, J. (1974). 'A strategy of ambiguity in locational conflicts'. In K. R. Cox, D. R. Reynolds and S. Rokkan (Eds.), *Locational Approaches to Power and Conflict* Halsted Press, New York. pp. 275–300.
Sennett, R. (1973). *The Uses of Disorder*, Penguin Books, Harmondsworth.

Simmons, J. (1968). 'Changing residence in the city'. *Geographical Review*, **58**, 622–651.
Suttles, G. D. (1968). *The Social Order of the Slum*, University of Chicago Press, Chicago.
Suttles, G. D. (1972). *The Social Construction of Communities*, University of Chicago Press, Chicago.
Stutz, F. P. (1974). 'Interactance communities versus named communities'. *The Professional Geographer*, **26**, 407–411.
Tryon, R. C. (1967). 'Predicting group differences in cluster analysis: the social area problem'. *Multivariate Behavioral Research*, **2**, 453–475.
Webber, M. M. (1964). 'Culture, territoriality, and the elastic mile'. *Papers, Regional Science Association*, **13**, 59–70.
Whyte, W. H. (1960). *The Organization Man*, Penguin Books, Harmondsworth.
Williams, P. (1975). *The Role of Institutions in the Inner London Housing Market: The Case of Islington*. Paper to the Institute of British Geographers' Conference, Oxford, January 1975.
Wolpert, J., Mumphrey, A., and Seeley, J. (1973). *Metropolitan Neighborhoods: Participation and Conflict over Change*, Resource Paper No. 16, Association of American Geographers, Commission on College Geography, Washington, D. C.
Yeates, M. H. (1972). 'The congruence between housing space, social space and community space'. *Environment and Planning*, **4**, 395–414.

Chapter 1

Social Bases to Social Areas

D. W. G. Timms

THE IMAGE OF THE URBAN MOSAIC

The notion of the city as a mosaic of social worlds has become part of the general intellectual imagery with which both social scientists and citizens interpret the phenomena of contemporary urbanism. A concern with the residential differentiation of the urban population is common to investigators from a variety of disciplines. To those working within the traditions of social area analysis and factorial ecology, residential differentiation is a prime focus of attention; to many others, concerned with the understanding of urban social behaviour, residential differentiation is important as a contextual variable. A belief in the significance of residential differentiation informs discussions of crime and delinquency, psychiatric disorder, formal and informal social relationships, educational achievement, social stratification and a wide variety of attitudinal and belief systems. Outside academic circles much of the impetus behind the demands for community power and neighbourhood schools, as well as much of the activity of both planners and residents' associations, reflects a similar belief in the differentiated nature of the urban mosaic. In the United Kingdom, the promotion of community councils as part of the reorganization of local government in the 1970s represents an official recognition, even if somewhat blurred, of a similar conception of the urban system.

Popularity is no guarantee of validity. The images associated with the notion of residential differentiation are powerful in the sense that, like all such images, they predetermine and prestructure attempts to apprehend reality. The validity of the image of the city as a residential mosaic is difficult to disentangle from its acceptance as part of the commonsense order of things, part of the taken-for-granted bases of the folk order. Moreover, as Suttles (1972, p. 4) points out:

> To a large extent the folk models we have for urban communities have become the operating bases for both the urban planner and the citizen selecting a place to live. Our technical, sociological models of the urban community are drawn largely from these folk images and have added to their diffusion and acceptance as realistic or 'scientific' portraits. Both kinds of cognitive maps can become self-fulfilling prophecies which help to tailor the urban landscape into a more discrete and stereotypic pattern.

To establish the validity of the images requires the analysis of the data of residential differentiation and of the implications of residence in one part of the city rather than another for the life-styles and life-chances of the population. To possess significance, the concept of residential differentiation must enter into the explanation of many other phenomena.

THE EXTENT OF RESIDENTAL DIFFERENTIATION

The residential differentiation of the urban population is well documented. Analyses of the residential patterning of groups categorized according to such criteria as colour, nationality and birthplace, religion, socioeconomic status, age and a variety of 'deviant' labels have revealed widespread and distinctive forms of differentiation. Variations in the nature of the data base and in the summary measures used to depict differentiation make rigorous comparisons difficult, but studies utilizing the index of dissimilarity, a measure of net displacement which varies from 0.0—indicating two similar distributions—to 100.0—two completely dissimilar distributions (Taueber and Taueber, 1965, Appendix A), have shown that large proportions of the varying populations which constitute cities in the developed world would need to change their place of residence if all are to share the same general residential pattern.

In an analysis of United States cities, using 1960 data, Taueber and Taueber (1965) show that the median index of dissimilarity between blacks and whites is 87.8 at the city block level and 79.3 at the census tract level. Kantrowitz (1973) demonstrates the continued existence of high index values for European migrant groups in New York forty years after the cessation of large-scale immigration. In 1960, the average index of dissimilarity between northern Europeans and 'native born whites of native parents' is reported as 41.1 at the census tract level, while that between northern and southern Europeans is 51.6. Many individual comparisons reveal considerably higher figures (e.g. 72.9 between Norwegians and Russians). In Brisbane, Australia, data on the residential differentiation of the eight largest immigrant groups in 1961, at the census enumerator's district level, reveal indices of dissimilarity between the Australian-born and the overseas-born, ranging from 10 in the case of those born in the United Kingdom to 68 for those from Greece and 77 for those born in Yugoslavia (Timms, 1969). Very similar findings are reported for other Australian cities (e.g. Jones, 1965). In Belfast, Poole and Boal (1973) calculate an index of 70.9 for the street-by-street segregation of Catholics and Protestants, and point out that this figure is likely to have increased considerably in the wake of the major displacements of population which have accompanied the cataclysmic events since 1969. The continued significance of religious differentiation, especially when combined with other ethnic factors, has also been demonstrated in United States settings (Laumann, 1973).

The extent of residential differentiation exhibited by varying ethnic categories is closely related to the extent of their differentiation in other institutional spheres, such as education and occupation, to the expressed desirability of their association and to such behavioural indicators of association as intermarriage and friendship (Laumann, 1973; Timms, 1969). Similar findings have been reported in studies of the differentiation of socioeconomic status categories (Laumann, 1966). In an analysis of census tract data for eight central cities in the United States, Fine, Gleen and Mants (1971) found indices of residential dissimilarity of 27 between professional and clerical workers, 50 between professional and unskilled manual workers, and 36 between the latter and clerical workers. An analysis of the 1961 residential patterning of five broad occupational categories in Brisbane, Australia, with data at the enumeration district level, shows similar levels of differentiation, with index values of 35 for the dissimilarity between professional and managerial workers and clerical workers, 46 between the professional and managerial group and unskilled manual workers, and 32 between the latter and clerical workers. In a pioneering study, Duncan and Duncan (1955) show that the residential dissimilarity of occupational categories in Chicago closely parallels their social distance and that the most segregated categories are those possessing the clearest rank, i.e. those at the top and the bottom of the socioeconomic scale. In a more detailed examination of the differentiation of occupational categories in the middle of the socioeconomic scale, they are able to demonstrate that clerical workers, who on average earn less than skilled manual workers, are more similar to the other non-manual workers in their residential distribution than are the skilled manual workers. Duncan and Duncan (1955, p. 503) suggest that 'in general, it would appear that "social status" or prestige is more important in determining the residential association of clerical with other white-collar groups than is income, although the latter sets up a powerful cross-pressure'. Similar findings are reported by Tilly (1961). Duncan and Duncan (1955) also find that residential dissimilarity parallels dissimilarity in occupational origins to an even higher degree than it does current socioeconomic status. They offer the hypothesis (p. 503) that this may reflect the fact 'that preferences and aspirations concerning housing and residential patterns are largely formed by childhood and adolescent experiences in a milieu of which the father's occupation is an important aspect'.

Not only do populations living in various sub-areas of the city differ in attributes but so also do they differ in behaviours. Rates of church attendance, attendance at public houses and football matches, visits to the physician and the pawnshop all vary by residential area. So also do patterns of informal association and participation in voluntary organizations, and attitudes to a variety of concerns including education, politics and marriage (see Bell, 1968, for a general review). Concern with the problems of 'skid row' and with other 'deviant areas' reflects the residential variation in official rates of such problem behaviours as suicide, crime and delinquency and psychiatric disorder (see Herbert, 1972, pp. 187–221, for a review). Whether such variations rest upon real differences in the behaviour of those in the problem areas, whether they instead reflect differences in the policing practices of the agencies of social control or, most likely, whether they depend on a combination of the two sets of influences, it remains the case that the urban mosaic is differentiated not just in terms of the social, demographic and economic characteristics of its residents but also in terms of their perceived behaviours.

THE DIMENSIONS OF RESIDENTIAL DIFFERENTIATION

Residential areas differ from one another in innumerable ways. They differ in terms of physical structure and age of development, in geographical position and public reputation, in ownership and political power, in the characteristics of their inhabitants and in a host of associated behaviours and sentiments. In order to interpret this mass of differences, it is necessary to simplify. Only in this way can the actor conduct himself around the city. Rather than stressing the uniqueness of each area, the search instead is for significant similarities. Areas are grouped together on the basis of their similarity, a grouping justified in terms of the significance of the properties in which the similarity is exhibited (see Timms, 1971, pp. 36–47, for an extended discussion). The choice of differentiating properties necessarily reflects the theoretical predilections of the classifier—classification is not a passive activity but an active imposition of order.

The search for the dimensions of residential differentiation is a search for those properties in terms of which neighbourhood variation has greatest significance. Establishment of significance is not, however, an easy matter. Two distinct approaches to residential differentiation have produced two distinct sets of differentiating dimensions. To those who stress a subjective, cognitive map approach to the urban mosaic, the major dimensions of residential differentiation revolve around such concepts as 'reputation', 'respectability', 'security', 'beauty' and 'harmony with nature'. To proponents of factorial ecology and other techniques based on the statistical manipulation and interpretation of small area census data (see chapter 6), the concern is with the  constructs of social rank or economic status, ethnicity and family life-cycle.

The difference between the two perspectives is partly grounded in their choice of data, but, more importantly, reflects a deep-seated difference in philosophy. To those adopting the cognitive map approach, residential differentiation is part of the social construction of reality, an attempt by the city's residents to impose order on reality. To social area analysts and factorial ecologists, on the other hand, residential differentiation is an objective concomitant of industrial urbanization, readily interpretable in terms of positive methodology. Each group of investigators can point to evidence justifying its stand. Those basing their analyses on information collected in national censuses can point to the success of social area analysis and factorial ecology in providing summary descriptions of a mass of data which is, *presumably*, collected because administrators and legislators consider it useful. The stability of the basic social area dimensions of social rank, ethnicity and family life-cycle across a wide variety of data sets has encouraged considerable belief in their validity as general differentiating properties of Western cities and has generated an expanding volume of *a posteriori* theory construction. At the same time, however, proponents of the subjective approach to residential differentiation are able to point out that there is massive support in social psychology and sociology for the proposition that humans act not in terms of some external 'objective' environment but, rather, in terms of the environment as perceived and subjectively interpreted. It is therefore likely to be the case that the symbolic impressions and images which provide the basis for the cognitive maps with which urban residents conceive their habitat are at least as important in guiding behaviour as are the 'facts' collected by the census. In view of this, it is unfortunate that the ready availability of census data has resulted in the great majority of the research on residential differentiation being confined to studies of the external environment.

THE EFFECTS OF RESIDENTIAL DIFFERENTIATION

That residential differentiation exists in the modern capitalist city is indisputable. The significance of the phenomenon for other aspects of human behaviour remains, however, somewhat contentious. The basis for the argument lies in the differing views held concerning the implications of locale for social interaction. On the one hand are those who claim that the combination of high personal mobility and modern communications techniques has rendered the notion of territorial constraints on human association obsolescent. To proponents of this view the concept of community itself becomes devoid of territorial content (e.g. Janowitz, 1967; Webber, 1963). To many ecologists and geographers, on the other hand, location remains a major determinant of interaction patterns and the concept of community is firmly anchored on a territorial base. To believe otherwise, according to Kantrowitz (1973, p. 3):

> . . . is to believe that a random network of varying directions and distances to the people and institutions in which people live the most meaningful parts of their face-to-face lives is only mildly disadvantageous when compared with short walks or automobile or bus rides within a circumscribed area.

Evidence on which to decide the issue is surprisingly hard to come by. Frequently, as in the case of those studies purporting to show the effects of propinquity on the choice of marriage partners (see Ramsøy, 1966, for a review), lacunae in methodology make it difficult to interpret the apparent results. The place of the telephone and the letter in interpersonal contact has largely been ignored in sociological studies of association patterns. The emphasis which Cooley (1929) placed on the face-to-face relationship may have blinded later investigators to the importance of other forms of contact in 'forming the social nature and ideas of the individual'. At the same time, however, further study of interpersonal behaviour has demonstrated the great power of face-to-face contact in the transmission of attitudinal and other emotively laden information, and, for a large proportion of the population, the residential locale remains a major arena for face-to-face contacts. Only a minority of the population leave their residential neighbourhood in order to go to work, while a large proportion—notably the very young and the very old, the infirm and the caretakers—spend the preponderance of their time within a small geographical radius of their dewlling. Most of their behaviours are set within a neighbourhood context and, even if their patterns of association are with actors outside the immediate locale, their neighbours remain a constraint to be reckoned with. Even if they are not seen and not known, the neighbours may still be a powerful source of social influence (e.g. Young and Willmott, 1957, pp. 135–136; see also Keller, 1969).

The contextual implications of residence in one part of the city rather than another are, perhaps, most obvious in the case of children. The differentiation of the urban environment necessarily impinges on the child's opportunities for social learning (Oates, 1974, pp. 129–132). For much of the first decade or so, the great majority of the individual's experiences are gained within close proximity to his home. The local area provides the base for informal play-groupings in which the child first comes in contact with peers. As the child matures, these playgroupings may form the basis for territorial gangs. More generally, school catchment areas, particularly those of primary schools, are so designed that school mates are likely also to be neighbours. Many of the adult models available for imitation will also be drawn from the local area, albeit in competition with the more fanciful figures depicted in television and other media. The fact that a schoolteacher is or is not the sort of person who might live next door in a particular area may have much to say about the development of attitudes towards the formal educational system. Apart from occasional family visits to friends and relatives in other areas and the formalized interaction with schoolteachers, the child's adult contacts outside the home are primarily with the parents of his street-group friends and with the immediate neighbours. The child's conception of social reality is built up in the process of his interaction with his family, his peers, the other adults in his community and those agencies of the wider society, particularly the school, with which he comes into contact. He can obtain consensual validation of his experience and beliefs by comparing his situation with that of his peers. The availability of adult models enables him to anticipate future life-patterns and to incorporate a variety of roles into his future repertoire. By conforming to the normative expectations embodied in the local culture, he can gain acceptance into the group. In each case, the earliest experiences help to determine much of what follows and these earliest experiences may be expected to take place within the bounds of the local area. The potential for a neighbourhood effect on socialization is high.

In common with the very young, the old and the infirm must also obtain much of their experience from a restricted area. Rosow (1970, p. 64) has demonstrated a strong but complex relationship between the territorial concentration of the aged, their social integration and their ability to withstand crises: 'The overall principle is clear: residential concentration of the aged significantly increases their social integration and group supports'. As in the case of several other writers concerned with the relationship between the local area and patterns of informal social interaction, Rosow distinguishes between individuals possessing *local* and *cosmopolitan* orientations (see also Merton, 1957). The localite, the individual who is positively orientated towards involvement in the local community, is particularly sensitive to the presence or absence of neighbouring possibilities, personal morale varying directly with the concentration of age-peers. The cosmopolitan, on the other hand, may feel 'hemmed in' and unduly coerced if he is surrounded by his age-mates. His orientation is to the wider world outside the immediate locale and he may be expected to object to attempts to confine him to the local territory. The varying responses serve as a valuable reminder that any attempt to predict behaviour according to contextual variables is likely to be seriously misleading, unless attention is also paid to the individual's attributes and orientations and to the degree of fit between these and those of the people and institutions around him.

It is perhaps the result of a pervading male bias in the social sciences that little attention has been paid to the third major category of the population who may spend much of their lives within the confines of a relatively small residential area—housewives. The proportion of women working outside the home has shown a steady increase in the last few decades, but, for significant periods of their lives, it remains the case that the great majority of women are home-centred. Young mothers, in particular, may expect to be subjected to strong pressures making for an essentially home-and-neighbourhood oriented existence. The assertion that one of the distinguishing characteristics of modern urbanization has been the geographical separation of home and workplace ignores the living and working locale of the largest single occupational category.

The fact that many residential areas, especially those in the suburbs, are essentially female preserves during the working day has occasionally been commented on (e.g. Seeley, Sim and Loosely, 1956), but has been little further investigated. The importance of neighbourhood gossip and helping relationships in the social integration of housewives is also given brief mention in the literature, but with little substantive backing. What data there are suggest that the local area remains an important source of self-affirming interaction for large numbers of women. A study of a small Australian housing estate, in which the values of 'neighbourliness' and 'togetherness' were heavily emphasized, found a close association between the personal morale of housewives and the extent of their integration into the local friendship network (Timms and Timms, 1972). Little effect was experienced by those women who left the estate to go to work, but for the large majority who stayed at home there was a high association between the feeling of self-alienation and such indicants of relative isolation as being unnamed by others as a friendship choice and getting together with neighbours rarely or never. The evidence appeared to suggest that it was the experience of isolation which led to feelings of failure and alienation rather than vice versa. In view of the apparent commonness of feelings of loneliness amongst housewives (Oakley, 1974), the significance of the neighbourhood as a source for interaction may require greater emphasis than it has recently been accorded. The mobility of association which is often said to be characteristic of modern man may, in fact, be characteristic only of a relatively small proportion of the population—the higher income, middle age group male.

TERRITORIAL CONSTRAINTS

The territorial constraints experienced by the very young, the aged and housewives are likely to be given even greater force if those concerned are the members of a population which is discriminated against on religious, ethnic or racial grounds. Where the discrimination is sufficiently pronounced, residence may become prescribed, as in *apartheid*, with an elaborate system of pass laws to govern movement from one designated residential area to another. If the discrimination is accompanied by open hostility, territories may be marked off by barbed wire and vigilantes. In Belfast, 'many of the boundaries between rival Catholic and Protestant areas have been clearly de-marcated by the British army's "peace line" barricades erected at potential flash-points' (Poole and Boal, 1973, p. 3). The walls separating private from local authority housing areas in some British cities (e.g. Collison, 1963) and the jealously guarded private estates of some American cities serve as a reminder that hostilities in Western society are not simply confined to questions of race and religion.

Concentration and the demarcation of a territory may, of course, reflect choice rather than coercion (see chapter 2). Segregation enables a group both to heighten its visibility vis-à-vis other groups and to preserve its distinguishing characteristics (Lieberson, 1961). Concentration of the group within a small area enables it to support such institutions as parochial schools, specialist foodshops and own-language professional services. Probably of even greater importance, it enables the older members of the group to monitor the behaviour of the younger and to continue to enforce traditional customs, such as those surrounding the choice of marriage partners and the rearing of children. Grandmother may be as powerful a conservative force in an ethnic enclave within an Australian or American city as she was in her original Greek village. The higher the degree of segregation of a minority group, the higher the proportion of its population resisting assimilation to the cultural norms of the dominant society.

Developments in transport and communications technology may have lessened territorial constraints, but place of residence remains a major factor in allocating life-chances and guiding interaction patterns. Given that distance is a constraint on access, the relationship between residence and the locations of such diverse goods as parks, hospitals, bus routes and welfare centres necessarily involves a differentiation of opportunities. The whole notion of a territorial base to local and national government ensures that locality will continue to be of vital importance in the organization of society. A child born in one part of the city rather than another is likely to belong to a particular type of family, to grow up in a particular sort of environment, to attend a particular sort of school, and so on. The effects of the local residential area may be overlain by a great variety of other influences, but they remain of potential importance throughout the life-cycle. Neither neighbours nor the neighbourhood may be the object of much regard, but both are difficult to escape. The residential differentiation of the urban mosaic provides a matrix for the development and maintenance of urban society. It is for this reason that it is important to analyse the nature of residential differentiation and of the bases of which it rests.

THE BASES OF RESIDENTIAL DIFFERENTIATION

Attempts at the explanation of residential differentiation have been made at both a microsocial and a macrosocial scale. In the microsocial approach, attention is focused on the relationship between residential location and patterns of individual decisions and behaviour, generally at a household level. In the macrosocial approach, focus is on the relationship between residential differentiation and certain global characteristics of the encompassing society, generally those relating to the distribution of power and the organization of the division of labour. In yet a third approach, attention is focused on the role of a series of intermediaries or urban gatekeepers in the allocation of residences.

A satisfactory explanation of residential differentiation must draw upon each approach. Individual decisions about choice of residential area take place against a framework of opportunities and constraints which reflect the structure of society and the manipulation of scarce resources; in its turn, the existing structure reflects the aggregate of previous behaviours and decisions, and becomes manifest through individual patterns of behaviour.

The macrosocial approach of the classical ecologists

The theoretical underpinning to a large proportion of the studies concerned with residential differentiation is provided in the approach of the early Chicago ecologists. To Park and his followers, residential differentiation is the natural result of impersonal competition. The struggle for a favourable location gives rise to a characteristic pattern of land rents which, through the market mechanism, acts as a template for the sifting and sorting of people and of land uses. Different types of people are segregated according to their ability to meet the rents associated with differing locations. Economic segregation is the basic form of residential differentiation.

At the most general level, the approach of the classical ecologists is based on a conception of economic competition closely modelled on the Darwinian struggle for existence. At times the Chicago school seems to have been unduly dazzled by the brilliance of their biological analogies and to have ignored the substance with which they worked. But in the application of their theoretical perspectives, they generally reveal too strong a commitment to the data they gather in their intimate involvement with the life of Chicago to be guilty of crude biological determinism. Even if the process of residential differentiation is seen as resting on impersonal competition, it is recognized that the resulting pattern is much more broadly based: 'The physical or ecological organization of the community, in the long run, responds to and reflects the occupational and the cultural. Social selection and segregation, which create the natural groups, determine at the same time the natural areas of the city' (Park, 1954, p. 170). Critics such as Alihan (1938) and Firey (1945), who claim that the use of a biological analogy blinds the Chicago ecologists to the role of sentiment and values in determining land use and residential location, confuse the heuristic perspective of human ecology with the substantive descriptions of the urban mosaic which form perhaps the most notable feature of the Chicago school's output (see Short, 1971, for a review). The biological analogy is always present in the background, but is rarely obtrusive.

The role of values

In the late 1930s and early 1940s a severe reaction set in to what was seen as the overmechanistic and organismic view of urban ecology promulgated by the Chicago school (e.g. see Alihan, 1938; Gettys, 1940; Hollingshead, 1947). With the benefit of hindsight, much of the criticism seems ill-directed; the Chicago ecologists were by no means as wedded to a single factor view of the community, nor were they as guilty of reification, as their critics suggest. What the criticisms do highlight, however, is the role of sentiments and values in residential differentiation.

The city conceived by the Chicago school appears to be inhabited by an agglomeration of ahistorical individuals on a virgin site who make their locational decisions on the basis of rational economics. This conception has little in common with actuality. Instead, as Firey (1945) most notably points out, both the inhabitants and the locations of cities are replete with historical tradition and symbolic value. Analyses of the movement of ethnic groups (Jonassen, 1949; Myers, 1950), of cities outside the United States (e.g. Caplow, 1949; Dotson and Dotson, 1954; Musil, 1968) and of the development of new housing areas (Jones, 1960; Tait-Davis, 1965) have added further support for the position that a knowledge of the social values involved is an indispensable component of any attempt at understanding residential differentiation.

The notion of social values is extremely wide. It covers a range of phenomena stretching from the nature of dominant political systems and ideologies, as in the contrast between 'capitalist' and 'socialist' forms of organization, to questions of individual motivation. Herein lies both the strength and the weakness of the concept. As an explanatory tool, the notion of values is too all-embracing; as a heuristic device, however, it directs attention to the importance of the 'nonobjective', subjective world in the ordering of human affairs. In order to understand residential differentiation, it is necessary to understand the pattern of meanings which various groups of actors attach to residence in one part of the city rather than another.

Residential differentiation and social change

It is characteristic of both classical urban ecology and much of the work conducted by those espousing the social values approach that urban phenomena are taken as being *sui generis*. Little attempt is made to relate what is happening within the city to the more general changes taking place within the encompassing society. The growth of a comparative perspective in the social sciences, the diffusion of urban studies from their Mid-West birthplace and a closer examination of the nature of urbanism have led to a conscious attempt to relate the form of the urban community to the characteristics of the society in which it is embedded. Much of the impetus for this attempt is provided in the theoretical rationale developed in connection with the body of techniques known as social area analysis.

Social area analysis is a set of operations for classifying the sub-areas of cities according to certain indexes, which are said (Shevky and Bell, 1955, p. 18) to be the 'logically demonstrable reflections of those major changes which have produced modern, urban society'. In the initial formulation of the model, three broad and interrelated trends are identified as correlates of changes in the scale of society: changes in the bases of reward and rank, changes in the nature of productive activity as these affect family life-styles and changes in the composition of the population. Each trend is said to give rise to one of the three constructs of social rank, family status and ethnic status, which are used in the classification of urban sub-communities.

The Shevky–Bell schema has encountered considerable criticism (see Timms, 1971, chapter 4, for an extended discussion). The notion of societal scale is vague; social change is represented in overly economic terms; and little play is given to differences in value orientations, to the distribution of power or even to organizational matters, except as these are seen as the consequences of changes in the nature of productive activity. Most importantly, no explanation is given of the way in which the three structural trends give rise to the three dimensions, in terms of which residential differentiation is said to take place. In the words of some early reviewers (Hawley and Duncan, 1957, p. 340): 'One searches in vain among these materials for a statement explaining why residential areas should differ one from the other or be internally homogeneous'.

At attempt to overcome some of the more glaring shortcomings in the original social area model is provided in a revision of the scheme by McElrath (1968). Greater attention is given to organizational considerations and the concept of societal scale is subject to redefinition. In addition to the constructs of social rank, family status and ethnic status, from the initial formulation, McElrath introduces a fourth construct—migrant status—to tap the effects of mobility. Each construct is seen (McElrath, 1968, p. 33) as providing a basic dimension of social differentiation: 'those categories into which people are divided, and in whose terms they receive differential treatment by others'. The connection with residential differentiation is made via the assertion (McElrath, 1968, p. 40) 'that important social differentia result in residential clustering of like populations'. Little attempt is made to spell out the process of residential clustering.

The equation of residential differentiation with social differentiation is similar to Park's observations on the relation between physical distance and social distance. It gains credence from the large number of studies which have shown the correlation between the residential differentiation of class and ethnic groups and measures of their social distance (see above). In addition, it opens up a rich field for comparative study. Changes in the nature of social differentiation should show clear relationships with changes in the bases of residential differentiation and in the association between the bases. Attempts to illustrate these relationships with data from societies exhibiting widely varying forms of social differentiation are as yet in their infancy, but seem highly promising (see especially Abu-Lughod, 1969; Timms, 1971, pp. 142–149). Rather than being a theory of residential differentiation, social area analysis has turned out to be essentially a global model of social change.

Choice and constraint in residential location

The explanations of residential differentiation attempted by the classical ecologists, proponents of the social values approach and those working within the tradition of social area analysis are couched in relatively abstract terms. They are concerned to establish general principles of community form. To the classical ecologists, residential differentiation reflects an impersonal competition for location, determined by the ability to pay rent; to those stressing the importance of social values, in reflects differences in the interpretation of what constitutes a desirable location, differences which may rest on little more than historical accident; to social area analysts, it is a reflection of the patterns of social differentiation characteristic of the encompassing society. None of the approaches provides a satisfactory explanation of the process of residential differentiation, the way in which different areas of the city come to be associated with different types of people. In order to approach this task, it is necessary to focus on the decisions and constraints involved in determining the characteristics of residential areas and the location of different types of household.

The concentration of decision-making power varies widely from society to society. In a community dominated by laissez-faire policies, decisions about the characteristics of residential areas may be widely diffused amongst a large number of individual households, the consumers, and a somewhat smaller number of builders, financiers and estate agents, the suppliers and brokers. Turn-of-the century Chicago may have approximated such a structure, at least as far as native-born whites were concerned. In a totalitarian society, decisions about the allocation of houses to households may be concentrated in the hands of a small élite group. In an extreme case, like Feudal Japan (Yazaki, 1963), a single person may become the decision-maker, planning the community in accordance with his own desires. Carter (1970) provides an example of a British town, Llandudno, whose early form and development was strictly controlled by a single family. In the typical 'Western' situation, in which aspects of private enterprise and property are combined with public planning and ownership, decisions about the nature of residential areas may be taken by many different individuals and agencies, acting in complex interrelationship. The aspirations, knowledge and resources of the individual household, the building programmes of the private developer and of public agencies, the promotion activities of real estate agents, the management policies of housing departments, the financial policies of building societies, banks and insurance companies, the planning activities of a variety of local and national government agencies, the image-building activities of promoters and mass media, and the attitude of government to a wide range of questions relating to housing; all of these help to structure the decision-making process and the resulting patterns of residential differentiation. Given so complex a web of activities, attempts to provide a simple description of the bases of residential differentiation must be treated with great caution.

Decisions about the nature of residential areas and about the allocation of people to locations finally impinge on the individual household. As Wurster (1966) has pointed out, the assumption that the individual householder has ever exercised a dominant influence in the housing market is a myth. Nonetheless, it seems reasonable to enter a discussion of the decision-making processes involved in the residential differentiation of the urban population at the level of the individual consumer. Although the household may have little freedom of choice, the decision to locate in a particular house and neighbourhood is one of the most important which it has to take, having implications for a wide range of behaviours and sentiments. The decision-making involved may be analysed in terms of the household's definition of what constitutes a desirable location and of the constraints which it has to overcome if it is to convert its aspirations into actuality.

An address locates the household both in physical space and in social space. Each aspect enters into judgements concerning the desirability of differing residential areas, although one may be stressed by some households to the virtual exclusion of the other.

Two major aspects of the physical environment appear to be important in determining preferences: the nature of the residential development and its accessibility to the places the household needs or wishes to visit. The physical characteristics of the residential units themselves are probably the most important single criterion of desirability (Kaiser, 1968). The fact that houses tend to be built in clusters, rather than individually, and that different types of house are more or less adapted to the needs of households at different stages of the family life-cycle helps to account for the widespread importance of differences in family structure as a major dimension of residential differentiation. According to Rossi (1955), the changing housing requirements of a household as it undergoes developmental changes in structure and activities form the most important general stimulus to residential mobility. Powerful inertia factors, particularly pronounced in the later years of a household's existence, introduce an error term in the equation of housing need and residential preference, but the general effect is strong. Evaluation of the house itself is closely related to that of its immediate environment. Studies of several populations in the English-speaking world (e.g. Peterson 1967; Wilson, 1962) have shown a very general preference for moderately low residential densities with single family houses set in country-like environs. The close-to-nature theme is particularly pronounced amongst those espousing a familistic way of life (Bell, 1968). With the spread of automobile ownership and the construction of suburban estates on a mass scale (see chapter 3), suburban residence has become a possible goal for a majority of the population. Both rich and poor, native-born and immigrant can aspire to a new house in a new 'garden' suburb. Only a small minority of the population, those whom Gans (1962) terms the 'cosmopolites' and the 'childless', appear to want the combination of high densities and restricted living space characteristic of most inner city areas.

Aggregate patterns of accessibility are closely related to other physical attributes of residential locations. Frequently there is an inverse relationship between the amount of living space which is available for a given outlay and location towards the city centre. A household must weigh the benefits of accessibility to central city amenities against the probable sacrifices which central location may entail in the supply of living space and country atmosphere. More particularly, a household must weigh accessibility to its workplaces against other desirable features of the location being considered. As with many other criteria, the higher the income of the household the freer it can be in its relative ranking of the criteria of quality and accessibility.

Residential areas possess social identities as well as physical locations and address is an important item in the identity of the urban resident. The address of a person immediately identifies him, to those who hold the relevant cognitive maps, as probably being a certain sort of person. In the absence of more detailed knowledge about an individual, knowledge of his place of residence may play an important role not only in identifying his probable social rank and ethnic identity (Ross, 1962) but also in establishing his respectability and credit-worthiness. The stigmatizing effect of being born 'on the wrong side of the tracks' may be powerful and long-lasting. Damer (1974) illustrates the variety of ways in which the inhabitants of a stigmatized corporation housing estate in Glasgow are discriminated against by other citizens and public officials. Writing about the general public stigmatization of public housing projects in the United States, Onibokun (1973 p. 471) quotes the tenants as believing that 'The public . . . is misinformed that all public housing projects are the concentration camps for the "poor", the irresponsible and the "dregs of the society"; and as a result of such misinformation the public looks down upon the tenants as second class citizens'.

Identities are organized in terms of the major criteria of social differentiation. In Western society, two of the most crucial factors involved are social rank and ethnicity. Each serves as a major basis for the evaluation and differential treatment of individuals and groups. Each also serves as a major basis of residential differentiation. Rossi (1955, p. 179) points out the close connection between changes in social rank and changes in residence:

> Residential mobility also plays a role in 'vertical' social mobility. The location of a residence has a prestige value, and is, to some degree, a determinant of personal contact potentials. Families moving up the 'occupational ladder' are particularly sensitive to the social aspects of location and use residential mobility to bring their residences into line with their prestige needs.

Similar processes characterize ethnic identities. In order to 'pass' from one category to another, it may be necessary to change from one area of residence to another. According to Hawley (quoted in Lieberson, 1961), it is only when what was previously a subjugated minority group is residentially indistinct from members of the core society that one can talk of its assimilation. Residential location is a means of claiming a certain public identity. Desirable locations are, therefore, those which are conceived as embodying the most desirable public identities.

The development of identities, either of people or the neighbourhoods, is a complex process. In each case, however, the crucial feature of the process is its heavy reliance on the propositions of others. Just as the sense of personal identity is built up in the looking-glass of significant others, so is that of residential areas in the dialogue between residents and significant outsiders. Even the names of residential areas—titles which are redolent with images—are generally coined by outsiders, particularly developers and planners. Labelling according to the connotations associated with the name chosen may thus take place prior to the arrival of the first settler. Residents in 'Ashgrove' are likely to be thought very different from those in 'Market Street'. Imagery builds upon reality, largely by exaggerating differences and using these as the basis for typification. Areas which have slightly more than the average number of high ranking residents come to be known as high rank; areas with slightly more than the average proportion of immigrants may be referred to as ethnic ghettos. A polarization takes place in which residential areas are typified in terms of their most apparent differences from one another (see Suttles, 1972).

There is a close association between a household's conception of its identity and its preferences for social interaction. Others who are perceived as personifying desirable identities are desirable associates. Since association demands contact and contact may be seen as a function of spatial proximity, it follows that the manipulation of residential location may be regarded as a strategy for optimizing the probability of identity-enhancing association. Social distance and spatial distance can both be seen not only as symbols of social standing but also as techniques for maintaining the existing distinctions between individuals and groups. The more intimate the relationship, the greater are its implications for the identities of the actors involved. Beshers (1962 p. 106) suggests that the concern of northerners in the United States for the residential 'purity' of their neighbourhood may be based on the same concern as that expressed by southerners in terms of who should marry their daughters: 'Who daughter marries has something to do with who daughter meets. Daughter will not come into contact with Negroes in an integrated school because residential segregation of non-whites effectively yields segregation of school districts. Residence choice and marriage choice may be closely connected'. In order to preserve social distance, it may be necessary to institute physical distance.

However clear a household may be about its housing and locational needs and about the identities it wishes to claim, it may be able to do little about its actual residential location. The attempt by a household to bring its residence into line with its aspirations—either by migration or by changing the characteristics of its location—may be frustrated by a variety of constraints. Particularly important are the financial resources of the household, the opportunities which exist and its knowledge of them, and its relationship with a number of urban gatekeepers, the manipulators of access to opportunities.

Desires can only be indulged if the household can afford to meet the attendant costs. As Hawley (1950, p. 286) puts it: 'If a family can pay the costs then it may exercise any conceivable motive'. For most households, a compromise must be made between the desirable and the practical. In assessing the costs which it can meet, the household has to take into account not just the rent or purchase price of the accommodation itself but also the ancillary costs—mainly those connected with travel—which a particular location entails. Attractive low rent houses on new local authority housing estates may have less practical appeal to many low income families than old inner-city dwellings, simply because their peripheral location may entail excessive time and money costs in journeying to work or shop. In general, housing behaves as a superior good: the higher the financial resources available, the higher the proportion tending to be spent on housing and the more weight that is given to marginal preferences (Goodall, 1972). Even at lower income levels, there is some evidence (Tilly, 1961) that households which are particularly sensitive to the prestige connotations of residence in desirable parts of the city may be prepared to devote abnormally high proportions of their income to housing costs.

Even if a household can afford to change its residential environment, it can only do so if suitable alternatives are available and it possesses the relative information. The great majority of housing choices are made from existing stock. In the United Kingdom, only some 2 per cent. per annum is added to the housing supply. The individual consumer is largely restricted to the distribution of existing development and existing reputations (for an analysis of the housing market see Grigsby, 1963). Previous evaluations of residential areas provide the framework for current choices. In a similar fashion, new information about the characteristics of neighbourhoods is structured by prior knowledge. A household which is involved in an active search for alternative locations is likely to concentrate its activities in those areas of which it was previously aware (Brown and Holmes, 1971). Different sources of information about residential alternatives are themselves subject to bias: newspapers are aimed at particular readerships, estate agents tend to specialize both by area and price of property, and personal contacts are anchored in the idiosyncracies of personal networks.

Information flows are constrained by the overall patterning of social differentiation. The effect is perhaps most pronounced in the case of those residential moves—half of the total, according to Rossi (1955)—which come about as the result of personal contact. The transmission of information via personal networks tends to amplify existing residential differentials. In selecting a new residence, the potential mover is particularly sensitive to the information provided by earlier movers who belong to his reference groups. The extent to which they are satisfied with an area will make it take on attractive qualities. The process of chain migration may set up a positive feedback system in which what may initially have been chance, and possibly even illusionary, differences in the characteristics of different areas become highly systematic.

Information is not freely available and like other scarce goods is subject to the control and manipulation of its producers and distributors. The power to withhold or to pass on information about alternative possibilities is one of the main weapons employed by those organizations and agencies which act as arbiters of the housing market. Access to housing opportunities is manipulated by a great variety of gatekeepers: public and private developers, estate agents, housing committees and factors, the mass media, rent collectors, local authority and national planning authorities, politicians, financial institutions and a large number of functionaries engaged in the day-to-day management of housing. The ability of differing agencies to control access to residential opportunities varies greatly from situation to situation. The greater the housing shortage and the greater the concentration of ownership and management, the greater is likely to be the influence of the gatekeepers. In large areas of British cities, the local authority may exercise almost monopolistic power, local authority councillors and officials effectively controlling access to housing opportunities. Differences in housing policy, for instance whether to concentrate or to disperse 'problem' families, may have immediate implications for the patterning of residential differentiation. Differences in the day-to-day administration of official policies may introduce yet further effects. Not all categories of the population are equally exposed to the power of the urban gatekeepers. The concept of housing classes (Rex, 1968), based on a combination of tenure and type of accommodation, attempts to systematize the variation in housing situations within British cities. Seven classes are recognized, ranging from the outright owners of large houses in desirable areas to lodgers in inner-city rooms. Information about alternatives tends to be confined within classes and considerable difficulty may be experienced in moving from one class to another. In consequence, the residential market may behave not as a single entity but, rather, as a series of relatively autonomous sub-markets, each of which may again be geographically divided.

In practice, residential location is likely to be more effected by the constraints of the urban system than it is by the preferences and cognitive maps of urban dwellers. Residential mobility is frequently forced rather than voluntary, and the opportunities which are available are restricted by costs, by knowledge and by social access. There is, in general, a remarkable stability in the urban residential system. The preference maps of urban residents are themselves guided by their conceptions of the constraints and opportunities of the urban system. Migration and attempts to alter the local habitat take place in terms of the overall system of differentiation characteristic of the community concerned. Whether by coercion or by choice, particular types of people are located in particular sorts of areas. The complex of individual preferences, housing needs and financial capabilities, existing housing supply, information flows and market manipulations leads to a sifting and sorting of the population into distinct residential clusters, organized in terms of basic social differentials. The attractions and repulsions between groups, differences in life-cycle and life-style, and variations in housing ideology are translated into residential differentiation.

CONCLUSION

The urban mosaic is highly differentiated. Different parts of the city are associated with different types of people and different forms of behaviour. The effects of residence in one area rather than another are pronounced and long-lasting, especially on those whose daily movements are more or less confined to a small radius of their home. The role of the local community in childhood socialization and as a contextual reference ensures that a neighbourhood effect is felt across a wide range of behaviours and sentiments.

Residential differentiation is both an objective phenomenon and part of the social construction of reality. Attempts at the explanation of residential differentiation must take account both of the sentiments of all those involved in the housing market and of the structures and constraints within which they must operate. At the level of the individual household, the search for a suitable residential location may be viewed as an attempt to satisfy the environmental needs of its way of life and stage in the life-cycle, and the identity needs related to its position on the main bases of social differentiation extent in the encompassing society. To convert its residential desires into actuality, the household must have access to sufficient financial resources and to information about suitable opportunities, and be sufficiently powerful to overcome the constraints which urban gatekeepers may put in its way. Residential differentiation is not just a symbol of social differentiation, but represents one of the major forms which the latter takes.

Attempts to develop a systematic model of the process of residential differentiation are, as yet, in their infancy. Much of the effort to date has been concentrated on attempts to explain the process in relatively mechanistic and 'objective' terms. In the future, it is suggested that more attention should be paid to subjective materials. Residential images are negotiated in ongoing social relationships, rather than simply being imposed by external economic or historical forces. As an aspect of social differentiation, the residential differentiation of the urban fabric reflects beliefs about the differences between people and about the way in which they should be treated. To understand the process of differentiation and the effects which it has, it is necessary to clothe the bare bones provided by objective data with the substance of human meanings. This is a task which is only just beginning.

REFERENCES

Abu-Lughod, J. L. (1969). 'Testing the theory of social area analysis: the ecology of Cairo, Egypt'. *American Sociological Review*, **34**, 198–212.

Alihan, M. A. (1938). *Social Ecology: A Critical Analysis*, Columbia University Press, New York.

Bell, W. (1968). 'The city, the suburb and a theory of social choice'. In S. Greer, D. C. McElrath, D. W. Minar and P. W. Orleans (Eds.), *The New Urbanization*, St. Martins Press, New York, pp. 132–168.

Beshers, J. M. (1962). *Urban Social Structure*, The Free Press, New York.

Brown, L. A., and Holmes, J. (1971). 'Search behavior in an intra-urban migration context: a spatial perspective'. *Environment and Planning*, **3**, 307–326.

Caplow, T. (1949). 'The social ecology of Guatemala City'. *Social Forces*, **28**, 113–133.

Carter, H. (1970). 'A decision-making approach to town plan analysis: a case study of Llandudno'. In H. Carter and W. K. D. Davies (Eds.), *Studies in the Geography of Wales*, Longman, London, pp. 66–78.

Collison, P. (1963). *The Cutteslowe Walls*, Faber and Faber, London.

Cooley, C. H. (1929). *Social Organization*, Scribner, New York.

Damer, S. (1974). 'Wine Alley: the sociology of a dreadful enclosure'. *Sociological Review*, **22**, 221–248.

Dotson, F., and Dotson, L. O. (1954). 'Ecological trends in the city of Guadalajara, Mexico'. *Social Forces*, **32**, 347–374.

Duncan, O. D., and Duncan, B. (1955). 'Residential distribution and occupational stratification'. *American Journal of Sociology*, **60**, 493–503.

Fine, J., Glenn, N. D., and Monts, J. K. (1971). 'The residential segregation of occupational groups in central cities and suburbs'. *Demography*, **8**, 91–102.

Firey, W. (1945). 'Sentiment and symbolism as ecological variables'. *American Sociological Review*, **10**, 140–148.

Gans, H. J. (1962). 'Urbanism and suburbanism as ways of life'. In A. H. Rose (Ed.), *Human Behavior and Social Processes*, Houghton Mifflin, Boston, pp. 625–648.

Gettys, W. E. (1940). 'Human ecology and social theory'. *Social Forces*, **18**, 466–476.

Goodall, B. (1972). *The Economics of Urban Areas*, Pergamon, Oxford.

Grigsby, W. G. (1963). *Housing Markets and Public Policy*, University of Pennsylvania Press, Philadelphia.

Hawley, A. H. (1950). *Human Ecology*, Ronald Press, New York.

Hawley, A. H. and Duncan, O. D. (1957). 'Social area analysis: a critical appraisal'. *Land Economics*, **33**, 337–345.

Herbert, D. T. (1972). *Urban Geography: A Social Perspective*, David and Charles, Newton Abbott.

Hollingshead, A. B. (1947). 'A re-examination of ecological theory'. *Sociology and Social Research*, **31**, 194–204.

Janowitz, M. (1967). *The Community Press in an Urban Setting*, 2nd ed., University of Chicago Press, Chicago.

Jonassen, C. T. (1949). 'Cultural variables in the ecology of an ethnic group'. *American Sociological Review*, **14**, 32–41.

Jones, E. (1960). *A Social Geography of Belfast*, Oxford University Press, London.
Jones, F. L. (1965). 'Ethnic concentration and assimilation: an Australian case study'. *Social Forces*, **45**, 412–423.
Kaiser, E. J. (1968). 'Locational decision factors in a producer model of residential development'. *Land Economics*, **44**, 351–362.
Kantrowitz, N. (1973). *Ethnic and Racial Segregation in the New York Metropolis*, Praeger, New York.
Keller, S. (1969). *The Urban Neighborhood: A Sociological Perspective*, Random House, New York.
Laumann, E. O. (1966). *Prestige and Association in an Urban Community*, Bobbs Merrill, Indianapolis.
Laumann, E. O. (1973). *The Bonds of Pluralism*, John Wiley, New York.
Lieberson, S. (1961). 'The impact of residential segregation on ethnic assimilation'. *Social Forces*, **40**, 52–57.
McElrath, D. C. (1968). 'Societal scale and social differentiation'. In S. Greer, D. C. McElrath, D. W. Minar and P. W. Orleans (Eds.), *The New Urbanization*, St. Martins Press, New York, pp. 33–52.
Merton, R. K. (1957). *Social Theory and Social Structure*, 2nd ed., The Free Press, New York.
Musil, J. (1968). 'The development of Prague's ecological structure'. In R. E. Pahl (Ed.), *Readings in Urban Sociology*, Pergamon, Oxford, pp. 232–262.
Myers, J. K. (1950). 'Assimilation to the ecological and social systems of a community' *American Sociological Review*, **15**, 367–372.
Oakley, A. (1974). *The Sociology of Housework*, Martin Robertson, London.
Oates, J. (1974). *People in Cities: An Ecological Approach*, Open University (Urban Education E351 Block 3), Milton Keynes.
Onibokun, A. G. (1973). 'Environmental issues in housing habitability'. *Environment and Planning*, **5**, 461–476.
Park, R. E. (1954). *Human Communities*, University of Chicago Press, Chicago.
Peterson, G. L. (1967). 'A model of preference'. *Journal of Regional Science*, **7**, 19–31.
Poole, M. A., and Boal, F. W. (1973). 'Religious residential segregation in Belfast in mid-1969'. In B. D. Clark and M. B. Gleave (Eds.), *Social Patterns in Cities*, Institute of British Geographers, London, pp. 1–40.
Ramsøy, N. R. (1966). 'Assortative mating and the structure of cities'. *American Sociological Review*, **31**, 773–786.
Rex, J. (1968). 'The sociology of a zone in transition'. In R. E. Pahl (Ed.), *Readings in Urban Sociology*, Pergamon, Oxford, pp. 211–231.
Rosow, I. (1970). 'Old people: their friends and neighbours'. *American Behavioral Scientist*, **1**, 59–69.
Ross, H. L. (1962). 'The local community: a survey approach'. *American Sociological Review*, **27**, 75–84.
Rossi, P. H. (1955). *Why Families Move*, The Free Press, Glencoe, Illinois.
Seeley, J. R., Sim, R. A. and Loosely, E. W. (1956). *Crestwood Heights*, Basic Books, New York.
Shevky, E., and Bell, W. (1955). *Social Area Analysis: Theory, Illustrative Application and Computational Procedures*, Stanford University Press, Stanford.
Short, J. F. (Ed.) (1971). *The Social Fabric of the Metropolis*, University of Chicago Press, Chicago.
Suttles, G. D. (1972). *The Social Construction of Communities*, University of Chicago Press, Chicago.
Tait-Davis, J. (1965). 'Middle class housing in the central city'. *Economic Geography*, **41**, 238–251.
Taueber, K. E., and Taueber, A. F. (1965). *Negroes in Cities*, Aldine, Chicago.

Tilly, C. (1961). 'Occupational rank and grade of residence in a metropolis'. *American Journal of Sociology*, **67**, 323–329.

Timms, D. W. G. (1969). 'The dissimilarity between overseas-born and Australian-born in Queensland'. *Sociology and Social Research*, **53**, 363–374.

Timms, D. W. G. (1971). *The Urban Mosaic*, Cambridge University Press, Cambridge.

Timms, D. W. G., and Timms, E. A. (1972). 'Anomia and social participation among suburban women'. *Pacific Sociological Review*, **15**, 123–141.

Webber, M. (1963). 'Order in diversity: community without propinquity'. In L. Wingo (Ed.), *Cities and Space*, Johns Hopkins Press, Baltimore, pp. 23–56.

Wilson, R. L. (1962). 'Livability of the city: attitudes and urban development'. In F. S. Chapin and S. Weiss (Eds.), *Urban Growth Dynamics*, John Wiley, New York, pp. 359–399.

Wurster, C. B. (1966). 'Social questions in housing and community planning'. In W. L. Wheaton, G. Milgram and M. E. Meyerson (Eds.), *Urban Housing*, McGraw-Hill, New York.

Yazaki, T. (Trans. by D. L. Swain) (1963). *The Japanese City: A Sociological Analysis*, Japan Publications, Tokyo.

Young, M., and Willmott, P. (1957). *Family and Kinship in East London*, Routledge and Kegan Paul, London.

Chapter 2

Ethnic Residential Segregation

F. W. Boal

Ethnic residential segregation is a very common characteristic of cities. Many authors take such segregation to be an indicant of the relationship between a particular ethnic group and some other segment of the urban population. The basic underpinning of such an interpretation derives from the early claim of Robert Park (1952) that 'social relations are . . . frequently and . . . inevitably correlated with spatial relations'. More specifically, in terms of ethnic group relationships, Duncan and Liberson (1959) find, from a study carried out in Chicago, that ethnic residential segregation is inversely related to assimilation. This, they claim, confirms an earlier hypothesis stated by Halbwachs (1932) that 'plus une population d'immigrants est concentrée moins elle est assimilée'. This chapter explores the relationships between three elements: ethnic groups, degree of assimilation, and degree and spatial form of residential segregation. It also attempts to examine the factors underlying those situations where ethnic residential segregation is marked.

ETHNIC GROUPS

First, some definition must be given to the term 'ethnic group'. Cohen (1974) provides a very broadly based statement that an ethnic group can be operationally defined as a collective of people who share some patterns of normative behaviour and who form a part of a larger population, interacting with people from other collectivities within the framework of a social system. Gordon (1964) takes the term ethnic group to mean 'any group which is defined or set off by race, religion or national origin or some combination of these categories'. He claims that all these categories have a common social-psychological referent, in that they serve to create a sense of peoplehood. This broadly based interpretation of 'ethnic groups' has recently been reinforced by Glazer (1975), who takes the term to refer to the vertical divisions of society, in contrast to the horizontal divisions of social class. Further backing for Gordon's interpretation is provided by Andrew Greeley (1969) in his use of Max Weber's definition that an ethnic group is a human collectivity based on an assumption of common origin, real or imaginary.

Thus, the basis for ethnic categorization can be racial, religious or national in origin, and the categorization can be employed both by the group itself and by the larger social matrix of which it is a part. In the urban context, some groups may be described by a clearly defined set of characteristics from the very beginning of their urban residence. For others, this may not be the case initially, but force of circumstances can create or reinforce ethnic consciousness and ethnic characteristics. An example of this is provided by Chinoy (1967, p. 212): 'to the extent that persons with a similar biological endowment conceive of themselves as a race, whether more or less spontaneously or because they are so considered by others, they become an ethnic group . . . for their conception of themselves now binds them together into a social whole . . . '. A further example is provided by Kramer (1970), who indicates that many migrant groups to the United States did not, in fact, found a replica of the original community, but created a new grouping that was an adaptation to minority status.

The association between ethnic groups in cities and migration into these same cities is a strong one. If we return to the definition of ethnic group given by Cohen, which requires that the ethnic group be set in the context of a larger population, then the most likely way for such a juxtaposition to occur will be where the ethnic group is formed of persons who have entered the urban social and spatial structure as migrants from outside. It does not follow, however, that ethnic status is necessarily a temporary phenomenon, 'a stage in the adaptation of the group to its new environment and in the final assimilation of its members within the new society' (Cohen, 1974, p. xiii). In some cases, this is a correct viewpoint; in others, the ethnic group, originally formed by in-migrants, takes on a degree of permanence within the urban social fabric. It should be noted that in this discussion the term 'in-migrant' will be employed to cover both people who have moved to a city from another part of the same country and also those who are immigrants from another country.

Charter group

If we accept that each ethnic group in a city has its origin through in-migration, then the initial relationship between the in-migrant group and the host population takes on critical importance for the subsequent development of social and spatial relationships. John Porter (1965, p. 60), in discussing the social structure of Canada, provides a useful framework:

> In a society which has to seek members from outside there will be varying judgements about the extensive reservoirs of recruits that exist in the world. In this process of evaluation the first ethnic group to come into previously unoccupied territory, as the effective professor, has the most to say. This group becomes the *charter group* (my italics) of the society, and among the many priviliges and prerogatives which it retains are decisions about what other groups are to be let in and what they will be permitted to do.

The charter group, then, provides the dominant matrix into which the new ethnic groups are inserted, though Porter's definition is a little too restrictive, in that he imputes dominance to the *first* ethnic group to enter an area; there are examples of later ethnic groups establishing themselves as dominants.

The degree of perceived social distance between the charter group and the other in-migrant ethnics will be a critical determinant of the degree to which assimilation occurs and, consequently, if we accept the initial relationships posited between assimilation and segregation (Duncan and Lieberson, 1959), the degree to which the subordinate in-migrant ethnic group is residentially segregated from the 'host' population. Since our focus in this chapter is on cities in the English-speaking world, it will be evident that the dominant charter group in almost all situations (though not quite all) is or was strongly Anglo-Saxon in character.

Since we have noted that an ethnic group is distinguished by a sense of 'peoplehood', it follows that the charter group is itself an ethnic group (Abramson, 1973). In the discussion that follows, however, most examples will be provided by ethnic *minorities*, where a minority is defined as a group which, regardless of where it is on the class ladder, faces barriers to the pursuit of life's values that are greater than the barriers faced by persons otherwise equally qualified (Yinger, 1965). Nonetheless, we must bear in mind that the processes causing minority ethnic group segregation also produce segregation for dominant groups as well.

Assimilation

The maintenance of the ethnic in-migrant group as a distinctive social and spatial entity will depend on the degree to which assimilation occurs. Assimilation itself is by no means a simple or unambiguous concept. An important distinction can be made between behavioural and structural assimilation. The former, having a similar meaning as acculturation, is taken to imply a process whereby the members of a group acquire the memories, sentiments and attitudes of other groups and, by sharing their experience and history, are incorporated with them in a common cultural life (Richmond, 1969). Structural assimilation, on the other hand, refers to the distribution of migrant ethnics through the groups and social systems of the society, including its system of occupational stratification. Gordon (1964) suggests that behavioural assimilation is likely to occur first, with structural assimilation, if it occurs at all, coming subsequently.

Clearly, assimilation is a temporal process. It can take place at different speeds for different groups and one type of assimilation can occur quite rapidly while another lags behind. Beshers makes this latter point when he notes that the barriers to social interaction may go at one speed, while the ethnic group's access to highly rewarding occupation roles may be created at quite a different speed (Beshers, Laumann and Bradshaw, 1964); the significance of this for residential segregation will be seen later. Furthermore, assimilation is by no means an inevitable process that only requires sufficient time. Cohen (1974) goes so far as to claim that in many situations the reverse can occur. In this instance, a group adjusts to the new situation by reorganizing its own traditional customs or by developing new customs to enhance its distinctiveness within the contemporary situation.

The assimilability of an in-migrant urban group will be a function of charter group attitudes and internal group cohesiveness. Social distance measurements of the Bogardus type appear to correlate highly with degree of ethnic residential segregation (Duncan and Lieberson, 1959). This is reinforced by the correspondence between Trlin's (1971) social distance measurements in New Zealand and Curson's (1970) study of Pacific islander segregation in Auckland. Since the degree of assimilation and of segregation of an ethnic group is a function of both internal and external factors, it is usually difficult to determine—in those circumstances where segregation is high—the extent of choice in the matter available. Here the temporal factor further confuses the issue because a high degree of segregation existing at one point in time may only be an early phase in the assimilation of an ethnic group which appears separate for the moment but which will be assimilated within a generation or so (Rex, 1970).

Ethnic institutions

It has been noted that those urban ethnic groups who maintain a strong identity generally have succeeded in creating and maintaining a comprehensive set of ethnic institutions (Driedger and Church, 1974). These organizations may be of various sorts: religious, educational, political, recreational, etc. The ethnic group succeeds in holding its members' allegiance by preventing their contact with the native community or, indeed, by making such contact unnecessary. This is achieved by a process of substitution, whereby ethnic institutions rather than those of the 'native' community take hold in the immigrants' social life (Breton, 1964). Driedger and Church (1974) demonstrate from a study of Winnipeg that those ethnic minorities with the highest degree of institutional completeness display the highest levels of residential segregation. They claim that crucial to the maintenance of segregation is the ability of the group to perpetuate its institutions. At the same time, it is clear that the institutions can be most effectively maintained by the perpetuation of segregation.

With this strong association between institutions and ethnic clusters, it is not surprising that the appearance of an ethnic institution in a residential area containing relatively few members of that particular ethnic group is taken by other residents as a signal of invasion. Consequently, the locating of the institution is resisted in the first place. Warner and Srole (1945, p. 45) give several examples of this from their study of 'Yankee City' (Newburyport, Massachusetts):

> When the Irish built their church here they had to have someone else buy the land for them because no Protestant would have sold them the land in that place. And when the people found out about it, they were very sore. Some 80 years later, when the Jewish community came to buy a vacated church building . . . for use as a synagogue, the families in the area again 'were very sore', and a petition was circulated to influence the mayor 'to keep the purchase from being made'. (By permission of Yale University Press)

FUNCTIONS OF ETHNICALLY SEGREGATED RESIDENTIAL AREAS

Ethnic residential clusters in cities seem to be basically defensive and conservative in function. One perspective suggests that we adopt a conflict interpretation (Hannerz, 1974), just as Cohen has in his approach to ethnic groups themselves, when he claims that they are interest groups engaged in struggle with other groups for resources in the public arena. Neuwirth (1969) suggests that community solidarity is not purely the result of common residence but also a response to outside pressures.

Conflict situations in cities lead people to feel threatened. This will particularly apply to recent in-migrants, who may vary culturally and indeed racially from the 'host' population. It will also apply to ethnic groups who have retained their distinctive characteristics long after the initial arrival in the city as in-migrants. The perceived threat may materialise in the form of physical violence or may remain as psychological threat. At the same time, and indeed sometimes because of the threat, the ethnic group may have a strong urge to internal cohesion, so that the cultural 'heritage' of the group may be retained (i.e. in order that total assimilation may be prevented).

Defensive functions

The ethnic residential cluster emerges as a complex mechanism for providing defence, for preserving culture and, indeed, for launching attacks on the host society (Boal, 1972). Firstly, we can consider the physical defensive role of the cluster. By joining the ethnic cluster, members of a particular group reduce their isolation, and the existence of the group itself within a clearly defined area enables an organized defence to be developed. Historically, the Jewish 'ghetto' clearly functioned in this way. As Wirth has (1928, p. 19) noted: 'in some instances it was the fear of the remainder of the population, perhaps, which induced them to seek each other's company for the sake of security'. The long history of communal conflict in Belfast illustrates time and again the importance of the ethnic cluster as a defensive arrangement. Isolated households have withdrawn into the heartland of their own group, and that group, in turn, has been able effectively to defend its own segregated area (Boyd, 1969; Northern Ireland Community Relations Commission Research Unit, 1971). A report on disturbances in Northern Ireland in 1969 notes that 'the two communities . . . fell apart into their respective "ghettos", where at least they had a sensation of security' (Tribunal of Inquiry, 1972).

Physical security can be increased by residing in an area of relatively homogeneous ethnic characteristics. The equating of homogeneity with security is one of the factors lying at the heart of suburban flight of many white Americans. This point is made by Gold (1970, p. 154) in a recent paper on urban violence and contemporary defensive cities: 'suburban neighbourhoods, geographically removed from the central city, would be safe areas, protected mainly by racial and economic homogeneity and by distance from population groups with the greatest propensities to commit crimes'. Jackson (1971, p. 11) makes the same point in the Northern Ireland context when he says that 'the family packs its belongings and seeks the security of living among its own kind, where there is both group and territorial protection'.

The ethnic community grouping as a defensive structure can, however, become counterproductive under certain circumstances. The concentration of Jews in the medieval 'ghettos' meant that they could more readily be controlled. The Jews of the Warsaw Ghetto during the Second World War could gain some security from their areal concentration and could even use the 'ghetto' as a basis for insurrection. At the same time, the very fact that they were concentrated in one part of the city meant that their opponents could subject them to an intensive level of attack that would not have been possible if the Warsaw Jews had resided throughout the city. This weakness inherent in residential concentration has been touched on by Taber (1970, p. 138) in his treatise on guerrilla warfare, when discussing the insurrection in Algeria: 'the Draconian methods used by the French in Algiers virtually stamped out the FLN underground there, but only because the Moslems of the Casbah were already separated, racially and physically, from the French population'.

Avoidance functions

A second form of defence occurs as avoidance. At the same time, avoidance of outside contact by means of ethnic residential concentration emphasizes the supportive functions of such concentrations. They provide havens, and for many ethnic groups they have served as 'ports-of-entry' into the larger society. Fried and Levin (1968, p. 67), in a discussion of the slum, make several points of considerable importance in regard to the ethnic cluster (whether physical slum or not):

> One of the most important (functions of the slum) is . . . as a haven. Whether or not individuals living in family based slums are occupationally and socially mobile, the slum serves as a port-of-entry and a place which provides many links with the past. In this respect the working class slum provides an environment of relatively low pressure for social adaptation and change. . . . (From chapter 4 of *Urban Planning and Social Policy*, edited by Bernard J. Frieden and Robert Morris, (© 1968 by Basic Books, Inc., Publishers, New York.)

The emphasis on haven or avoidance can be found in many writings that deal with urban ethnic groups. For instance, Kramer (1970) indicates that the ethnic 'minority' community may be the only place in which its members feel at ease. According to her, they opt for ethnic enclosure in an alien world, finding it a 'haven of refuge in unfriendly surrounding'. Hiro (1973) refers to a common tendency among immigrants to stick together due to the unfamiliarity and insecurity that they feel on arrival in a new country; he claims that the West Indians in England are no exception to this patterns. Nicolas Deakin (1970,

p. 122) when discussing coloured immigrant concentrations in British cities, comments:

> . . . there are, after all, a number of good reasons for choosing the familiar surroundings in preference to the dubious honour of integrating a housing estate, with the possibility of hostile or at best anxious neighbours. It is psychologically supportive to have neighbours from a familiar background.

The Ministry of Housing and Local Government (1969, p. 134) report on council housing in England and Wales, when discussing West Indians, says: 'there are (those) who will not want to leave the concentration in the inner city either through fear of the unknown or because they feel threatened by the hostility they have increasingly perceived among the majority'.

The black ethnic concentrations in American cities would appear to have a similar cushioning function against external hostility. Drake and Cayton (1945) claim that black people 'escape from the tensions of contact with white people', and 'the pressure of the white world is lifted' by residence in the ethnic cluster and its associated social networks. Kenneth Clarke (1967) notes that 'there is considerable psychological safety in the "ghetto"; there one lives among one's own and does not risk rejection among strangers'.

The supportive nature of the ethnic concentration has been reinforced, in many instances, by the development of welfare institutions specifically to serve the local ethnic clientele. Richmond (1969) claims that in the nineteenth century immigrant families, through their extended family networks, provided the only support, material and social, upon which the newcomers could rely. This seems somewhat of an overstatement in that the immigrant communities did tend to establish welfare institutions of their own. A more recent example of this comes from 'New Commonwealth' immigration to Britain (Hiro, 1973, p. 127):

> The function of the Gurdwara (temple) does not cease after Sunday service. It remains open to Sikhs at all times of the day and night. A hungry Sikh can walk in and cook a meal for himself in the refectory, if one is not already prepared. A homeless Sikh can sleep there during the night and stay during the day. (By permission of D. Hiro, *Black British, White British*, Eyre and Spottiswoode (Publishers) Ltd.)

Hiro also refers to Moslem mosques, which, though first and foremost places of worship, also tend, in the present British context, to become part of the Pakistani community's social welfare system.

The avoidance of outside contact and the development of areas of substantial ethnic concentration with their own particular culturally based needs serve to provide what Hannerz (1974) calls 'protected niches' for entrepreneurs. In such niches, some members of the ethnic groups have been able to advance themselves through ethnic enterprise in the form of shops, or the provision of professional or personal services. Hannerz also notes that the ethnic cluster can provide a niche for less legitimate entrepreneurship in the form of organized crime. He develops this argument in relation to the Cosa Nostra and Italian concentrations in American cities (Hannerz, 1974, p. 52):

> . . . the relative success of organization members, and their ability both to provide certain benefits and to enforce sanctions against those within the community who act contrary to the will of the organization, seem together to have given the Cosa Nostra a relatively safe harbour in the Italian–American communities, the members of which may have been somewhat reluctant to cooperate with outsiders against their own countrymen. (By permission of U. Hannerz in A. Cohen (Ed.), *Urban Ethnicity*, Tavistock Publications Ltd., London.)

The parallels between this function for the ethnic cluster and its role in connection with the urban guerrilla are striking (see below).

The avoidance functions of the ethnic residential cluster can be significantly reinforced where chain migration has been operative. Chain migration has been defined as that movement in which prospective migrants learn of opportunities, are provided with transportation, and have initial accommodation and employment arranged by means of primary social relationships with previous migrants (Macdonald and Macdonald, 1964). Chain migration, consequently, will tend to maintain group homogeneity at a high level. Where chain migration involves the families of initial in-migrants, this particularly can create very strong close-knit communities (Dalton and Seaman, 1973). Several studies have suggested that the degree of residential clustering (Scott, 1965) and the degree of resistance to assimilation (Trlin, 1971) can be closely correlated with the significance of migration chains. Chain migration can even lead to segregation within what might otherwise be viewed as homogeneous ethnic areas, as illustrated by Burnley's (1972) analysis of Italian areas in Wellington, New Zealand; and it can also be an important factor in the preservation functions of the ethnic residential cluster.

Preservation functions

Although ethnic group solidarity and geographical coherence may be promoted by outside pressures, there also appears to be a desire amongst many urban ethnics to preserve and promote their own cultural heritage. This, of course, may be part of the avoidance mechanisms discussed above, but it also appears for many groups as something more positive. A number of examples can be provided from varying temporal and cultural contexts.

Jewish groupings seem frequently to be a consequence of the desire to conserve identity. Louis Wirth (1928, p. 19), in his book on the 'ghetto' says:

> . . . to the Jews the geographically separated and socially isolated community seemed to offer the best opportunity for following their religious precepts, of preparing their food according to the established religious ritual, of following their dietary laws, of attending the synagogue for

> prayer three times a day, and of participating in the numerous functions of communal life which religious duty imposed upon every member of the community.

This comment was made in reference to the medieval 'ghetto' in Europe. Interestingly, it seems to indicate a function for the ethnic residential concentration that parallels that ascribed by Erving Goffman (1959) to what he calls the 'back region'.

The same desire for conservation can be found in present-day Chicago, where it has been suggested that Jewish parents favour residence in a neighbourhood that has such a high density of Jewish families that the probability of their children marrying a Jewish person approaches certainty (Rosenthal, 1961). It has been noted that in Auckland, New Zealand, among immigrants from the Pacific Islands proximity to persons of the same ethnic background provides an important means of preserving traditional cultural patterns and group identity (Curson, 1970). In a general comment on ethnic residential clustering in the United States, Kramer (1970) states that the 'principle of closure' in the 'ghetto' operated to protect its cultural insulation and social isolation. Avoidance of all but the most impersonal economic contact with the dominant group minimized the potential for conflict *and* thus helped to preserve the distinctive values of the ethnic group.

Residential clustering as an aid to the conservation of ethnic characteristics has also been noted in Britain. For instance, Kearsley and Srivastava (1974) refer to Asians in Glasgow as 'living in self-segregating communities (tending) to retain as much of their way of life as possible, and not to value social integration'. Dahya (1974, p. 95), in his discussion of Pakistani ethnicity in industrial cities in Britain, gives us this important statement:

> ... the immigrant community's ecological base serves several important functions which are related to the community's need to create, manifest and defend its ethnic identity. During the early stages of the community's settlement, the ecological base is closely interwoven with the immigrants' participation in ethnic socio-economic institutions and mutual aid, and with the community's need to define its identity, both for its members and outsiders. Reinforced by endogamy, the ecological base with its concomitant institutions serves as an instrument for the transmission of the community's culture, values and identity to the second generation and for maintaining ethnic boundaries and for avoiding (or minimizing) ambiguities with regard to ethnic identity. (By permission of B. Dahya in A. Cohen (Ed.) *Urban Ethnicity*, Tavistock Publications Ltd., London.)

'Attack' functions

Spatial concentration of an ethnic group can provide it with a base for action in the struggle of its members with society in general. This struggle may take a peaceful political form or may become violent. In terms of political action, spatial concentration may enable the group to elect its own representatives, who can then attempt to fight their group's battles in the political arena. The Black Power movement in America wishes to take advantage of this by tapping what Stokely Carmichael calls 'the potential power of the "ghetto"' (Carmichael and Hamilton, 1968). A similar function for the ethnic residential concentration exists, at least potentially, in Britain: 'the geographical concentration in the incipient "ghetto" provides a framework within which to organize, and the preoccupation of most immigrants with bread and butter issues becomes a conscious policy of economic development' (Deakin, 1974, p. 290). Hiro (1973) refers to the political power base of American blacks and suggests the existence of similar (if incipient) posibilities in Britain.

The significance of the ethnic residential concentration extends beyond institutional politics. Such areas also provide potential bases for urban insurrection or guerrilla warfare. Hobsbawm (1969, p. 308), reviewing the relationship between city layout and urban insurrection, suggests just such a role for the black concentrations in American cities:

> . . . the 'ghettos' lap round the city centre like dark and turbulent seas. It is this concentration of the most discontented and turbulent in the neighbourhood of a relatively few unusually sensitive urban centres which gives the militants of a smallish minority the political importance which black riots would certainly not have if the 10 or 15 per cent of the U.S. population who are Negroes were more evenly distributed throughout the whole of that vast and complex country.

Urban ethnic residential concentrations provide a milieu closely equivalent to the classic guerrilla situation favoured by Mao Tse-tung—the guerrilla is the fish and the people are the sea (Kitson, 1971). Taber (1970) notes that 'even in well policed, large cities, a sympathetic population can protect active insurgents' (shades of the Cosa Nostra). Certain areas in Belfast have functioned in this way from time to time; rioters and members of insurrectionary groups 'disappear' into such areas, protected by the silence of the inhabitants—a silence based on either sympathy or intimidation.

The ethnic residential cluster as a base for attack has international ramifications. For instance, only partly assimilated Catholic Irish ethnics in the United States (e.g. Boston) are thought to provide financial support for the insurrectionary IRA operating in the ethnic conflict situation in Northern Ireland. Irish ethnic clusters in English cities are also not uninvolved in the same conflict.

In concluding this discussion of the functions of ethnic residential concentrations, it is worth nothing that such concentrations display all the basic features ascribed to territory—they provide a source of identity, they are characterized by substantial degrees of exclusiveness and they act to compartmentalize activity spatially (Boal, 1969; Soja, 1971).

SEGREGATION

We have focused attention on the functions of the ethnic residential cluster. The term cluster implies some degree of segregation of the ethnic group concerned from other groups or from the remainder of the population. The term residential segregation must now be examined and, in addition, a number of measurement problems must be discussed.

Definitions

The customary academic definition of residential segregation is that a particular ethnic group is completely unsegregated when its members are distributed uniformly, relative to the remainder of the population. Any deviation from such uniformity represents a situation characterized by segregation, and the greater the deviation the greater the degree of segregation. This concept of segregation implies an inverse which, following Marcuse (1969), can be referred to as 'residential mixing'. Thus, the closer an ethnic group is to being distributed evenly relative to the total population, the greater the degree of residential mixing (Poole and Boal, 1973).

Segregation and its inverse, mixing, must be clearly distinguished from two other concepts, both of which involve examination of the relative numerical balance between two groups in a given area. The first regards complete residential mixing as occurring when two ethnic groups are found in equal numbers in a particular area. It may be hypothesized that this is a particularly important concept to people themselves, for it seems likely that the fact that an ethnic group is found in the same proportion in a particular neighbourhood as in a city as a whole is of little perceptual relevance to the residents, especially since they are probably unaware of the overall proportion in that particular city anyway. What probably matters to the residents is which ethnic group is in the majority and by how much. This notion must be related to desired levels of homogeneity for a residential area and also to the function of 'tipping-points' (see below). In order to minimize semantic confusion, it would be best to restrict the segregation–mixing dichotomy to descriptions of uniform distributions and deviations from such uniformity, and to employ the terms 'dominance' and 'equality', albeit in a strictly numerical sense, as an analogous dichotomy for use in the context of describing deviation from the situation where each ethnic group is found in equal numbers in a particular area.

The second of the two concepts, which are alternatives to the definition given of residential segregation and residential mixing, is exemplified in the work of Sudman, Bradburn and Gockel (1969), in which they define racially integrated housing, not with reference to the racial composition of the entire group of residents in a neighbourhood at a particular cross-section through time but in relation to the racial affiliation of the new residents moving into the neighbourhood during a particular period of time. This can be considered as a balanced flow definition of segregation.

The segregation–mixing definition is that most frequently employed, and the degree of segregation existing is usually measured by the index of segregation (Taeuber and Taeuber, 1965), which takes the form:

$$\text{Index of segregation} = \left(\frac{Ao}{At} - \frac{Bo}{Bt}\right)100$$

where A represents a particular ethnic group, B represents the rest of the population, o represents those data sub-sets (see below) where the ethnic group is overrepresented relative to its proportion in the city, and t represents the total population of A and B. The index can range from 0 (complete mixing) to 100 (complete segregation). It will be clear that the index is a measurement of deviation from a state of even distribution. It thus has a residual quality which provides a 'catch-all' for the operation of a number of different segregating processes—basically economic factors and ethnic factors which may be voluntary or involuntary in nature (Lee, 1973b; Zelder, 1970). As we shall see later, this residual quality of the index raises problems in its use for policy purposes.

Scale of analysis

Reference has been made to the existence of certain ethnic group proportions in particular unit areas within a city. This raises the whole question of the unit areas to be employed in any ethnic segregation analysis. Employing the terminology of Poole and Boal (1973), we can discuss this question under the heads of data set and data sub-set. The data set refers to the area of study, while the data sub-sets are subdivisions of the data set made for purposes of spatial analysis.

The likely data set to be adopted can take one of three basic dimensions. The smallest data set will be the core city of a larger urban area, an intermediate data set will be the whole urban area, while the largest set will be that segment of space which functions both as a relatively closed and as a highly integrated system in relation to the multitude of flows which characterize urban living. If the core city alone forms the data set, any degree of segregation for a particular ethnic group that exists between the core city and the rest of an urban area will be lost. If the urban area forms the data set, segregation for an ethnic group between it and the more extensive urban system will be lost. The actual data set to be employed in any study is as likely to be determined by data availability as by more conceptual considerations.

The scale of data sub-sets employed in a segregation study can fundamentally influence the values for segregation indices obtained (see, for instance, Poole and Boal, 1973; Taeuber and Taeuber, 1965). The smaller the size of data sub-sets, the larger the segregation index values. The discussion as to whether or not 'coloured ghettos' exist in Britain is bedevilled by this scale problem. For instance, E. J. B. Rose (1969) claims that the degree of 'New Commonwealth' immigrant concentration is much less than popular opinion believes, supporting his statement by reference to the fact that only six local authorities had more than 5 per cent. of their population coloured. More recently, the 1971 census returns, which showed that only five wards in Greater London had more than one-third of their population born in the 'New Commonwealth', were interpreted as demonstrating that 'hardly yet a "ghetto" situation existed' (New Society, 1974). Hiro (1973, p. 63), on the other hand, claims that 'substantially, or dominantly, coloured enclaves have already formed . . . and these will get blacker as years go by and today's children grow up'.

Whether ethnic group concentrations exist or not seems to be related not to the geographic realities but to the scale of the spatial analysis. In this context, Deakin and Ungerson (1973) note that since 'immigrants' form such a low percentage of the London population, the proportion of one particular group living in a specific area would have to be very high indeed to fill it. It must be added, however, that this only applies where the defined area is quite large (such as boroughs or wards). In an unpublished paper, Jones and McEvoy (1974) go further in a discussion of Asians in Huddersfield, demonstrating that when the Asian community is analysed at a scale appropriate to its size it is seen to be acutely separated from the total population. Indeed, at the scale of individual streets they calculated a segregation index of 81.6, which indicates as high a level of segregation as the average block-level segregation for blacks in a sample of American cities (Taeuber and Taeuber, 1965). Perhaps one should not attempt to establish an appropriate scale level for data sub-sets for any particular ethnic segregation analysis; rather one should analyse the segregation over a range of sub-set scales from a coarse to a very fine mesh.

The suggestion that ethnic residential segregation should be examined over a scale range of sub-sets leads to a further suggestion. Much emphasis has been given in the literature to the significance of the ethnic composition of individual streets. Lee (1973b) suggests that what is perhaps the most crucial level of concentration and dispersal from a behavioural or perceptual viewpoint is the proportion of a street or block population belonging to a minority group. It seems possible to go further than this, however, and attempt to define a hierarchy of areas which will have different degrees of significance to the individual resident. A sequence of areas might emerge running from the area encompassing proximate neighbours, through the street or face-block (Suttles, 1972), neighbouring street, rest of neighbourhood, to neighbouring communities. Particular ethnic group composition may well vary in significance through each of these sub-sets. Wolpert, Mumphrey and Seley (1972) developed an approach parallel to this in their study of resident reaction to the introduction of a wide range of facilities in Philadelphia. In the ethnic segregation field, no quantitative work involving this approach is to hand at present.

Homogeneity

In the study of ethnic residential segregation, two questions in regard to homogeneity arise. The first refers to the homogeneity of any group of persons subsumed under an ethnic label. The second question refers to the possibility that a particular ethnic group may desire some specific level of ethnic homogeneity for its area.

When we use an ethnic label such as 'Asian' in Britain, how homogeneous is this group? Perhaps such a classification is not very meaningful in ethnic group terms and may well hide fundamental internal differences (e.g. Indians, Pakistanis or Bangladeshis—or even finer distinctions—see Lee, 1973b). A further example of this problem is provided by Jackson (1964) and by Lee (1973a), who both treat the Irish in London as a homogeneous group; one would think that the ethnic conflict in Ireland would drive home the profound lack of ethnic homogeneity of a group labelled 'Irish'. Sometimes ethnic groupings are forced on researchers by the nature of available census data, but where this is the case conclusions should be interpreted with the greatest circumspection.

The question of the level of ethnic homogeneity desired by members of a particular group is a complex one. For instance, in the United States the minimum level of homogeneity required by whites vis-à-vis blacks cannot readily be established. Rose (1970) gives some clue when he suggests that whites will seek housing in a particular area until black occupancy attains a level of approximately 30 per cent., but at the same time he states that no general agreement on what whites perceive to be an acceptable residential mix can be achieved.

The concept of 'tipping-point' relates to notions of desirable levels of homogeneity. In this instance, it has been hypothesized that when one group begins to displace another in a particular neighbourhood, a tip-point may be reached beyond which the initially dominant ethnic group begins to leave in large numbers. One definition of the tip-point in the American interracial situation has been given by Grodzins' (1958) claim that once the proportion of non-whites exceeds the limits of the neighbourhood's tolerance for interracial living (this limit being the tip-point) the whites move out. Wolf (1963) suggests that the tip-point does not apply to any current level of interethnic mixture but to the residents' estimation of what the situation will be in the future.

A number of writers, such as Spengler (1967), Gans (1972) and Downs (1973), support the notion that a considerable degree of homogeneity is a basic requirement for a satisfactory set of social relationships to exist in a neighbourhood. Spengler (1967) claims that when that degree of homogeneity is not fully attained the local residential habitat becomes unstable. From this we may conclude that too much ethnic heterogeneity will be disruptive of social relations, but that at present it is impossible operationally to define what the required level of homogeneity actually is (Gans, 1972). Downs (1973, p. 63) has succinctly stated the situation that may confront households of a particular ethnic group:

> Without effective means of changing the behaviour of non-conforming households, the conforming ones can maintain their quality of life mainly in two ways. One is to prevent the entry of many non-conforming households into their neighbourhoods. The other is to move to where few

conforming households are present. (By permission of Yale University Press.)

These two alternative strategies have been called respectively 'voicing' and 'exit' by Orbell and Uno (1972). The outcome of both strategies is to maintain ethnic residential homogeneity. Downs (1973) supports the view that residential discrimination of some type among urban households is an inevitable characteristic of effective urban living. He goes on, however, to say that such discrimination does not mean 'racial or ethnic' discrimination. One can accept this distinction on theoretical grounds, but in practice ethnic group affinity may well be a most useful short-cut indicator of the likely compatibility of households to each other.

Social stratification

One feature that is frequently a fundamental factor in the relationship between an ethnic group and its social matrix is that of social stratification. On the one hand, a given ethnic group may be disproportionately represented in a particular segment of the social class spectrum and, on the other, the same ethnic group may be internally differentiated along social class lines. Thus, on initial immigration into a city, a particular ethnic group may be composed predominantly of relatively poor people. Social class differentiation from the host society will therefore in itself be a basis for segregation. If social mobility occurs over time for certain members of the group, then the members will become differentiated from their ethnic compatriots in social class terms, though they may retain strong ethnic affinities. Gordon (1964) suggests that a series of sub-societies are created by the intersection of the vertical stratification of ethnicity with the horizontal stratification of social class. He calls each of these sub-societies an *ethclass*. He continues (p. 53):

> One may say that the ethnic group is the locus of a sense of historical identification, while the ethclass is the locus of a sense of participational identification. With a person of the same social class but of a different ethnic group, one shares behavioural similarities but not a sense of peoplehood. With those of the same ethnic group but of a different social class, one shares the sense of peoplehood but not behavioural similarities. The only group which meets both of these criteria are people of the same ethnic group and the same social class—the ethclass. (By permission of M. M. Gordon, *Assimilation—in American Life*, Oxford University Press, New York.)

On this basis, each ethclass has the potential for residential segregation from other members of the same social class on the basis of ethnic differences, and from other members of the same ethnic group on the basis of social class.

The fact that any 'ethnic' segregation situation may be due to a particular combination of ethnic factors and of social class factors leads one to posit two alternative segregation models. Where segregation of an ethnic group can be attributed predominantly to socioeconomic factors, a social class model of ethnic segregation can be taken to be operative. Where ethnic segregation persists over an extended period of time due to ethnic as opposed to class factors, then an ethnic model of residential segregation can be accepted (Marston, 1969).

Given that both social class and ethnic factors may explain the degree of segregation of a particular group, a number of studies have attempted to control for social class, interpreting any residual segregation as being due to ethnic factors. For instance, Taeuber (1968) and Berry (1971) have calculated that if blacks, in Cleveland and Chicago respectively, were distributed purely on the basis of the existing economic structure of society, segregation would still be very high indeed. The conclusions reached indicate that ethnic rather than social class factors are predominant. In Toronto, on the other hand, Marston (1969) only goes so far as to say that an 'unqualified social class model of ethnic segregation' is unsupportable. Furthermore, in London, Lee's (1973b) analysis of the segregation of West Indians, which controlled for ethnic status rather than social class, also takes a middle-of-the road interpretation when he states that if there was no segregation on racial and ethnic grounds ('voluntary and involuntary') the social class characteristics of the West Indian-born population would ensure a marked concentration of that group in inner London. Thus, the two studies by Taeuber (1968) and Berry (1971) of black segregation in the United States indicate that the low socioeconomic status of that ethnic group has little to do with its high level of residential segregation. Marston's (1969) and Lee's (1973b) studies, on the other hand, suggest that social class is an important contributor to ethnic segregation, but that purely ethnic factors are also of considerable significance. The extent to which the ethnic factor operates as a source of voluntary as opposed to involuntary segregation remains undefined.

An ethnic group, though concentrated predominantly in the lower levels of the socioeconomic structure, may well still contain members at all levels of the society. Such internal socioeconomic differentiation of an ethnic group can have two residential spatial outcomes. On the one hand, socioeconomic mobility may release certain ethnic group members from the ethnic residential cluster and they may consequently disperse residentially. On the other hand, ethnic factors may maintain such members within the cluster. In this instance, some socioeconomic internal spatial differentiation of the cluster may be expected (see, for instance, Boal, 1970; Marston, 1969), creating what we may call ethclass segregation.

SPATIAL OUTCOMES

Our discussion to this point has established that the ethnic group can be racial, religious or national in origin, or some combination of these. In the urban context, we interpret the ethnic group as having its initiation through in-migration, and we assume that its subsequent social and spatial experience

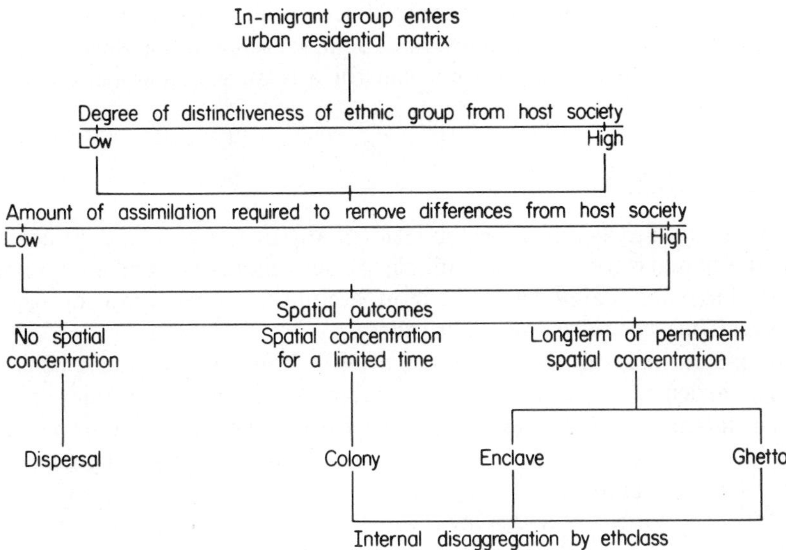

FIGURE 2.1 Ethnic groups, assimilation and residential spatial outcomes

will be a function of the degree and speed of assimilation that occurs. We have also noted that the ethnic vertical divisions of society are likely also to display internal horizontal differentiation on the basis of social class or economic status characteristics. We can now proceed to examine the spatial outcomes of the various social processes. Figure 2.1 shows the suggested relationships between ethnic group distinctiveness, degree of assimilation and these spatial outcomes.

If the entering group has very few differences from the host society, rapid dispersal into the urban spatial structure is to be expected. If host group–ethnic group differences are initially important, the ethnic group will display spatial concentration. In some instances, this will only be a stage in the assimilation of the group into the urban sociospatial fabric and it is suggested that such concentrations be called 'colonies'. In other instances, the condition of concentration may be long term in nature. The maintenance of such a condition is likely to be the outcome both of cohesion factors within the ethnic group and external pressures from the host society. Where the situation suggests that the dominant factor is internal cohesion, the ethnic spatial concentrations will be called 'enclaves'; where external factors severely limit the possibilities for dispersal of the spatial concentrations, the concentrations will be called 'ghettos'. It is realized that 'enclave' and 'ghetto' are ideal types, but the distinction, though operationally difficult to make, is conceptually important.

The links we have suggested earlier between assimilation and ethnic residential segregation indicate that such segregation must be viewed not only spatially but temporally. In other words, we need to be able to examine the evolution of any individual pattern. Only in this way can we obtain spatial clues as to the underlying processes operative. Lack of temporal perspective will not only exist where the record is incomplete but also in those situations where a particular ethnic group has only been resident for a relatively short period of time (Johnston, 1971).

The spatial record

Where data are available on the residential patterns of ethnic groups over time, the spatial record may be available in one or more of a number of different forms. Some forms are likely to be more useful than others for a comparative analysis. The principal forms are as follows:

1. Simple dot maps of the occurrence of households or individuals belonging to a particular ethnic group. The spatial pattern of the dots can be examined and statements can be made about the distribution relative to some particular area, such as that defined by the corporate limits of a city or by the area of residential land use.
2. Maps which attempt to display the distribution of the ethnic group population relative to the population of a given city as a whole. These can take a number of forms:
   (a) Choropleth maps showing the percentage of the population in each data sub-set which belongs to the ethnic group being analysed.
   (c) Choropleth maps showing the proportion of the population in each data sub-set belonging to the ethnic group being analysed relative to some 'expected' proportion. The 'expected' proportion is generated by making one or more assumptions, such as that of an even distribution.
3. Choropleth maps which indicate, for each data sub-set within a particular city, the proportion of the ethnic group in the city that is resident within each sub-set.

In the analysis that follows we have had to draw upon a varying set of records.

Figure 2.1 attempts to indicate the spatial outcomes of the social processes operative in the city insofar as they might influence ethnic residential patterns. This gives a number of outcomes which have been labelled dispersal, colony, enclave and ghetto. To place a particular ethnic distribution into one of these categories requires that the distribution be viewed over time. It also requires that where ethnic clustering exists we have some indication of the voluntary or involuntary nature of such clustering. In reading the spatial record, we must also take note of the 'fabric' effects.

'Fabric' effects

We have laid considerable emphasis on internal group cohesion as a key factor in ethnic residential segregation. However, the cohesion may in part be due to external pressures and also to obstacles in the urban housing fabric to the free movement of ethnic groups. We can view any particular city as presenting to the ethnic group household a physical and social housing fabric within which it can move with varying degrees of difficulty. The influence of the fabric can be briefly indicated.

A high proportion of inmigrants into cities tend, at least initially, to occupy relatively unfavourable position in the economic structure of the particular society. For ethnic groups, the average household economic position may vary with time (social mobility), but some groups remain relatively disadvantaged for generations. Given relatively low economic position, a very considerable proportion of a particular city's housing stock is consequently unavailable to the in-migrant ethnics. Thus, only the lowest cost (and frequently poorest quality) housing can be entered by these groups. Harvey (1973) explains the black ghetto in American cities in this way. It should be noted, however, that his emphasis on economic competition in the housing market provides no explanation for the segregation that exists *between* ethnic groups, each of which may suffer considerable economic disadvantage.

The poorest quality housing locations are almost invariably to be found in the innermost portions of cities or, where redevelopment is significant, in a ring immediately outside the expanding redevelopment zones. Some examples of concentration in peripheral locations also exist, for instance in Australia, where it has been suggested that such concentrations are due to the prevalence of low land values and the absence of local government regulations prohibiting the building of low-grade housing. Proximity to certain industrial job opportunities also seems to be a factor (Scott, 1965; Stimson, 1970). The evidence available in this instance, however, does not enable us to be sure that such peripheral locations are the initial ones subsequent to entry to the city or whether they are secondary in nature. Another example, drawn deep from the historical record, is the extramural/peripheral locations for Catholics in the early days of urban development in Ireland (Jones, 1960; Orme, 1971).

The significance of spatial access to certain types of relatively unskilled employment available predominantly in the central business district has also been stressed by several writers (Kearsley and Srivastava, 1974; Ward, 1971) as giving added significance to inner-area housing locations for low income in-migrant ethnics.

High status in-migrants are not likely to form ethnic residential clusters, but rather to disperse within the relevant socioeconomic spatial context. This will be particularly true where the inmigrant has close cultural affinities with the host population or with a particular occupational segment of it. Sheer numbers may also be important, in that high status inmigrants are likely to be few. Even where relatively low status ethnic households are concerned, it has been suggested that some minimum number is necessary before ethnic clustering becomes viable or is forced upon the groups concerned (Driedger and Church, 1974; Jakle and Wheeler, 1969).

Superimposed on the economic constraints, it is possible to find evidence of other factors operative. For instance, in the British context, with the production of large quantities of public ('Council') housing, where priorities are given to low income families in poor existing dwellings, one would expect low income ethnics to be a significant element in the vast peripheral public housing estates. Since this is not the case, questions must be raised about the constraints that operate. Rex and Moore (1967), in their discussion of Birmingham, suggest that the five-year waiting period before a household can get its name placed on a council waiting list at all, operates greatly to the disadvantage of the in-migrant (black or white). They also claim that specific discrimination against 'coloured immigrants' is evident. On the other hand, a number of studies suggest that certain in-migrant groups have, in fact, no desire to obtain rented council housing. Kearsley and Srivastva (1974), for example, state that the imperative towards the ownership of property is very strong among Asians in Glasgow and that this has had a powerful influence on their residential location patterns. They even go so far as to write of the emphatic rejection of renting as a mode of household tenure. Dahya (1974) also emphasizes Asian desire for house purchase as a means of saving rent, as a means of obtaining a steady source of income by taking lodgers and as an expression of status. He is also critical of Rex's explanation of the absence of coloured immigrants from council estates in Birmingham, referring to a study by Plant (1971) where a claim is made that 'to date no Asian immigrant in Birmingham has put his name down for a local council house'. This Asian emphasis on house purchase, consequently, is a factor explaining the absence of Asian from public housing estates. In addition, since one reason for house purchase is to enable the owner to take in lodgers, it is the larger older houses of the inner ring of British cities that prove the most attractive. Here again, we see the housing fabric constraining the locations of the ethnic clusters.

West Indian migrants, on the other hand, do not appear to be opposed to renting council housing *per se*, and the explanation for their low numbers in outer council estates must lie with some combination of preference for spatial cohesion and the effects of the operation of the council house allocation system.

Some ethnic groups are neither excluded from public housing nor do they display self-excluding tendencies. Two groups specifically come to mind here—Catholics in Nothern Irish cities and blacks in American urban areas. However, these two groups also display quite different patterns because public housing in American cities is highly concentrated in inner city areas, while public housing in Northern Ireland conforms to the general British pattern of inner city redevelopment and large-scale peripheral estates.

Economic constraints, and constraints of allocation and preference in the public housing sector, greatly reduce the proportion of the urban housing 'fabric' open to ethnic households. A further constraint exists in 'blocking'. In this case, areas that are within the economic/preference outreach of particular ethnic groups are blocked by the resistance of existing occupants. Examples of this have been noted by both Kantrowitz and Clark. Kantrowitz (1969) claims that in New York City the greatest opposition to Negro dispersion comes from specific white ethnic groups. Clark (1964) gives us the following:

Examples of such roadblocks to Negro movements could be seen in St

> Louis around 1930 when German Jews, Poles and Italians bounded the Negro district near the Mississippi. 'The Polish Principality' of Hamtramck in Detroit has for years been impenetrable by Negros. The ethnic ghettos along Franklin Street in North Philadelphia have long prevented the eastward movement of Negros.

Thus, existing tightly knit ethnic clusters are the most resistant to invasion, or perhaps one could say that they are least liable to retreat. Areas occupied by groups that are more mobile socially also tend to be more mobile geographically, and the blocking effect of such groups is much less significant. In this way, the expansion of a particular ethnic group's territory is steered into specific limited segments of the urban housing fabric.

Institutional factors in the housing market may also introduce 'fabric effects'. If financial institutions that operate in the housing field employ policies that discriminate against certain ethnic groups on non-economic grounds or if real estate agents operate selective steering policies, then the array of housing stock available to these ethnic groups is consequently restricted (Daniel, 1968; Helper 1969; E. J. B. Rose, 1969).

Fabric effects create limited niches for ethnic group occupation. At times the niches are shared by a number of groups. This would be true, for instance, of the Addams area of Chicago (Suttles, 1968) and also of parts of inner north-west London (Jones and Sinclair, 1968). However, at a detailed scale level, the common niche may be found to display internal ethnic segregation.

Spatial generalizations

Anderson (1962) has produced the most succinct set of generalizations covering the spatial patterns of ethnic groups. He suggests two alternative patterns, the one being sectoral and associated with groups displaying numerical growth, the other not displaying extensive sectoral features, this latter being associated with static or declining groups. Anderson claims that what he calls 'ethnic' groups do not display markedly sectoral spatial patterns, both because restrictions on immigration (recently in the United States) prevent the influx of great numbers of new recruits and because acculturation and assimilation into the broader social structure cause these groups to lose many members, thus effectively preventing their growth. Anderson does not treat racial groups under the ethnic rubric. He does discuss black residential patterns in American cities, however, and concludes that they are an exception to his rule that growing groups display sectoral spatial patterns. In this instance, he says that black expansion tends to be concentric to a much greater extent, though 'some sectorial development is characteristic even in this extreme case however'.

The importance of Anderson's contribution does not lie in the patterns he suggests but in the distinction he makes between growing and static or declining ethnic groups. The growing group is one where assimilation is of

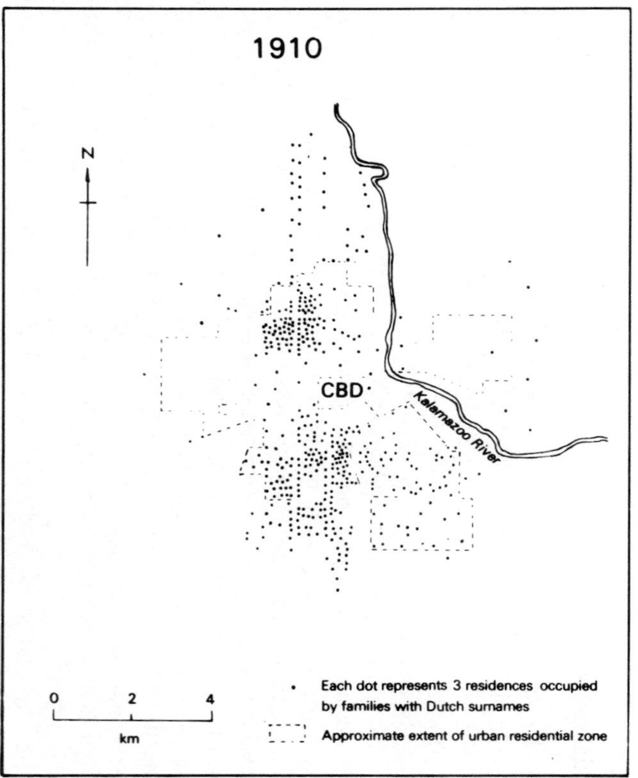
1910
N
CBD
Kalamazoo River
0
2
4
km
Each dot represents 3 residences occupied by families with Dutch surnames
Approximate extent of urban residential zone

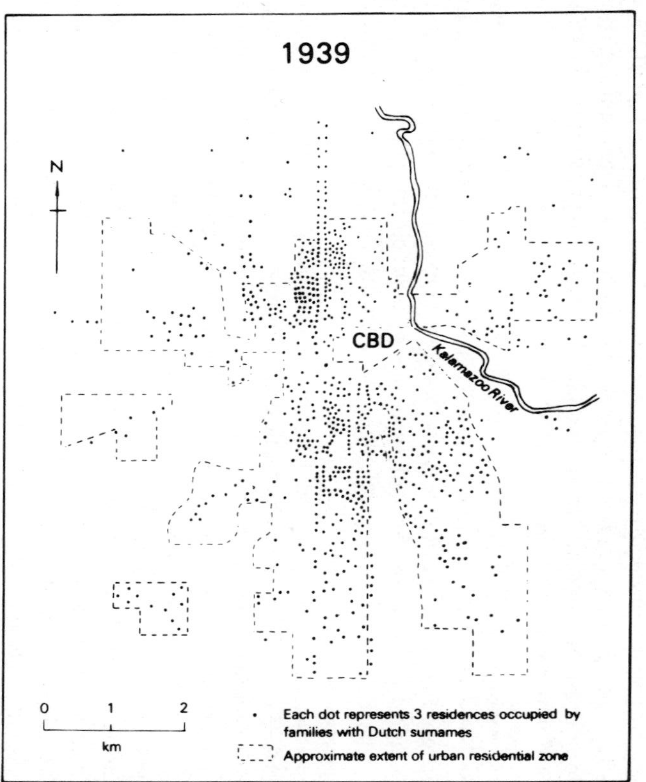
1939
N
CBD
Kalamazoo River
0
1
2
km
Each dot represents 3 residences occupied by families with Dutch surnames
Approximate extent of urban residential zone

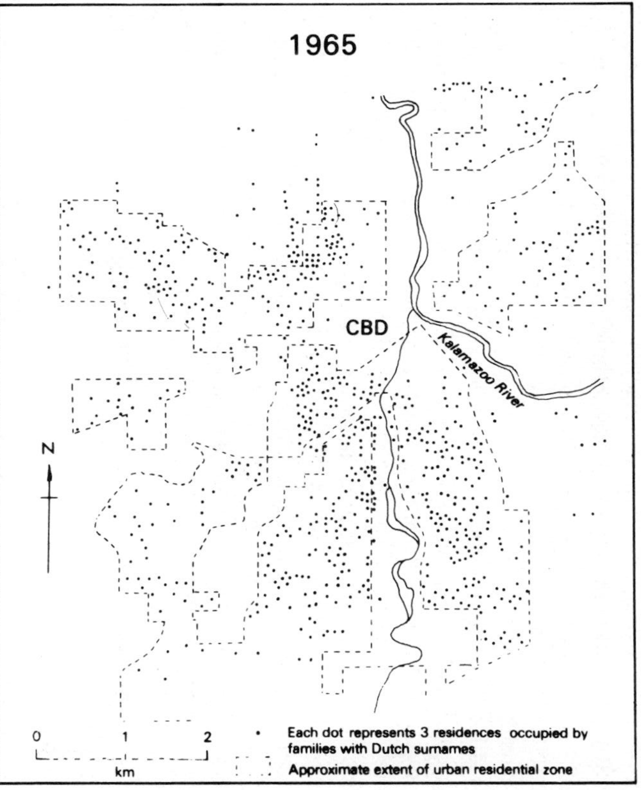

FIGURE 2.2 The ethnic colony: households with Dutch surnames in Kalamazoo, Michigan. (Reproduced by permission of the Association of American Geographers, from Jakle and Wheeler, 1969)

little importance or where the assimilation of a limited number of group members is more than counterbalanced by new members being added to the group, either by inmigration or natural growth processes.

Colony

We can now turn to examine the spatial outcomes suggested in Figure 2.1. The dispersed outcome does not require discussion because it does not represent segregation. The colony outcomes refers to those situations where a particular area of a city serves as a port of entry for an ethnic group. The colony provides a base wherefrom ethnic group members are culturally assimilated and spatially dispersed. The colony may be a relatively short-lived feature or it may have a considerable longevity, the latter state being largely dependent on a continuing input of new ethnic group members. Figure 2.2 shows the distribution of 'Dutch' households in Kalamazoo, Michigan, at three dates between 1910 and 1965. The 1910 pattern shows two marked Dutch clusters, whereas 1939 shows considerable dispersal, though with evidence still of the original clusters. The 1965 distribution is highly dispersed. It is suggested that this sequence would be fairly typical of the operation of the colony situation. The only unusual feature is that the initial colonies were not located in the inner city but on the then edge of the town, due to Dutch attachment to certain agricultural activities, though there are parallels to this in the distribution of Italians in Wellington, New Zealand (Burnley, 1972). A full reading of the paper by Jakle and Wheeler (1969) will fill in the details of both pattern and process in this instance. Other cartographic examples of the colony type of ethnic concentration (and subsequent dispersal) can be found in Warner and Srole (1945). In all these cases, initial clumps have functioned as colonies, but with assimilation and also with a decline of in-migration dispersal has occurred, accompanied by the final disappearance of the clumps.

Enclave–ghetto

The enclave and ghetto outcomes must be treated together. Earlier it has been established that the distinction between enclave and ghetto lies in the extent to which the particular ethnic concentration can be viewed as a voluntary or involuntary phenomenon. It is very difficult to make this distinction operational, though particular ethnic concentrations do seem to lie at varying points along a voluntary–involuntary continuum. Complexity is increased because it would appear that the enclave–ghetto can take a number of quite distinctive spatial forms.

The first form is particularly associated with Jewish residential areas in many North American cities. In this case, the original location took the form of one or more clumps in the inner city. These clumps did not function as colonies from which dispersion to the wider city fabric occurs, however, but as bases for the subsequent formation of new clumps, invariably in more suburban

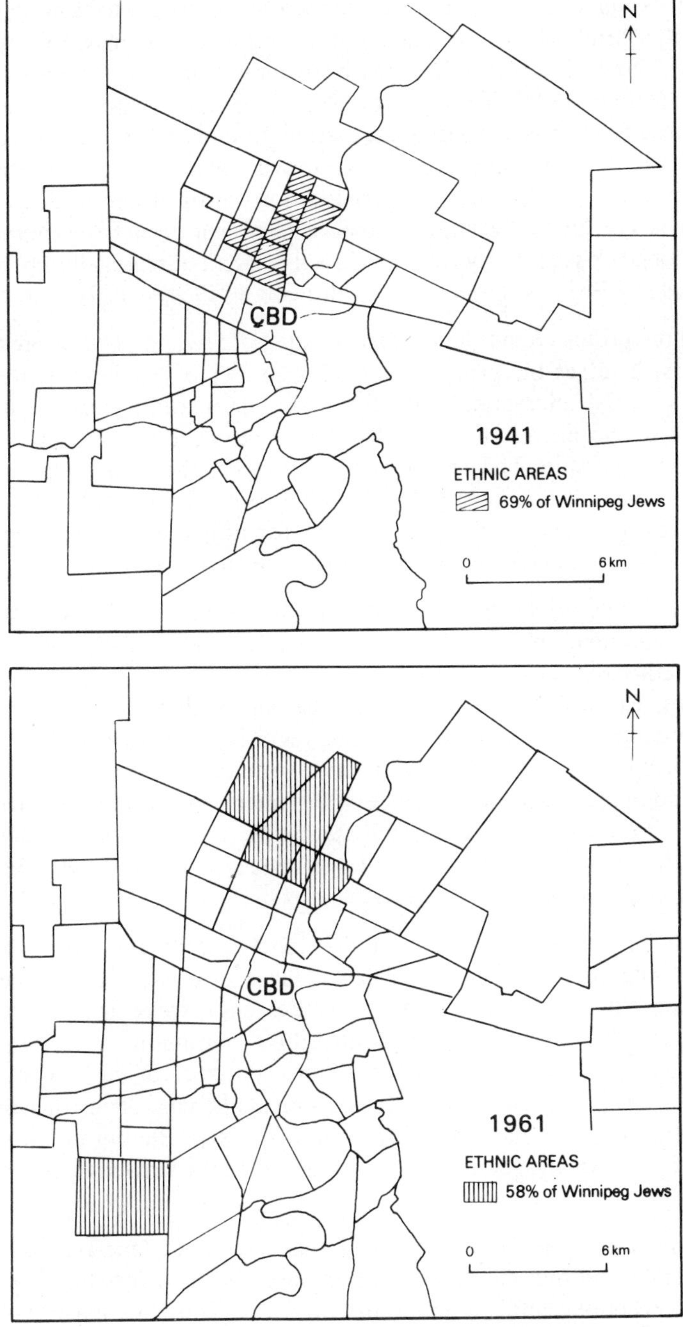

FIGURE 2.3 The ethnic enclave: Jews in Winnipeg, Manitoba. (Reproduced by permission of the Canadian Sociology and Anthropology Association, from Driedger and Church, 1974)

locations. Thus, over time the inner clumps were abandoned and new outer-city clumps established. One cartographic example is provided by Figure 2.3, which shows the shifts of the Jewish cluster in Winnipeg, Manitoba (Driedger and Church, 1974). Though upwardly mobile in social class terms, this did not become the basis for complete assimilation or for geographical dispersal of the Jews. The Winnipeg Jews also moved their ethnic institutions and Driedger and Church feel that this perpetuation of institutions in a new location was and is crucial to the maintenance of segregation. The combination of upward social class mobility with continued residential segregation reinforces a point made by Beshers, Laumann and Bradshaw (1964, p. 487), who write:

> An ethnic group's assimilation involves at least two important processes. The first involves the progressive disappearance of barriers to an ethnic group's 'social interaction' with the native population—i.e. the gradual erosion of the norms of social distance contingent on ascriptive ethnic group membership. The second process involves the improvement in the ethnic group's access to highly rewarding occupational roles. ... these processes operate at very different rates for different ethnic groups. (By permission of the University of North Carolina Press).

In the case of the Jews the improvement in the ethnic group's access to 'highly rewarding occupational roles' has not been accompanied by the erosion of social distance.

It seems reasonable from the evidence to suggest that a large component of this segregation is of a voluntary nature, which indicates that we can place these Jewish segregated clumps in the enclave category. Other examples of the pattern and of the underlying processes are given by Wirth (1928) and Rosenthal (1961) for Chicago. In particular, Rosenthal's paper provides a fascinating insight. The nature of the outer-city Jewish enclaves is further clarified by the following (Rosenthal, 1961, p. 287):

> A modicum of Jewish education and voluntary segregation are two parts of a three part device designed to forestall large scale assimilation. The third is residence in a high status area. ... Settlement there removes the stigma that is usually attributed to a separate ethnic community. ... Residence in a high status area indicates the voluntary nature of the settlement of Jews as well as non-Jews and lifts the burden of alienation from the younger generation in particular. (By permission of E. Rosenthal in the *American Journal of Sociology*, vol. **66**, p. 287, published by the University of Chicago Press.)

Finally, in passing, it should be noted that the Jewish enclaves in Chicago display a degree of internal differentiation based both on variation in degree of religious orthodoxy and on economic position. Thus, we have evidence of ethclass segregation (Rosenthal, 1961).

The second form for the enclave–ghetto is that where a particular ethnic group initially locates in a small segment of the inner city and where subsequent growth conforms basically to a concentric arrangement relative to the city centre. This results in a continuous or discontinuous ring, the discontinuities reflecting variations in the urban fabric in terms of house type and resistant groups (Jones 1970; H. M. Rose, 1969). Anderson (1962) has argued that the growth of black areas in American cities has tended to be concentric, as it has occurred (according to him) through encroachment into relatively stable or non-growing nearby population groups. The distribution of Catholics in Belfast has also, in part, taken the form of a discontinuous inner ring (Poole and Boal, 1973).

A cartographic example of the concentric enclave–ghetto is provided by Figure 2.4, which shows the distribution of Asians in Glasgow for 1951, 1961 and 1971. The spread of this population as it has grown numerically has been steered in a basically concentric fashion by the location of a particular type of tenement housing that situated the locational and tenurial requirements of the Asians—i.e. access to the city centre for jobs and desire for the ownership of property (Kearsley and Srivastava, 1974). The concentricity may also indicate the absence of strong resistance to Asian entry into housing in the inner tenement areas. Since our example shows a changing pattern for the comparatively short period of twenty years, it is difficult to make any predictions as to future evolution in terms of concentration and dispersal. The patterns displayed and the processes operative to date do suggest, however, that the concentration of Asians is due predominantly to voluntary factors. Thus, this example may be treated as lying on the 'enclave' side of our enclave–ghetto continuum.

One difficulty with the Glasgow data is that, while they clearly show the evolution of the spatial pattern of Asian residence, they do not indicate the extent to which Asians numerically dominate in areas at any scale level. The only clue to this is Kearsley and Srivastava's (1974) statement that only in a few limited areas do Asian households form more than 40 per cent. of the total, though they go on to record that it is quite common for a 'close' to house a predominance of Asians. (A 'close' is a set of apartments having a common street entrance and a common stairway.)

As we have already noted, Anderson (1962) has suggested that growing ethnic groups that maintain residential segregation are likely to display a sectoral spatial pattern. He also suggested that American blacks might be a partial exception to this generalization. H. M. Rose (1969) indicates that the rate of growth and the rent-paying ability of the black population strongly influence the completeness of the sectoral arrangement. If there is a disproportionate number of blacks with limited rent-paying ability seeking housing acommodations, a new 'ghetto' cluster is sometimes formed in an alternative low income sector. Thus, black concentrations are initiated in inner-city locations with subsequent growth under continued high segregation, leading to a combination of concentric and sectoral extensions. The cartographic evidence suggests, however, that the truncated sector is now the dominant form for black ethnic areas, the truncation being due to the fact that sectoral growth, under contiguity and socioeconomic constraints, has not reached the edge

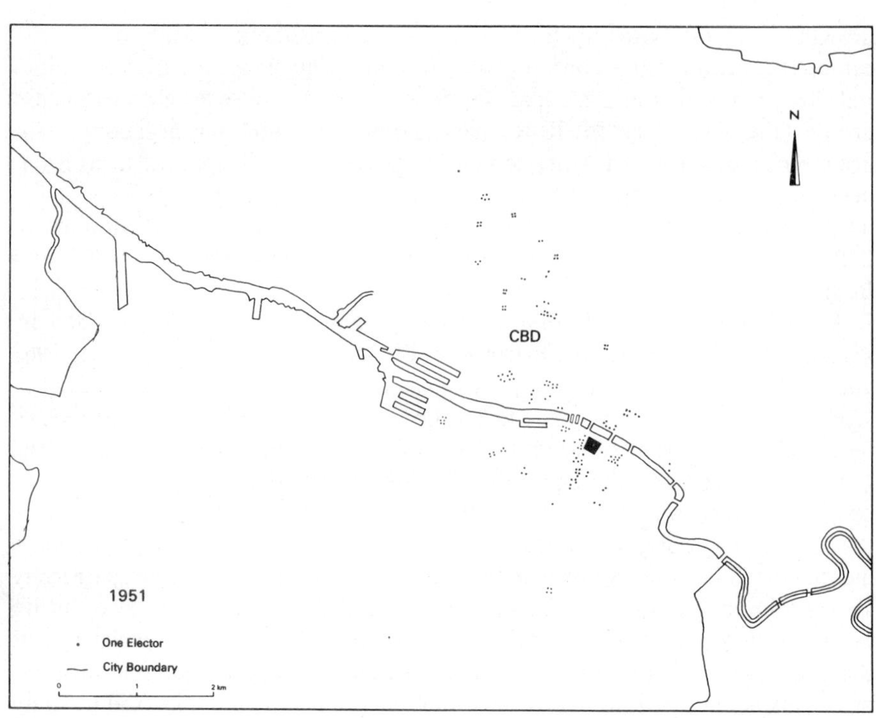
N
CBD
1951
One Elector
City Boundary
0
1
2 km

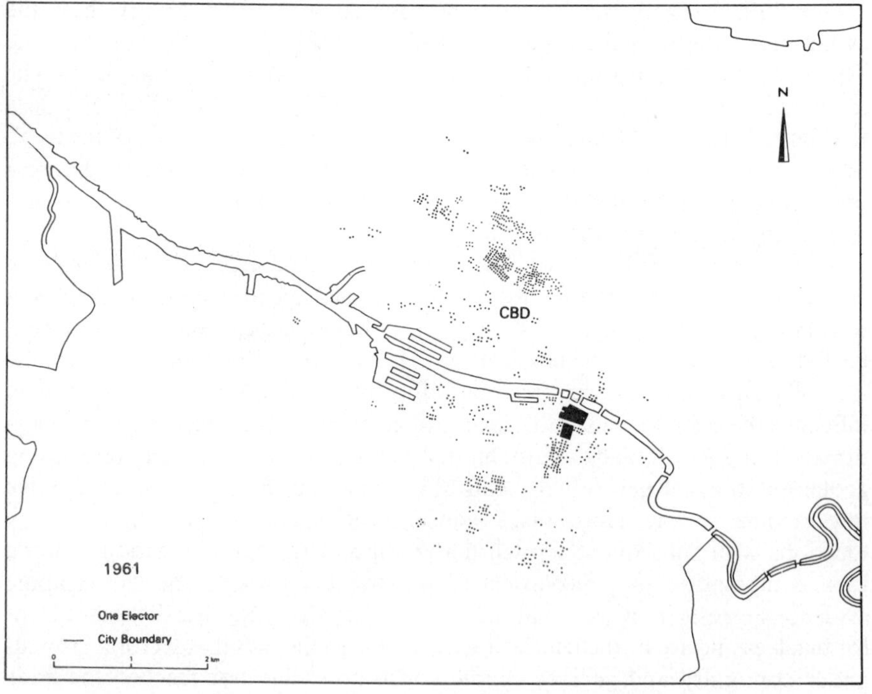
N
CBD
1961
One Elector
City Boundary
0
1
2 km

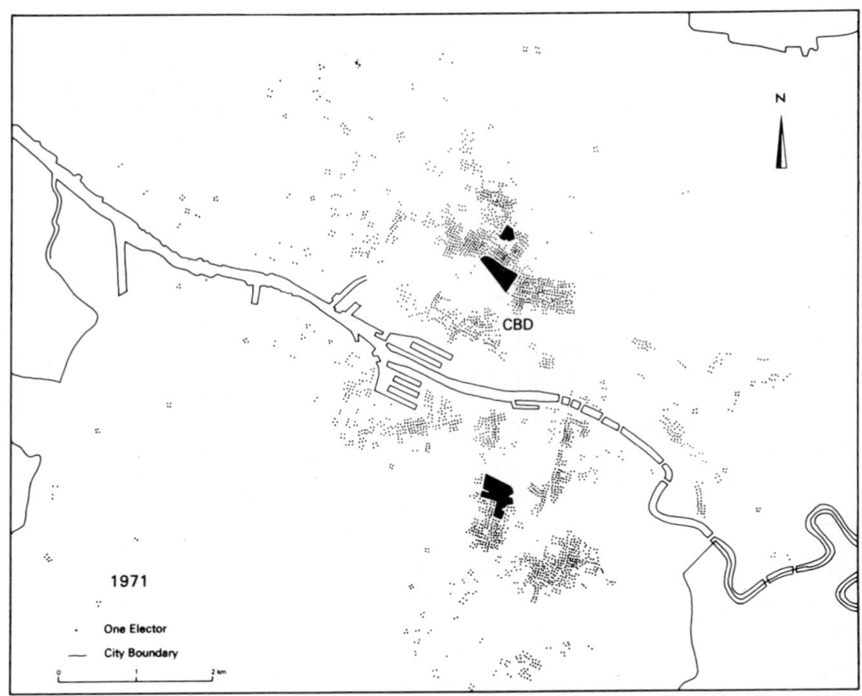

FIGURE 2.4 The concentric enclave–ghetto: households with 'Asian' names in Glasgow, Scotland. (Reproduced by permission of the Royal Scottish Geographical Society, from Kearsley and Srivastava, 1974)

of urban areas. Figure 2.5 provides an example of sectoral distribution for a numerically growing and spatially expanding ethnic group that has shown only a very slight desegregation tendency over the twenty-year period 1950–1970 (Table 2.1).

The black residential concentration in Grand Rapids, Michigan, is clearly sectoral in form. The sector is a truncated one, in that although it now approa-

TABLE 2.1 Black households and block-level segregation indices, Grand Rapids, Michigan, 1950–1970

	'Black' households	Percentage of all households	Block-level segregation index for black households
1950	1 646	3.0	90.3
1960	3 722	6.7	89.7
1970	5 992	11.4	85.7

Note. The area is held constant at the 1950 city limits. The census enumerated non-white households in 1950 and 1960 and Negro households in 1970. This change should have had only a very slight influence on the figures.

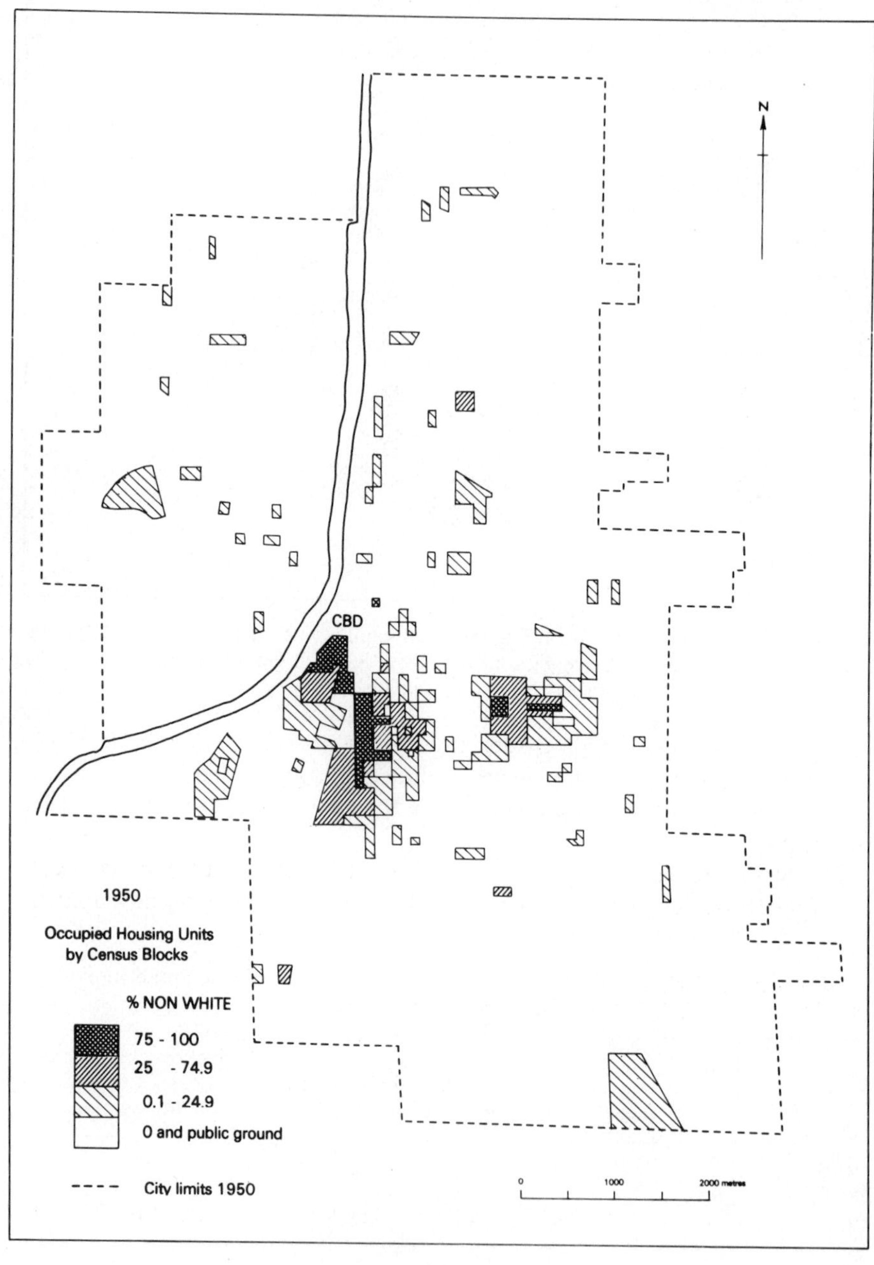
N
CBD
1950
Occupied Housing Units
by Census Blocks
% NON WHITE
75 - 100
25 - 74.9
0.1 - 24.9
0 and public ground
City limits 1950
0
1000
2000 metres

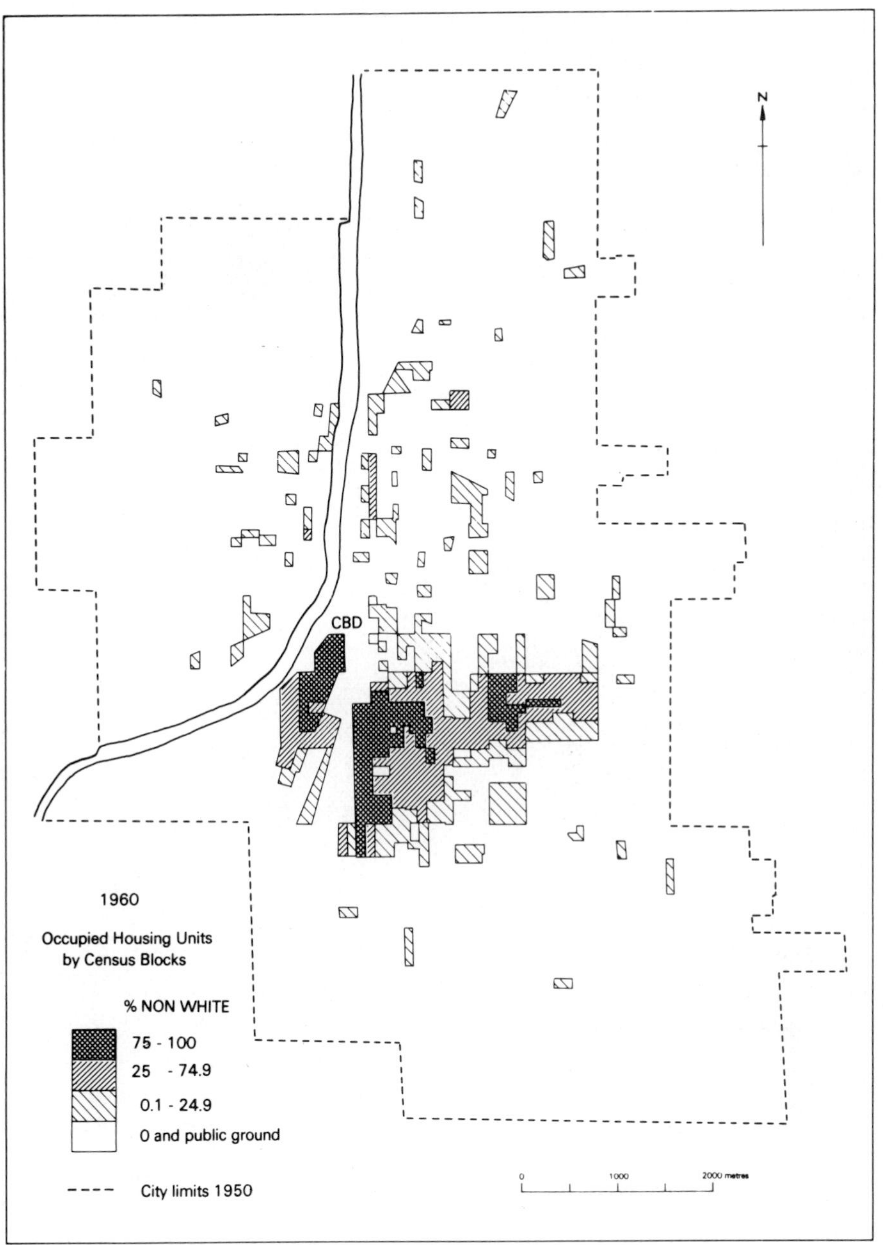
N
CBD
1960
Occupied Housing Units
by Census Blocks
% NON WHITE
75 - 100
25 - 74.9
0.1 - 24.9
0 and public ground
City limits 1950
0
1000
2000 metres

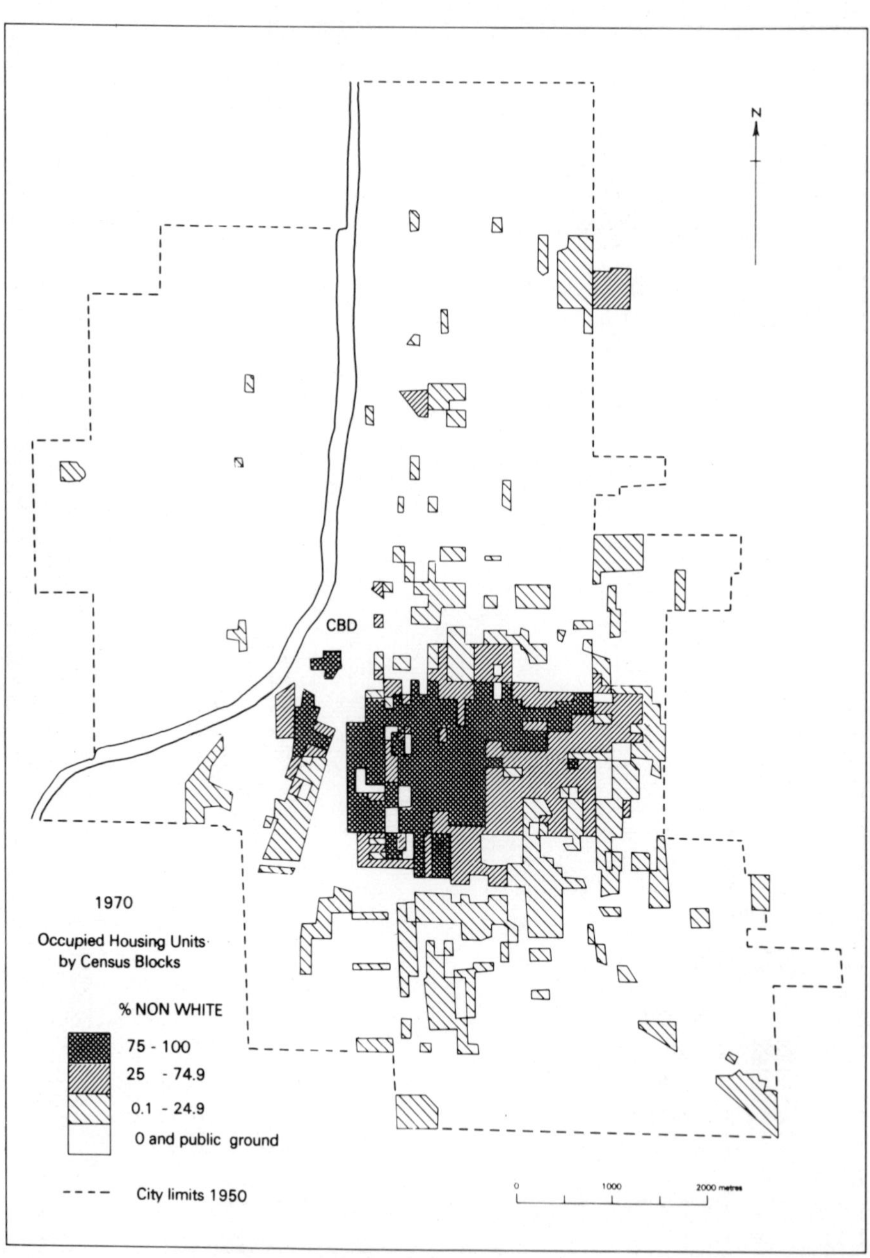

FIGURE 2.5 The sectoral ethnic enclave–ghetto: blacks in Grand Rapids, Michigan

ches the city limits these only define the 'central city', there being very substantial (and almost entirely white) suburbs beyond. Two other aspects of the Grand Rapids' distribution also deserve brief mention. Both refer to 'fabric' effects. First, it will be noted that blacks are virtually absent from the west side of the city. It may be significant that the west side is perceived as the 'Polish' segment and it has been observed for other cities that the Poles have been one of the ethnic groups particularly resistant to black invasion, or less likely to retreat before the possibility. The other fabric aspect refers to the break in the continuity of the black distribution in 1950. This is an area of large houses and it is reasonable to assume that they were economically beyond the reach of most black households. However, with the passage of time and the further build-up and expansion of the black areas, the intervening area became increasingly disfavoured in white eyes, while black entry was further facilitated by a degree of subdivision of the original large dwellings.

The segregation of Roman Catholics in Belfast has shown an even greater longevity than that of blacks in American cities. Institutional completeness is quite high and general assimilation to the majority population has been slight. The dominant spatial feature in this instance is one very large sector which extends right to the edge of the urban area. There are also several inner-area clumps that recently have shown tendencies to expand slightly in a sectoral manner. Thus, the Roman Catholic pattern in Belfast provides a further example of the basically sectoral nature of the ethnic area for a growing non-assimilating group. A key difference from the blacks in the United States, and indeed the Asians in Glasgow, is that Belfast Catholics have full access to peripherally located public housing. This is a further explanation for the completeness of the main sector (Poole and Boal, 1973).

Segregation in Belfast also reminds us of a point made early in this discussion, when it was pointed out (following Abramson, 1973) that ethnic status is not necessarily a function of minority status. Host communities frequently also display many of the features of ethnicity, and this is certainly true of the Protestant majority in Belfast. In this instance, perhaps, one should not talk of the Catholics being segregated *from* the Protestants, but of mutual segregation achieved simultaneously by both groups.

The ethnic sectors in Grand Rapids and Belfast both display internal differentiation on a social class basis. Thus, within each area, ethclass differentiation of the ethnic residential spaces can be recognized. The sectoral areas discussed above have been in existence for a substantial period. The extent to which the segregation is voluntary or involuntary determines whether we should call such spatial structures enclaves or ghettos. Since both choice and force are operative, all we can do is to suggest that these patterns can be subsumed under the enclave–ghetto label, but that they are closer to the ghetto state than is true for the Jews in Winnipeg or Chicago, or for the Asians (at least at present) in Glasgow.

The spatial patterns of ethnic groups in cities appear to be closely related to the degree and nature of the assimilation process. The examples provided illustrate what are taken, at this stage of our knowledge, to be the outcomes of three different degrees of assimilation. In one instance, full assimilation occurs over time and the spatial pattern evolves from clumped to highly dispersed. In the second instance, assimilation occurs along one dimension only (occupational), leading to a transference from an inner-city clumped pattern to a more suburban clumping. In the final instance, over the time spans examined, assimilation is slight, and concentric or sectoral forms evolve, or some combination of these develops.

POLICY ASPECTS

In the preceding discussion, we have emphasized the defensive, the supportive, the conservative and the power base functions of the ethnic residential grouping. In their own contexts, these functions are highly positive in nature and they provide a warning about the too ready adoption of an integrationist approach to urban residential geography. Indeed, Piven and Cloward (1967) have argued that if the American black is to enter the mainstream of national life then it is separation that will be essential to achieve results. They claim that the whole history of ethnic groups in the United States belies the utility of the integrationist view.

In the general suburban context, Downs (1973) has argued that the quality of life in every urban household is, in part, determined by the interactions of its members with other people in the vicinity of its dwelling unit. These interactions involved personal movement, normal child play with value reinforcement, school activities and the use of shared public facilities. To be most effective and least stressful, these interactions should be with people rather similar in life-style. Although Downs does not approve of residential discrimination on ethnic grounds, such an approach is probably an effective means of achieving these satisfactory interactions. Thus, some degree of ethnic homogeneity is desirable.

We have defined three basic types of ethnic segregated residential situations. The colony is a temporary phenomenon—a mechanism for achieving the integration of an ethnic group into the wider society. The enclave is much more permanent, but is viewed as basically voluntary in origin and maintenance; in the case of the Jewish enclave we have cultural pluralism with economic integration (Reubens, 1971). Only when we come to the ghetto does emphasis shift to the operation of involuntary factors. Most commentators hold the position that only forced segregation is bad, though some will interpret that part of ethnic segregation that may be apportioned to economic factors as also being undesirable.

In any policy approach to ethnic residential segregation, the strategy adopted will depend upon the realism of the causal assumptions (Reubens, 1971). Thus, it will be important to try and partition out the causal factors into the three main types of socioeconomic, voluntary ethnic and involuntary ethnic. As we have already noted, it is particularly difficult to evaluate the relative importance of the latter two sets of factors. Even further, it can be argued that economic differentials that contribute to residential segregation may also have their roots in ethnic factors.

Choice

Increasingly it has been recognized that ethnic residential segregation has many positive features (see Deakin and Ungerson, 1973). Statements such as that by Jones (1970) which demands that the possibility that coloured immigrants in Birmingham might approach a majority position in certain clusters should be recognized, 'and appropriate action taken to avoid the establishment of such a degree of segregation' would now be considered excessively dogmatic. The emphasis has shifted to 'choice'. For instance, Cullingworth (1973, p. 127) states that 'dispersal of immigrant concentrations should be regarded as a desirable consequence, but not the overriding purpose, of housing individual immigrant families on council estates. The criterion of full, informed, individual choice comes first'. Deakin and Ungerson (1973, p. 238) adopt a similar stance when they write: 'the important thing is that everybody should be free to choose, and to move outside such circles (of broadly similar social characteristics) if they wish to do so; there should be as few constraints as possible on the exercise of choice by individuals'. In the American racial context, Petticrew (1969, p. 63) adopts a similar position: 'the democratic objective is not total racial integration and the elimination of the ghetto; the idea is simply to provide an honest choice between separation and integration. ... The longterm goal ... is the transformation of these ghettos from today's racial prisons to tomorrow's ethnic areas of choice'.

The emphasis on choice and the consequent removal of the ghetto form of ethic residential segregation is totally consistent with the interpretations of the functions of such segregation adopted in this chapter.

In any attempt to modify patterns of ethnic residential segregation, particular note will have to be taken of the nature of the urban spaces involved. In many instances, these spaces are profoundly territorial and the in-movement of 'alien' households will be viewed as invasion. In addition, the loss of such spaces to individuals or ethnic groups is likely to be traumatic and to be bitterly resisted (Boal, 1969; Fried, 1963; Suttles, 1968). Such territories may well play key roles in reducing interethnic conflict, in that an individual can recognize their existence and can refrain from going where he is likely to be involved in disputes (Sommer, 1969).

Three final comments arise from the preceding discussion. Firstly, I am very conscious of the fact that most of the supporting evidence for the arguments I have developed have been obtained from the works of writers who themselves, by and large, have been observers of the ethnic residential scene rather than active participants. Consequently, there is a need for much greater insight from within the ethnic areas and for interpretation of their functions by ethnic group members. Secondly, there is a great need for standardization of studies over a wide range of cities so that we can readily make comparisons. These studies may well be thought of by some as being less rewarding, in that they are unlikely to demonstrate the use of 'new' techniques, but they are likely to provide a much sounder basis for generalization than exists at present. Finally, I am conscious of the fact that in all the ethnic residential situations discussed above, 'Anglo-Saxon' culture and power provided the host community contexts—this being true whether we are discussing Chicago, Winnipeg, Auckland, Birmingham or Belfast. It is perhaps a nice historical irony that after providing the dominant cultural and economic contexts for a variety of subsequent in migrant ethnic groups in widely flung parts of the world, the tolerance of the Anglo-Saxon host community is probably now being most fully tested in Britain itself.

REFERENCES

Abramson, H. J. (1973). *Ethnic Diversity in Catholic America*, John Wiley, New York.

Anderson, T. R. (1962). 'Social and economic factors affecting the location of residential neighbourhoods'. *Papers and Proceedings of the Regional Science Association*, **9**, 161–170.

Berry, B. J. L. (1971). 'Monitoring trends, forecasting change and evaluating goal achievement in the urban environment: the ghetto expansion versus desegregation issue in Chicago as a case study'. In M. Chisholm, A. E. Frey and P. Haggett (Eds.), *Regional Forecasting*, Butterworths, London, pp. 93–117.

Beshers, J. M., Laumann, E. O., and Bradshaw, B. S. (1964). 'Ethnic congregation—segregation, assimilation and stratification'. *Social Forces*, **42**, 482–489.

Boal, F. W. (1969). 'Territoriality on the Shankill–Falls Divide, Belfast'. *Irish Geography*, **6**, 30–50.

Boal, F. W. (1970). 'Social space in the Belfast urban area'. In N. Stephens and R. E. Glasscock (Eds.), *Irish Geographical Studies*, Queen's University, Belfast. pp. 373–393.

Boal, F. W. (1972). 'The urban residential sub-community—a conflict interpretation'. *Area*, **4**, 164–168.

Boyd, A. (1969). *Holy War in Belfast*, Anvil Press, Tralee.

Burnley, I. H. (1972). 'Ethnic settlement formation in Wellington–Hutt'. *New Zealand Geographer*, **28**, 151–170.

Breton, R. (1964). 'Institutional completeness of ethnic communities and personal relations to immigrants'. *American Journal of Sociology*, **70**, 193–205.

Carmichael, S., and Hamilton, C. V. (1968). *Black Power*, Penguin, Harmondsworth, Middlesex.

Chinoy, E. (1967). *Society*, Random House, New York.

Clark, D. (1964). 'Immigrant enclaves in our cities'. In C. E. Elias Jr., J. Gillies and S. Riemer (Eds.), *Metropolis: Values in Conflict*, Wadsworth Publishing, Belmont, California, pp. 205–218.

Clarke, K. (1967). *Dark Ghetto*, Harper and Row, New York.

Cohen, A. (1974). 'Introduction: the lesson of ethnicity'. In A. Cohen (Ed.), *Urban Ethnicity*, Tavistock, London, pp. ix–xxiv.

Cullingworth, J. B. (1973). 'The social context of planning'. In *Problems of An Urban Society*, vol. 2. George Allen and Unwin, London.

Curson, P. H. (1970). 'Polynesians and residence in Auckland, New Zealand'. *New Zealand Geographer*, **26**, 162–173.

Dahya, B. (1974). 'The nature of Pakistani ethnicity in industrial cities in Britain'. In A. Cohen (Ed.), *Urban Ethnicity*, Tavistock, London, pp. 77–118.

Dalton, M., and Seaman, J. M. (1973). 'The distribution of New Commonwealth immigrants in the London Borough of Ealing, 1961–66'. *Transactions, Institute of British Geographers*, **58**, 21–39.

Daniel, W. W. (1968). *Racial Discrimination in England*, Penguin Books, Harmondsworth, Middlesex.

Deakin, N. (1970). 'Race and human rights in the city'. In P. Cowan (Ed.), *Developing Patterns of Urbanization*, Oliver and Boyd, Edinburgh, pp. 107–129.

Deakin, N. (1974). *Colour, Citizenship and British Society*, Panther Book, London.

Deakin, N., and Ungerson, C. (1973). 'Beyond the ghetto: the illusion of choice'. In D. Donnison and D. Eversley (Eds.), *London: Urban Patterns, Problems and Policies*, Heinemann, London, pp. 215–247.

Downs, A. (1973). *Opening Up the Suburbs*, Yale University Press, New Haven, Connecticut.

Drake, St. C., and Cayton, H. E. (1945). *Black Metropolis: a Study of Negro Life in a Northern City*, Harcourt Brace, New York.

Driedger, L., and Church, G. (1974). 'Residential segregation and institutional completeness: a comparison of ethnic minorities'. *Canadian Review of Sociology and Anthropology*, **11**, 30–52.

Duncan, O. D., and Lieberson, S. (1959). 'Ethnic segregation and assimilation'. *American Journal of Sociology*, **64**, 364–374.

Fried, M. (1963). 'Grieving for a lost home'. In L. J. Duhl (Ed.), *The Urban Condition*, Basic Books, New York, pp. 151–171.

Fried, M., and Levin, J. (1968). 'Some social functions of the urban slum'. In B. J. Frieden and R. Morris (Eds.), *Urban Planning and Policy*, Basic Books, New York, pp. 60–83.

Gans, H. J. (1972). *People and Plans*, Penguin, Harmondsworth, Middlesex.

Glazer, N. (1975). 'The universalization of ethnicity'. *Encounter*, **44**(2), 8–17.

Goffman, E. (1959). *The Presentation of Self in Everyday Life*, Doubleday, Garden City, New York.

Gordon, M. M. (1964). *Assimilation in American Life*, Oxford University Press, New York.

Gold, R. (1970). 'Urban violence and contemporary defensive cities'. *Journal of the American Institute of Planners*, **36**, 146–159.

Greeley, A. (1969). *Why Can't They Be Like Us*. Institute of Human Relations Press, New York.

Grodzins, M. (1958). *The Metropolitan Area as a Racial Problem*, University of Pittsburgh Press, Pennsylvania.

Halbwachs, M. (1932). 'Chicago, experiénce ethnique'. *Annales d'Histoire Economique et Sociale*, **4**, 11–49.

Hannerz, U. (1974). 'Ethnicity and opportunity in urban America'. In A. Cohen (Ed.), *Urban Ethnicity*, Tavistock, London, pp. 37–76.

Harvey, D. (1973). *Social Justice and the City*, Edward Arnold, London.

Helper, R. (1969). *Racial Policies and Practices of Real Estate Brokers*, University of Minnesota Press, Minneapolis.

Hiro, D. (1973). *Black British, White British*, Penguin Books, Harmondsworth, Middlesex.

Hobsbawm, H. E. (1969). 'Cities and insurrections'. *Ekistics*, **27**, 304–308.

Jackson, H. (1971). *The Two Irelands—A Dual Study in Inter-group Relations*, Minority Rights Group, London.

Jackson, J. A. (1964). 'The Irish'. In Centre for Urban Studies (Ed.), *London: Aspects of Change*, MacGibbon and Kee, London. pp. 293–308.

Jakle, J. A. and Wheeler, J. O. (1969). 'The changing residential structure of the Dutch population of Kalamazoo, Michigan'. *Annals, Association of American Geographers*, **59**, 441–460.

Johnston, R. J. (1971). *Urban Residential Patterns: An Introductory Review*, G. Bell, London.

Jones, E. (1960). *The Social Geography of Belfast*, Oxford University Press, Oxford.

Jones, E., and Sinclair, D. J. (1968). *Atlas of London and the London Region*, Pergamon Press, Oxford.

Jones, P. N. (1970). 'Some aspects of the changing distribution of coloured immigrants in Birmingham, 1961–66'. *Transactions, Institute of British Geographers*, **50**, 199–219.

Jones, T. P., and McEvoy, D. (1974). *Residential Segregation of Asians in Huddersfield.* Paper read at the annual conference, Institute of British Geographers, Norwich.

Kantrowitz, N. (1969). 'Ethnic and racial segregation in the New York metropolis'. *American Journal of Sociology*, **74**, 685–695.

Kearsley, G. W., and Srivastava, S. R. (1974). 'The spatial evolution of Glasgow's Asian community'. *Scottish Geographical Magazine*, **90**, 110–124.

Kitson, F. (1971). *Low Intensity Operations*, Faber and Faber, London.

Kramer, J. R. (1970). *The American Minority Community*, Thomas Y. Crowell, New York.

Lee, T. R. (1973a). 'Immigrants in London: trends in distribution and concentration 1961–71'. *New Community*, **2**, 145–158.

Lee, T. R. (1973b). 'Ethnic and social class factors in residential segregation: some implications for dispersal'. *Environment and Planning*, **5**, 477–490.

Macdonald, J. S., and Macdonald, L. D. (1964). 'Chain migration, ethnic neighborhood formation and social networks'. *Milbank Memorial Fund Quarterly*, **42**, 82–97.

Marcuse, P. (1969). 'Integration and the planner'. *Journal of the American Institute of Planners*, **35**, 113–117.

Marston, W. G. (1969). 'Social class segregation within ethnic groups in Toronto'. *Canadian Review of Sociology and Anthropology*, **6**, 65–79.

Ministry of Housing and Local Government (1969). *Council Housing: Purposes, Procedures and Priorities*, H.M.S.O., London.

Neuwirth, G. (1969). 'A Weberian outline of a theory of community: its application to the "Dark Ghetto"'. *British Journal of Sociology*, **20**, 148–163.

New Society (1974). 'Ghettoes or not?', *New Society*, **28**, 2nd May 1974.

Northern Ireland Community Relations Commission Research Unit (1971). *Flight: A Report on Population Movements in Belfast during August 1971*, Northern Ireland Community Relations Commission, Belfast.

Orbell, J. M., and Uno, T. (1972). 'A theory of neighborhood problem solving: political action versus residential mobility'. *American Political Science Review*, **66**, 471–489.

Orme, A. R. (1971). 'Segregation as a feature of urban development in medieval and plantation Ireland'. *Geographical Viewpoint*, **2**, 193–206.

Park, R. E. (1952). 'The urban community as a spatial pattern and a moral order'. In R. E. Park and coworkers (Eds.), *Human Communities*, The Free Press, Glencoe, Illinois.

Petticrew, T. F. (1969). 'Racially separate or together?'. *Journal of Social Issues*, **25**, 43–69.

Piven, F. F., and Cloward, R. A. (1967). 'The case against urban desegregation'. *Social Work*, **12**, 12–21.

Plant, M. A. (1971). 'The attitudes of coloured immigrants in two areas of Britain to the concept of dispersal'. *Race*, **12**, 323–328.

Poole, M. A., and Boal, F. W. (1973). 'Religious residential segregation in Belfast in mid-1969: a multi-level analysis'. In B. D. Clark and M. B. Gleave (Eds.), *Social Patterns in Cities*, Institute of British Geographers, London. Special Publication No. 5. pp. 1–40.

Porter, J. (1965). *The Vertical Mosaic*, University of Toronto Press, Toronto.

Reubens, E. P. (1971). 'Our urban ghettos in British perspective'. *Urban Affairs Quarterly*, **6**, 319–340.

Rex, J. A. (1970). *Race Relations in Sociological Theory*, Weidenfeld and Nicolson, London.

Rex, J. A., and Moore, R. (1967). *Race, Community and Conflict*, Oxford University Press, Oxford.

Richmond, A. H. (1969). 'Sociology of migration in industrial and post-industrial societies'. In J. A. Jackson (Ed.), *Migration*, Cambridge University Press, Cambridge, pp. 238–281.
Rose, E. J. B. (1969). *Colour and Citizenship*, Oxford University Press, Oxford.
Rose, H. M. (1969). *Social Processes in the City: Race and Urban Residential Choice*, Resource Paper No. 6, Association of American Geographers, Commission on College Geography, Washington, D.C.
Rose, H. M. (1970). 'The development of an urban sub-system: the case of the Negro ghetto'. *Annals, Association of American Geographers*, **60**, 1–17.
Rosenthal, E. (1961). 'Acculturation without assimilation? The Jewish Community of Chicago, Illinois'. *American Journal of Sociology*, **66**, 275–288.
Scott, P. (1965). 'The population structure of Australian cities'. *Geographical Journal*, **131**, 463–481.
Soja, E. W. (1971). *The Political Organization of Space*, Resource Paper No. 8, Association of American Geographers, Commission on College Geography, Washington D.C.
Sommer, R. (1969). *Personal Space*, Prentice-Hall, Englewood Cliffs, New Jersey.
Spengler, J. J. (1967). 'Population pressure, housing and habitat'. *Law and Contemporary Problems*, **32**, 191–208.
Stimson, R. J. (1970). 'Patterns of European immigrant settlement in Melbourne, 1947–1961'. *Tijdschrift voor Economische en Sociale Geografie*, **61**, 114–126.
Sudman, S., Bradburn, N. M., and Gockel, G. (1969). 'The extent and characteristics of racially integrated housing in the United States'. *Journal of Business*, **42**, 50–87.
Suttles, G. (1968). *The Social Order of the Slum*, University of Chicago Press, Chicago.
Suttles, G. (1972). *The Social Construction of Communities*, University of Chicago Press, Chicago.
Taber, R. (1970). *The War of the Flea*, Granada, London.
Taeuber, K. E. (1968). 'The effect of income redistribution on racial residential segregation'. *Urban Affairs Quarterly*, **4**, 5–14.
Taeuber, K. E., and Taeuber, A. F. (1965). *Negroes in Cities: Residential Segregation and Neighborhood Change*, Aldine, Chicago.
Tribunal of Inquiry (1972). *Violence and Civil Disturbances in Northern Ireland in 1969*, H.M.S.O., Belfast.
Trlin, A. D. (1971). 'Social distance and assimilation orientation: a survey of attitudes towards immigrants in New Zealand'. *Pacific Viewpoint*, **12**, 141–161.
Ward, D. (1971). *Cities and Immigrants*, Oxford University Press, New York.
Warner, W. L., and Srole, L. (1945). *The Social Systems of American Ethnic Groups*, Yale University Press, New Haven.
Wirth, L. (1928). *The Ghetto*, University of Chicago Press, Chicago.
Wolf, E. P. (1963). 'The tipping point in racially changing neighborhoods'. *Journal of the American Institute of Planners*, **24**, 217–222.
Wolpert, J., Mumphrey, A., and Seley, J. (1972). *Metropolitan Neighborhoods: Participation and Conflict over Change*, Resource Paper No. 16, Association of American Geographers, Commission on College Geography, Washington, D.C.
Yinger, J. M. (1965). *A Minority Group in American Society*, McGraw-Hill, New York.
Zelder, R. E. (1970). 'Residential desegregation: can nothing be accomplished?'. *Urban Affairs Quarterly*, **5**, 265–277.

Chapter 3

Institutional Forces that Shape the City

J. E. Vance, Jr.

Within the compass of a single chapter it is clearly impracticable to account for all the various forces that give the city the form it has. Of the three ways that city forms are shaped—through institutional forces, by natural environmental processes and through inheritances from urban morphology in previous times only the first is considered here. In this viewing of human institutions, we must comprehend two scales of action, that of the institution working as a body and that wherein the institution is the instrument of an individual will.

Before turning to such an appraisal of institutional forces at work in urban morphology, we must call attention to the product itself. Recent work in geography has heavily discounted the concrete physical form of the city, turning its attention instead to assumed normative processes of locational distribution and social regionalization and treating the city as an economic or social institution rather than a physical entity. If the all-too-substantial form of the city might be effectively disregarded, this narrowing of attention would still be of dubious intellectual justification: as the impact of the morphology of cities is both direct and undeniable, it seems irresponsible to act as if only economic and social processes have validity in the shaping of both cities and the nature of urban life. I do not wish to assert a new form of physical determinism, in the guise of the impact of city forms on urban life, but yet to deny some substantial role to the bricks and mortar and physical layout of cities in the existence of urban people is as silly as to deny the matter of rainfall as a force in agricultural geography.

THE SHAPING OF THE CITY BY INSTITUTIONS

Cities are shaped by institutions of several general types: social, economic, governmental, religious and cultural (Vance, 1976). Here only two types will be considered, governmental and financial institutions, though only in the first type is the history very long. If we accept the argument of this chapter that to study the city only in the present is unwise and unreliable of truth, then the role that financial institutions play becomes one confined to the third act of the drama, perhaps crucial in the outcome but not part of the establishment of the plot.

Because the shaping of the city may come from many moulding hands, it is essential to distinguish between those places created with a fixed form already extant in someone's mind and those where there is a continuing and democratic evolution of the form, organically, as the city grows and prospers. Topsy said it without academic prolixity: 'I 'spect I growed. Don't think nobody never made me.' Many cities must, in fact, acknowledge a similar ontogeny and, in doing so, make clear that the impact of government, in particular, will be very different from that found in a preconceived town shaped by an all-powerful sovereignty. Organic growth is more commonly found in democratic than autocratic cities and history affords us many examples of the differences in the morphogenetic processes between the two types. The Renaissance was the point in our era of preconception and it was, as well, the age of absolute monarchies, tyranny and despotism in church and state. In turn, it was in the New World that democracy took hold most fundamentally in the governance of towns and it was there that true organic evolution of morphology was to be found, a fact reinforced by the strong role that American cities came to play, in the last hundred years, as the truly innovative force in the introduction of functional urban forms, which have been copied widely from a prototype first encountered in Chicago in the 1880s.

HOUSING IN THE STRUCTURE OF THE CITY

With our objective of looking at the roots of city patterns, their current bloomings and the processes of organic growth, as in the United States and other New Lands, it is essential to spell out how housing will be viewed. First, our concern will be with the cellular unit from which residential areas are built, with houses rather than with those statistical aggregations commonly called 'social areas', census tracts or the like. Such aggregations often obscure truth through the lumping of dissimilar details and they tell us little about the housing provision as shaped by governmental and financial institutions. Finally, it is the house, or its apartmented equivalent, through which housing provision is made, and in the forces shaping that basic housing unit we find the real expression of the institutional impact on cities. This is especially true when we must deal with the past, a time when the details of actual policy may no longer be available to us but through whose outcome we may reconstruct its nature. Next comes the assemblage of the basic housing units into larger urban physical patterns, which may in turn respond to processes somewhat different from those at work on the house itself and express a different impress of government, the banks and builders.

If we look at the development of housing as one of the fundamental concerns of mankind and houses as one of man's most widespread artifacts, it should not surprise us that housing is provided either by the basic social unit—the family, nuclear or extended, or the clan—or by the basic economic unit—the manor, or craftman's or merchant's establishment. In the past, housing was far more commonly provided by the economic than by the family unit. The medieval manor furnished employment and also shelter, as did the merchant's house for his journeymen and apprentices. In rural areas, the tie was traditionally and legally maintained, to the extent that the social dependency of vassalage had an attached geographical restriction of serfdom which passed down through succeeding generations, a social practice, as we shall see, that Germany in the Third Reich attempted to restore. When we examine the morphology of the medieval city, we find that the fundamental residential unit was the house of a master of an occupation, often a high and narrow structure divided by floors among the several activities carried on there: selling on the ground floor, workships behind or on the second floor, and housing and storage in the higher storeys, assorted in the case of workers by their rank within the occupational 'family'. In such a system, there was little chance for residence within the city for those occupationally unattached, a fact that shunted the floaters and other pariahs beyond the walls into the shacks and stews of the 'suburbs', in their original meaning.

One other aspect of medieval housing should be mentioned here, largely because of its ancestry of certain current practices with respect to housing: the tendency in the cities of Italy toward clustering of political and ethnic factions. Within these Italian city republics, certainly urbane for their time but hardly very republican in most cases, were the roots of the notion of social and political clustering. In Europe north of the Alps the basic clustering of houses was in terms of occupations—occupation districts were the result—but south of the Alps there was more commonly a political or ethnic base at work. The tower houses of Sienna, Bologna or San Gimignano were such urban political citadels, around which the houses of lesser henchmen were collected. Under such a philosophy of housing structure, the emergence during the counter-reformation of the ghetto quarter of Venice as the home for the Jews is more easily understood and less loaded with justifications for cries of mistreatment. There most commonly were ethnic and political groupings when the provision of housing was highly specialized and there was no general body of 'rental' housing. Recently, such ethnic and political districts of cities have reemerged as 'areas of opposition' in American cities.

The occupational structuring of housing that was the norm for the medieval merchant's and craftsman's town became the common practice in colonial America. For that reason, under such a system there was no real need for government involvement. But even more, there was no necessary practice of institutionalized lending to provide urban housing. The state had always played a role of sorts, either in its formal expression as the government or in its *alter ego* as the state religion, when it provided for those who we would today call 'welfare cases', the elderly in particular, as the common presence of alms houses in English towns shows us. And it is clear there were individual borrowings by merchants and craftsmen for use in the provision of housing. These were not strictly instances of real estate lending so much as they were tied to the general matter of commercial credit and borrowing, which came with the development of banking practices in the High Middle Ages in Italy and then in the North.

Up to the time of the industrial revolution of the eighteenth century, the medieval pattern of housing provision both obtained and worked with reasonable success, but as ports developed, some component of rental housing was necessary for the families of merchant sailors and dock workers. It seems to have developed in the larger ports, no doubt as a minor activity of merchants whose wealth was expanding rather rapidly. Esther Forbes (1942) furnishes a picture of these still rather medieval practices found even in the later decades of the eighteenth century. Houses were built by artisans and used by them during their lifetime to shelter both their work and their workers, who seem more commonly to have been charged board than rent. It was inherited property that perhaps first entered the rental market and, given the short lifetime of residents and fairly stable population of these colonial ports, such a provision may well have sufficed.

The fundamental disruption of these practices was brought on by a siege of urban growth that was unusual. Already in Elizabethan times English ports, most notably London with its enlarging monopolies of overseas trade, were being strained by increases of population due to quickening migrations city-ward from the countryside and not to any fundamental change in the negative balance of births over deaths among the townspeople. We all know of the Virgin Queen's efforts to contain London's growth and the practices she had established. Houses were not to be built, save, interestingly, those for workers engaged in port functions. But because the economic growth was not stopped, neither was the physical extent of the city, which became the Elizabethans' main concern. In the end, a new system of housing provision had to be devised. In London it came through the 'pestering' of medieval houses, that is their being broken up into strictly rental units in the original building and crowded on the lot by additions perched upon or leaned against them (Byrne, 1925).

At the other end of the social spectrum, there had come finally the establishment of an outright house-building trade. John Summerson (1946) holds that it was Nicholas Barbon who began it all in earnest during the late seventeenth century, when he started the first successful creation of actual houses for sale or lease. Before that, as early as 1636, several noble landowners just outside London's walls began bruiting the division of their lands into leaseholds to be let out for house construction. And there were speculators who took up leases and built houses for sub-leasees. Roger North (Summerson, 1946, p. 29) drew attention to the significant change that Barbon introduced: 'It was not worth his while to deal little. . . . That a bricklayer could do. The gain he expected was out of great undertakings, which would rise lustily in the whole.' Without expanding further on this incident, it may suffice to note that with Barbon's generation house-building became an undertaking of capitalists, both actually and philosophically; Marx used Barbon's considerable economic writings to secure definitions of 'commodities' and 'use value' in *Das Kapital.*

If port expansion was the first disruption of the slow and orderly growth that had characterized the city in the Middle Ages, the onset of major industrialization in the eighteenth century led to the total extinction of the old order. No half-measures such as pestering or the laying out of aristocratic quarters could relieve the pressure once factories began to cluster in cities. There were some initial attempts to patch up the older system of occupational housing provision, but they were soon abandoned (Vance, 1966). For a time, some industries could borrow the housing provisions of others by employing the unengaged members of families already housed (Vance, 1967). In the end, the main solution came through enlarging the role that capital was to play in the provision of housing. This led in the first instance to the generalization of housing in disruption of its former ties to a specific trade, and usually a particular employer. Soon it also set location as the determinant of housing design and utilization the economic return to be gained by the private investor. There was a complete dismissal of any previous ties to human welfare and the exercise of personal or institutional responsibility by employers, civic bodies or ecclesiastics. The main body of urban residents were cast adrift to become the closest thing to economic man yet to live on Earth.

This is not the place to recount the appalling results; the observations of reformers, radical economists and realistic writers during the last hundred years are legion and nearly unanimous in condemning the notion that an economic standard can be used in housing provision. Note, I did not say a capitalist standard, for it is not so much the specific economic system that is at fault as it is the idea of a housing policy established solely in terms of 'rent-paying ability'. That pernicious term can be used both to justify capitalist 'slums' and socialist people-warrens, such as those devised by Le Corbusier and other anticapitalists.

THE OUTCOME OF ECONOMIC STANDARDS FOR HOUSING

There is a great tendency to concentrate on the assumed deterioration of workers' housing that is thought to have come from the industrialization of urban populations. Yet when we look back at housing in the Middle Ages, it is very hard to make such an indictment of capitalism and industry stick. Rather, the middle and upper classes, which were made sufficiently numerous by industrialization to begin to be geographically significant in the shaping of cities, began to 'take off' and gain a distinctly different housing provision from what they had previously had and from that of the urban proletariat. The contrast between the housing provision of the economic classes increased, but it did so by raising the top rather than lowering the bottom. There were places and times when new depths were reached—Dickens and Friedrich Engels both observed industrial Britain at such a grim low point—but in general the working class simply failed to benefit from new improvements in the material standard of living, specifically of housing, that began to come with industrialization. If one doubts that, any account of the housing of magnates in medieval or even Elizabethan times will correct the misapprehension (e.g. Origo, 1957).

The great problems of housing in the industrial era came from the vastly increased size of cities and the generalization of housing, to such an extent that there was no residue of the welfare concept that had entered into the housing of workers by employers in former times. Taking the first of those changes, the vast scalar growth of cities, its impact on housing had a particularly geographical expression. In previous times, the working-class population had very little space for its shelter—the one-room *cenacula* was common in classical Rome and the sharing of rooms and houses was the general practice in medieval times—but so long as cities were reasonably small, or well sewered, as Rome was when she was larger, the health hazards were kept within bounds. Even so, in the plagues of the Middle Ages, there was a tencency to flee the cities in epidemic times, a practice not abandoned even during the cholera epidemics of mid-nineteenth century America. When cities became large in total population, they had, of necessity, to become densely built up, and in that there was a great danger to health.

The key to the greater densities at which housing was built in the industrial cities is found in the greater concentration of employment required by the introduction of factories and the enlargement of the foreign trade passing over the docks. Factory jobs clustered together in great numbers, as did the casual employments on the docks, so the housing of the working class had to exist in both great quantities and close proximity. Jobs were long with few free hours, so little time could be taken up by the journey to work. Jobs were often casual in origin, requiring close-by residence so the worker could quickly accept odd employment that might be offered. There was, for the first century of industrialization, no economically attainable transportation for the workers. Steam railroads were able to operate neither over such short distances nor at a price the proletariat could pay. Omnibus lines were introduced in Paris and London in the 1820s and horse-car lines in New York in the 1830s, but the charges they made were beyond the purse of wage employees.

The only practicable solution in large industrial cities was to pile up the workers in small housing units stacked at high densities on land as close to the factories or docks as they could find. In different countries, various approaches were tried: England built endless carpets of tiny houses of brick, often with only a single outside wall, into which great numbers were crowded; the United States, particularly in the big New England textile towns, went in for three- and four-storey wooden structures broken into tenements and crowded, rather without order, into the areas adjacent to mills; and Scotland, the Continental industrial districts across Germany, and the Austro-Hungarian Empire went in for tall masonry flats with single rooms for a family and long stairs endlessly to be climbed. The form differed, but the geographical approach was always the same: crowd as many people together as close to the places of employment as was physically possible.

In doing this, the conditions for the class segregation of urban housing were strengthened. The middle and upper class need not tolerate such crowding because they had the money and the means to travel farther to work. The suburban house—a villa in central Europe—was the most common solution for these groups, but in some large cities even the prosperous could no longer be individually housed. London solved the problem, at least in part, before the coming of city transportation, and thereby took recourse in the eighteenth century to laying out of the squares and terrace (row) houses of Bloomsbury and Mayfair. The row house became the local norm even for the prosperous, so, as the city spread, it did so in the terraces of suburbia such as those that Dyos (1966) has considered in South London. On the Continent, the row house was not normally the solution to housing the middle and upper classes, even though it had been so initially in the Place Royale (des Vosges) in Paris, when Henri IV had it constructed to house silk merchants brought from Milano. Instead, the nineteenth century saw the prosperous housed in *appartements* in Paris, Vienna and Milan. In that way, the medieval notion of the social élite living at the centre of things could be maintained. In America, there were several approaches to the housing of the middle and upper classes: in Boston, New York, Philadelphia, Baltimore and Washington, there was much use of the Georgian terrace as brought over from England, but there and in most more western cities the single-family detached house played an increasing role. Only in New York City has the 'brownstone house' of the long unbroken façade been used by the prosperous right down to the present time. After flirting with English practices in the row houses and Continental ones in the apartment houses (such as the *Dakota* in New York, which survives on Central Park, built in the 1880s), prosperous Americans rejected central-city living for the suburb. This was an act of the late nineteenth century not merely of recent years and in response to black in-migration, as radical 'rhetoric' has it.

To understand the movement to the suburbs which is so much the twentieth century pattern of American urbanization, and increasingly the pattern of world urbanization in more recent decades, we must return to the matter of what happened to housing when its occupational provision disappeared with the industrial revolution. There were two problems: the increase in city scale and the decline of the welfare concept that had attached to housing provision in medieval times. We should not be misled into envisaging medieval housing as light, airy, roomy and comfortable. It was almost none of those things, but for its time it was as good as was to be had, whatever your status and income. Masters perceived the importance of good housing, by contemporary standards, for their workers, and if they did not the guild and the civic corporation commonly corrected the error in their ways. The question of caring for the welfare of workers was intimately tied up with the notion of 'establishment of residence', a fundamental point in much of the legislation to care for the poor. The guild had a geographically defined area of privilege and responsibility, as did the city corporation. For those within the area of jurisdiction, they bore responsibility; for those outside, none. The critical point to make is that those born outside and later coming into the city stood in a questionable status with respect to guild and civic welfare. Until the industrial revolution, these aliens to the city were not too numerous, but with factory production they flooded in. The existing system of caring for misfortune, unemployment and illness was totally inadequate, as few in need had the legal 'settlement' of the denizen needed for consideration. This welfare statelessness was a sorry state, only increased when housing was split from employment and thrown into a general economic institution of house-building for return on investment. By the early nineteenth century, the welfare and housing practices of the city of the Middle Ages had disappeared and nothing but a capitalist solution had come to take their place. The result was an almost wholly economic structuring of Western urban society, throwing out the economic security of the medieval trades and the geographical classlessness of those times.

Once the middle class became separated from the lower class, there was the possibility of a separate salvation unknown in earlier times. This chance assumed greater importance as the germ theory of disease emerged in the minds of physicians during the last century. It was clear that increased personal space was a road to health, so those financially able to gain space could find an argument (for moving out of the city) in terms so emotional and intimate as caring for the health of their families, Any reading of the housing reform literature of the last century will convince the reader of the central position that health played in that movement. In the report of the Royal Commission set up in England in the 1840s to consider the state of the 'large towns and populous places', most of the evidence is given by 'medical officers for health' and concerns the state of the towns in terms of their healthfulness. The conclusion was constantly drawn that, whatever urban prophylaxis was undertaken, only continued massive rural population implosion would biologically maintain cities. Adna Ferrin Weber (1899, p. 475) concludes that it is only in the 'rise of the suburbs' that we find the solution 'which furnishes the solid basis of a hope that the evils of city life, so far as they result from overcrowding, may be in large part removed'. And he was certainly right, as has been shown by the sometimes frightening ability of suburbs to maintain and increase their numbers. This was the solution to the problem of cities for the prosperous members of society, and they took to suburbanization with the vigour that had already raised their individual status to the middle class.

For the working class, the problem was different: they had been abandoned by the past and as yet unfound by the present. In that past, a host of concerned observers found them and sought to set forth the way to the separate salvation of the lower economic class. Engels' observations on Manchester in the 1840s joined with Marx's organization of history to propose a radical transformation of the socialism that had first been shaped a generation earlier by Robert Owen. The American George Peabody and the Earl of Shaftesbury sought a solution in a socially responsible capitalism that would take over, as the medieval guild had done, the care for the poor and unfortunate. In contemporary America, during its Civil War, a different solution was proposed—that of encouraging the urban poor to return to the countryside, which was one of the fundamental arguments for the Homestead Act of 1862. As Hrothgar Habbakuk

(1962) has shown, this solution was far more successful than has usually been understood in raising the overall lot of the working class. But the real solution to the problem for most countries was the emergence of a less radical form of socialism than that of Marx and Engels and a less moralistic form than that of the enlightened English businessmen and clerics. At that time, the reassertion of civic responsibility for welfare, regardless of settlement, was seldom called so, even though we might justly now term it municipal socialism, and we should note that it was the first functioning expression of that great political philosophy of the contemporary world.

What transpired was the assumption of social responsibilities by individual civic councils, as in the Middle Ages. Some would argue that the case is very different because the role of the city government in more recent times has been so much larger than was that of the general council of some medieval town, but the difference is commonly not one of degree of responsibility so much as one of heightened concern for certain aspects of life. Housing in general is so much more ample today that we could hardly expect that public housing would not be more ample as well.

In the late nineteenth century, the first phase of civic concern for housing was expressed mainly along the lines of extinguishing nuisances. It was commonly thought that destruction of areas with bad conditions would force a general improvement in the fabric of the city, particularly that of housing. In city after city, railroad stations were built in formerly insalubrious areas, with the idea of doing away with them. In several English cities—Birmingham with the Corporation Street Scheme and London with Shaftesbury Avenue as prime examples —new arterial streets were cut through stews to force their demolition. The philosophy was so unrelievedly one of physical determinism (bad houses make bad people) that we must cringe in reading the arguments advanced in support of the plans; and even more we must wonder how the proponents envisaged that those who were displaced would improve the conditions of the housing of the poor elsewhere in the city by moving in on them. But the motive behind these schemes was that of taking responsibility for the lot of the poor in housing. In most cities, the responsibility came largely in adopting legislation that would condemn housing beyond human tolerance and would seek to set a basic standard for newer housing.

This was not city planning as we now use the term; the cellular base of the city was being controlled and transformed, but the grouping of those cells was left largely to chance and the operation of economic and social institutions. The Peabody houses of London were spotted around the city, often hidden behind older buildings. Shaftesbury Avenue was not so much a building scheme as a clearance scheme, with the route for the arterial street determined by the location of existing bad housing. In New York, the individual cells of the urban fabric changed—with the introduction of the 'New Law' tenements in 1901—but the street pattern remained that of the first half of the last century. The unit of construction normally remained the house lot, sometimes carried down from the burgage plot of the Middle Ages and sometimes from the pre-revolutionary (political or industrial) time of the city. In New York, these lots often had dimensions of 25 by 100 feet, which made for grim tenement buildings, even under the 'New Law'. We would be utterly misled if we were to deal with great aggregations of housing as our basis of analysis. Government began to play a rapidly increasing role in the matter of housing for the lower classes, but only in the matter of new construction on existing lots, and it still played almost no role in the housing of the middle and upper classes and in the broad-scale social and physical planning of the city.

The experiment with higher standards for individual houses was only partially successful, for it did not transform society as the reformers thought it would. Their error was the assumption that environment fully shapes man, but at the turn of the century no one was willing to question the fundamental basis for middle-class involvement in housing. That involvement was based on the notion of 'enlightened self-interest', wherein we are all members of society and the health of society affects us all. Thus, we must assure that the poor are sufficiently well housed as not to constitute a breeding ground for social illness. If rehousing in the city could not suffice, then that favourite hygienic institution of the late nineteenth century, the isolation hospital, had to be brought to bear in housing. In the inter-war years, both the Netherlands and France experimented with notions of creating isolated housing areas for 'undesirables' and the asocial family, where they were removed from contact and conflict with the ordinary public-housing population, in turn to be sheltered in specially designed austere and durable buildings (Gray, 1946, p. 74).

THE PROBLEM OF SPACE IN CITIES

The conclusion that social reformers of the last century drew, with respect to housing, has a particularly geographical importance: they came strongly to the view that the fundamental problem of housing provision was that once it had been transformed into a strictly economic undertaking it was impossible to give to the working classes an adequate amount of space at a rent they could pay. The problem really had two aspects, that of rent-paying ability and that of area open to the housing of the lower economic classes. The middle and upper classes could gain reasonable space by moving toward the edge of the city, but the poor could not, not because they were priced out of the land market there but because they could not afford the cost of commuting back and forth to such areas. This fact was already acknowledged by the running of 'parliamentary trains' on the lines entering London, a practice begun in the mid-nineteenth century to try to open the suburbs to those displaced by station building, at fares of no more than a penny a mile. But for the poor that was too high and these so-called 'workman's trains' were, in fact, trains for clerks and other petty salary employees. The problem of space for the lower classes had to be solved either within the core of the city or by revolutionary destruction of the clustering of economic activity there.

Ebenezer Howard played an interesting role in the shaping of the second of those solutions to the space problem. As a young man, he had gone to Chicago in the early 1870s to work as a court reporter just when the city was being rebuilt from its disastrous fire of 1871. The reconstruction took two forms, the earliest considerable use in America of 'French flats', that is *appartements* (though Richard Morris Hung had built such a structure in New York in 1869, it had been rather unsuccessful), and the even more vigorous development of single-family housing in outlying sites. The availability of horse-car lines operating easily and cheaply across the flat prairie lands, even before the fire made dispersal of housing logical, and the fast introduction of cable-car lines after their invention in San Francisco in 1873 confirmed this trend. In large measure, the Chicago that emerged from the fire was the first modern city possessed of a core given over to apartment houses and a vast periphery of suburbs. It was in Chicago that the technology of iron building and the elevator made its start; it was there that the idea of a densely built-up city with at least marginally acceptable personal space in tall apartment houses could be seen as a practicality; and it was there that the suburb first came into its own, located along steam rail lines for the more prosperous, and along cable and, later, trolley lines for the stable working class.

Chicago even provided an early experiment in the notion of the 'machine for living' which became so much the property of the Continentals—the Germans, the Swiss and some French. In the early 1880s George M. Pullman became greatly concerned with the intemperance and restiveness of his employees living in the city of Chicago, so he set about laying out a fully integrated town on the prairie south of the city. Housing was well planned and constructed, shopping and recreation were created for, and the plants for building railroad cars were modern and efficient and located within an easy walk from the housing. Like Letchworth, at a later time, this town was shielded from temptation by law, was carefully organized as to social practice and aimed high in its thinking. Richard T. Ely (1885), in describing the place at the time, came to the ultimate conclusion, though the general impression was one of thrift and order, that 'it is benevolent, well-wishing feudalism, which desires the happiness of the people, but in such a way as shall please the authorities'. And he argued that Pullman would, in fact, best please the Iron Chancellor.

Thus, when Ebenezer Howard returned to England, he had already witnessed in Chicago the first city of suburbs, and to that image he might well have added information gained from a continuing attention to the pace of Pullman's experiments after his own departure in 1876; there were similar undertakings closer to home at Saltaire and Port Sunlight. It is not necessary to expand on the influences that lay behind the Garden City movement of the turn of the century; instead, we may merely note that there was a strong affinity between those detached towns that were built in the late nineteenth century by industrialists, seeking to improve the housing of their workers as well as also to reorder their lives, and the towns built in this century by academic Utopians and Fabian socialists, striving to wrench the honest working class from the evil influences of the city.

There was a highly doctrinal quality to all of this, and that quality of morphological right-thinking has grown over the years. Garden City advocates denigrated real cities with a hate only the self-righteous can muster. Believers in physical determinism of social conditions planned on paper personally rational complexes of apartment buildings lumped into a *unité de habitation* of Le Corbusier or an 'arcology' (Soleri, 1969). The suburb lacked the fervour of the other solutions and grew through settlement, not by protagonists but by pragmatists. Yet it has become the *bête noire* of the intelligentsia in most countries, perhaps as much for political as for any other reasons. Who can really believe in the suburb as a citadel of either 'soul' or socialism? And most Europeans and too many American intellectuals would heartily agree with 'Corbu' that 'the suburb is the great problem of the U.S.A.' (Blake, 1964, p. 98). Perhaps we should examine just why he and they are so very wrong in this.

THE THREE SOLUTIONS TO HOUSING

At the end of the last century three different solutions to the problem of housing the urban working class were being followed. Within the city, philanthropists, and subsequently city governments, were trying to improve the quality of housing and thereby in part 'reform' the urban poor. Starting in 1889, the London County Council commenced a modest programme of public housing in belated recognition of the locus of responsibility, as proposed in Shaftesbury's Common Lodging Houses Act of 1851. For many years, private philanthropy had had to fill the gap. Between 1846, when the Metropolitan Association erected the first block of philanthropic housing, and 1890, over 70 000 dwellings had been built by private trusts in London (Gray, 1946, p. 58). But once the city authorities took over there were few additions to the housing built by trusts, and their properties slowly were replaced by public projects of one sort or another. They were the first conscious efforts at improved working-class housing provision.

The second solution to the housing problem came in devising a way to permit the greater proportion of the working population to engage in suburban living. This remedy has, in fact, been both the most common and the most important of the three. But because an understanding of the housing provision in the suburbs requires a discussion of both government policies and lending practices, it is best to look first at the third and least important solution before taking up private provision in the suburbs. That third possible solution can be summarized as one of planned institutional reconstruction under deliberate disintegration of the city. As first proposed by Ebenezer Howard in the Garden City movement, the 'solution' to the urban housing problem was really that of turning your back on the city: employment, shopping, recreation, education and living were all to be had in a single, detached village, certainly no more urbane than the meanest suburb. This device was practical if one were willing to accept the reimposition of a parochial existence and if there were no need for great groupings of people for any economic activity. There was an innate preciosity to much of the Garden City thinking—sale of liquor was forbidden and leasehold tenancy of land kept the controls firmly gripped from above, so any earthy backsliding could be dealt with effectively. In these conditions, only one Garden City was really built; Welwyn and Hampstead Garden Suburb were just that, suburbs of a special sort, and A. T. Stewart's Garden City on Long Island predated Howard's by nearly forty years.

Oddly enough, the fundamental Letchworth goals were far more widely accomplished in the United States than in Britain. To begin with, it was the massive availability of electric trolleys, even in the 1890s, that allowed the working class to move outward and the factories to follow in their wake: or the reverse of that procedure, as the case might be. Those American suburbs may not have been so isolated or so self-consciously designed as Letchworth, but in the provision of reasonable housing with adequate personal space inside and out they were fully a match for Raymond Unwin's designs for the First Garden City. And Riverside, which is so like Letchworth, but outside Chicago, was laid out in 1871, while Ebenezer Howard was starving on the Middle Western homestead he had emigrated to, soon to move to Chicago to become a court stenographer.

There is a considerable literature detailing the role of the street-car in shaping American residential areas, of which Sam Warner's *Streetcar Suburbs* (1962) is the best known. In his book, he shows how the opening of blocks of land for development by small builders combined with the provision of circumferential public transit to make it possible for the working class to move out of the centre, earn a living locally and create a proletarian suburban society. Only to a much lesser degree was this possible in Europe, so the more pretentious 'garden cities' had to be used to accomplish this morphogenesis that free development brought far more widely in American cities.

The problem of space persisted in the centres of all cities, for the reason that much of the housing provision was old and had been built before any standards were enforced. Obviously, the larger the city in the nineteenth century, the greater the redevelopment problem in the twentieth. London was particularly a problem, but Birmingham, Manchester, Paris, Amsterdam, Cophenhagen and the larger German cities all had great crowding. In the United States, New York was the main problem city and the only one to require solutions as vast as those in Europe.

RELIEF OF CENTRE CROWDING

Without here entering into detail, the programmes to alleviate centre crowding went two ways: some sought redevelopment in place and others peripheral substitution. Taking London as an example, between 1889, when the London County Council took over the matter of housing reform, and 1912 only some 15 000 persons were rehoused *in situ*, or at least in the centre, whereas 20 000 were located in new cottages at the edge. On the Continent, programmes were in scale. The cities had assumed responsibility for providing adequate working-class housing, but had not accomplished any wonders by 1914, probably because redevelopment in place is exceedingly hard to carry out and peripheral construction of replacement houses was very difficult in a society without cheap and widespread city transit. In the Austro-Hungarian Empire and in Germany, trolley lines were well developed, but neither French nor British cities were so well served, with both Paris and London plagued by problems. Paris seems to have been slow in adopting electric traction. In 1910 her largest company, *Compagnie Generale des Omnibus*, had thirty lines, of which only part of one had modern electric operation; of the twenty-nine others, eight were horse-drawn, ten steam-operated, nine run by compressed air and only two by electricity, and then by batteries rather than by power lines or third-rails (Robert, 1959, p. 74).

Although there were tramways to the *banlieux* of Paris as early as the turn of the century, they were poorly integrated, plagued with the need to operate differently intra-muros from the way they did extra-muros, and probably beyond the reach of the working poor. The effective control of the *Chemin de Fer Metropolitain* by the city of Paris meant that none of its lines extended significantly beyond the walls of 1870.

DEVELOPMENTAL FREEDOM THROUGH SPACE: EUROPE

To understand the basic question of space and its constraint of housing development, we must reflect briefly on the question of the 'contained' as opposed to the 'open' urban frontier. Throughout Europe, there was actual physical containment of cities during much of their history up to the nineteenth century. In England, constraint came more from the reluctance of wealthy landowners to sell land for working-class housing development than from walls. However, on the Continent, many cities were ringed by a fixed wall, as in Paris and Vienna, until the late nineteenth century, with the supposedly empty *glacis* beyond it, or even until after the First World War by a network of forts, as in Antwerp, Belfort and Paris. If these fortifications did not constrain, they did push the possible suburb even farther away from the centre. In Paris, shacks had been built beyond the current wall soon after the Franco-Prussian War, but the defensive structure actually remained until dismantling began in 1922. Similar conditions prevailed in other cities; although, in Britain, it was the interjection of the state into the building of working-class housing that forced the opening of peripheral lands to development through heavy pressure on landowners or outright condemnation of land under eminent domain (compulsory purchase). In any event, during the 1920s it was clear how much housing reform depended upon the newly available peripheral sites of cheap land for the construction of housing of a price sufficiently low to allow the migration of slum residents.

Much as governments might seek to re-use cleared central sites '(t) he difficulties of town planning in central areas with proper zoning to avoid the mistakes of the past, and the fact that cleared sites were generally small in area and scattered, caused progress in this direction to be slow' (Manzoni, 1939, p. 25). It was so much easier, cheaper and more effective to develop outlying sites that most cities took that course, leaving the centre to be cleared more than reconstructed. Not least among the appeals of peripheral sites was the lower cost of land and site preparation there, which commonly allowed the government subsidies that stood as a fixed sum per unit to stretch to larger or better dwellings. The main rub came in gaining access to workplaces from these estates at the city frontier. In Paris, the dismantling of the walls came adjacent to the various *portes*, which were the termini of the *metropolitain* lines, thus opening practical sites for inter-war housing and shaping the 'Red Ring' of workers' developments already named and in evidence in the 1930s; this band of public housing projects had older private developments on both sides. In England, the pattern was somewhat different because the extension of public transport was very rapid in the same period. The London Underground, quite unlike the Paris Métro, pushed its lines well out into open country and Green Line and other buses gave reasonable mobility to the working class in the suburbs. In Birmingham, 50 000 houses were built by the city corporation between the wars and only around 750 of these were in the older city, the others being connected by bus with the centre or to adjacent outlying automobile, small arms and other factories.

In Germany and Sweden, suburbanization was equally as strongly pursued in the inter-war years. The Nazis became smitten with many of the environmentalist notions of Howard, the Fabians and the back-to-the-land movement in America, calling for the development of *Kleinsiedlungen* (perhaps best rendered as small-holdings), on which there was 'the linking of the German worker to the soil'. Gray (1946, p. 97) quotes German officials at a conference in 1937 to the effect that 'the program is intended to make possible for the maximum number of workers to own their own homes, become loyal non-communistic citizens and to increase the subsistence supplies of the country, while maintaining a steady supply of labour for industry'. This appeal sounds rather similar to one of the legislative justifications of the Homestead Act in the United States in 1862, though then it was riots and disorders rather than communism they sought to forfend. The Government of the Third Reich went several steps farther backward than had been the case with Pullman, and no doubt Bismarck would nod still greater approval from his grave, when it established that 'these homesteads were sold (to the small holder) on long-term monthly payments by (his) signing a contract to work with the (adjacent) industry the remainder of his working life and by entailing one son to take his place when his own work ceased' (Gray, 1946, p. 97). The Scandinavians, in contrast, depended heavily on the cooperative movement to furnish the organization and the funds for inter-war housing, though they also offered small-holdings at the edge of the city to those families with the health to do the job of building a house on it.

The land economics of the 1930s were particularly conducive to the areal spread of cities. Because the notion was still strongly held that the centre was the place of most men's desire, exterior sites were fairly cheaply had, leading to a large element of private working-class housing development in that decade. There were many contributing factors: the reasonable cost of land, the increased availability of capital (in Britain, interest rates on building were subsidized and building societies had large sums to invest) and, rather late in the day, the catching up of public transport to the needs of the working class. Between the wars, Britain added 2 249 000 private houses in a spurt of building never before witnessed, and ever since held down by planning prohibitions. So long as the users of land continued to view the city's centre as far more valuable than its edge, the private sector of housing provision could furnish there, even to workers, a large amount of shelter. But in the post-war years, the great rise in land values, which is simply a measure of the new way we look upon the utility and desirability of land, has come in areas of urban expansion. While central-city values are stable or even declining, the inflation in land values near the edge has been so great that working-class housing has had to disappear in most parts of Europe as a consideration in the private sector.

THE ROLE OF FINANCIAL INSTITUTIONS

While all of this was going on in Europe, the pattern in the United States was distinctly different. To understand this contrast, we must look briefly at the roles that financial institutions and governments play in shaping the residential fabric of the city. The influence of financial institutions is extremely difficult to generalize for the simple reason that we must consider both the private and the public sources of funds and the great contrasts that are found among political jurisdictions in the matter of banks and banking procedures. Although banking dates back to the Middle Ages, and certainly merchant bankers must have invested in real property at an early date through granting loans to individuals who used the money in turn to buy land or build structures, it seems only at the end of the eighteenth century that specialized financial institutions were created to deal specifically with real-property investment. A century earlier, in a London rebuilding itself from the Great Fire of 1666, Nicholas Barbon and similar land developers had begun the practice of actually building houses on speculation—where needed to advance their larger land schemes. But much of their financing was from their private fortunes; it was only with the shaping of 'building societies' in England (which began with a 'building club' in Birmingham in 1795 and flowered with legislation for 'friendly societies' in 1836) and 'building and loan associations' in the United States (the first, the Oxford Provident Building Association, was set up in Philadelphia in 1831) that institutions intended for financial support of housing provision were in existence. Throughout the nineteenth century, these were the main instruments available for the individual mortgaging of private housing. Industrialists had, on occasion, furnished capital for worker housing, at least from the time of Jedidiah Strutt in the eighteenth century, but that practice was made more unusual with the development of the worker's lodging house, as devised under the Waltham System that Francis Cabot Lowell pioneered in 1817 (Vance, 1966).

When public support for worker housing was first legislated in England, under Shaftesbury's Common Lodging Houses Act of 1851, it was this sheltering of unattached individuals that was first proposed as a shift from private to public concern. Building societies continued to finance house construction, but only in small measure and at the top of lower-class provision, and what impact they had was entirely with respect to family housing. In London, private philanthropy took up much of the burden below this threshold of building loans. Fourteen major trusts were established there in the nineteenth century to build worker housing for rent, of which perhaps the most important, the Peabody Trust (founded in 1862), built 7 200 dwellings. It was estimated at the turn of the century, when the expansion of the programme had ended, that the philanthropies in London had constructed dwellings for around 150 000 persons (Encyclopaedia Britannica, 1911). But this programme was essentially a reciprocal of public endeavours along those lines; when the employment-tied housing disappeared with the industrial revolution, deterioration in urban dwellings was so great that private philanthropies were created in an attempt to reverse the evil tide. But it flowed too strongly and in the 1890s a new and more direct form of government participation had to be instituted; it caused the housing charities in a reciprocal fashion to disappear.

We may gain some rough measure of the adequacy of private finance for housing in Britain and America by looking at the assets of those banking institutions intended specifically for building at the time that this shift from private to public housing provision was taking place in Britain. In 1895, when the urban population of Britain was nearly twenty million (1891 population of all towns over 5 000 was 19 763 264), the total capital of building societies there was £43 million [around $215 million] whereas in the United States in 1892, with a nearly identical urban population [1890 population of all cities over 5 000 was 19 829 258], the assets of building and loan associations was $473 million. There may have been some difference in the costs of construction that would influence the comparison, but it seems reasonable to argue that in rough measure there was at least twice as much money for lending on housing by American associations as there was in Britain. At a time when the older country was resorting to public provision of worker housing the younger was still confidently going ahead with private construction. And this contrast must be substantially increased when we take into account how much more personal mobility American workers had and how far advanced were the trolley systems of the Great Republic.

EUROPE AND AMERICA: CONTRASTING COURSES AND THE EFFECT ON PERSONAL SPACE

In the period after the First World War, two basic approaches to housing evolved in the Western democracies: the first represented an acceptance of the belief that housing could not be provided by the market place, as it had had to be in most countries during the nineteenth century once the provision was generalized under the industrial revolution; the second approach argued that housing could be provided by the traditional economic institutions of Western society so long as they were prodded in places and aided by the government in others. These might appropriately be called respectively the notion of the *social welfare provision of housing* and the notion of the *economic market provision of housing*. Obviously, neither approach was absolute; there was some private provision even when state construction dominated and some public activity even though market institutions did most of the work, and there were experiments and shifts in policy that seemed to go back on previous policy commitments. But in the end, there came to be these two long-term policy trends which became political philosophies and party doctrines.

In the United States, a number of things led to the adoption of economic market provision of housing. Geographically, we might relate this to one of the seeming fundamentals for a market provision of housing, to the continually expanding availability of low-cost development land, which seems essential to keep the economic-class threshold of housing low enough to make the market an acceptable mechanism as a national policy. Even in the social welfare countries, there will be market provision for the more prosperous, but that hardly constitutes a basic policy so much as a tolerated survival accepted in the interests of diversity. But where land is cheap at the edge of the city, there can be enough private housing to allow its adoption as the basic national provision of dwellings.

Cheap land is not the only question, though perhaps the most important, as the evidence from Europe shows that cheap internal transit is also needed, preferably as flexible as possible so that the cheap land, that normally at the edge of the city, can be used for housing without unduly constraining the area in which work can be sought. It was this absence of cheap and flexible transportation that seems as much as anything to have thrown Western Europe into the public or social welfare provision of housing. The test of that assertion is furnished through looking at the British policies in the inter-war period, which took a turn toward social welfare but accompanied it with a strong persistence of market provision. In Birmingham, the social welfare provision of houses worked very much as the market supply would have: virtually all building was on cheap, open land at the edge of the city, though the density of houses—12 to 15 per net acre—was higher than would have been the case in private developments in America. But in that distinction the difference was national rather than economically sectoral as the row (terrace) housing of the North London suburbs then being built by private developers was at densities similar to public housing estates in the West Midlands. And while Birmingham was building 50 000 municipal houses (almost all at the edge of the city), London was building somewhat over a million new houses during the inter-war years, most at the edge of the city but built by private enterprises. The keys as to public or private housing for the working class seem to lie in cheap land outside the city and the effective use by the larger London developers of building society funds in a 'Builders' Pool', which allowed families to occupy

£800 houses for as little as £25 down, rather than the traditional 25 per cent. (Johnson, 1964). To this selling edge, the large builders added great advantages in construction costs due to better utilization of labour and cheaper bulk-buying of materials. 'As a result it is almost true to say that by the 1930s the suburban speculative builder (in London) was either relatively large or defunct.' And site costs were made up of two components—cost of land and cost of site preparation—of which the second could be the more weighty. James Johnson has shown that where land might range between £500 and £1 000 per acre (an exceedingly low price by current standards) the cost of laying streets, sewers, water and the like might be greater per lot, but still so long as neither cost was exorbitant the lots would be costed at from £140 to £180, a very low sum in light of the present. It was on such a cheap land-base that privately-built worker housing could rise. Unfortunately, by 1939 most of the accessible and reasonable parcels of open land within practical distance of London had been taken up (Johnson, 1964, p. 159). While all of this private development in and around London was probably supplying nearly 1.2 million houses, the government added a total of 119 879 dwellings in Greater London between 1919 and 1945, a rather small figure when matched against Birmingham's 50 000 for a shorter period and a city one-tenth the size. It seems that the advantages of mass building on cheap sites within the municipality, and with good commuting access to work, could be used by the city as effectively as by the private developers. But as in the case of London where the London County Council (L.C.C.) had little open land within its boundaries, it was the private sector unconcerned by such niceties as local jurisdiction that had then to take over the job. The L.C.C. did, at Becontree and elsewhere, build outside its boundaries, but not so readily as Birmingham did within its own.

In either case, it was the low land costs that determined where the houses would be built in large numbers, and basically the morphology of the houses themselves. So long as land was reasonably plentiful, single-family houses were built—separated from one another, semi-detached or in rows, as the buyers' income permitted. It was only in the older city, where land for redevelopment came at a higher price, that the single-family house was abandoned in favour of tenements or apartments. Because these apartments were so foreign to the desires of the tenants, even London sought to continue to build separate dwellings, though it meant building most of its housing estates outside the L.C.C. boundary. The British governments of the 1930s forced a change on tenants when they increasingly restricted subsidies to apartmented housing in the overcrowded central areas, thus signalling a shift from the concept of meeting the individual desires of tenants to the concept of a housing geography shaped in the image of doctrinal social welfare. It seems that by 1930 the notion of potential space in the centre was beginning to enter into the formulation of policies.

While the urban frontier in Europe was closing during the inter-war years this was not the case in the United States. During the 1920s private development of housing was essentially complete. What little experimentation there was with mass housing, as at Sunnyside Gardens in Queens in New York City in 1925, was conducted by an insurance company or, in other projects, by labour unions building for their own members. Otherwise, privately built apartments took over the role of residential provision in the centres of cities and single-family houses were built for sale in the suburbs. There was a strong land-rent sorting of uses fostered by tax assessment practices which made central land too valuable for single-family housing. The 1920s saw many apartments built, but they were virtually confined to the edge of the downtown or to innermost suburbs in truly large cities. New York was the exception, when the Bronx in particular became the New World replica, and thereby a scalar exaggeration, of the great apartmented cities of the German and Austrian empires from where so many of the settlers came. Outside the heart of cities, car ownership was fast reaching the level of at least one per family and those newly mobile families were flooding into suburban towns located on cheap lands at the frontier with the country. Unlike the situation in Europe, the democratic mobility of America made such vast areas available that the main planning complaint of the inter-war years was the 'excessive subdivision of land' which left vacant more building sites than those for which there was a market.

There was in the central cities a group largely unable, because of income, to participate in suburbanization, though in some ethnic groups, Jews in particular, there was considerable resistance to accepting the North American norm of residential morphology in the suburban house. Recent immigrants tended to cling to the central city because cheap rents were to be had there, which led to a persistence of the slum conditions that reformers sought to improve. In the 1920s, not much was accomplished in a positive sense: the cutting off of immigration merely reduced the numbers of the most obvious slum tenants as they died off with age. Perhaps the combination of immigrant quotas and ageing would have 'solved' the problem but for the soon-to-come transformation of the economy of the Cotton Belt and the hyper-reproduction of Puerto Rico, which introduced substitute floods of poor whose implosion on the city ended the experiment. In the 1930s blacks and Puerto Ricans began moving to northern cities, filling and again crowding the old tenement and apartment structures at the centre.

THE NEW DEAL PUTS GOVERNMENT TO WORK

Government entrance into the question of housing provision, as opposed to the much longer-standing one of setting minimal standards for health and safety, came only during the 1930s in America. In 1932, the Federal government created the Federal Home Loan Bank System, whose purpose was avoiding the total collapse of the existing private investment system of housing provision. It effectively accomplished that goal, but only with the advent of the Roosevelt administration were active programmes undertaken. The New Deal witnessed two general approaches to housing with one for each of the housing sectors. To try to maintain and stimulate the private sector in its building of new houses the Federal Housing Administration (F.H.A.) was created in 1934 to make low-interest and guaranteed mortgages available to the lower-income segments of the private market. Later F.H.A. got into the refurbishing of the already existing house through home improvement loans. In the rental component of housing, governmental policies took two forms: as many apartment buildings had been built by business corporations before 1933 and had, along with other corporations, suffered extreme difficulties, the Reconstruction Finance Corporation was authorized to aid in their business reorganization, which meant a modest subsidization of private investment rental housing. More important, however, was the federal assistance for public housing construction in some fifty slum clearance projects in thirty-seven cities as part of the 'pump-priming' activities of the Public Works Administration programme of employment relief. These were the first instances of actual public housing construction in the United States and they ran afoul the strict constructionists then sitting on the Supreme Court. In 1937, these housing programmes were found unconstitutional. Only by new legislation and decentralizing public housing to the states and cities was the programme continued.

At the end of the 1930s, the American housing policy stood as a very small and shaky programme of public housing (only in the larger cities and with most rigid means tests applied to potential tenants) and a large and increasing programme of Federal encouragement of the private housing market through mortgage moneys and guarantees, which were tied in vast measure to the building of new mass housing tracts on cheap peripheral land.

POST-WAR CONTRASTS

After the Second World War, in the United States the emerging success of the F.H.A. programme of the late 1930s (in stimulating large-scale private construction of housing for sale to those with a steady job) was taken as the guide. Aid to returning veterans and aid to the lower and middle income groups in general fell into the pattern of mortgage support—easy money at relatively low interest rates to cover all (the G. I. Bill housing) or virtually all of the cost of purchase. In Britain, no such programme was thought possible. The rub came in two ways, one political and the other essentially geographical. In 1945, a Labour government succeeded to power when the wartime coalition was dissolved, and it sought to encourage a quasi-municipalization of housing by confering the main powers of new construction on cities and urban districts. The reconsideration of pre-war conditions had led planners and government reformers to propose a green belt to constrain further peripheral spread of London and other large cities. Only those cities or the national government could effectively either invade or jump over the green belt in housing provision and only they could stand the cost of redevelopment within the older city, the two possible locations of new housing. The overvaunted 'new towns' schemes of the post-war years were essentially the only available leap over the wall for the working class, not so much the case for the more wealthy, so these places finally made certain a geography of economic class in housing unknown even in the nineteenth century. Thus, in the period from 1945 to 1948 the United States took one course and Britain almost the diametrically opposed one. Economic market provision would rule in the first and social welfare in the second. In broad scale, this was the division that came to rule between the extra-European democracies and those within her borders.

There were doctrinal reasons for the split, but certainly two measures of space and geography played major roles in shaping the two courses. Outside Europe the great democratic demand during the nineteenth century was for increased personal space. Homesteading laws were widely adopted; government aid to transportation was vastly encouraged long before this became a principle of socialist planning; and in numerous other ways American society built space into its practices and used the unearned increment of cheaply bought land to accumulate capital to fuel a free enterprise society. People asked for and received larger houses, larger yards, wider streets, more parks and a myriad other demands that depended essentially on the cheapness of land and its having no cachet of class or aristocracy. Thus, personal space and cheap space in which to grow were cardinal aspects of democracy in America and the other New Lands. In Britain and on the Continent, space had been extremely constrained throughout the Middle Ages, leading to an ever-increasing cramping of the city person's personal space, a constriction that even increased in some cases under industrialization. And so long as public transit was less widely and well developed than in the New Lands, space at the edge of the city might be cheap but it was broadly inaccessible. In this context of thought, the relatively cheap and accessible urban frontier of the inter-war decades in Europe was most exceptional in her normal processes of morphogenesis. The 1920s and 1930s were a time when because of past constraints on class and personal space, leading to a cramping to the bottom of society in both measures, there was a pent-up demand for housing and space that caused cities to grow so rapidly that the social and governmental élites feared for the future.

In the 1920s, London, Paris and other big European cities witnessed a rapid expansion of their rural frontiers. So long as this growth came from the outward spread of the middle and upper classes, the encroachment on the fields was modest and widely accepted. But in the 1930s, in both London and Paris, the working class began to gain ground they had never before enjoyed. At Marly and other areas along the Seine above Paris, and in the North London and West Middlesex suburbs, the working class began to occupy suburban lands. The result was a fast expansion that deeply frightened both traditionalists and futurists. Thus, when the Second World War closed, there was a broad coalition, oddly most deeply entrenched in the planning mystique of the British Labour party, which called for government constraint of further geographical expansion of the city. Because cheap land had made millionaires of some developers in the inter-war years, it seems to have been concluded that free use of that commodity was against the interests of the working class.

SPACE, GOVERNMENT POLICY, AND INVESTMENT

In the years just before the Second World War, the availability of rather cheap land at the edge of the city was the operative force in most Western countries, the fundamental support for which was the concept of the single-centred city with that focus thought to lie in the central area. This notion maintained a clear-cut boundary to the city with only the industrial satellite lying beyond it. Within the urban frontier, it was likely that railroad suburbs would be most distant from the core. But in the United States at the very end of the inter-war period, developments were taking place that foretold a major shift in the forces shaping cities. In the suburbs of Boston as early as 1930, in those in the New Jersey part of New York City at the same time and in the Los Angeles basin in the late 1930s, experiments seeking a form for express highways internal to the city were undertaken. The culmination came in 1940 in Los Angeles when the Arroyo Seco Freeway was completed between Pasadena and downtown Los Angeles, a road whose modest proportions belie its great significance. Justifications for its construction made at the time held, firstly, that it would allow faster travel within the city and, secondly, that it would allow seekers of suburban residence to get farther away from the city centre, opening new and larger tracts for development and thereby keeping down the land costs for building.

In the late 1940s, Western Europe and the United States entered upon quite contrasting housing strategies. In Europe, the war had destroyed much of the urban fabric, a quarter of a million houses in Britain, for example, requiring strenuous efforts at restoration of buildings and services. Most European countries placed the emphasis on gaining as much shelter as quickly as possible and on restoring pre-war transportation. In Britain, for example, it was not until 1958 that private development, heavily weighted toward middle-class housing, caught up with public development, with its skew toward working-class housing. Until that change came, there was a strong force toward standardization in housing provision with the government doing the rather modular job. For Americans, it is critical to note that British public housing utilizes no 'means test' for residents, so, though the houses must be working class, the residents need not necessarily be so. Yet class will out, and when private housing began to be reasonably available in the 1960s most who could afford it moved from the public to the private sector.

The role of transportation in these post-war policies tends to be overlooked. Economic stringency was such that most European governments repressed the desire for automobiles and forced a massive and exceedingly costly reconstruction and improvement of pre-war public transit. The combination of this transportation policy with that for public housing meant an absolute rejection of the pre-war strategy of 'cheap land and your own house'. After 1945, to keep public investment in mass transit under even minor control, the outer edge of the city had to be fixed and held constant. There were other motives—concern for open space, maintenance of the aristocratic quality of the countryside around cities and the effort to avoid overtaxing roads by mass car use—but they all gained expression by tying the city form to transit planning. In sum, the poor and middle class were to be walled within the city and only a small élite would be allowed to live in the nearby countryside. They could do it because they could pay the scarcity prices for housing already found there, could afford the longer commuting journey to the city and could manage the trip by car or car and train. The classical Chicago School model, as refined by William Alonso (1965), was pressed down firmly on European cities that had previously known neither in a fully developed form.

In the United States, the course was quite different; pre-war trends were encouraged and used as a rather unformulated national policy. The key was still cheap and readily available land, with the availability encouraged both by peripheral accretions of formerly unurbanized land and by the outward dispersal of a great part of previously central commercial and manufacturing activities. People now could justly argue that to live near the edge was to live in the centre of their own particular personal space. Planners seem never to have understood this truth and, instead, have constantly castigated suburban America for lacking the centralized qualities of Western Europe. To maintain the private provision of housing, it was necessary in the United States to adopt freeways as a means of opening ever more land, thus keeping land prices within reason, and of providing circulation in the 'new city' that grew up in the suburbs. This city was not centred as was its earlier ancestor, so it required good transport not merely to and from the centre but across the city from one edge to the other and circumferentially within the sector. European planning has almost totally overlooked the existence of such a 'new city' in the hearts and minds of men, and planners there have been startled and disturbed by its emergence once free will was allowed to enter into the shaping of European cities, as it did when private housing provision returned to a reasonably important role, thus allowing a competitive test between popular will and planning fiat.

The post-war housing strategy in the United States has been equally confounded, but in this instance by the absolute inability of the private sector to provide for more than the middle and upper components of the housing provision, admittedly the make-up of a far larger part of the market in the United States than in almost any other country. This trend has exaggerated in the last five years, creating a true housing crisis, because the threshold has risen so rapidly in that period. The rise in the floor for private provision has come for several reasons, some of which will gain rather than wane in strength in the near future. Most fundamental in raising the floor has been the sharp rise in land prices in the last ten to fifteen years, to the point that land now makes up a far higher part of the cost of housing than ever before and those costs are rising faster than even the quickly inflating construction and materials costs. And national and worldwide inflation can be expected further to shift investment toward land and thereby continue its inflationary rise.

Although land costs have increased faster than the other components of housing provision, those other components have all risen enough, so a great structural change has taken place in the form and location of private housing. Not only has loan capital become increasingly expensive but also it has become absolutely scarce. There has not been the money to continue the financing of a private single-family house for most Americans with a reasonable job. During the last ten years, the housing industry has shifted from a dominance by house builders for sale to that by developers of rental property in multiple-unit structures. Even much of the sale property that is being offered comes in condominium structures wherein the morphology of the residential quarter is more akin to the apartment areas of the 1920s than to the single-family housing areas of the 1950s. Note it is the morphology but not the location that bears the resemblance.

The current rental and condominium properties seem to be the last inheritors of the tradition of cheap land shaping housing for the lowest strata of society purchasing their own. For a complexity of reasons that can only be suggested here, single-family housing has declined very sharply in this decade, but the virgin fields on which it was built in the forty years from 1920 to 1960 have remained the let-out for the housing of the middle of the economic spectrum, the great mass market that has existed for more than a century in private housing. Although the land is no longer relatively cheap, still it has had what might be termed an 'unearned development increment' which can be used to provide housing for those not fully able to bear its entirely capitalized cost. Many have castigated this use of development land at the edge of the city, arguing that it rapes the countryside and enriches the few developers, leaving the house buyer with no share in the unearned gain. Yet, rather, the reverse seems the case: that buyer has been able to substitute commuting and further improvement of the property at his own hands for purchase capital he does not possess. This feature has been retained in the 'apartment boom' of the last few years when, quite in the face of traditional land economics, we have seen the edges of American cities ringed by apartments and row houses which are bordered toward the centre by the more-expected single-family housing and away from it by open fields.

The apartment building that has been the American pattern for a decade has been a morphological rather than a spatial substitution, occurring in the fabric of the city where housing incrementation was to be expected. But in the last couple of years, a startling new force has begun to loom over the morphogenesis of housing districts; that is the imposition of truly repressive restraints on internal movement. These restraints can be repressive because they are completely a matter of economics which governments have not been able to treat as a question of social welfare. The apparent secular rise in the price of petroleum in the Western nations has meant that the economic feasibility of great personal mobility is rapidly declining. The trade-off between relatively cheap land at the edge of the city and lack of personal capital is no longer so easy. As a result, the fundamental basis of American housing policy is shaky indeed and will probably have to be greatly revised in the next several years.

Public housing provision can no longer be thought merely a question for those families at or near the poverty line, but it must now become a question of governmental policy concern that reaches well within the broad middle class. Once the mobility of the middle class is reduced, the ability to use cheaper land to keep their provision of housing within the private sector, even if it is a condominium rather than a house, is so reduced as to make much of the middle class a prey to disruption by swings of the money market.

It is in this context that the United States will very soon be faced with making some of the absolutely central policy decisions that Western European countries faced either in 1919 or in 1946. And the problem here may be far more painful of resolution because Americans have been able to enjoy for two to four decades a level of personal space that will be hard indeed to see reduced.

The 'environmental movement' has been no help in all of this as it has created a ridiculous belief that suburban land is cancerous and unremitting in its growth. It is neither; and who can sensibly argue that we should destroy the lives of people for the abstract goal of keeping land, often scrubby and unattractive land, in its natural state? In a country such as the United States, cities make up only a couple of parts out of a hundred of the land use and the actual acreage in farms has increased rather than decreased since 1940. To add to the allaying of the current land fright, we should note also that most Western societies are fast approaching a level of zero population growth, under which it will be the hyper-procreation of the rural lands—Mexico, Brazil, India and the African nations—rather than the most modestly expanding suburban population on which the legions of reform should descend and spit. Experience would seem to suggest that if we wish to defuse the population bomb, what we need is a higher proportion of our population living in cities.

CONCLUSIONS

There is no possibility of concluding this discussion of the roles played by governmental and financial institutions in the shaping of the city in a summary way. Those roles have been diverse and shifting. Before the industrial revolution, there were no very clear policies advanced by governments with respect to housing, as that activity was not then thought to be independent of a broader interest in economic production. With industrialization (in the period 1760–1860), this tie of employment and housing provision was broken, leaving cities socially and physically in a most distressed state. For much of the last half of the nineteenth century, various lines of reform were undertaken: setting minimum standards of health and safety, destroying the bad in housing in the hope that the good would replace it, turning towards philanthropy to make up for the medieval notion of enlightened self-interest on the part of the employing master, which disappeared with factory industry, and finally a turn toward public housing provision. By 1900, in most of Western Europe governments were assuming some responsibilities for the care of the poor and the unfortunate, though most housing still came from the private sector either as rentals or purchases. After the First World War, and its sobering evidence that national armies need vast democratic backing to win, most European countries sought to assure decent shelter to all, regardless of income, so public housing became the norm in most working-class areas. With this reliance upon public housing two geographical locations gained attention, but each received a different physical solution:

1. The older areas of the centre were redeveloped *in situ*, normally with multiple-unit housing to cover the higher land costs found there—all of this in the interests of maintaining the traditional functional geography of the city.
2. New housing was built at the city's edge on cheaper land, in the interests of trying to provide more personal space and openness, with the public housing following in style as closely upon the private market as costs permitted.

The American picture differed both geographically and institutionally. In the United States, there was no governmental policy, until the depression years of the 1930s, looking toward housing beyond the application of the police power to try to assure health and safety. Then a very modest programme of public housing was begun, more as an economic pump-priming operation than as a true housing measure. Only the most impoverished were in any sense eligible. The result was that, starting in the 1930s public housing became firmly tied in the American mind to great poverty, social-pariah status and physical reconstruction of former slums in large central city projects. Public housing became an urban microenvironment, dispiriting to the residents and shunned by general society. In America, recourse to public housing was viewed as an act of social and economic desperation, so the private sector continued to be used for all but a most fractional part of housing provision. In that private sector, astounding successes were shaped through a combination of reasonable and plentiful mortgage lending, nearly universal personal mobility that made housing location a very free process and cheap land which allowed housing to grow in size—because most of the investment could go into the building rather than the plot on which it stood. Americans became the best housed nation on Earth, not so much for the physical quality of the house as for the surpassing quality of their space, personal within the house and external within the neighbourhood. There was little living with in-laws as in Sweden or Britain, there was private and useful access to open space beyond the Parisians' wildest dreams and there was a broadening of the realm of social intercourse that would have popped the eyes of any urban Hollander. There were faults; they have been as bannered by the American press as the European, so there is no need to repeat them here. Instead, we should come down heavily on the great spatial successes of American housing policies which were much greater than critics admit. But not all was success, and we can properly note America's grievous failure—that of providing decent social conditions for the poor and the ethnic. Note I did not say bad physical conditions, for in most cases the physical quality of public housing in the United States is not inferior to that in Europe—

the Pruitt-Igoe project of St. Louis, which had to be blown up as a social nuisance, began as an architecturally distinguished public housing project. The great failure of American housing has been in creating a healthily *social* environment in public housing and a positive acceptance of its role in housing provision for an ever-widening band of the working population.

While American policy has been suffering at its lower end, which though terribly obvious and very unacceptable is fortunately rather small in relative terms, European policy has been sick in its middle. Most Western European cities now lack slums and have rich and elegant countrysides around them. It is the broadly defined middle class that has been badly cared for in Europe, and unfortunately that is an expanding group. Crowding is a reality in these Western cities and personal space is so cramped as to throw an undesirable burden on public space. The crowding of highways around European cities is terrifying, even to a Californian, and perhaps even worse is the intemperant, vicious competitiveness of driving on them, which seems perhaps to reflect the outcome of a cramping housing policy that places national goals too high above personal goals; a policy which has argued that men must live cooped up in physically limited cities not for their own protection and good, as in the Middle Ages, but rather for the protection of a 'plan' and the good of those 'few' who can escape from the city to live in the countryside. For those who can live in that countryside, perhaps the benefit is commensurate with the cost, but it seems highly doubtful in Britain or in France that the weekend tripper or the vacationer has a very good bargain. An informative sidelight on this situation is furnished by the post-war developments in Germany, where most fortunately the *kleinsiedlungen* of Hitler's time have gone into eclipse as social engineering but have persisted as personal open space. Around most large German cities there are truly extensive allotments of land given over to productive gardening, and often dotted with garden houses, where it is possible to escape the planned packing of the city. These small-holdings seem not to have improved the quality of local driving, but they have somewhat reduced its incidence, and perhaps as well they have preserved a bit of what the housing reformers of the turn of the century had in mind.

For those reformers of 1900, the planning of housing provision had most strongly to be related to health, and from that came the suburb, private or public, in Europe or America. But because of large changes in governmental policy and in the availability of capital and land, housing provision has lost that hygienic quality and has taken its role instead from national economic planning. The assumption is made that we have conquered questions of health, and therefore we may think in terms of those of wealth, planning the most efficient and productive uses of resources. In such terms, the densely built-up city is thought the best, a notion encouraged by an increasingly reactionary concern for population in Western countries. Unfortunately, there has been no real questioning of what this social engineering that crowds men together as in the Middle Ages does to mental if not physical health. The evidence of the desires of people as we have seen them here suggests that the quality of personal space should be one of the fundamental concerns of our future housing provision. In this, we may yet again reinvest the provision of a reasonable personal space with the hygienic qualities with which it was vested when government intervened in housing at the turn of the century.

REFERENCES

Alonso, W. (1965). *Location and Land Use*, Harvard University Press, Cambridge, Massachusetts.

Blake, P. (1964). *Le Corbusier: Architecture and Form*, Penguin Books, Baltimore.

Byrne, M. St. Clare (1925). *Elizabethan Life in Town and Country*, Methuen, London.

Dyos, H. J. (1966). *Victorian Suburb*, Leicester University Press, Leicester.

Ely, R. T. (1885). 'Pullman: a social study'. *Harper's New Monthly Magazine*, **70**, 452–466.

Encyclopaedia Britannica (1911). 'Housing', 11th ed.

Forbes, E. (1942). *Paul Revere and the World He Lived In*, Houghton Mifflin, Boston.

Gray, G. H. (1946). *Housing and Citizenship: A Study of Low-Cost Housing*, Reinhold, New York.

Habbakuk, H. J. (1962). *American and British Technology in the Nineteenth Century: The Search for Labour Saving*, Cambridge University Press, Cambridge.

Johnson, J. H. (1964). 'The suburban expansion of housing in London, 1918–1939'. In J. T. Coppock and H. C. Prince (Eds.), *Greater London*, Faber and Faber, London, pp. 142–166.

Manzoni, H. J. (1939). *The Production of Fifty Thousand Municipal Homes*, The City of Birmingham, Birmingham.

Origo, I. (1957). *The Merchant of Prato*, Alfred A. Knopf, New York.

Robert, J. (1959). *Les Tramways Parisiens*, R.A.T.P., Paris.

Soleri, P. (1969). *Arcology: The City in the Image of Man*, The M.I.T. Press, Cambridge, Massachusetts.

Summerson, J. (1946). *Georgian London*, Charles Scribner, New York.

Vance, J. E., Jr. (1966). 'Housing the worker: the employment linkage as a force in urban structure'. *Economic Geography*, **42**, 294–325.

Vance, J. E., Jr. (1967). 'Housing the worker: determinative and contingent ties in nineteenth century Birmingham'. *Economic Geography*, **43**, 95–127.

Vance, J. E., Jr. (1976). *The Scene of Man: The Physical Evolution of the Western City*, Harper and Row, New York. (In press).

Warner, S. B., Jr., (1962). *Streetcar Suburbs: The Process of Growth in Boston, 1870–1900*. The M.I.T. Press, Cambridge, Massachusetts.

Weber, A. F., (1899). *The Growth of Cities in the Nineteenth Century*, (Reprinted 1963). Cornell University Press, Ithaca, New York.

Chapter 4

Housing Supply and Housing Market Behaviour in Residential Development

L. S. Bourne

Houses are things other people live in. To the cabbie a house is a street number; to the tax office a revenue source; to the school so many desks; to the speculator an investment; but, to the occupant, it is home. Housing, in other words, is a multidimensional entity, with strongly personal ties. It must be seen as holding several roles simultaneously in the working out of life-styles and residential patterns in the city.

Three interrelated aspects of urban housing are examined in this chapter: aggregate supply considerations, the operation of local housing markets and the role of supply factors in residential change. Given the complexity of the issues involved, the discussion begins with a review of definitions and elementary concepts, not because these are unknown but rather because they are so often misused or overlooked. The review also wanders beyond the role of the supply industry in residential patterning to look at housing as a social phenomenon and as the source of innumerable social conflicts.

Alternative approaches

There are at least three approaches to the study of housing in the context of urban residential structure. One begins with the production or supply side. First, examine the exogenous determinants of construction by type, value and location, including the effect of business cycles, the investment climate and government policy. Then determine the demand and income elasticities for housing, consumer preferences, the behaviour of the industries, builders and unions which deliver housing to the market, as well as the role of public and financial institutions which determine its eventual allocation to the population. Then, finally, one might study the processes by which households sort themselves out (or are sorted out by others) within the stock, and assess the various consequences of that sorting. A second approach reverses the above. It begins with a household's residential choice process and uses surrogates of housing demand (incomes) to construct a pattern of market areas in the city based on social characteristics. Questions of supply and housing industry behaviour are only brought into account for anomalies in the developed socio-ecological landscape of the city. The latter approach typifies most research in the social sciences concerned with intera-urban residential location.

A third approach treats supply and demand components at the same time. While obviously preferable and more realistic, it is (even) more frustrating. The two components are seldom in balance in the aggregate, and are less so in spatial or temporal terms. Supply considerations may shape the market at certain times, limiting intra-urban mobility and neighbourhood choice, and in specific sectors and areas at different times. Demand may dominate in other situations. And both are linked, in many and complex ways, with other variables we might wish to study, such as income. Research is not very close to isolating what these interrelationships are, nor to establishing their ultimate social importance.

The organization of the present chapter primarily follows the first approach. Emphasis is given to the processes by which the supply of housing is adjusted to demand (and vice versa), the types of housing sub-markets, the economic and behavioural underpinnings of the supply side, and the impact of housing supply in its broadest sense on the evolution of urban sub-areas. Because it is difficult to shed any new light on any of the above approaches, this chapter raises more questions than it answers.

The literature review in the paper is selective. In aggregate, the housing literature, particularly in economics, planning and design, is too enormous and detailed to document in the limited space available. Fortunately, there is now a number of excellent reviews (W. F. Smith, 1970), readers (Page and Seyfried, 1970; Pynoos, Schafer and Hartman, 1973; Wheaton, Milgram and Meyerson, 1966) and bibliographies (Real Estate Research Corporation, 1973; Silzer, 1972; Zeitlin, 1972) to assist the beginning student of housing. Unfortunately, there is relatively little analytical literature on the spatial aspects of intra-urban housing provision and the processes of urban housing market behaviour.

DEFINITIONS

The first step is to clarify our terminology. What do we mean by the terms housing stock, services, markets and sub-markets? Housing itself, as noted earlier, has many interpretations: as an economic or social good, a public or private resource, a physical container, or a function or service performed. Housing also has a considerable symbolic importance and a direct role in shaping human behaviour, both inside and outside the home (Michelson, 1972). In this paper, the term is defined broadly in order to encompass as many of these dimensions as possible.

Housing stock and services

Specifically, the concept of the housing stock applies to a physical facility (i.e. the building) and is usually differentiated from that of housing services

(Audian, 1972; De Leeuw, 1972). The latter deals with the flow of outputs from that stock in terms of what services it provides for the occupant and/or the owner (shelter, satisfaction, status, equity). Although a large number of such services could be enumerated, four are sufficient here:

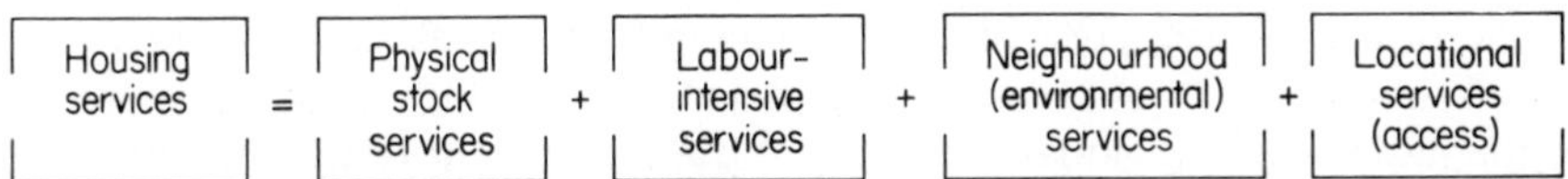

All but the second component, labour-intensive services, are self-explanatory. Isler (1970) defines this component to include maintenance, custodial and protective services (as in rental accommodation); these are commonly paid for either in rent or rates (taxes) and are the essence of housing standards legislation in most Western countries. The importance of each component varies with the tenure position of the unit—that is owner-occupied or rented, and for the latter whether the unit is public sector or private, furnished or unfurnished—and with the income of the occupant. In the case of owner-occupied housing, the first two of these services, at least, are generally performed by the owner himself, but eventually return income to that owner through capital gains on improvements.

These distinctions are critical for several reasons. First is the recognition that housing consists of a mix of attributes, the housing 'package' or 'bundle', some of which are external to the structure itself but each of which delivers its own output. Defining that bundle can become complicated. Kain and Quigley (1970a), for example, used thirty-nine variables to obtain measures of the physical, social and visual qualities of housing in a study of St. Louis, covering three different spatial scales: the dwelling, adjacent properties and the block face. A second reason is that the concept of a flow of services from housing removes the typically sharp distinction between the producers and consumers of housing, except in reference to the rental market. Owner-occupants, by this definition, become producers as well as consumers because of their labour inputs and equity accumulation. Third is the recognition given to neighbourhood and locational factors. Services deriving from these sources stress the importance of analysing housing in terms of environmental or spatial externalities, and in terms of the different values attached to each service by individual households and by groups of households. Interestingly, discussions of housing supply usually refer to the physical stock of dwellings, while studies of demand talk more frequently of the demand for housing services. Not surprisingly, the two concepts do not coincide.

Housing markets and sub-markets

A housing market, like other economic markets, is a set of arrangements for bringing together buyers and sellers for purposes of exchange. It may involve a very informal series of negotiations or highly complex transactions involving numerous participants. In any case, the private-sector housing market may be characterized as dealing with a range of services rather than a single commodity and with rights rather than property. It is a market directed primarily by price for the purpose of allocating scarce resources. Note, however, that this terminology is misleading; there is not one housing market, but many.

The principal distinction made in defining housing markets is between the macro- and micro-level. In the case of macro-level studies, housing is a sector of the national (or regional) economy and a component of national financial accounts. Research at this aggregate level (Grebler, 1951; Grebler and Maisel, 1963; W. F. Smith, 1970) is primarily directed at explaining the volume of construction activity (housing starts), shifts between housing and other sectors (investment flows) and the responsiveness (elasticities) of housing demand and supply with respect to current mortgage availability, interest rates, price and income. Surprisingly, there are few studies of interregional differences in housing market behaviour (Lee, 1972; Mittelbach, Saxer and Klaassen, 1967). Although beyond the scope of this paper, the outcomes of these macro-national and regional markets are what one eventually studies as the micro-patterns of urban residential development and redevelopment. Clearly, one cannot understand housing without considering the broader national context, particularly as it affects financing and urban and regional growth rates.

Although the concept of housing markets itself is straightforward, their delimitation is not. There is no market-place in the traditional sense. Buyers move to the goods, rather than the reverse. Definitions of markets depend on how one defines the housing commodity and also vary with one's perspective, even between traditional supply and demand sides. To take an extreme example, the housing markets of Los Angeles and New York, or of Glasgow and London, are separate from the viewpoint of most households in the two cities, but are not in the view of the major building and investment firms. The former are considered to be localized micro-markets while the latter are macro-markets. For some households and firms, this distinction could be reversed, of course.

Further complicating the issues, these definitions vary widely between countries. Wide differences appear in the existing stock and use of housing in each country (Table 4.1), and cultural attitudes to housing also differ. Variations in social aspirations, in the manner of reporting changes in the needs and quality of housing, and in government policy, defy simple cross-national generalizations. For this reason, further descriptive statistics on urban housing stock, by country or urban area, are not included here; a number of national and international inventories serve that purpose (Cullingworth, 1965; DiMaio, 1974; Karn, 1973; L. B. Smith, 1970; United Nations, 1974; United States Department of Housing and Urban Development, 1973). Even these are quickly dated by massive shifts in supply composition (Figure 4.1) and price (Figure 4.2) within relatively short periods of time.

These attributes raise two further and specific concerns: the relative uniqueness of urban housing markets as economic markets and the definition of appropriate sub-markets. The properties of housing as an economic good are

TABLE 4.1 Selected national indices of housing stock and supply[a]

Index (date)	United Kingdom	United States	Canada	Sweden
Total dwellings, 1970–1 (in 000s)	19 418	68 678	6 035	2 997
Population, 1971 (millions)	55.7	207.1	21.6	8.1
New dwellings built, 1971 (in 000s)	371.7	1 434.0[b]	201.3	107.2
Construction cost per sq. metre, 1971	£53.71 (council)	$158.34 (single-detached)	$164.56 (single-detached)	Kr. 930.00 (one-family, 1967)
Owner occupants (%)	49 (1971)	62 (1960)	60 (1971)	48 (1965)
Dwellings with fixed bath or shower (%)	77 (1971)	88 (1960)	80 (1961)	65 (1965)
New dwellings in apartments or flats (%)	28 (1967)	43 (1970)	45 (1971)	72 (1967)
Average number of rooms per dwelling[c]	4.6 (1971)	5.0 (1970)	5.4 (1967)	3.8 (1971)
Average hours of work[d] for house purchase	7 725 (1970)	5 744 (1970)	7 308 (1970)	n.a.
Average price: new housing (owner-occupied)	£8 456 (1972)	$25 206 (1971)	$25 206 (1972)	Kr 92 100[e] (1967)

Notes.

[a]For some indices more recent data are available but are less compatible across national boundaries.

[b]Private sector only.

[c]New dwellings.

[d]Average manufacturing earnings, male employees (United Kingdom), male and female (United States and Canada); for new dwellings only.

[e]Based on average size of 99 sq. metres.

Sources. Varied: United Nations; O.E.C.D., national sources; Karn (1973); United States Department of Housing and Urban Development (1973); Social Trends (1972), H.M.S.O., London.

well known, but their uniqueness is still hotly debated (W. F. Smith, 1970). Among these properties the most relevant to the present context are:

1. *Exogenous sensitivity.* As noted above, urban housing supply is heavily dependent on conditions external to local markets: e.g. business and construction cycles, money supply and investment alternatives.
2. *Durability.* The long-term nature of housing as an investment and the long (anticipated) life-span of the physical facility itself.
3. *Inflexibility.* The relatively slow response of the housing stock to changing demands (although the flow of services may change much more quickly).
4. *Immobility.* The housing stock generally remains in place in the short-term (occupants often move, houses seldom do).

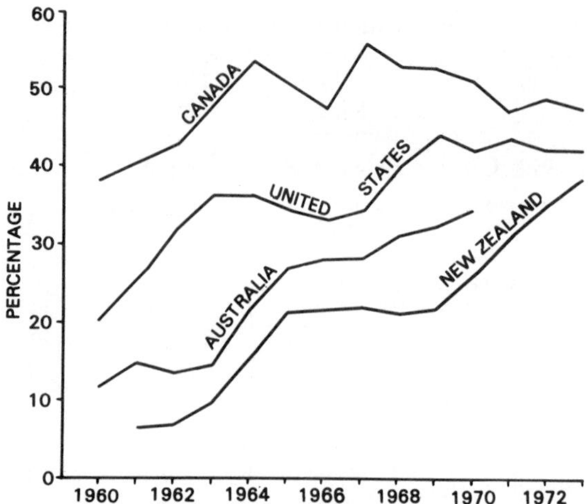

FIGURE 4.1 The changing composition of housing supply: the proportion of multi-family construction. (Extended from Nahkies, 1974)

5. *Institutionalization.* Housing is subject to a bewildering array of titles, rights, liens and policy constraints, which are superimposed on the land and on the design and use of housing to a greater extent than in most economic markets.
6. *Inhomogeneity.* The highly variable character of the stock itself and of the services it produces.
7. *Spatial externalities.* These are the 'spill-over' effects typical of urban land markets, which link the fortunes of any given housing unit to the fate of the environment in which that unit is located.

Each of these has a direct impact on urban social structure, to which we return later in the chapter. Their immediate effect is to encourage the operation of many different underlying sorting mechanisms, each subject to diverse operating constraints, leading to the creation of distinct sub-markets and housing environments.

Defining urban sub-markets

The essence of any study of housing is to define the most appropriate sub-markets. Aside from the problem of scale, the reason disaggregation is necessary is that housing is severely compartmentalized. The behaviour of builders, estate agents and developers is responsive to a differing mix of production factors for specific areas and housing types. Groups of consumers are also seeking different bundles of housing services, within the overall housing stock. Restrictive planning policies then ensure the separation of available housing into sub-markets.

In theory, housing sub-markets are defined by 'substitution'. That is, any unit within some larger set of units within a city is considered to be a potential substitute for any other. However, this definition does not advance us very far.

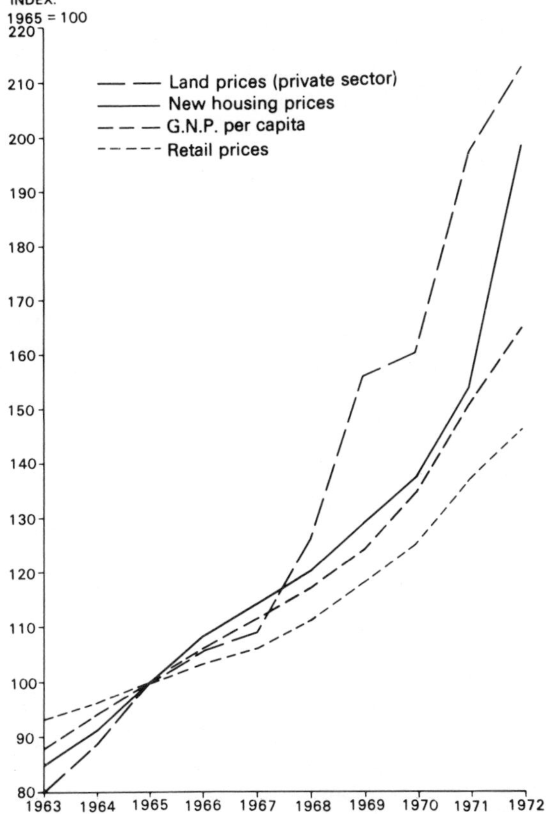

FIGURE 4.2 Housing prices and related indices in the United Kingdom, 1963–72

Substitution is extremely limited in reality, by price, location, tenure and legal restrictions, not to mention through race, ethnicity and social class barriers on mobility and choice. And, although substitution may be physically possible in all directions, it is seldom practical in terms of the economic and sociophysiological costs involved. Then there is the difficulty of defining substitution in space. Should spatially contiguous sub-markets be delimited? If so, how? Are they simply neighbourhoods in the traditional sense?

Because of these problems there is no consistent approach to, or criteria for, the definition of housing sub-markets in either spatial or aspatial contexts, Table 4.2 suggests a range of alternative definitions for the identification of sub-markets, drawn from studies in three different countries. Clearly, each classification is tailored to the particular purpose of the study, as well as to the cultural, economic and political conditions in which the research is set. Grigsby (1963) provides the most generally applicable criteria: location, tenure, value (price) and race, with the latter reflecting the existence of dual housing markets for whites and non-whites in most large United States cities. Maisel (1963), instead, emphasizes the difference between the market for newly constructed

TABLE 4.2 Definitions of housing sub-markets: selected examples

Author (date)	City	Principal criteria for classification	Types: Number	Types: Examples
Grigsby (1963)	Philadelphia	Location Tenure Value Race	Many	Central city/suburban Owner occupied/rental High/medium/low price Black/white
Maisel (1963)	Los Angeles	New Existing Owned Rental	4	Newly constructed single-family, unoccupied Previously occupied, resale Previously occupied, up for rental Newly constructed rental, unoccupied
Needleman (1965)	London	Tenure	4	Local authority Privately rented (furnished) Privately rented (unfurnished) Owner-occupied
Lithwick (1970)	Toronto	Price Type Ethnicity	9	High/middle/low price Age and family status/with children Anglo-Saxons/recent immigrants (non-English)
Cripps and Cater (1972)	Reading	Tenure Size Condition	12	Public–private/owned–rented Small/large Poor/good
Straszheim (1973)	San Francisco–Oakland	Municipal jurisdictions Race Homogeneity of stock	Many	(a) Central city, old housing, high density (b) Established suburbs, newer housing ...through... (f) Suburban industrial area, older housing, black population
Harvey (1974)	Baltimore	Location Ethnicity Income Turnover rates Financing	12	Grouped into eight areas or general types primarily on the basis of housing prices and finance: i.e. ethnic South Baltimore
Kain and Quigley (1974)	Pittsburgh	Density Quality (age) Size Tenure	30	Basically structural: fifteen types cross-classified by interior size, building type, lot size and tenure, for each of two time periods: post-1930 and pre-1930

TABLE 4.2 *(Contd.)*

Author (date)	City	Principal criteria for classification	Types: Number	Types: Examples
Maher (1974)	Toronto	Social status	5	Regions: stable single-family; increasing ethnicity; increasing social status; increasing population and crowding
		Tenure	2	Owned/rented; high turnover

units and that for housing previously occupied but up for resale. In Britain, the most common differentiation of sub-market types is that based on tenure (Doling, 1973; Donnison, 1967b; Needleman, 1965), notably between local authority (public sector), private sector rental and owner-occupied housing. In Canada, interest has centred on the structural typology of single-family row housing and high-rise apartments (L. B. Smith, 1969), and on ownership (Maher, 1974) and ethnicity (Lithwick, 1970). The latter criterion recognizes the effect of massive immigration on the housing markets of Canada's larger metropolitan areas. To this list could be added the indirect identification of urban housing sub-markets in terms of the analysis of neighbourhood types, such as through social area and factorial ecology techniques.

Following a quite different tack, Harvey (1974) and Harvey and Chatterjee (1974) look at the behaviour of housing finance institutions within different ethnic and income districts as a basis for identifying housing sub-markets in the city of Baltimore. This contribution is sufficiently different from previous research to warrant some elaboration here. Table 4.3 provides a summary of some of the properties of their eight sub-market types, with the types ranked by their average selling price; the spatial pattern of the sub-markets is mapped in Figure 4.3. The body of the table contains the proportions of sales transactions involving financial assistance from different sources. The essence of the classification of sub-markets is in the behaviour of financial intermediaries. Note that most house sales in low-income inner-city neighbourhoods are based on cash purchases or loans from private sources. Public lending agencies, both Federal and State, and the banks finance higher proportions of purchases in middle- and upper-income areas where presumably mortgage investments are most secure. The implications and injustices are obvious. As will be noted later, financial institutions are but one of many groups of actors involved in the delivery of housing services to areas and social groups within the city.

Despite this diversity of criteria, a common set of descriptive guidelines for delineating sub-market types can be identified. Figure 4.4 displays three dimensions of such types defined with reference to (a) the housing stock, (b) households and (c) location. A fourth dimension, the decision agents and

TABLE 4.3 Properties of housing sub-markets, Baltimore City, 1970

Examples of sub-markets	Percentage transactions by source of funds							Sales insured by F.H.A. (%)	Average sale price (in 000s $)
	House sales per 100 properties	Cash	Private	Federal S & L	State S & L	Mortgage and savings banks	Other		
1. Inner city	1.86	*65.7*	15.0	3.0	12.0	2.9	1.7	2.9	3.5
2. Ethnic	3.34	*39.9*	5.5	6.1	*43.2*	3.7	2.2	2.6	6.4
3. Hampden	2.40	*40.4*	8.1	18.2	*26.3*	7.0		14.1	7.1
4. West Baltimore	2.32	*30.6*	12.5	12.1	11.7	*27.0*	6.0	*25.8*	8.7
5. South Baltimore	3.16	*28.3*	7.4	*22.7*	13.4	19.3	9.0	*22.7*	8.8
6. High turnover	5.28	*19.1*	6.1	13.6	14.9	*39.7*	6.2	*38.2*	9.9
7. Middle income	3.15	*20.8*	4.4	*29.8*	17.0	19.2	9.0	17.7	12.8
8. Upper income	3.84	19.4	6.9	*23.5*	10.5	*36.9*	2.8	11.9	27.4

Note. S & L—Savings and Loan Associations; F.H.A.—Federal Housing Administration.
Source. Harvey (1974).

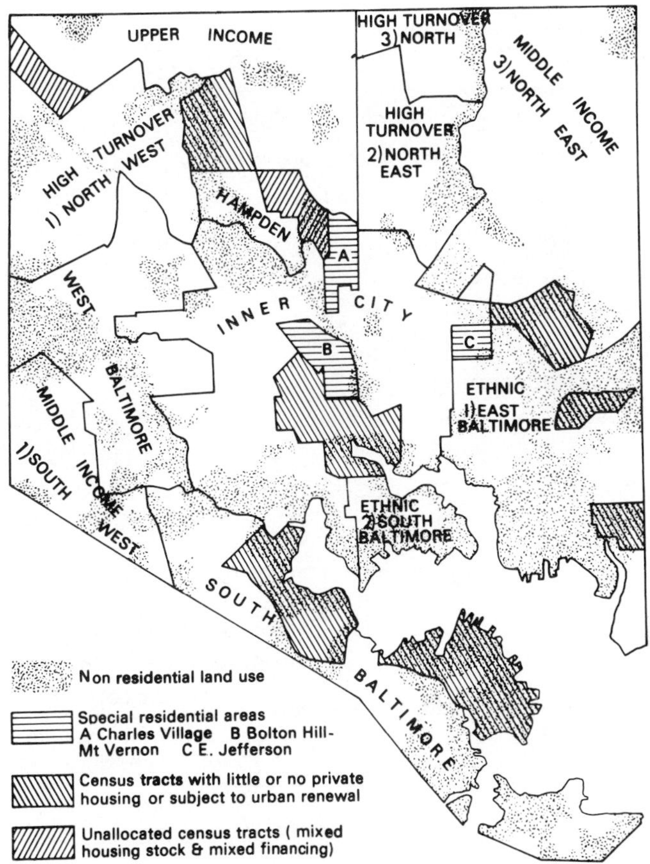

FIGURE 4.3 The distribution of housing finance sub-markets in Baltimore. (From Harvey, 1974)

actors influencing the market, is left to a later section. The first two each have three subdivisions: housing by type of structure, ownership and costs; households by their age and family status (stage in life-cycle), income and occupational status; and ethnic origin. The latter could be replaced by race in United States cities, by class in British cities (Mabry, 1968; Rex and Moore, 1967; Robson, 1969), or it might simply be dropped, as in Sweden (Holm, 1967; Wendt, 1963). The third dimension of sub-markets added to Figure 4.4, by location and neighbourhood type, follows from the above definition of the housing bundle as consisting of both environmental (neighbourhood) and structural attributes. Since most housing is fixed in location, and its use is dominated by externalities, sub-markets are generally considered to be highly localized in spatial extent. Harvey's example of housing finance sub-markets in Figure 4.3 and Table 4.3 is a clear illustration of one such localization effect.

The purpose of this elaboration of definitional problems is not to demonstrate

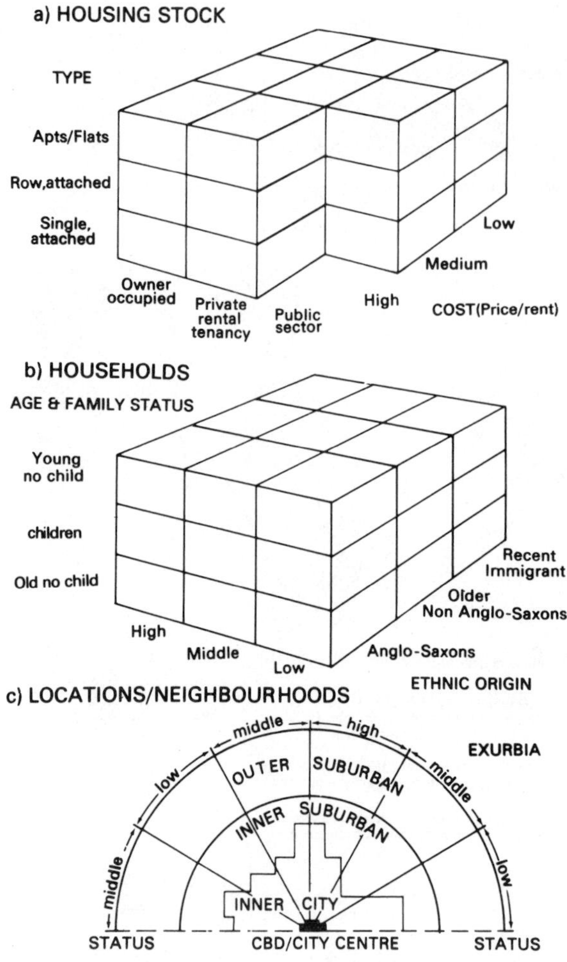

FIGURE 4.4 Intra-urban housing sub-markets: traditional definitions

that one can delimit 9, 27 or n^2 types of housing sub-markets. Rather it is to suggest the diversity of approaches which are possible and the inevitable limitations of each. Specific definitions must be tailored to the needs of each study, but should emphasize social service criteria rather than strictly physical criteria. And the above examples say nothing about the interactions or linkages between sub-markets which Grigsby (1963) attempted to introduce; nor are they based explicitly on the mechanisms by which households and houses are matched through the operation of the markets themselves. As is so often the case, to define housing sub-markets one must understand how the market operates in the aggregate; but one needs to define sub-markets effectively to understand the larger market context.

THE OPERATION OF HOUSING MARKETS

Many areas of research concerned with the operation of urban housing markets contribute to the analysis of supply and its social and spatial impacts. Only three are discussed here, and even this review is brief and specific to residential patterning. The three areas are: microeconomic theory, urban development modelling and behavioural studies of the producers of housing services.

Microeconomic theory

Microeconomic models are probably the most widely known approach to housing market research. An extensive literature has developed in economics, emanating primarily from the provocative work of Muth (1961, 1968, 1969), Alonso (1963), Mills (1967), Olson (1969) and Kain (1969). In general, these are elaborations of the von Thünen agricultural model. Such studies attempted to replicate the pattern of residential land consumption in urban areas through an analysis of the pricing mechanism for land and location. To do so, they sought to model the residential location-decision process by merging neoclassical theories of the behaviour of households and firms into a general equilibrium framework. This framework seeks to explain, at one and the same time, variations in location rent, population densities and substitutions among factors of production in housing, across an urban area.

The analyses are subject to a number of limiting assumptions. Housing is considered to be a unidimensional product, competition is perfect, household tastes are invariant, market price information is widely available and legal restrictions on the land are non-existent. For the suppliers of housing, profit maximization is the behavioural norm. The housing stock itself is assumed to adapt immediately to new needs. Space has only one dimension (distance from the city centre as measured by accessibility costs). And since, traditionally, all employment (and shopping) is assumed to be concentrated in the city centre, the costs of commuting are known.

The demand for housing in the aggregate is determined by essentially the same factors as that for other goods—population, income levels, prices, the cost and availability of credit, consumer preferences and policy changes. While, in the long-term, demographic structure, income and preferences are considered to be the key factors, in microeconomic models the household's budget allocation schedules are taken as the principal ordering mechanism in measuring demand. A household's equilibrium is defined based on the household's consumption of housing against consumption of all other goods. Housing is essentially a derived demand. That is, the household consumes land (size of site) and a housing location (distance, in time and money costs) according to its preferences for both, and subject to an overall budget (income) constraint.

The market process implied in such models is basically a mechanistic one. Households distribute themselves among locations in the city according to income, their desire for accessibility to employment (i.e. distance from the city centre), and a set profile of preferences for all goods other than land and location (i.e. housing), including leisure. Interestingly, the housing market has an outer geographic boundary under the latter assumption: the distance from the city centre at which all leisure time is consumed in commuting to work.

There is, however, no agreement in the literature about the complex trade-offs the household has to make. Evidence is inconsistent, for example, on the size of income elasticities for housing expenditures, on the marginal propensities of households to spend on housing and on the cross-elasticities between different household budget items. Nevertheless, it is generally agreed that housing expenditures increase at a faster rate than permanent (long-term) income, at least up to a certain level (Straszheim, 1972), and that income elasticities of housing expenditure are typically higher among low income groups. One result of these differences is that the response of different income groups to any given change in housing supply will vary widely, even if all other factors are held constant, and the poor will pay more for the same housing bundle.

The supply of housing in most microeconomic models is not considered to be much of a problem. Supply, under the assumptions of profit maximization and a totally fluid housing inventory, follows automatically from the structure of demand. The decision to build or not to build, and what type to build and where, depends on the builder's assessment of the expected yield on invested capital, reflecting the balance between expected selling or rental price on the one hand and construction and carrying costs on the other. Real estate, like other long-term investments, depends on the calculated net cash flow over the life of the property. Mortgage market conditions, taxation policies and financing practices exert an immense influence on the direction this investment takes. This investment flow also differs in the aggregate between the owner-occupied and rental markets (L. B. Smith, 1970), with the latter (at least in Canada) most sensitive to the availability of credit.

The typical output of such micro-models is directly relevant to the housing supply theme of this chapter. They provide, simultaneously, a market equilibrium distribution of location rents (which are, in effect, housing prices) and an equilibrium residential pattern for groups of households based on individual utility maximization. In spatial terms, the results may be summarized as follows: (a) population densities decrease regularly with distance from the city centre; (b) lot sizes increase with distance; (c) income increases with distance; and (d) lot size increases with income. Housing supply patterns must then be inferred from what are essentially two identical patterns—of land use and income.

In economic theory, a housing market performs efficiently when demand matches supply. Efficiency, in the terms ascribed to the Italian economist and social philosopher, Vilfredo Pareto, is that situation in which every participant in the market has satisfied his wishes and for which any other solution would mean some others are not as well-off. This Pareto equilibrium is very difficult to rationalize in the context of urban housing, and is impossible to find.

Recent extensions to this area of research, in attempting to relax the highly restrictive assumptions, have added innumerable new wrinkles to the theory and new explanatory variables to the empirical models. Among these are attempts to measure a fuller range of housing services (Evans, 1973; Isler, 1970; Olson, 1969); to relax the assumption of a single employment centre (De Leeuw, 1972); to incorporate different forms of household utility and production functions (Menchik, 1973) and varying tastes (Beckmann, 1974); to introduce environmental quality (Kain and Quigley, 1970b), racial discrimination (Kain and Quigley, 1972) and tenure choice (Doling, 1973); to include discontinuities (i.e. heterogeneity) within the housing stock over both space and time (Straszheim, 1973); to include the costs of moving (Muth, 1974) and the effects of taxes on land rent and subsidies to housing (Beckmann, 1974); and to measure the disbenefits and well as the benefits of differing residential environments (Berry and Bednarz, 1974)—to name only a few.

What do these extensions tell us of the actual prices at which housing is supplied at different locations within the city? Many, but not all, of the above models have been tested empirically (Evans, 1973; Kain and Quigley, 1970a, 1970b; Muth, 1969), with varying results. While it is neither possible nor appropriate to review these results in detail, selective summaries are provided in Table 4.4, as well as by Ball (1973), Richardson, Vipond and Furbey (1974), Berry and Bednarz (1974) and Kain and Quigley (1974).

Despite wide differences in the hypothesized determinants of urban house prices in Table 4.4, most can be grouped under one of three broad headings: those relating to (a) the characteristics of the units themselves, (b) the neighbourhood and (c) the location (accessibility). These correspond to three of the four components of housing services defined previously. The specific kinds (and numbers) of variables chosen to measure each of these determinants vary with data availability, purpose, social context and level of generality (house, block or census tract). Consequently, the analytical results vary. Studies in United States cities might emphasize differences in racial composition and crime rates between areas (Kain and Quigley, 1970a) or pollution (Berry and Bednarz, 1974), while those set in the United Kingdom might identify social class as an environmental determinant of price and the prevalence of central heating and inside toilets (Wilkinson and Archer, 1973) as important structural determinants. In most cases, structural characteristics (house size, type and improvements) dominate the statistical results.

More important perhaps for this review, these studies demonstrate the imprint of spatial interdependencies affecting urban housing markets and the importance of defining housing as a package of interdependent services. Their results also indicate why sub-market definitions are so tenuous and potentially unstable. Despite the analytical precision of many of the preceding studies, much of the spatial variability of housing prices escapes easy measurement and explanation. The relationships between variables are not all linear or log-linear; differences within census tracts (or other recording areas) tend to be

TABLE 4.4 Determinants of housing value: a sample of recent studies

Author (date)	City	Dependent variable	Location variables	Neighourhood variables: Race/ethnic/class	Neighourhood variables: Neighbourhood characteristics	Neighourhood variables: Environmental quality	Housing variables: Housing characteristics	Housing variables: Housing improvements
Muth (1969)	Chicago	Housing expenditures per month	—	% Black	No. of manufacturing establishments % Housing built before 1940 % owner-occupied % Population over 20 Income Migration Median -years school % workforce, white collar Population growth rate	—	—	—
Kain and Quigley (1970a, 1970b)	St. Louis	House price	Distance to C.B.D. (central business district)	% white	Median schooling Crime index	—	Five factors produced from thirty-nine variables Age No. of rooms Lot area	No. of baths
				Same variables as above plus the following:				
		Monthly rent	Distance to C.B.D.				Type of building structure	Heat Water Appliances Hot water Central heating

Apps (1971, but see 1974)	Reading	House price	Access to employment and schools	—	—	—	Floor area Stories Age Condition Lot area Structure type	Garage
Evans (1973)	London	Asking price	Distance to C.B.D.	—	—	—	Floor area No. years of lease expired	—
Wilkinson and Archer (1973)	Leeds	Factor analysis results	Distance to C.B.D.	Socioeconomic index	Residential density No. of schools/ population	—	House type Age No. of rooms Area	Attics Bedrooms Garage Bath Inside toilet
Berry and Bednarz (1974)	Chicago	House price	Distance to C.B.D.	% Black % Cubans/ Mexicans % Irish	Median family income % Apartments Migration rate	SO_2 levels Particulates	Sq. Feet Age Lot area	Air conditioning Garage Improved attic Basement No. of baths
Grether and Mieszkowski (1974)	New Haven	House price	Distance to New Haven Green (C.B.D.)	% White in schools	Pupil/teacher ratios Traffic flows Density	—	Size stories Age Lot area Building materials	Appliances Heating Garage Rooms Fireplace Electrical outlets

Source. Adapted and extended from Ball (1973) and Berry and Bednarz (1974).

overlooked; subtle differences in price changes are blanketed by the methodologies employed; and the dynamics of price behaviour are still not a logical component of the model's construction and solution.

Urban development models

Housing sub-models, and specifically those concerned with housing supply, have frequently been major components in the massive urban development models typical of urban research in the early 1960s. These provide useful insight for any student of housing, not for their results as such but for their attempts to conceptualize the operation of urban housing markets. Among the better-known 'first generation' examples are the housing demand sub-models contained in the Penn-Jersey study (Herbert and Stevens, 1960) and the explicit supply-oriented approach of the San Francisco Community Renewal Program (Wheaton, Milgram and Meyerson 1966). Space does not permit a full description of even one such model here. What can be done, however, is briefly to summarize the approach, extensions to and limitations of the models, in reference to housing supply.

These models, and the generations which followed, were primarily spatial allocation models. That is, given H^{kv} housing units of type k and value v, and U_{ir} households of income level i and with an ordering r of housing preferences, the problem was to allocate those households to the units spread over j regions of the city. The allocation was made on the basis of a set of assumptions on growth rates, forecasts of public actions subject to simple locational parameters (i.e. accessibility) and constraints on allowable densities in each region. The purpose was to replicate an existing pattern of housing occupance and to provide a forecasting device for testing policy alternatives. In some cases, such as the San Francisco model, the demand side incorporated both an ordered set of household preferences by households for different housing types and minimum–maximum budget limits on expenditures for housing by those households.

Figure 4.5 is a schematic flow chart for such a model. Given the above assumptions, households are allocated to the existing stock according to their first choice in housing, then their second, etc., until demand and supply are exhausted. If supply matches the (hypothetical) demand, a second iteration begins with new population growth forecasts. If they are not in balance, needed changes in supply are specified and preferences are reassessed.

This and other models, however, have been widely criticized for failing to encompass the processes by which the existing stock is actually adapted to different needs and, more generally, for their failure to model the market and policy mechanisms involved in housing supply. Note that in Figure 4.5 the supply side is at least partially recursive and partly responsive to the effects of public actions, in that it allows for some readjustment of the flow of new units to accommodate changing household demands. Few such studies allow for a realistic determination of housing prices, however, nor for the

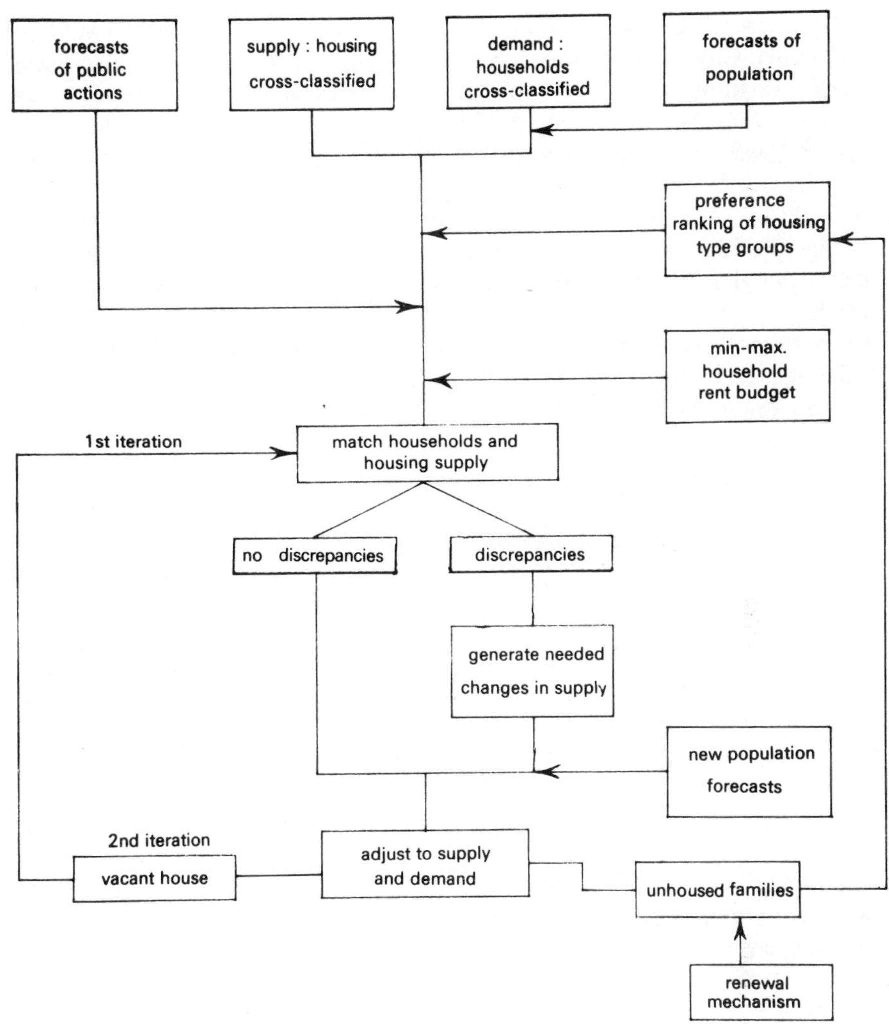

FIGURE 4.5 Hypothetical housing supply component of an urban development simulation model

competition between residential and non-residential uses of urban land. Also, in the American context, such models have traditionally been colour-blind (Kain, 1969), as well as largely oblivious to the important role of public and financial institutions (Harvey, 1974; Noursey, 1973).

Recent large-scale modelling efforts have generally attempted to encompass both supply and demand considerations within a multidimensional competitive housing market. Most models, however, are increasingly tailored to a specific purpose and urban context, and consequently lack generality. Examples include the CERAU model of French housing markets (Kirwan and Martin,

1970), those of the Greater London Council (Dear, 1970), the Rand study of New York City (Lowry, de Salvo and Woodfill, 1971) and the United States Urban Institute and Bureau of Economic Research housing models (De Leeuw, 1972). While most of the earlier models were essentially accounting systems, with only strictly mechanical changes permitted, more recent versions have depended increasingly on probabilistic simulation. A number of geographers have attempted to outline an extensive accounting system for housing change paralleling that developed for models of household and population migration (Batty, 1973; Cripps and Cater, 1972; Echenique, Crowther and Lindsay, 1969; Echenique and coauthors, 1974; Rees, 1972). While these are valuable, precisely as accounting techniques for housing change, they still fail to encompass the diverse and overlapping nature of housing sub-markets and the highly variable character and influence of the standing stock of dwellings.

Behavioural considerations

The supply side of urban housing markets is not, as assumed in most micro-economic models, characterized by optimal decision-making within a uniform and unconstrained environment. The housing industry itself, and the various private and public agents responsible for the provision of housing, are not homogeneous in character or behaviour. This complexity, well known to students of the city, is a major determinant of the changing residential geography of urban areas.

Understanding such changes necessitates getting 'inside' the development process, on both demand and supply sides. Paralleling attempts to outline the actual sequence of decisions and the factors involved in a household's selection of a new residential location are efforts to describe the behavioural underpinnings of decision-making on the producer side. While a great deal has been written on the economic behaviour of the firm, much less has been done on the broad spectrum of processes involved in the delivery of housing to the consumers. The most relevant perspective here is that which focuses on the process of site-selection for new residential development or redevelopment. The work of Pahl and Craven (1970) and Drewett (1970) on the land development process in England; of Neutze (1971) on Sydney and Melbourne; of Bourne (1969) and Chamberlain (1972) on Toronto; of Clawson (1971) on Philadelphia and New York; and of Harvey (1974) on landlords in Baltimore, are examples. Many have their origins in the work of Weiss and coauthors (1966) and Kaiser (1972) and their associates at the University of North Carolina.

The essence of this approach is that supplying land for housing purposes is not a single unitary transition from rural to urban (from undeveloped to developed) states. Instead, land areas (sites) are seen to pass through a set of complex processes, involving a sequence of stage of 'preparedness' and, eventually, delivery. The sequence begins with the initial rural state and ends with occupance of the unit by a new household. More important, at each stage in the sequence, a different set of what Wheaton (1964) called 'primary' decision agents may be involved. Each has varying criteria for making its decisions, each has differing objectives, and the constraints on how they behave also differ. Market outcomes (i.e. patterns of new housing) may therefore be shaped by conditions or actors prevailing at one or a few stages in the development process.

Figure 4.6 illustrates one view of this sequence of states. Five states are identified, and for each the specific key (priming) decisions involved and the factors affecting those decisions are shown (Kaiser, 1972; Kaiser and Weiss, 1970). The most important factors influencing the decisions to develop land relate to the environment (contextual characteristics), the specific site (properties) and the attributes of the decision agents involved. Superimposed on this process are a lattice of public policy constraints on the use of urban land and housing. Empirical evaluations of the relative weights to be attached to the roles of different agents and location factors have, however, produced inconsistent results. And, as one study (Bourne and Berridge, 1973) of the developers' choice of locations for high-rise apartments (flats) demonstrated, these weights will shift over time as the structure of the city evolves, as social preferences change and as policy controls mature.

Although most of this research is still in the formative stage, a number of important lessons have already been documented. One is the obvious point that macro-level models of residential development are inadequate to grasp the complexity of the supply process. Also, the housing market is far from perfectly competitive. Even though the number of agents in the provision of housing is very large (Clawson, 1971), the inherent monopoly properties of land (being fixed in location) allow for some agents, particularly on the supply side, effectively to dominate the market. Third, the role of public agencies and institutions, rather than being passive as in traditional economic models, does fundamentally shape the geography of residential development in a city. Marriott (1967) has demonstrated the prevailing role of oligopoly in the redevelopment process in London; Harvey (1974), as noted earlier, has argued that institutional finance policies in Baltimore have acted '. . . to create distinctive submarkets within the urban residential structure'; and Bourne and Berridge (1973) have shown the increasingly powerful force of zoning and planning permissions on the location of new residential construction in Toronto. What effect do these supply factors have on conventional descriptions of how a city's residence structure evolves? Are new concepts needed?

DESCRIPTIVE CONCEPTS OF HOUSING CHANGE

One of the specific failings of such models worthy of elaboration here is the difficulty of incorporating the various forms of adjustment which occur in the housing stock. These adjustments include the locational impact both of new units and of modifications within the standing stock. The former are usually obvious; the latter are not and are frequently ignored. Since most people live in second-hand houses, and the majority of residential moves and neighbour-

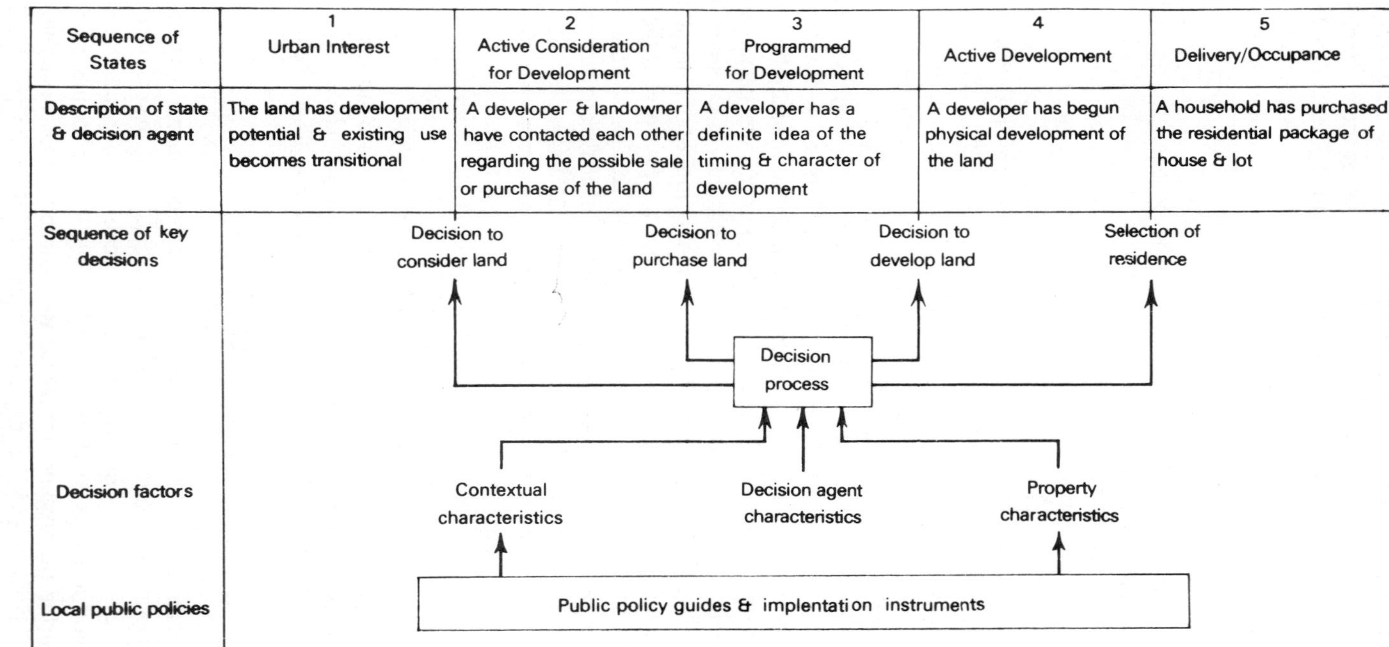

FIGURE 4.6 The residential land development process. From Kaiser and Weiss (Reprinted by permission of the *Journal of the American Institute of Planners*, **36**, 1, 1972)

hood transitions are accommodated within this stock, then such adjustments become central in understanding residential differentiation as documented in subsequent chapters. In this section, three descriptive concepts of housing stock change are selected for review: development cycles, filtering and vacancy chains. Before doing so, a typology of the different forms of structural adjustment to change is provided.

Forms of structural adaptation

Any elementary text on urban land economics cites a range of possible adaptations in the building stock of a city over time. Each building (and dwelling) unit has a particular historical profile and a varying record of occupancy; each ages in a different way and obsolesence has a varying impact; and each unit also occupies a given relative position, in terms of value, type of occupancy, tenure and, more generally, in the flow of services, within the 'matrix' of housing opportunities (i.e. sub-markets) in any given city at any point in time.

Figure 4.7 summarizes a range of possible adjustments; it focuses specifically on changes involving the housing stock and the generalized outcomes of such changes. Housing units can be added either (a) by new units on previously undeveloped land, (b) through modifications in the form and usage of the existing stock or (c) by replacement of existing units with new construction. Each of these three types in turn can take different forms, depending on location (as extensions to the built-up area or as in-filling), on the scale of modification (in price, occupancy, use) or in the origin of the investment decisions involved (public or private renewal). This range of adjustments, in turn, conforms roughly to a time scale (from initial construction to demolition and replacement) and to a spatial scale (moving from the city centre redevelopment to peripheral extension). Each type of adjustment can also be viewed at different levels of spatial aggregation—the individual dwelling or building unit (or site), city blocks or even as broad neighbourhoods or socioeconomic regions within an urban area. Changes in relative housing value (filtering) or occupancy (density), and duration (turnover) or tenure, for example, are expressed at each of these levels. Yet what is missing from the above is evidence of how changes in the stock at these levels interact.

Despite our initial presuppositions, such changes in supply can be considerable, even over short periods of time. In the construction of new towns, the types and arrangement of several thousand dwellings built in the first few years will permanently shape the new city's social geography. In existing metropolitan areas, the scale of new construction may also be substantial, in both absolute and relative terms, when aggregated over several years. In Toronto, the base of the author's perspective on housing, over 300 000 new dwelling units were completed in the ten years from 1964 to 1973. During that time, the population of the census metropolitan area (which probably underestimates the full spatial extent of the Toronto housing market) increased from 1.8 to 2.7 millions.

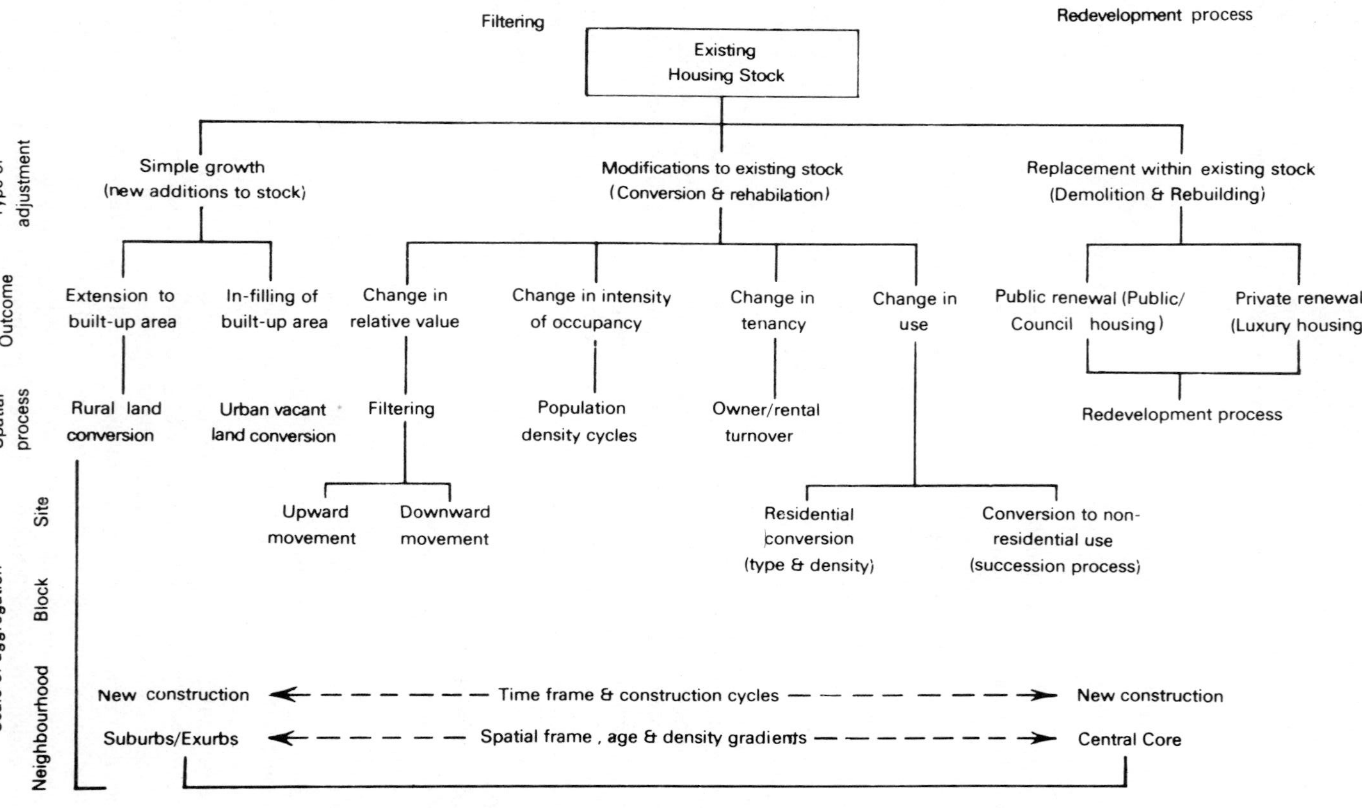

FIGURE 4.7 Summary of structural adjustments in urban housing markets

More important, the composition and price (and location) of this construction, and thus the choice it provided for households, was substantially different from that of the existing stock. From 50 to 60 per cent. of the additions in each year were apartments (flats; 190 000 units), most of which were in high-rise, high-density and privately rented buildings, compared to less than 20 per cent. of the existing stock in apartments at the beginning of the period. Now nearly 40 per cent. of the total stock is in apartments, and housing choice is declining.

Thus, both the character and the operation of housing sub-markets has changed dramatically, and it has been largely ignored by research (Wright, 1971). The visual and physical impact on the differentiation of residential sub-areas has been equally dramatic. Other rapidly growing cities have witnessed similar magnitudes of change (Nahkies, 1974), although the directions of impact will almost certainly differ. Similarly, the scale of deletions from the existing housing stock, through non-residential succession (Bourne, 1971), urban renewal and slum clearance (Cullingworth, 1973), through 'white-painting' and rehabilitation (Listokin, 1973), or, in recent years, through large-scale housing abandonment, as in some large American cities (Berry, 1973; Sternlieb and Burchell, 1973), may also significantly alter the distribution of housing opportunities.

The point of these examples is to argue that housing supply can no longer (if it ever could) be treated as a direct consequence of the spatial distribution of demand. Variability within the existing stock and shifts in the parameters of new housing construction cannot be ignored—shifts which alter the social landscape of the city through the choice of housing and residential environments provided.

Urban development cycles

Implicit in Figure 4.7 is the notion that regularities occur in housing and urban development changes over time and in the residential life-histories of buildings and neighbourhoods. Two effects, that of ageing and obsolesence on residential change, on the one hand, and of the timing of construction, on the other, are the bases for this idea. We know that individual buildings go through an ageing process (Clawson, 1968), which is reflected either in standardized housing depreciation curves (Grigsby, 1963) or in condition deterioration curves (Wolfe, 1969) in most economic models. Needleman (1965) has attempted to construct housing life-tables. Previously, Miles Colean (1950) proposed a 'universal' urban development cycle in which a building itself moves through a series of states from new construction, a long period of gradual decline and depreciation, to a state when it is economically feasible (and socially appropriate?) either to convert the building to a new use (often non-residential) or to replace that building with a new structure (inevitably at higher densities). With redevelopment, a new 'cycle' then begins, but on a different economic plateau.

The concept of development cycles can be generalized more broadly in at least two directions: in reference to neighbourhood changes and in terms of the wide historical fluctuations in construction activity. As for the latter, the construction industry is, as everyone knows, notoriously cyclical, in part because of its use by most Western governments for purposes other than housing (i.e. as a Keynesian economic growth regulator) and in part because urban housing construction, in particular, appears to be highly sensitive to the flow of migrants into urban areas (Johnson, Salt and Wood, 1974; Wyatt and Winger, 1971) and thus to rates of overall employment growth in the economy. The inefficiencies in the industry itself and in its financial sources are also well known. In any case, temporal instability in the housing industry adds an important element of uncertainty to the operation of urban land and housing markets, which affects the behaviour of both the suppliers and consumers of urban housing. In particular, it encourages short-term and largely speculative responses by developers, financers and the purchasers of new and existing housing. It also discourages mobility in the city by encouraging the creation of closed housing sub-markets through inflated house prices and restrictive zoning.

Equally important is the simple fact that differences in the timing of development, enforced by building cycles and prevailing economic conditions, can produce markedly different residential patterns within and between cities. Each city is layered with housing stocks added under varying economic (and social) conditions and must be examined in terms of that historical record. Jane Jacobs once remarked that slums could not escape the misfortune of having been built at the same time. But then how else could urban areas be built? Examinations of the imprint of actual building cycles on the spatial structure of specific cities, such as Ward's (1964) comparison of nineteenth century Boston and Leeds, Adams' (1970) study of Minneapolis, Whitehand's (1972) work on Glasgow and Gonen's (1972) analysis of the role of high growth rates and extensive public housing construction in shaping Israeli cities, point to very different residential fabrics evolving as a result of differences in the scale, timing and character of new construction. Both Ward (1964) and Adams (1970) also tie construction cycles to the timing of changes to or improvements in the transport systems within cities, as Isard (1942) did twenty years earlier. Each new system increases the differentials in the area available for development and thus in the space for augmenting housing supply. The automobile is but one of these conditioning factors shaping the form of housing construction.

The patterns resulting from these varied cycles then determine the broad parameters and set the stage for studies of residential growth and change. Figures 4.8 and 4.9 are examples taken from Adams' (1970) study of Minneapolis. The isolines in Figure 4.8, for instance, delimit the spatial extent of most housing construction during each period in time and thus the addition of new sub-markets. As sub-markets, based on age of housing as well as location, these isolines also act as catchment areas within which most intra-urban residential mobility takes place. What Figure 4.8 masks, however, is the renewal or redevelopment process identified in Figure 4.7. This process may be of enormous importance, as Gayler (1971), Haynes and Pinsky (1971), Bourne and Berridge

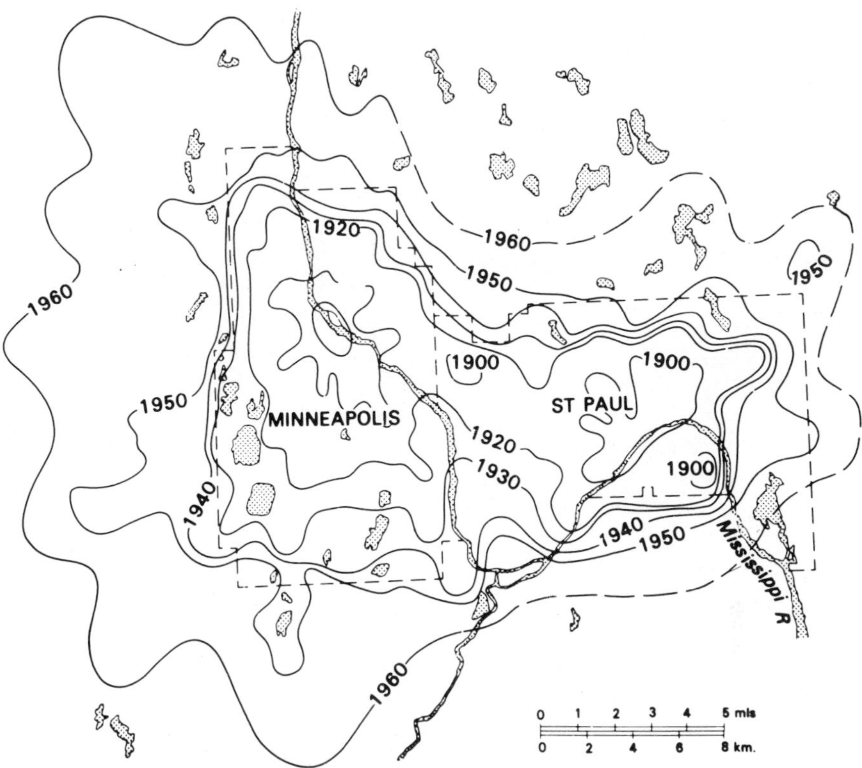

FIGURE 4.8 Pattern of housing supply: median age of housing in Minneapolis and St. Paul. (Adapted from Adams, 1970, Figure 16, and from the Comparative Metropolitan Analysis Project, Association of American Geographers, 1974, with the author's permission)

(1973) and Murphy (1973) have demonstrated for different Canadian cities, because of the type of construction (high-rise, rental apartments) and the portion of the market (highly mobile, non-family households) for which this construction is largely intended.

Attempts have also been made, since the classic work of Hoover and Vernon on New York, to identify regular characteristics and/or stages in the historical profile of neighbourhood change (see Birch, 1971; Birch and coauthors, 1974). This profile is extended here to include housing change. The stages are thought to represent periods of time when neighbourhoods display a particular mix of social and physical attributes, such as in age and demographic structure, income, and migration flows, as well as in building type, condition and change. The latter, paralleling the 'developmental' sequence suggested earlier by Colean (1950) for individual buildings, includes systematic changes in both the rate and character of new construction and in the general condition and occupancy of the existing building stock, and in that area's relative position in the city's housing mosaic. Ageing is clearly the driving force in this evolutionary sequence.

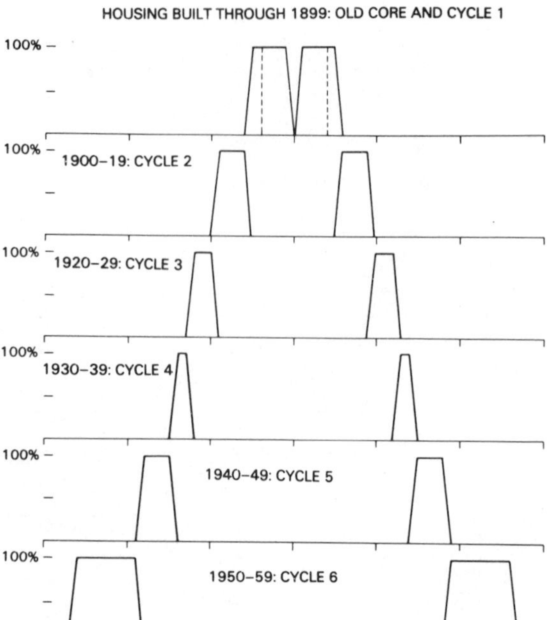

FIGURE 4.9 Pattern of suburban housing construction: a traverse through the centre of a hypothetical city. (After Adams, 1970, Figure 17. Reproduced by permission from the *Annals Association of American Geographers*, **60**, 1970)

Table 4.5 enumerates some of these characteristics for each of the five stages suggested by Hoover and Vernon. Attempts to evaluate such stages empirically, at least when measured primarily in terms of social change, have not been very successful, however (Guest, 1974). Clearly, the same stock of housing can accommodate differing social structures, and vice versa. Yet the recognition of supply changes as a continuous and integral portion of neighbourhood structure, throughout the history of those neighbourhoods, whether falling into discrete stages or not, is an important step in developing more comprehensive perspectives on urban and residential change.

The filtering process

One form of adjustment noted in Figure 4.7 which has received the most attention in housing research is the filtering process, which Grigsby (1963) refers to as '... the principal dynamic feature of the housing market ...'. The concept is of concern here since it is basically through one form or other of the filtering process that most changes in neighbourhood status and housing

TABLE 4.5 Summary of neighbourhood life-cycles

	Physical changes			Social changes			Other changes
Stage	Dwelling type (predominate additions)	Level of construction	Population density	Family structure	Social status income	Migration mobility	Other characteristics
1. Suburbanization (new growth) 'homogeneity'	Single-family (low-density multiple)	High	Low (but increasing)	Young families, small children, large households	High (increasing)	High net in-migration, high mobility turnover	Initial development stage; cluster development; large-scale projects, usually on virgin land
2. In-filling (on vacant land)	Multi-family	Low, decreasing	Medium (increasing slowly or stable)	Ageing families, older children, more mixing	High (stable)	Low net inmigration, low mobility turnover	First transition stage—less homogeneity in age, class, housing first apartments; some replacements
3. Downgrading (stability and decline)	Conversions of existing dwellings to multi-family	Very low	Medium (increasing slowly), population total down	Older families, fewer children	Medium (declining)	Low net out-migration, high turnover	Long period of depreciation and stagnation; some non-residential succession
4. Thinning out	Non-residential construction—demolitions of existing units	Low	Declining (net densities may be increasing)	Older families, few children, non-family households	Declining	Higher net out-migration, high turnover	Selective non-residential succession
5. Renewal	(a) Public housing	High	Increasing (net)	Young families, many children	Declining	High net inmigration, high turnover	The second transition stage—may take either of two forms depending on conditions
	(b) Luxury high-rise apartment	Medium	Increasing (net)	Mixed	Increasing	Medium	
	Townhouse conversions	Low	Decreasing (net)	Few children	Increasing	Low	

quality occur. Equally important, filtering has been a principal rationale for the approach taken by most Western governments to financing housing supply. The initial difficulty concerns how this process is to be defined.

Most generally, the term filtering implies any change in either (a) the house, (b) the household or (c) the matching of the two. More specifically, it refers to a change in the position of a housing unit (or household) in the matrix of units in any given market area. Beyond that there is no agreement on what it means, as evidenced by a lengthy and often bitter debate in the literature, particularly the American literature (Fisher and Winnick, 1951; Grigsby, 1963; Klaassen, 1966; Kristof, 1972; Lowry, 1960; W. F. Smith, 1970; Weathersby, 1970). At least five definitions of filtering emerge: (a) a change in both value and occupancy, (b) a change in relative price (or rent), (c) a change in absolute price (or rent), (d) a change in occupancy by income of the household and (e) an improvement in housing condition. To some observers, the latter is the only situation in which filtering can be said to have occurred at all. The problem is the confusion between what constitutes the process (market change) and the possible results (housing improvements) of that process.

The simplest definitions used relate to price (or income). If we array dwellings (or households) in a city along a continuum of price (or income), cross-classified for each of two or more points in time (i.e. as a matrix), filtering is said to have occurred if a given unit (household) has changed its position within the matrix. While buildings obviously age with time, it is also assumed that ageing implies a relative decline in housing attractiveness and value. Older units or those in unattractive neighbourhoods will then move downward within the matrix as new units are added. These declining units are then, in theory, available to households of increasingly lower income with each time period. If the rate of upward filtering of households (through income growth) exceeds the rate of depreciation or decline of the stock, then households have improved their housing quality, in absolute if not relative terms.

Take the simple example given below. Eighteen housing units in existence at the beginning of the period are grouped into three classes on the basis of value (price): five in the lowest category (I), ten in the middle category (II) and three in the highest category (III). During the period under study, three new units were added to the stock in that area, all in the high value category, and one unit, in the lowest category, was removed. Moreover, two of the seventeen remaining initial units increased their relative position in the value matrix (one moving from I to II, and one from II to III), and one other declined (II to I). The final frequency tally of housing units by value category with twenty units then becomes 4–9–7 instead of 5–10–3 as at the initial point in time.

Real-world examples become substantially more complex and difficult to interpret. Note that the frequencies in each cell could also represent households cross-classified by income or housing values rather than houses by value as in this example. In short, these matrix formulations are useful in a number of ways: as descriptive summaries of housing price change (Grigsby, 1963; Straszheim, 1973), as measures of rates of neighbourhood quality change

Initial			Final value category				
			I	II	III	Removed	Total
housing	Low	I	3	1	0	-1	5
value	Medium	II	1	8	1	0	10
category	High	III	0	0	3	0	3
	Added		0	0	3		
	Total		4	9	7		

(Clark, 1965) and as operational policy models (Berry, 1970) for monitoring and forecasting movements between sub-markets.

Recent extensions have examined the measurement of filtering in various terms: as standardized deviations from the average transaction prices of the stock (Maher, 1974) or through changes in household utility (Little, 1974a, 1974b), whether anyone moves or not. Little, for example, argues that households filter not units, and that utility can be improved either by staying put while increasing the flow of housing services through neighbourhood change or rehabilitation (passive filtering), or by moving to a location with a preferred housing bundle (active filtering). Clearly, each approach has merit and each contributes to understanding the complexities of housing market behaviour. But the question remains: why does filtering (however defined) occur more rapidly in one area than in another?

Chains of vacancies

A variant of the study of housing change is to examine the sequence of household moves generated by the addition of vacancies. Such vacancies may be introduced to the housing stock as new units or by the release of existing housing through the migration of households outside the market (Kristof, 1965; Lansing, Clifton and Morgan, 1969; Watson, 1974; White, 1971). The effect of a vacancy is wave-like. Those households moving into old units, from which the occupants of the newly vacated units originated, leave behind units available for a third group to occupy; they in turn for a fourth group; and so forth. This sequence, or chain, of moves can be used to measure the multiplier effects of new construction, possibly the effect on improving housing standards, and to monitor the impact of supply changes on the choice of residential locations available. The latter impact is clear and substantial.

Consider a hypothetical city. Of 100 housing units on the market at any one time in this city, 30 to 40 on average are likely to be newly constructed. Of the other 60 to 70 units on the market, drawn from the existing stock of older units, 25 to 30 may be available for resale or rental because their previous owners (renters) moved into new units. The remaining units represent opportunities generated by the exchange of older units and existing residents. In reality,

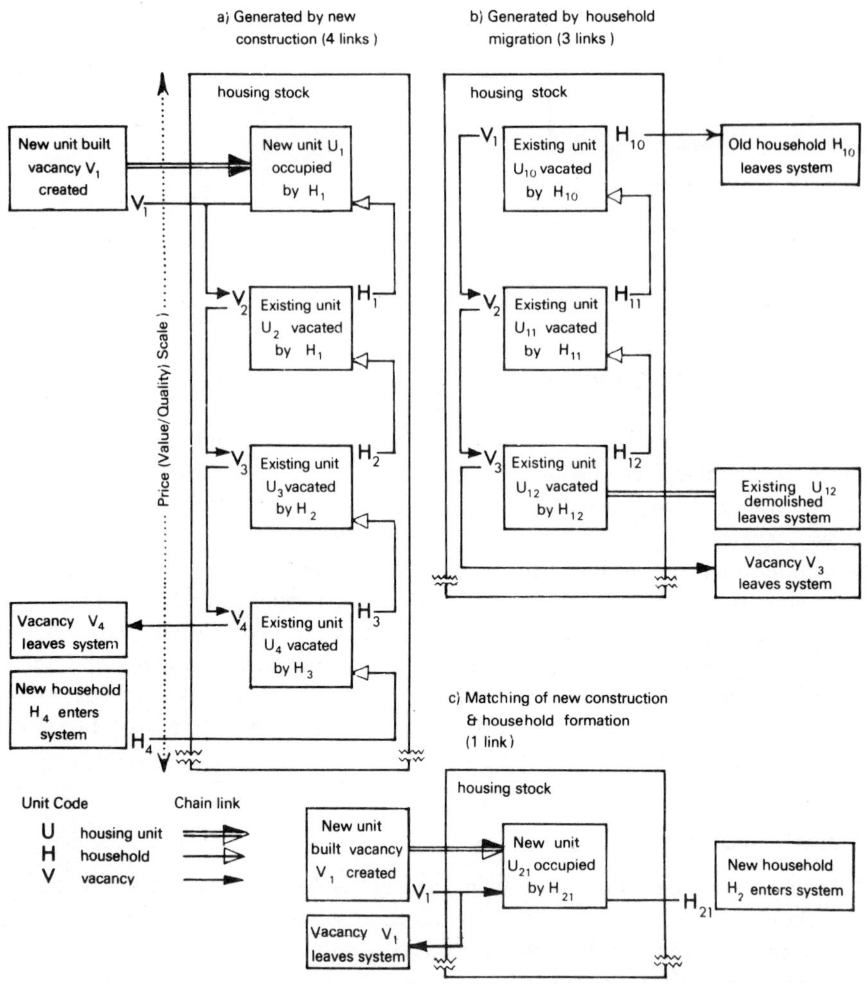

FIGURE 4.10 Intra-urban housing vacancy chain models: schematic examples

measuring the impact is more difficult. The United Kingdom Department of the Environment (1973), for example, established that of between 440 000 and 470 000 sales of existing houses in Britain during 1969, from 160 000 to 179 000 were directly connected through chains of sales with the sale of newly constructed units.

Three different examples of such links in the chain of supply are demonstrated in Figure 4.10. Flow diagrams are given for chains initiated by (a) new construction and (b) household out-migration, and one terminated (c) when a new unit is immediately occupied by a new household (an in-migrant or newly formed household). Note that these sequences follow the vacancy, not the household, through the housing stock. The number of links in such chains (i.e. the response of the market to a new supply) varies from one (Figure 4.10c) to many (Figure 4.10a), although four is about the longest common chain.

Most chains are considerably shorter. Again citing the United Kingdom Department of the Environment's (1973) study (Table 4.6), over 47 per cent. of all such chains had one link, 29 had two, while only 23 had three or more. On average, the number of movements generated by new construction in Toronto, for example, seems to be about two (Sharpe, 1974, Table 4.7), and is of course lower within the public sector, as Watson (1974) found in Glasgow. There is, however, a considerable loss rate in reconstructing the residential histories necessary to identify the links in the chains, which affects these figures. Many chains terminate abruptly when the older unit is removed from the market (demolition or conversion), or because the original unit is still occupied by a member or members of the former household (undoubling, separation, new family formation, etc.). As to income level and house value, there is little empirical evidence that the chains involve a consistent downward movement or 'trickling' down of vacancies through the price scale, as Figure 4.10 intentionally suggests, or that chain lengths or their multiplier effects (i.e. the spread of new housing opportunities) are greater for higher than for lower price units. Thus, new housing, as measured by the length of movement chains and their directions within the market, does not necessarily result in increased housing opportunities for society's disadvantaged. But that is one outcome, and a debatable one, of the process and is not the process itself.

Two questions then remain unsolved. One is the relationship between vacancy chains and filtering. If one uses the broadest definitions of filtering as given above (i.e. any change in relative housing position), then vacancy chains are, in effect, one measure of filtering. For more restrictive definitions of filtering (i.e. a change between sub-markets), vacancy chains are not directly relevant. The other question is whether the units linked by the chains are, in fact, interdependent or just accidental groupings. The answer to this question depends on the perspective taken and on the level of generalization employed. Such chains are independent accidental groupings from the perspective of most households, or in reference to the market behaviour of individual housing units. With a more macro-perspective, however, the chains do offer descriptive

TABLE 4.6 Chains of sales in the private housing market in Britain, 1969

Chain length	Number of chains involved (in 000s)	Percentage	Number of older homes involved (in 000s)
One link	85.9	47	—
Two links	53.6	29	53.6
Three links	19.5	11	39.0
Four or more links	22.7	12	72.4
Totals	181.7	100	165.0

Source. United Kingdom Department of the Environment (1973).

TABLE 4.7 Household movements generated directly by housing supply changes

City or cities	Author (date of survey)	Size of sample	Average length of housing chains in sequence	Reasons for termination of chain: Removed from stock (%)	Reasons for termination of chain: Still occupied by relatives, friends (%)
New York, N. Y.	Kristof (1965)	65⁻	2.4	*	*
New Haven, Connecticut	Pack (1970)	94	2.3†	19.7	48.3
Columbus, Ohio	Brueggeman (1972)	1 007	2.3†	*	*
Christchurch, New Zealand	Duffy (1972)	300	2.3†	7.1	12.3
London, England	United Kingdom Department of the Environment (1973)	363	1.5	n.c.	n.c.
Toronto, Ontario	Sharpe (1975)	263	1.5	15.0	27.1
Glasgow, Scotland	Watson (1974)	945	2.1 (owned)	8.0	43.0
			1.6 (local authority)	50.0	23.0
United States Standard Metropolitan Statistical Areas	Lansing, Clifton and Morgan (1969)	*	3.5	20.0	63.0

Note. Some considerable differences appear in the measurement of the above proportions.
*not compatible.
n.c. not completed.
†recalibrated as weighted mean chain length by Sharpe.
Source. Adapted from Sharpe (1975).

measures of the degree of interdependence in terms of aggregate housing markets, in the sense that the supply of housing opportunities are linked, and in the transference of those opportunities between sub-markets. As such, the chains become useful as social indicators (Marcuse, 1971; Smith, 1972) and as means of evaluating public policy (Solomon, 1972), if not as one approach to empirical research (Moore and Gale, 1973).

MARKET FAILURES

No discussion of urban housing markets can be concluded without reference to housing as a social problem and to the influence of public attitudes on housing supply. Clearly, there is no 'housing problem' as such. Instead, there are many; and they vary depending on who you talk to (Welfeld, 1972). Briefly, reference is made here to three problem areas: the quality and distribution of supply, market discrimination, and changing attitudes and social aspirations.

Shelter and equity

The most serious problems in urban housing relate to the quantity, type and price of shelter provided at different locations. Housing supply has always been a problem (Tarn, 1968), and, to a degree, that problem is intractable. Part of the difficulty is that few societies have defined what role housing should play in terms of social priorities and how it should be provided. Also, the difficulty is one of balancing a seemingly unlimited demand (rather than needs) for housing services with the supply provided by conventional methods of production for consumer durable goods. Donnison (1967a, p. 23) writes: 'It is technically feasible to produce about as much bread, bedding or ballpoint pens as a nation can use. But the best-housed countries have found no limit to the quantity or quality of housing they want.'

The supply problem takes several forms. Firstly, as noted, not enough housing of sufficient quality has been provided in any modern society to satisfy social demands. Secondly, and more serious, is the problem of distribution. Housing supply has been very unequally distributed, by location, tenure and income level. And, despite massive improvements in the quality of urban housing, particularly since the second World War, the allocation of new supply has been largely insensitive to certain obvious social needs. This applies both in capitalistic (Harvey, 1972) and in socialistic societies such as Poland (Ball and Harloe, 1974) and the Soviet Union (DiMaio, 1973). A map of housing prices (and vacancies) in any large city attests to the limited choice in residential location for lower-income groups. They live where they do because housing opportunities are so limited. The poorest (or at least some of them) are relegated to public sector housing—filed for future reference. They are generally packed into unattractive inner-city renewal projects or exported to the outer-suburban fringe, or even beyond. Within the public sector, mobility is severely restricted or non-existent. Public policies can inadvertently reduce housing opportunities for the poor even further by limiting production (Nourse, 1973), by increasing costs (Davis, Eastman and Chan-I Hua 1974) or by the inadequate delivery of housing services (Ahlbrandt, 1974), to name but a few. Research on residential change must be more cognisant of these policy inputs and and constraints.

A related problem stressed in the body of this paper is the impact of externalities on the supply of housing available at different price and quality levels within the city. Housing, as noted in the introduction, is a bundle of 'environmental' as well as structural attributes. Therefore, it delivers a flow of services to the neighbourhood as well as to the occupant. Housing improvements and additions to the stock will likely extend net positive benefits through increased equity to other units in the immediate area, largely at no cost to the owners of those units. Deterioration, on the other hand, spreads negative benefits or costs. The process involved has been variously described as a contagion effect, ghettoization or simply neighbourhood interdependence. Often these externalities are accentuated by restrictive zoning practices and by the collective behaviour of large landowners and developers—as Lorimer (1972) has argued in Toronto. While empirical measurement has proven difficult (Crecine, Davis and Jackson, 1967; Schall, 1971; Stull, 1974), they do have obvious effects on polarizing housing quality between areas which are appreciating and those which are depreciating, and between those households with the social power to influence environmental change and those without such power.

Finally, housing investments, or more particularly the ownership of the supply and the land on which it stands, also seem to have a strongly regressive effect on patterns of income distribution within society itself. The very rapid increase in housing and land prices in the early 1970s, post-dating most published statistics (Bruce-Briggs, 1973; Eversley, 1972; King, 1973; Neutze, 1973; Real Estate Research Corporation, 1973) as well as the empirical analyses cited above (Table 4.4), has among other effects also increased social polarization—between those groups in the housing market and those not in that market. The latter include those in public sector housing, renters in the private sector and the homeless. Also, property tax and mortgage interest deductions (common in Britain and the United States), are subsidies to the upper half of the income profile, subsidies which would appear, given recent inflation rates, to be almost limitless. One result is that existing home-owners generally consume more housing (and land) than the economic models might suggest, often more than they need, and at lower cost relative to income. The same applies between high and low income areas within the city (Walzer and Singer, 1974).

Discrimination: closed and biased markets

A glance at statistics on immigrant housing in most European cities, on black housing in American cities (Berry, 1973; Meyer, 1973) or on housing for the poor in any city (Downs, 1970) indicates that access to the market is not ubiquitous, even when income differences are taken into account. Discrimination, either enforced or self-selected, is widespread but equally difficult to document. In any case, one obvious consequence is the physical separation in most Western cities of ethnic, class and income groups into distinct clusters—separation operating primarily through controls on the distribution of housing choice.

American cities provide the most obvious (but not the only) example of the widespread extent of housing market discrimination. A flood of academic literature has sought to identify the extent of racial discrimination in housing (Kain and Quigley, 1972, 1974; Zedler, 1970) and to measure its effects on rents

(Rapkin, 1966), on prices (King and Mieszkowski, 1973; Lapham, 1971; Marcus, 1968) and on access to employment opportunities (Quigley, 1973). Recently, Kain (1973b) has argued, in reviewing American economic research on housing to date, that the major deficiency of existing theoretical models is their inability to account for the full impact of housing discrimination by race. Housing and housing supply have become vehicles for achieving individual or group goals other than those concerned with housing, often at the expense of the residential location desires of other groups in the city, including those of the next generation.

That discrimination exists is obvious; its consequences are not, though we might assume that most are negative. At best, the considerable evidence now available suggests that in United States cities, black households typically pay from 5 to 20 per cent. more than white for the same housing bundle (Kain and Quigley, 1972). Moreover, black Americans consume less housing measured in terms of neighbourhood attributes and housing quality than do whites at any given income level (Straszheim, 1974); they also are much less likely to be home-owners (Kain, 1973b) and therefore to receive capital gains, than would be the case without extensive discrimination. The housing situation for American blacks is no doubt improving, as Kristof (1972) and Berry (1973) note, and some researchers have argued that the combination of filtration and the abandonment of older units will eventually erase the bulk of deteriorated housing and the problem of black housing quality. It is, however, debatable (Harvey, 1972) whether the capitalistic system with private ownership of urban land as its foundation can produce satisfactory solutions, even in the longer term, to questions of the equitable distribution of supply.

Discrimination, of course, takes forms other than those evident in racial segregation. Such forms, whether by class (Robson, 1969), ownership (Pickvance, 1974) or more subtle social pressures (Spengler, 1967), or simply by the distortion of information on housing needs and opportunities, need to be studied at least as thoroughly as that of race. Planning policies, the practices of estate agents (Clawson, 1971), financial institutions (Gillies, 1965; Harvey and Chatterjee, 1974), and government housing and taxation policies in general (Nourse, 1973), have also been prime determinants in enforcing and reinforcing market segregation through social discrimination. As Kain (1969, 1973a) again noted, housing segregation leaves an overriding imprint on the pattern of urban development which, in turn, facilitates further social segregation. Each feeds on the other in the classic self-reinforcing pattern of public action and the private market.

Housing attitudes and aspirations

Despite these inherently complex problems, changes in social attitudes and in housing preferences and aspirations can produce dramatic changes in the supply side of the housing market. No long list of examples is necessary. It is not generally recognized, however, how persuasive attitude changes can be in altering supply as well as the distribution of housing needs and demands. The very few existing cross-national studies of housing attitudes (Canter and Thorne, 1972; Cullingworth, 1973; Donnison, 1967a; Rose, 1968; Solomon, 1972; Wendt, 1963) demonstrate the very wide differences among countries in the importance attached to housing, in the means of accommodating social needs in the supply of new housing and in setting priorities for public policy. Some authors have also warned of an emerging conflict in attitudes between the ecological-environmental quality movement and the desire for more housing. Babcock and Callies (1973) even suggest the need for a 'housing impact statement' to accompany each environmental impact statement on development proposals, particularly in urban areas, indicating the effect on housing supply.

Although this subject cannot be taken up in detail here, it is worth noting one example of possible responses to a shift in the composition of increments to the housing stock, increments which in turn provide the physical framework for extending social areas within the city. The example is the high-rise revolution in housing construction. Although by no means a recent phenomenon (see Woodbury, 1930), it has by its sheer scale resulted in a drastic redesign of urban residential structure, particularly in North America and Western Europe (Bourne, 1968; Murphy, 1973; Nahkies, 1974; Neutze, 1968). The consequences on land value gradients (Wright, 1971), the structure of urban neighbourhoods (Bourne and Murdie, 1972), life-styles (Wellman, 1974) and social pathologies (United Kingdom Ministry of Housing and Local Government, 1970), as well as their highly inflated speculative qualities (Barker, Penney and Seccombe, 1973)—not to mention the type of housing choice available—have been the subject of belated but growing research interest. The evidence is inconsistent on a pro-or-con basis as to the desirability of high-rise construction on any of the above grounds. Yet its predominance, at least in many cities of North America and Europe, is a valid subject for growing social concern (*The Economist*, 1971) and research (Schafer, 1974).

How have attitudes influenced such supply changes? In many European cities, the predisposition against high-rises was so strong (in government and among the public generally) as to preclude extensive high-rise construction (except for public sector housing). In most of North America, on the other hand, there has been almost a fatalistic acceptance that high-rises are here to stay in at least the same proportion as at present. Planners, politicians, financial institutions, builders, and even the media, all seem to have accepted this premise. The result is a self-fulfilling prophecy.

In other countries, the rapid increase in apartments and flats, particularly high-rise, has led to sharp conflicts between housing policies and long-standing social attitudes. In one case at least (Sweden), this conflict has produced a shift in the new construction pendulum back to lower-density and largely owner-occupied housing. Sociologist Bill Michelson is currently investigating the factors behind this policy shift, and the structural and political changes which facilitated its realization; he has entitled the study the 'dynamics of the inevitable'. Whatever reasons eventually emerge as critical, it is clear that the stock of housing and the flow of services from that stock are both socially as well as economically determined. They can and do respond to attitudinal changes, even in the short term. More studies are needed of what such attitudes are, how they change and how urban residential structure changes accordingly.

CONCLUDING REMARKS

Most economic models of residential location (following Alonso, Mills and Muth) assume that population and housing stock distributions (i.e. supply and demand) are one and the same. The output of these models provides, simultaneously, a market equilibrium pattern of location rents (which are, in effect, short-term housing prices at the margin) and an equilibrium distribution of households based on utility maximization between housing consumed and access to city-centred jobs. Even the trade-off between accessibility to work and living space is determined as if the latter were plastic, tastes were invariant and workplaces were either fixed at one location (city centre) or ubiquitous, instead of becoming concentrated at several nodes within the city. The resulting patterns (of housing, population) are, in fact, identical to those which would be obtained if an urban area was constructed again each year in a systematic form around the city centre.

No one, of course, now believes these results. The housing stock persists and ages. Once built, it constrains the pattern of housing opportunities, shapes the price geography of the city and sets the framework for the evolution of social areas for a long period of time. Although the same inventory can be used for many different types of service and function (shelter, social and economic) and permits a wide latitude of locational change for certain high income (and social) groups, it effectively channels residential mobility and change for all groups (Simmons, 1974). Increments to the stock provide one means of improving social mobility and one specific direction for extending and reordering the residential landscape. These increments, in turn, are shaped in large part by the standing stock of dwellings in the city. Further, the extreme heterogeneity of the stock itself and the extensive externalities which tie groups of housing units (and services) together, defy simple generalization. The relationships between housing construction, occupancy and patterns of residence change are too complex to submit to strictly economic explanations. And some authors (Harvey, 1972, 1974) have questioned even the economic premises of such models. No doubt, the market is myopic and inconsistent.

Recent trends in supply seem to inflict even further damage on both the econometric and ecological formulations regarding the spatial structure of housing markets. They undermine the implications (or inferences) drawn from factorial ecology studies that the spatial distribution of households (by choice or force) can be accounted for strictly on the basis of family status (life-cycle), income (class) and ethnicity (segregation). Housing is represented as a set of variables in these studies, but there is no sense of the dynamic interdependence between supply and demand. Numerous studies have documented the overriding importance of spatial restrictions on supply (through financing, zoning and planning permissions), of changing housing preferences, of the availability of sufficient parcels of land (in public or private hands) and of increasing local community resistance to change.

ACKNOWLEDGEMENTS

The author acknowledges the valuable comments on an earlier draft of this paper by John Bossons, Ron Johnston, Bill Michelson, Chris Sharpe and Jim Simmons. These individuals, of course, bear no responsibility for any errors or omissions. The cartography was done in the Departments of Geography at the University of Toronto and the University College of Swansea. Bev Thompson typed an excellent final copy.

REFERENCES

(This listing is a full bibliography and thus includes details not referred to in the text)

Adams, J. S. (1970). 'Residential structure of Midwestern cities'. *Annals, Association of American Geographers*, **60**, 37–62.

Adams, J. S. (1973). *New Homes, Vacancy Chains, and Housing Submarkets in the Twin City Area*, Center for Urban and Regional Affairs, University of Minnesota, Minneapolis.

Ahlbrandt, R. J., Jr. (1974). 'Delivery systems for federally-assisted housing services: constraints, locational decisions and policy implications'. *Land Economics*, **50** (3), 242–250.

Alonso, W. (1963). *Location and Land Use*, Harvard University Press, Cambridge, Massachusetts.

Apgar, W. C., Jr., and Kain, J. F. (1972). 'Neighbourhood attributes and the residential price geography of urban areas'. Paper presented to Annual Meetings of the Econometric Society, Toronto, 28–30 December 1972.

Apps, P. F. (1974). 'An approach to urban modelling and evaluation: a residential model: 3. Demand equations for housing services'. *Environment and Planning*, **6**, 11–32.

Arrow, K. J. (1973). 'The effects of the price system and market on urban economic development'. In *Urban Process*, National Academy of Sciences Symposium, The Urban Institute, Washington, pp. 11–20.

Audian, M. (1972). 'Transforming housing into a social service'. *Plan*, **13** (2), 91–111.

Azcarate, J. (1970). 'A model of a local housing market: SMALA'. In *Urban Housing*, Seminar Proceedings, Planning and Transport Research Ltd., London.

Babcock, R. F., and Callies, D. L. (1973). 'Ecology and housing: virtues in conflict'. In M. Clawson (Ed.), *Modernizing Urban Land Policy*, Johns Hopkins, Baltimore, pp. 205–220.

Ball, M. J. (1973). 'Recent empirical work on the determination of relative house prices'. *Urban Studies*, **10**, 213–223.

Ball, M. J., and Harloe, M. (1974). *Housing Policy in a Socialist Country: The Case of Poland*, Research Paper No. 8, Centre for Environmental Studies, London.

Barker, G., Penney, J., and Seccombe, W. (1973). *High-rise and Superprofits*, Dumont Press, Kitchener, Ontario.

Batty, M. (1973). 'A probability model of the housing market based on quasi-classical considerations'. *Socio-economic Planning Sciences*, **7**, 573–598.

Beckmann, M. J. (1974). 'Spatial equilibrium and the housing market'. *Journal of Urban Economics*, **1**, 99–107.

Berry, B. J. L. (1970). 'Monitoring trends, forecasting change and evaluating goal achievement in the urban environment: the ghetto expansion versus desegregation issue in Chicago as a case study'. In M. Chisholm, A. E. Frey and P. Haggett (Eds.), *Regional Forecasting*, Butterworths, London, pp. 93–115.

Berry, B. J. L. (1973). 'What really happens when tenants leave'. *American Institute of Architects Journal*, December **1973**, 34–38.

Berry, B. J. L., and Bednarz, R. S. (1974). *The disbenefits of neighbourhood and environment to urban property*. Paper presented to the Fiftieth Anniversary Conference, Department of Geography, University of Michigan, Ann Arbor.

Birch, D. (1971). 'Toward a stage theory of urban growth'. *Journal, American Institute of Planners*, **37**, 78–87.

Birch, D., and coauthors (1974). *Patterns of Urban Change: The New Haven Experience*, D. C. Heath, Lexington, Massachusetts.

Bourne, L. S. (1968). 'Market, location and site selection in apartment construction'. *Canadian Geographer*, **12**, 211–226.

Bourne, L. S. (1969). 'Location factors in the redevelopment process: a model of residential change'. *Land Economics*, **45**, 183–193.

Bourne, L. S. (1971). 'Physical adjustment processes and land use succession: Toronto'. *Ekistics*, **32**, 77–83.

Bourne, L. S., and Berridge, J. D. (1973). 'Apartment location and developer behaviour: a reappraisal'. *Canadian Geographer*, **17**, 403–411.

Bourne, L. S., and Murdie, R. A. (1972). 'Interrelationships of social and physical space in the city'. *Canadian Geographer*, **16**, 211–229.

Bruce-Briggs, B. (1973). 'The cost of housing'. *The Public Interest*, **32**, 34–42.

Brueggeman, W. B., *et. al* (1972). 'Research Report: Multiple Housing Programs and Urban Housing Policy'. *Journal, American Institute of Planners*, **38**, 160–167.

Canter, D., and Thorne, R. (1972). 'Attitudes to housing: a cross-cultural comparison'. *Environment and Behavior*, **4**, 21–36.

Carey, G. W. (1969). 'The regional interpretation of Manhattan population and housing patterns through factor analysis'. *The Geographical Review*, **59**, 551–569.

Cave, P. (1969). 'Occupancy duration and the analysis of residential change'. *Urban Studies*, **6**, 58–69.

Chamberlain, S. (1972). *Aspects of developer behaviour in the land development process*, Research Paper no. 56, Centre for Urban and Community Studies, University of Toronto, Toronto.

Chapin, F. S., Jr., and Weiss, S. F. (1965). *Some Input Refinements for a Residential Model*, Center for Urban and Regional Studies, University of North Carolina, Chapel Hill, North Carolina.

Clark, W. A. V. (1965). 'Markov chain analysis in geography: an application to the movement of rental housing areas'. *Annals, Association of American Geographers*, **55**, 351–359.

Clawson, M. (1968). 'Urban renewal in 2000'. *Journal, American Institute of Planners*, **34**, 173–179.

Clawson, M. (1971). *Suburban Land Conversion in the United States: An Economic and Governmental Process*, Johns Hopkins, Baltimore.

Clawson, M., and Hall, P. (1973). *Planning and Urban Growth: An Anglo-American Perspective*, Resources for the Future, Baltimore.

Colean, Miles (1950). *American Housing: Problems and Prospects*, Social Science Research Council, New York.

Commonwealth Department of Housing, Australia (1968). *Flats: A Survey of Multi-unit Construction in Australia*, G.P.O., Canberra.

Crecine, J. P., Davis, O. A., and Jackson, J. E. (1967). 'Urban property markets: some empirical results and their implications for municipal zoning'. *Journal of Law and Economics*, **10**, 79–99.

Cripps, E. L., and Cater, E. A. (1972). 'The empirical development of a disaggregated residential location model: some preliminary results'. In A. G. Wilson (Ed.), *Patterns and Processes in Urban and Regional Systems*, London Papers in Regional Science no. 3, Pion, London, pp. 114–145.

Cullingworth, J. B. (1965). *English Housing Trends*, Occasional Papers on Social Administration No. 13, G. Bell, London.

Cullingworth, J. B. (1969). *Housing and Labour Mobility*, O.E.C.D., Paris.

Cullingworth, J. B. (1973). 'Housing'. In *Problems of an Urban Society*, Allen and Unwin, London, Vol. 2.

Daly, M. T. (1972). '*The Residential Land Market: Newcastle, N.S.W.*, Research Paper No. 13. Department of Geography, University of Sydney, Sydney.

Davis, J. T. (1971). 'Sources of variation in housing values in Washington, D.C.' *Geographical Analysis*, **3**, 63–76.

Davis, O. A., Eastman, C. M., and Chan. I Hua (1974). 'The shrinkage in the stock of low-quality housing in the central city'. *Urban Studies*, **11**, 13–26.

Dear, M. J. (1970). 'A model for predicting the growth of London's housing stock'. In *Urban Housing*, Seminar Proceedings, Planning and Transport Research Ltd., London, pp. 21–24.

De Leeuw, F. (1971). 'The demand for housing: a review of cross-sectional evidence'. *Review of Economics and Statistics*, **35**, 1–11.

De Leeuw, F. (1972). *The Distribution of Housing Services*, Urban Institute Paper, Washington.

DiMaio, A. J. Jr. (1974). *Soviet Urban Housing: Problems and Policies*, Praeger, New York.

Doling, J. F. (1973). 'A two-stage model of tenure choice in the housing market'. *Urban Studies*, **10**, 199–211.

Donnison, D. V. (1967a). *The Government of Housing*, Penguin Books, Baltimore.

Donnison, D. V. (1967b). 'Research and policy in housing: current developments in Britain'. *Journal, American Institute of Planners*, **33**, 123–126.

Downs, A. (1970). 'Housing the urban poor'. In *Urban Problem and Prospects*, Markham, Chicago. pp. 165–175.

Drewett, R. (1970). 'Land values and urban growth'. In M. Chisholm, A. E. Frey and P. Haggett (Eds.), *Regional Forecasting*, Butterworths, London. pp. 335–357.

Duffy, D. J. (1972). *The nature and characteristics of the intra-urban migration process in Christchurch*. M. A. Thesis, University of Canterbury, Christchurch.

Echenique, M., Crowther, D., and Lindsay, W. (1969). 'A spatial model of urban stock and activities'. *Regional Studies*, **3**, 281–312.

Echenique, M., Feo, A., Herrera, R., and Riquezas, J. (1974). 'A disaggregated model of urban spatial structure: theoretical framework'. *Environment and Planning*, **6**, 33–64.

Engle, R. F., Fisher, F. M., Harris, J. R., and Rothenberg, J. (1972). 'An econometric stimulation model of intra-metropolitan housing location'. *American Economic Review*, **62**, 87–97.

Evans, A. W., (1973). *The Economics of Residential Location*, Macmillan, London.

Eversley, D.E.C. (1972). 'Rising costs and static incomes'. *Urban Studies*, **9**, 347–368.

Fisher, E. M., and Winnick, L. (1951). 'A reformulation of the filtering concept'. *Journal of Social Issues*, **12**, 47–58.

Frieden, B. J. (1961). 'Locational preferences in the urban housing market. *Journal, American Institute of Planners*, **27**, 316–324.

Freiden, B. J. (1964). *The Future of Old Neighbourhoods*, The M.I.T. Press, Cambridge, Massachusetts.

Gayler, H. J. (1971). 'Private residential redevelopment in the inner city'. *Journal of the Town Planning Institute*, **57**, 15–20.

Gillies, J. (1965). 'The structure of local mortgage markets'. *Journal of Finance*, **10**, 363–375.

Goldstein, G. S. (1973). 'Household behaviour in the housing market: the decision to move and the decision to buy or rent housing'. In E. G. Moore. (Ed.), *Models of Residential Location and Relocation in the City*, Northwestern University, Evanston, Illinois. pp. 101–118.

Gonen, A. (1972). 'The role of high growth rates and of public housing agencies in shaping the spatial structure of Israeli towns'. *Tijdschrift voor Economische en Sociale Geografie*, **63**, 402–410.

Grebler, L. (1951). 'The housing inventory: analytical concept and quantitative change'. *American Economic Review*, **45**, 555–568.

Grebler, L., and Maisel, S. J. (1963). 'Determinants of residential construction. A review of present knowledge'. In D. B. Suits and coauthors, *Impacts of Monetary Policy*, Prentice-Hall, Englewood Cliffs, New Jersey, pp. 475–620.

Grether, D. M., and Mieszkowski, P. (1974). 'Determinants of real estate values'. *Journal of Urban Economics*, **1**, 127–146.

Grigsby, W. G. (1963). *Housing Markets and Public Policy*, University of Pennsylvania Press, Philadephia.

Guest, Avery M. (1974). 'Neighbourhood life cycles and social status'. *Economic Geography*, **50**, 228–243.

Hartshorn, T. A. (1971). 'Inner city residential structure and decline'. *Annals, Association of American Geographers*, **61** (1), 72–96.

Harvey, D. (1972). *Society, the City and the Space Economy of Urbanism*, Resource Paper No. 18, Commission on College Geography, Association of American Geographers, Washington.

Harvey, D. (1974). *Class-Monopoly rent, finance capital and the urban revolution*, Papers on Planning and Design No. 4, Faculty of Architecture, University of Toronoto, Toronto; also in *Regional Studies*, **8** (1974), 239–255.

Harvey, D., and Chatterjee, L. (1974). 'Absolute rent and the structuring of space by governmental and financial institutions'. *Antipode*, **6** (1), 22–36.

Haynes, K. E., and Pinsky, B. (1971). 'The distribution of multi-occupancy residential housing in the Montreal area'. *Revue de Geografiede Montreal*, **25**, 173–178.

Herbert, D., and Stevens, B. (1960). 'A model for the distribution of residential activity in urban areas'. *Journal of Regional Science*, **2**, 21–36.

Holm, Per. (1967). 'A disaggregated housing market model'. In A. A. Nevitt (Ed.), *The Economic Problems of Housing*, Macmillan, London.

Isard, W. (1942). 'A neglected cycle: the transport-building cycle'. *Review of Economics and Statistics*, **24**, 149–158.

Isler, M. (1970). *Thinking About Housing*, Urban Institute, Washington.

Johnson, J. H., Salt, J., and Wood, P. A. (1974). *Housing and the Migration of Labour in England and Wales*, Saxon House, Farnborough, Hampshire.

Johnston, R. J. (1971). *Urban Residential Patterns*, Praeger, New York.

Kain, J. F. (1969). 'Effects of housing market segregation on urban development'. In *Savings and Residential Financing*, United States Savings and Loan League, Chicago, Illinois, pp. 89–108.

Kain, J. F. (1973a). *Housing segregation, Negro-employment and metropolitan decentralization: a retrospective view*, Discussion Paper No. 81, Program on Regional and Urban Economics, Harvard University, Cambridge, Massachusetts.

Kain, J. F. (1973b). *What should America's Housing Program Be?*, Discussion Paper No. 82. Program on Regional and Urban Economics, Harvard University, Cambridge, Massachusetts.

Kain, J. F., and Quigley, J. M. (1970a). 'Measuring the value of housing quality'. *Journal of the American Statistical Association*, **65**, 512–519.

Kain, J. F., and Quigley, J. M. (1970b). 'Measuring the quality of the residential environment'. *Environment and Planning*, **2**, 23–32.

Kain, J. F., and Quigley, J. M. (1972). 'Housing market discrimination, homeownership, and savings behavior'. *The American Economic Review*, **62**, 263–277.

Kain, J. F., and Quigley, J. M. (1974). *Housing Markets and Racial Discrimination: A Micro-economic Analysis*, National Bureau of Economic Research, New York and London.

Kaiser, E. J. (1972). 'Decision agent models: an alternative modeling approach for urban residential growth'. In D. C. Sweet (Ed.), *Models of Urban Structure*, D. C. Heath, Lexington, Massachusetts, pp. 109–122.

Kaiser, E. J., and Weiss, S. F. (1970). 'Public policy and the residential development process'. *Journal, American Institute of Planners*, **36**, 30–37.

Karn, V. A. (1973). *Housing Standards and Costs*, Occasional Paper No. 25, Centre for Urban and Regional Studies, Birmingham.

King, A. T. (1973). *Property Taxes, Amenities and Residential Land Values*, Ballinger, Cambridge, Massachusetts.

King, A. T., and Mieszkowski, P. (1973). 'Racial discrimination, segregation and the price of housing.' *Journal of Political Economy*, **81**, 590–607.

Kirwan, R., and Martin, D. (1970). *The Economic Basis for Models of the Housing Market*, Working Paper No. 62, Centre for Environmental Studies, London.

Klaassen, L. K. (1966). 'Some theoretical considerations for the structure of the housing market'. In *Essays in Urban Land Economics*, Real Estate Research Program, University of California, Los Angeles, pp. 69–75.

Kristof, F. (1965). 'Housing policy goals and the turnover of housing'. *Journal, American Institute of Planners*, **31**, 232–245.

Kristof, F. (1972). 'Federal housing policies: subsidized production, filtration and objectives, Part I'. *Land Economics*, **48**, 309–320.

Lansing, J. B. Clifton, C. V., and Morgan, J. N. (1969). *New Homes and Poor People: A Study of Chains of Moves*, Institute for Social Research, University of Michigan, Ann Arbor.

Lapham, V. (1971). 'Do blacks pay more for housing?' *Journal of Political Economy*, **79**, 1244–1257.

Lee, R. (1972). *A Multivariate Analysis of Interurban Housing Stock Variations in Ontario and Quebec*, Report No. 7, Centre for Urban and Community Studies, University of Toronto, Toronto.

Lewis, J. P. (1965). *Building Cycles and Britain's Growth*, Macmillan, London.

Listokin, D. (1973). *The Dynamics of Housing Rehabilitation: Macro and Micro Analyses*, Rutgers University, New Brunswick, New Jersey (mimeo).

Lithwick, N. W. (1970). *Urban Canada: Problems and Prospects*, Research Monograph No. 1, Canadian Mortgage and Housing Corporation, Ottawa.

Little, J. T. (1974a). *Household Preferences, Relocation and Welfare: An Evaluation of the Filtering Concept*, Working Paper HMS2, Institute for Urban and Regional Studies, Washington University, St. Louis.

Little, J. T. (1974b). *Residential Preferences, Neighborhood Filtering and Neighborhood Change*, Working Paper HMS3. Institute for Urban and Regional Studies, Washington University, St. Louis.

Lorimer, J. (1972). *A Citizens Guide to City Politics*, James, Lewis and Samuel, Toronto.

Lowry, I. (1960). 'Filtering and housing standards: a conceptual analysis'. *Land Economics*, **36**, 362–370.

Lowry, I. S. de Salvo, J. S., and Woodfill, B., (1971). *Rental Housing in New York City: Volume 2 The Demand for Shelter*, The Rand Corporation New York.

Mabry, J. H. (1968). 'Public housing as an ecological influence in three English cities'. *Land Economics*, **44**, 393–398.

Maher, C. A. (1974). 'Spatial patterns in urban housing markets: filtering in Toronto, 1953–71'. *Canadian Geographer*, **18**, 108–124.

Maisel, S. J. (1963). 'A theory of fluctuation in residential construction starts'. *American Economic Review*, **53**, 359–383.

Marcus, M. (1968). 'Racial composition and home price changes'. *Journal, American Institute of Planners*, **34**, 334–340.

Marcuse, P. (1971). 'Social indicators and housing policy'. *Urban Affairs Quarterly*, **7**, 193–218.

Marriott, O. (1967). *The Property Boom*, Pan Piper, London.

Menchik, M. D. (1973). 'Income and residential location in Alonso's model of urban form'. In E. G. Moore (Ed.), *Models of Residential Location and Relocation in the City*, Northwestern University, Evanston, Illinois. pp. 1–48.

Meyer, D. R. (1973). 'Inter-urban differences in black housing quality'. *Annals, Association of American Geographers*, **63**, 347–352.

Meyerson, M. (1962). *Housing, People and Cities*, McGraw-Hill, New York.

Michelson, W. (1972). *Environmental Choice: The Social Bases of Family Decisions on Housing Type and Location*, Discussion Paper B-72–9. Ministry of State for Urban Affairs, Ottawa.

Mills, E. S. (1967). 'An aggregate model of resource allocation in a metropolitan area'. *American Economic Review*, **57**, 197–211.

Mills, E. S. (1972). 'Markets and efficient resource allocation in urban areas'. *Swedish Journal of Economics*, **74**, 110–113.

Mittelbach, F. G., Saxer, A., and Klaassen, L. (1967). 'Interregional differences in housing market activity'. *Annals of Regional Science*, **1**, 114–126.

Moore, E. G., and Gale, S. (1973). *Some Comments on Models of Neighborhood Change*, Renewal Paper No. 1, Studies in Intra-metropolitan Planning Problems, Department of Geography, Nouthwestern University, Evanstan, Illionis.

Murphy, P. E. (1973). 'Apartment location: the balance between developer and community'. In C. N. Forward (Ed.), *Residential and Neighbourhood Studies*, Western Geographical Series No. 5, University of Victoria, Victoria, pp. 149–177.

Muth, R. F. (1961). 'The spatial structure of the housing market'. *Papers and Proceedings of the Regional Science Association*, **7**, 207–220.

Muth, R. F. (1968). 'Urban residential land and housing markets'. In H. S. Perloff and L. Wingo (Eds.), *Issues in Urban Economics*, John Hopkins, Baltimore.

Muth, R. F. (1969). *Cities and Housing*, University of Chicago Press, Chicago.

Muth, R. F. (1974). 'Moving costs and housing expenditures'. *Journal of Urban Economics*, **1**, 108–125.

Nahkies, G. E. (1974). 'Multi-unit residential development in Christchurch'. *New Zealand Geographer*, **30**, 151–165.

Needleman, L. (1965). *The Economics of Housing*, The Staples Press, London.

Neutze, M. (1968). *The Suburban Apartment Boom*, Resources for the Future, Baltimore.

Neutze, M. (1971). *People and Property in Randwick*, Urban Research Unit, Australian National University, Canberra.

Neutze, M. (1973). *The Price of Land and Land Use Planning. Policy Instruments in the Urban Land Market*, O.E.C.D., Environmental Directorate, Paris.

Nevitt, A. A. (1967). *The Economic Problems of Housing*, Macmillan, London.

Nourse, H. O. (1973). *The Effect of Public Policy on Housing Markets*, Lexington Books, Lexington, Massachusetts.

Olson, E. (1969). 'A competitive theory of the housing market'. *American Economic Review*, **59**, 612–622.

Peck, J. (1970). *Movers' Survey: Some Dimensions of the Housing Market of the City of New Haven*, City Planning Department, New Haven.

Page, A. N., and Seyfried, W. R. (Eds.) (1970). *Urban Analysis: Readings in Housing and Urban Development*, Scott Foresman, Glenview, Illinois.

Pahl, R. E., and Craven, E. (1970). 'Residential expansion: the role of the private developer in the south east'. In R. E. Pahl (Ed.), *Whose City?*, Longmans, London.

Pickvance, C. G. (1974). 'Life cycle, housing tenure and residential mobility: a path analytic approach'. *Urban Studies*, **11**, 171–188.

Pynoos, J., Schafer, R, and Hartman, C. W. (Eds.) (1973). *Housing Urban America*, Aldine Publishing, Chicago.

Quigley, J. M. (1973). *The Influences of Workplaces and Housing Stocks Upon Residential*

Choice: A Crude Test of the Gross Price Hypothesis, Discussion Paper No. 80, Program on Regional and Urban Economics, Harvard University, Cambridge, Massachusetts.

Quigley, J. M. (1974). *Towards a Synthesis of Theories of Residential Site Choice*, Working Paper W4–22. Social and Policy Studies, Yale University, New Haven, Connecticut.

Rapkin, C. (1966). 'Price discrimination against Negroes in the rental housing market'. In *Essays in Urban Land Economics*, Real Estate Research Program, University of California, Los Angeles, pp. 333–345.

Real Estate Research Corporation (1973). *Environmental and Economic Effects of Alternative Development Patterns. A Bibliography*, The Corporation, Chicago.

Rees, P. H. (1972). 'The distribution of social groups within cities: models and accounts'. In A. G. Wilson (Ed.), *Patterns and Processes in Urban and Regional Systems*, London Papers in Regional Science No. 3, Pion, London, pp. 165–216.

Rex, J. A., and Moore, R. (1967). *Race, Community and Conflict*, Oxford University Press, Oxford.

Richardson, H. W., Vipond, J., and Furbey, R. A. (1974). 'Determinations of urban house prices'. *Urban Studies*, **11**, 189–199.

Robson, B. T. (1969). *Urban Analysis*, Cambridge University Press, Cambridge.

Rose, H. (1968). *The Housing Problem*, Heinemann, London.

Schafer, R. (1974). *The Suburbanization of Multi-family Housing*, D. C. Heath, Lexington, Massachusetts.

Schall, L. O. (1971). 'A note on externalities and property values'. *Journal of Regional Science*, **11**, 101–105.

Senior, M. L. (1973). 'Approaches to residential location modelling. 1: Urban ecological and spatial interaction models'. *Environment and Planning*, **5**, 165–197.

Sharpe, C. A. (1975). *Vacancy Chains and Residential Change*. Unpublished doctoral dissertation, Department of Geography, University of Toronto.

Silzer, V. J. (1972). *Housing Problems, Government Housing Policies and Housing Market Responses: An Annoted Bibliography*, Exchange Bibliography 344, Council of Planning Librarians, Monticello, Illinois.

Simmons, J. W. (1974). *Patterns of Residential Movement in Metropolitan Toronto*, Research Publication No. 13, Department of Geography, University of Toronto Press, Toronto.

Smith, L. B. (1969). 'A bi-sectoral housing market model'. *Canadian Journal of Economics*, **2**, 557–569.

Smith, L. B. (1970). *Housing in Canada. Market Structure and Policy Performance*, Research Monograph No. 2, C.M.H.C., Ottawa.

Smith, W. F. (1963). *Filtering and Neighborhood Change*, Research Report No. 24, Center for Real Estate and Urban Economics, University of California, Berkeley.

Smith, W. F. (1964). *The Low Rise Speculative Apartment*, Research Report No. 25, Center for Real Estate and Urban Economics, University of California, Berkeley.

Smith, W. F. (1970). *Housing: The Social and Economic Elements*, University of California Press, Berkeley.

Smith, W. F. (1972). 'The housing replacement rate as a social indicator'. *Plan*, **13**, 118–135.

Solomon, A. (1972). 'Housing and public policy analysis'. *Public Policy*, **9**, 443–473.

Spengler, J. J. (1967). 'Population pressure, housing and habitat'. *Law and Contemporary Problems*, **32**, 191–208.

Sternlieb, G. (1969). 'New York's housing: a study in immobilism'. *The Public Interest*, **16**, 123–138.

Sternlieb, G., and Burchell, R. W. (1973). *Residential Abandonment*, Center for Urban Policy Research, Rutgers University, New Brunswick, New Jersey.

Sternlieb, G. Burchell, R. W., Hughes, J. W., and James, F. J. (1974). 'Housing abandonment in the urban core'. *Journal, American Institute of Planners*, **40**, 321–332.

Stone, P. A. (1970). *Urban Development in Britain. Vol. 1, Population Trends and Housing*, Cambridge University Press, Cambridge.

Straszheim, M. (1972). *An Econometric Analysis of the Urban Housing Market*, National Bureau of Economic Research, Washington.

Straszheim, M. (1973). 'Modelling of urban housing markets and metropolitan change: an econometric approach'. In E. G. Moore (Ed.), *Models of Residential Location and Relocation in the City*, Northwestern University, Evanston, Illinois, pp. 49–99.

Straszheim, M. (1974). 'Housing market discrimination and black housing consumption'. *Quarterly Journal of Economics*, **88**, 19–43.

Stull, W. J. (1974). 'Land use and zoning in an urban economy'. *American Economic Review*, **64** (3), 337–347.

Tarn, J. N. (1968). 'The housing problem a century ago'. *Urban Studies*, **5**, 290–300.

The Economist (1971). 'Is high-rise the answer?'. 13 November 1971.

United Kingdom Department of the Environment (1973). *Chains of Sales in Private Housing*, Building Statistical Services, London.

United Kingdom Ministry of Housing and Local Government (1970). *Families Living at High Densities*, H.M.S.O., London.

United Nations, Centre for Housing, Building and Planning (1974). 'Housing Finance Sources and Methods in Eastern and Western Europe'. *Human Settlements*, **4** (2), 26–46.

United States Department of Housing and Urban Development (1973). *Housing in the Seventies*, United States G. P. O., Washington.

Walzer, N., and Singer, D. (1974). 'Housing expenditure in urban low-income areas'. *Land Economics*, **50**, 224–231.

Ward, D. (1964). 'A comparative historical geography of streetcar suburbs in Boston Massachusetts, and Leeds England, 1850–1920'. *Annals, Association of American Geographers*, **54**, 477–489.

Watson, C. J. (1974). 'Vacancy chains, filtering and the public sector'. *Journal, American Institute of Planners*, **40**, 346–352.

Weathersby, G. B. (1970). *Formal Models of Filtering in the Housing Stock*, Paper presented to the Annual Meetings of the Operations Research Society of America (mimeo).

Weiss, S. F., Smith, J. E., Kaiser, E. J., and Kenney, K. B. (1966). *Residential Developer Decisions*, Center for Urban and Regional Studies, University of North Carolina, Chapel Hill, North Carolina.

Welfeld, I. (1972). 'That "housing problem": the American versus the European experience'. *The Public Interest*, **27**, 78–95.

Wellman, B. (1974). *High Rise versus Low Rise: The Effects of High-Density Living*. Unpublished report, Centre for Urban and Community Studies, University of Toronto, Toronto.

Wendt, P. F. (1963). *Housing Policy: The Search for Solutions*, University of California Press, Berkeley.

Wheaton, W. L. C. (1964). 'Public and private agents of change in urban expansion'. In M. M. Webber and coworkers (Eds.), *Explorations into Urban Structure*, University of Pennsylvania Press, Philadelphia, pp. 154–196.

Wheaton, W. L. C. Milgram, G., and Meyerson, M. E. (Eds.) (1966). *Urban Housing*, The Free Press, New York.

White, H. C. (1971). 'Multipliers, vacancy chains and filtering in housing'. *Journal, American Institute of Planners*, **37**, 88–94.

Whitehand, J. W. R. (1972). 'Building cycles and the spatial pattern of urban growth'. *Transactions, Institute of British Geographers*, **56**, 39–55.

Wilkinson, R. K., and Archer, C. A. (1973). 'Measuring the determinants of relative house prices'. *Environment and Planning*, **5**, 357–367.

Wolfe, H. B. (1969). 'Models for the condition ageing of residential structures'. *Journal, American Institute of Planners*, **33**, 192–196.

Woodbury, C. (1930). 'The trend of multi-family housing in cities in the U.S.'. *Journal of Land and Public Utility Economics*, **6**, 225–234.

Wright, C. (1971). 'Residential location in a three-dimensional city'. *Journal of Political Economy*, **79**, 1378–1387.

Wyatt, G. L., and Winger, A. R. (1971). 'Residential construction, mover origin and urban form'. *Regional Studies*, **5**, 95–99.

Zedler, R. (1970). 'Racial segregation in urban housing markets'. *Journal of Regional Science*, **10**, 93–106.

Zeitlin, M. (1972). *Guide to the Literature of Cities: Part IV. Urban Housing*, Exchange Bibliography No. 308. Council of Planning Librarians, Monticello, Illinois.

Chapter 5

Household Location and Intra-urban Migration

John S. Adams and Kathleen A. Gilder

The housing construction process and the family life-cycle create and continuously transform the physical and social fabric of Western cities. A housing inventory is laid down in orderly annual tree-like rings around the old urban core. Individual housing units pass through stages of construction, ageing, obsolescence, abandonment and, finally, demolition. Thus, in most cities the oldest, most decrepit houses lie near the core, while newer houses are found on the outer margins of the built-up area.

The family life-cycle starts with household formation, followed by reproduction, ageing and eventually death. Households try to match up their housing needs during their lifetimes with the available stock of housing units. When needs expand to the point where they can no longer be met by the unit occupied because of changes in either the household or the house, the household attempts to move to another unit (Morgan, 1973). When housing needs decline, the household either moves to a smaller unit or remains in the house, maintaining or increasing the portion of income devoted to housing. For elderly households, the sharp reduction in many non-housing expenses permits the relative increase in housing outlays.

Intra-urban migration patterns tie together the housing process and the family life-cycle, raising a central geographical question: can the migration behaviour of households that move be predicted from information about their origins? In answering the question, this chapter discusses urban residential structure, the behaviour of migrants within this structure and the characteristics of migrating households as they decide to move and seek a new address. It concludes by describing how the housing market influences migration decisions and urban residential structure.

This chapter emphasizes the *high* mobility rates of American urban households, within an essentially *private* housing market, stimulated by steady progression of stages in the *family life-cycle*. Outside the United States and Canada a different picture emerges. In the United Kingdom, in most countries of Western Europe, in all Eastern European countries and in urban centres throughout the Third World, the rates of public ownership and operation of housing far exceed those commonly found in North America. Public sector intervention in urban housing markets means that a high proportion of households move to or between public housing estates, while other movers are affected indirectly by activity in the public sector when the occupation of a new housing estate releases private housing for other households.

Studies of residential mobility usually emphasize the reasons why households desire to move and the choices that are made among alternative destinations. Seldom is attention paid to the constraints that prevent a move or the limits on the range of housing choices. There are large numbers of households, especially in lower-income groups, who have all the motives and desires to move but lack the ability to do so at the relevant time. Moves may be delayed for varying lengths of time; then compromises are made when households confront the financial constraints on their range of choice. In a study of residential mobility in the South Wales city of Swansea, for example, the relatively immobile share of the population in low income areas, including local authority housing estates, was much larger than might be expected from North American studies (Herbert, 1973a, 1973b). Many more households were stayers than movers, suggesting that large sections of British cities probably possess stable and essentially local populations. Even neighbourhoods of 'mobile professionals' showed a strong locally based element of comparatively high stability.

As with other features of British cities, the public sector wields great influence in housing. Public housing activity triggers the residential mobility of many low income households. For many others, it offers the only genuine prospect of a change of residence. Life-cycle factors operate, but only over a protracted time scale, with direction and timing of moves conditioned by the availability of public housing units.

URBAN RESIDENTIAL STRUCTURE AND INTRA-URBAN MIGRATION

The relations between urban residential structure and intra-urban migration are only incompletely understood. Migration itself remodels urban structure, but the structure exerts some control over the intra-urban migration process. For example, the roads, rails and rivers that radiate outward from the downtown centre divide a typical American city into a series of pie-shaped wedges or sectors. Each sector displays a distinctive socioeconomic level of its residents and a corresponding level of rents and house values. Some sectors are traditionally high class and high rent, some are middle class and others remain low on all scores. As the city grows and each sector expands outward, the flavours of the inner precincts project outward.

Inside each sector a household's movement or kinetic space is usually sectoral. Activities matching the sector's tastes and social status, such as grocery and clothing stores, car repair shops, schools, recreation, and so forth, are normally available in the home sector. The resident quickly becomes familiar with opportunities in his home sector, makes his choices from among the known alternatives and thereby reinforces familiarity with those nearby opportunities. When the time comes to move, mobility patterns tend to be sectoral, as people seek to improve their housing while using information biased in favour of the home sector.

In–out directional bias of residential movements occurs in association with residential sectors, but only where sectoral structures are well defined. The best-defined sectors tend to be the highest social class areas, this class having a highly localized housing market and close ties with downtown, which maintain an in–out sectoral view of the city. Lower social class sectors show less sectoral bias (Clark, 1972). Where tastes place relatively less emphasis on oversized and opulent houses as a form of conspicuous consumption or, outside the United States, where access to large amounts of mortgage money or to earned or inherited wealth may be difficult, there may be great stability of high income sectors, and peripheral estates, when subdivided, may be more than sufficient to accommodate the young marrieds of the upper class (Johnston, 1969b).

Besides sectoral variations in housing values and social status of residents, the housing inventory in the American city forms a series of concentric rings. Each housing ring represents the legacy from a specific building boom that extended over several years. Incomes rose in good times, such as the years after 1900 and before the first World War, immigration increased and house construction boomed. Periods of war and economic recession cut the demand and supply of the housing almost to zero. Before the 1880s, movement was difficult in cities, so housing units were small and closely spaced in high densities to minimize the distances travelled by foot or horse-car. Arrival of the electric street-car meant that the next rings of new housing built around the compact city could sprawl outward at lower densities into areas served by street-car lines. Widespread ownership of the private car, coupled with the post-second World War prosperity and building boom, meant additional rings at still lower densities (Adams, 1970, Johnston, 1969a).

This residential structure of concentric rings was reinforced by a gradual process of invasion and succession by which alien groups slowly diffused into the suburbs as new housing was built on the urban fringe. During decades of heavy influx from Eastern, South-eastern and Southern Europe, city growth attracted migrants who concentrated at high densities in small housing units in central residential areas. Continued movement into the central areas prompted outward movement of acculturated groups.

In the succession of building cycles since the 1880s, new housing on the edge of the built-up area offered the lowest densities, plus more rooms per unit and a larger fraction of single unit structures than what came before. The typical first occupants were disproportionately white, native Americans, married with children, in the middle of the family life-cycle and with above-average incomes. The first generation of owners in a new neighbourhood have much in common. Heterogeneity increases with time, so that eventually almost as much heterogeneity develops within each concentric ring as between rings (Sanders, 1974).

Nevertheless, a general tendency exists for very young households without children and for old households beyond the child-rearing years to concentrate in the inner rings of smaller, cheaper housing. Families who prefer more space at lower densities and have the means to pay for it move outward, leaving behind a residual of families who want little space or who lack the means to purchase more.

Concentric rings around the downtown centre, when superimposed on axial sectors fanning out from downtown, partition a symmetrical city into neighbourhoods that often display a high degree of ethnic or racial homogeneity. The size of neighbourhoods corresponds to the size of the city. In cities with fewer than 50 000 people, the vaguely defined rings and sectors are so closely spaced that they define small neighbourhoods containing only a few hundred households. The homogeneity that may exist at this scale is swallowed up in census tracts defined so as to contain a thousand or more households. In smaller cities, a resident's normal movement paths take him outside his home area and into immediate contact with a wide range of neighbourhood types. At the other extreme, in massive cities the wide rings and sectors define huge neighbourhoods each with thousands of households. Sheer size insulates inner-city residents from the variety of metropolitan experience and encourages patterns of residential segregation to intensify over time. Each neighbourhood is so large it isolates many of its residents, preventing daily movement paths from ranging very far from home.

As described in chapter 7, a synthesis of these alternative views of urban structure assumes that a city's social structure is described in terms of a two-dimensional social space defined by socioeconomic status and stage in the family life-cycle (Berry and Rees, 1969). Households are arrayed along the first dimension or scale according to a summary measure of education, income and occupational level. On the second, they are differentiated according to household size. Meanwhile, the city's housing inventory may be described by a two-dimensional housing space defined by housing quality and by residential density. Housing units are distributed along the quality scale in terms of space available per person and price of the unit, and along the density axis in terms of yard space per unit and dwelling units per acre. Within the households distributed in a social space, and housing units arrayed in a corresponding housing space, the housing process is viewed as households matching their needs with the available housing supply. Each household has a social position that roughly corresponds with the type of house it occupies. Since each neighbourhood offers housing of a distinctive age, density, style and price range, it attracts people sharing similar housing needs, presumably a community of households with similar socioeconomic status and family characteristics.

Superimposing the social space and housing space implies the existence of a community space in which neighbourhoods are arrayed according to their average 'social status–housing quality' composite scores on one dimension, and their 'household size–open space per person' scores on the other axis. Each of the communities or neighbourhoods occupies a location in the city's physical space, centred on a central business district and partitioned into a series of concentric zones and sectors. High status neighbourhoods preempt the sector offering the most desirable residential land, growing outward and gradually attracting the commercial centre of downtown toward it. The lowest status sectors crowd near industrial corridors. Within each sector, there is a zonation of housing styles with younger families at the lowest densities on the margins, older families in intermediate zones and non-family households concentrated at higher densities in smaller units near the downtown.

Three factors often distort the complementary ring-and-sector description of the average city. The first of these is the presence of immigrant and minority groups, usually of low social status and often living in segregated communities. As socioeconomic status groups, they generally create a sectoral settlement pattern, within which zonal differences develop based on household age and family status. Secondly, the pattern is distorted by secondary nucleated workplaces scattered throughout the urban areas around which communities may cluster as they do around the downtown. Finally, the pattern is twisted and warped by the physical site of the city. River estuaries, sea coasts, lake shores and other physical discontinuities twist and warp the pattern of transport lines and interfere with the symmetrical sprawl of the city over a uniform transportation plane.

Observed migration patterns are moderated by the *shape* of the city. Classic ring-sector-neighbourhood models are based on a typical Mid-western city with constraint-free movement in every direction (Barrett, 1973). The range of mover choice is also constrained by city *size*. A comparison of migration patterns in Cedar Rapids and Minneapolis concluded that the larger the city, the greater the ignorance of housing opportunities in the sector, and the greater the likelihood of radial directional bias in mobility patterns (Brown and Holmes, 1971).

In cities outside North America, migration patterns are greatly modulated by public sector intervention in the housing market. The construction of *public housing* estates and the establishment of eligibility criteria for their occupance selectively promotes and inhibits intra-urban migration. In all free market economies, *financial institutions* regulate migration rates by establishing eligibility criteria for mortgage loans. Households who qualify for loans can borrow, buy *and move*. Disqualification for a mortgage loan may prohibit a move, regardless of a household's needs or desires.

Regarding the *age* of the cities, the factors producing concentric zonal patterns in older Northern and North-eastern cities have not been supplanted by new forces operating to produce a different pattern in newer cities of the South and West. Eventually, a zonal structure emerges regardless of the differences in technological regimes operating on different age cohorts of cities (Haggerty, 1971).

To summarize, the relations between urban residential structure and intra-urban migration are only incompletely understood. Study of the spatial patterning of moves should proceed side by side with that of the process, but this difficult task has seldom been attempted. From decennial census data and field observation, we describe average urban structure and common distortions from symmetry. From continued observation through time, we understand something of the structural changes brought on by rings of new construction, ageing and modification of existing stock, abandonment and removal of the of the worst housing, outward expansion of status sectors, and the creation and maintenance of distinctive neighbourhoods. One process transforming the spatial structure of cities is the steady modification of the physical stock of housing. The other is intra-urban migration which continuously redistributes a city's households among the available housing units. Each set of models describing the main dimensions of society—socioeconomic status, family status and minority status—includes intra-urban migration as a basic process. Each suggests that movement will usually be away from the downtown centre, but the socioeconomic status models argue that this comes from a desire to maintain or improve social standing in the city, the family status models trace movement to the changing space needs of households, and those concerned with minority groups associate intra-urban migration with either ghetto expansion or assimilation into society at large. Since the same geographical pattern of migration could be produced by a number of different processes, it is impossible to observe a migration pattern and infer its cause.

BEHAVIOUR OF MIGRANTS WITHIN THE STRUCTURE

Residential mobility rates, usually measured by the fraction of households changing their address during a one-year or five-year period, vary substantially between urban areas and from place to place within them. In the United States, 18 per cent. of the households change residence in the course of a year, with little difference in average rates between metropolitan (17.8 per cent. between 1970 and 1971) and non-metropolitan areas (18.1 per cent.). Within metropolitan regions, turnover in the central city (19.0 per cent.) slightly exceeds the rate outside (16.9 per cent.).

The proportion of 1970 households that changed addresses during the previous five years ranged from less than a third (about 6 per cent. per year) in North-eastern metropolitan areas of high stability or out-migration, such as Scranton (32 per cent.), Johnstown (32 per cent.) or Wilkes-Barre-Hazelton (30 per cent.), to over two-thirds in fast-growing high amenity settings in the West, South and Gulf Coast—areas such as Reno (68 per cent.), Anaheim-Santa Ana-Garden Grove (68 per cent.), Colorado Springs (70 per cent.) and Las Vegas (72 per cent.). Within urban areas, inner-city rooming house and apartment districts often show annual turnover of 70 per cent. A five-year turnover rate above 70 per cent. is common in neighbourhoods receiving immigrant minority groups and young persons. In the zone of stability surrounding the core, the rate falls well below 40 per cent., only to rise again in the newly built suburban margins. Population turnover is fast in the core because of rapid changes in family needs, the constant search for something better by people unlikely to leave the area where leases are short and rents high, and the continued in-migration of low income persons. Were it not for the normal lag between the increase in need for more space and the acquisition of the means to pay for it, the turnover rates near the core—and, indeed, throughout the city—might be even higher.

In general, mobility is high in the suburbs, despite large mortgages, because of adjustments of housing needs of growing families, transfers into the urban area by middle-class families due to changes in employment and aspirations pushing some families to acquire the best housing affordable. In the middle neighbourhoods straddling the boundary between the city and the contiguous suburban municipalities that emerged in the mid-twentieth century, turnover is lower because families are static or declining in size, career peaks have been reached and households are satisfied with their housing (Johnston, 1969c; Simmons, 1968).

These are general tendencies rather than precise rules. Households often undergo changes in their family status at the same time as they experience adjustments in income and social status, so it is hard to explain a move exclusively in terms of one or the other. The inconclusive impact of changes in socioeconomic status or of status aspirations on the propensity to move is hard to assess, because of its high correlations with other influencing variables such as age of household head and tenure. The reasons given for relocation are not related in any ordered fashion to ownership status, age, marital status, occupation, education and length of time in the city. Occasionally, the obvious extravagance of status-related moves is rationalized with references to family needs, much as purchasers of oversize cars hasten to explain their choice in terms of safety.

The cost of movement for high status households averages about 10 per cent. of the house value, and thus requires a substantial change in dwelling or environment to make it worthwhile. Low status households, with much lower move costs, require only a slight change in income or family structure to trigger a move (Simmons, 1968). Yet the highest mobility zones have a predominance of households in early or late stages in the family life-cycle, and age may be more accurate than life-cycle alone in predicting aspects of the mobility process (Figure 5.1). Much of the high mobility of non-whites is explainable by their lower incomes, fewer assets, poorer housing, larger and younger families, and the immigrant status of many households (Moore, 1972).

Where do people move?

When households move to new addresses, they move through *physical* or terrestrial space, but they also may relocate within the *community* space defined by the cardinal neighbourhood attributes: socioeconomic status and family status. Because there are two ways to view a move, a question about the nature of an origin or a destination can mean ‘What location on the map?’ as well as ‘What kind of place is it?’. In seeking regularities in move behaviour,

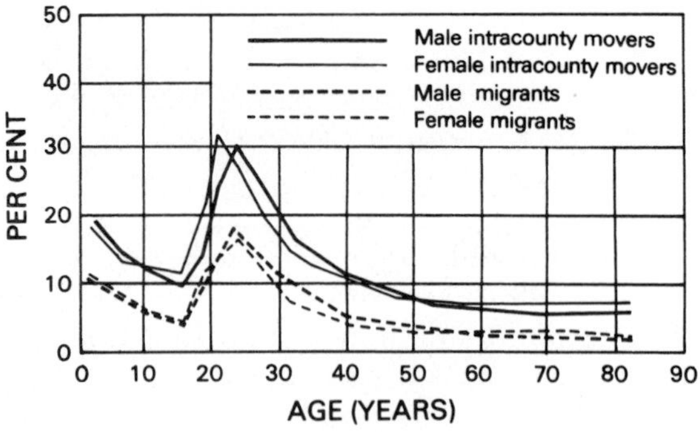

FIGURE 5.1 Annual mobility rate for intra-county movers and inter-county migrants. (From 'Mobility for the population of the United States, March 1964 to March 1965', *Current Population Reports, Series, P. 20 Population Characteristics,* No. 150, United States Bureau of the Census, Washington, D.C. 1966)

geographical research separates into these two streams as it asks how origins and destinations are associated. Central questions in the first stream include:

1. What is the likely geographical distribution of destinations of people moving from specific locations within the urban area?
2. What is the most probable distribution of origins of households moving to specific locations?
3. What are the geometrical attributes of the move paths described when lines connecting origins and destinations are traced on a map?

The complementary stream of research focuses on the internal characteristics of households, housing units and neighbourhoods, and asks:

1. What is the correspondence between the type of housing sought and the type of household seeking it?
2. How are households exchanged between similar types of neighbourhood?
3. How do patterns of household exchange differ among different types of urban neighbourhoods?

In virtually every study of intra-urban migration, most moves are short. Various samples of moves from Minneapolis are representative of other studies (Figure 5.2). In a national sample of United States households' moves between 1960 and 1966, almost a fifth stayed within the same neighbourhood, less than 2 per cent. moved to the central city from outlying towns or suburbs and 18 per cent. entered the suburbs from outlying towns or suburbs in the same metropolitan area. Almost 45 per cent. moved within the same central city. Of the most recent moves, 28 per cent. were short moves within the same neighbourhood, 58 per cent. stayed within the metropolitan area but changed neighbourhoods and 14 per cent. originated outside the metropolitan area (Butler and coauthors, 1969). Income, race and previous tenure best explain length of move. Higher-income, white households who previously owned

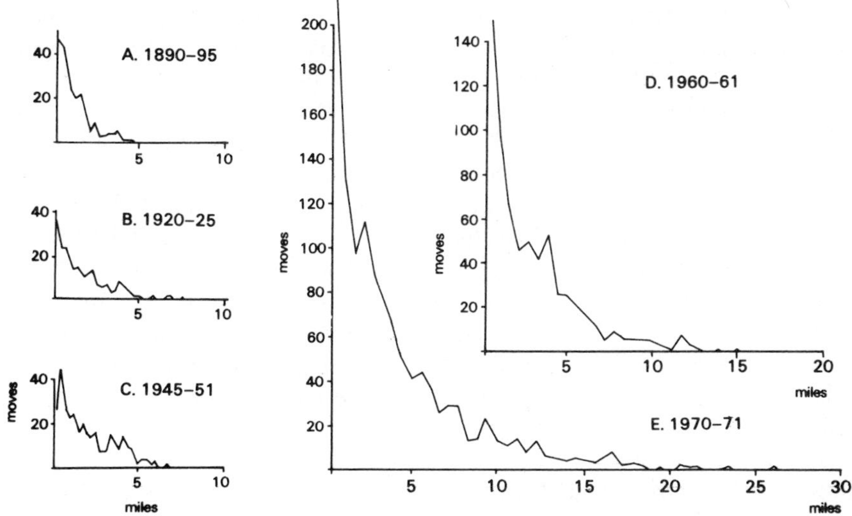

FIGURE 5.2 Distribution of moves in physical space by length of move from five Minneapolis area migration samples. (Reproduced by permission of Earl A. Nordstrand, 1973, p. 86)

houses, and those moving because of job change, are more likely to move across metropolitan boundaries. Intra-urban migration data from Swansea are consistent with United States evidence of variation in move patterns by social class of households. Virtually all the housing alternatives named by sample migrants to low cost areas were in the same residential district, while migrants to high cost areas nominated several locations elsewhere in the city where housing is of a similar quality and neighbourhoods are of similar socioeconomic composition (Herbert, 1973b). Non-white, low income and renting households are most likely to make short moves within the same neighbourhood, partly because of constraints on search behaviour, but also because minority areas, low priced housing and rental units are often confined to a few central-city areas.

Because of the wide ring of low turnover neighbourhoods near the edge of the central city and in the first-tier suburbs, many innercity movers unable to satisfy their status aspirations with short moves may have to jump the barrier to outward (and upward) progress which stable areas present. A residential ring of low turnover will be most pronounced in moderate-to-slow growth urban areas where forces of invasion and succession are weak, thus affecting the distances moved by promoting leap-frogging. The longer moves that result may be a function of a city's size, of special sentiment for an attractive area, or because high income households feel satisfactorily housed. They have stayed put because they have little desire for new housing or another neighbourhood. This barrier fosters development of middleclass suburbs or working-class satellites organized around decentralized industries (Johnston, 1969c).

The analysis of move directions is closely intertwined with that of places moved between because neighbourhoods of different styles occur at predictable locations in many cities. In fact, the geographical distribution of social status zones may be the main variable regulating the direction of migration flows (Greer-Wootten and Gilmour, 1972).

In a move sample from the 1950s, an average of 40 per cent. of all moves originated within the radial sector of destination. Considerable short distance movement in inner-residential areas contributes to this result. Of the intra-urban moves terminating in the suburbs, 54 per cent. stayed within the sector of origin. Moves from residences in outer sectors are even more likely to end within the same sector than those from the inner city, suggesting that once most households have lived in one segment of suburbia they seldom leave it for another. Residents of the central areas, however, fail to show an exclusive commitment to any one sector of suburbia. Those who decide to move display different preferences when leaving the inner city (Johnston, 1969c).

Destinations stay within the sector of origin because the majority of moves simply adjust housing while attempting to retain neighbourhood location and internal neighbourhood characteristics. About 80 per cent. of intra-city movement takes place within census tracts of the same class or adjacent classes (Simmons, 1968). That is, moves are not only short in terrestrial space but also in community space (Figure 5.3). To a considerable degree, distances in physical space are correlated with distances in community space because each place usually resembles its neighbouring places. Only one move in a lifetime might normally be explained by social mobility. More effective are changes in family status and income adjustments that permit the moves without altering relative social class (Simmons, 1968). Also crucial are differences in family spending and saving habits which allow early house purchases and rapid capital accumulation by some families, compared to overspending and a lifetime of debt for others.

Patterns of population distribution reflect migration patterns, suggesting that the family life-cycle model is the most useful explanation of intra-urban migration. Suburbs display the highest concentration of children and more married women as full-time homemakers. The proportion of households in early family-cycle stages with unmarried persons 15 years and older is twice as high in the central city than in the suburbs, and more women are in the work force (Johnston, 1969a). Up to the mid-1960s only those people who took familism as their dominant life-style chose to be the first residents of newly built suburbs of single-family houses (Bell, 1958). Since then, the increasing variety of suburban housing styles has increased the variety of households at different life-cycle stages.

Patterns of move attributes in physical space, in community space, and of the relations between them, are further complicated by variations in city sizes. In smaller cities, all variety is close at hand. In the Detroits and Chicagos, different kinds of neighbourhoods form different worlds, often located many miles apart. Research in Cedar Rapids, a smaller urban area, disclosed that a given zone type in community space is relatively accessible to a household,

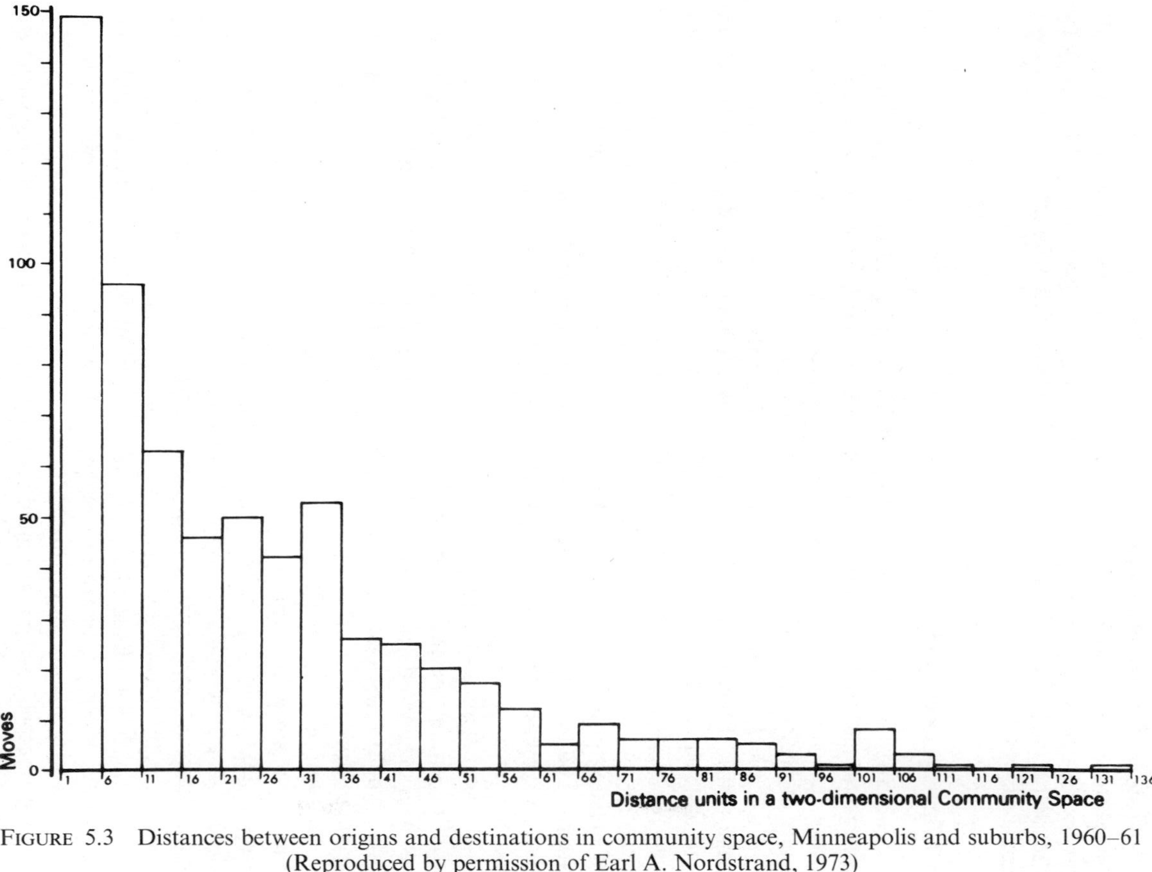

FIGURE 5.3 Distances between origins and destinations in community space, Minneapolis and suburbs, 1960–61 (Reproduced by permission of Earl A. Nordstrand, 1973)

whatever its origin zone type, but the nature of the origin zone influenced the volume of flow. Zones of middle life-cycle, middle-class households are likely to attract migrants from all over the urban area as well as from themselves. Zones with lower economic status, with unsound rented multi-family housing, were found more likely to attract migrants from themselves, from zones of low economic status but sound rented duplexes, and from downtown commercial areas. The latter two types appear to persist as independent entities. Perhaps they attract inter-urban migrants rather than being fed from other zones (Brown and Longbrake, 1970).

A Minneapolis example

Since the same spatial pattern of migrations can be produced by a number of processes, it is impossible to observe a pattern and infer back to its cause. A study of moves in Minneapolis and suburbs illustrates the need for the parallel study of process and of pattern.

A sample of moving households was compiled by examining names on each page of the 1970 Minneapolis area telephone directory and comparing them with corresponding persons in the 1971 directory to find the first person from each 1970 page who had changed addresses within the study area by 1971. Directories provide a good data source in Minneapolis since the proportion of unlisted phones is well below 10 per cent., among the lowest in the United States. The sample of 1 196 households excludes persons without telephones, those with unlisted phones and those whose reported addresses could not be located on base maps.

The next step was to plot each move on a separate map, recording the census tract of origin, the tract of destination, the length of the move, the distance between origin and central business district (C.B.D.), and the angle formed by two straight lines, one from the origin to the C.B.D. and the other from the origin to the destination.

The setting within which the moves were made consisted of 310 central-city and suburban census tracts described by twelve intercorrelated measures of household and housing characteristics. The degree to which the level of each variable is predictable from the others in the set (the squared multiple correlation) varies through time with societal changes, modification of the housing and changing tastes (Table 5.1). For example, income levels and racial composition of tracts are increasingly associated with other tract features, while the percentage of old persons or median price of rental units have become harder to predict from other tract attributes.

Each tract was given a weighted score on each factor based on the structure of each factor and the value of the variables for the tract (see chapter 6). Then each tract was plotted in a community space defined by family status and associated housing variables (Factor I), and socioeconomic status with related measures of housing value (Factor II, see Figure 5.4). The community space is divided into sixteen zones. On the horizontal dimension, tracts of type 4

TABLE 5.1 Variables used to describe 310 Minneapolis area census tracts, 1970

Tract attribute	Squared multiple correlation coefficients 1960	Squared multiple correlation coefficients 1970	Varimax rotated factor structure[a] I	Varimax rotated factor structure[a] II	Varimax rotated factor structure[a] III
Population per household	0.94	0.94	0.78	—	−0.54
Percentage under 18 years of age	0.95	0.94	0.84	—	−0.47
Percentage 65 years of age and over	0.83	0.75	−0.80	—	—
Median family income	0.85	0.88	0.41	0.55	0.64
Median years of school completed by persons 25 and older	0.77	0.72	—	0.81	—
Percentage of work force in white-collar occupations	0.76	0.66	—	0.83	—
Percentage foreign stock	0.65	0.66	−0.81	—	—
Percentage black	0.33	0.52	—	—	0.65
Percentage other races	0.52	0.66	—	—	0.73
Percentage single-family houses	0.82	0.83	0.49	—	−0.73
Median value of owner-occupied houses	0.74	0.76	—	0.75	—
Median contract rent	0.72	0.59	—	0.59	—

[a]Loadings smaller than 0.4 are ignored.
Reproduced by permission of Earl A. Nordstrand.

(Zones 4A, 4B, 4C and 4D) typically contain larger households, many young persons, few foreign-born or children of foreign-born, and few elderly. Incomes are above average and single-family houses predominate. At the other extreme are tracts of type 1 (Zones 1A, 1B, 1C and 1D) with concentrations of elderly, a high fraction of foreign stock and small households with few dependent children. These tracts also feature lower incomes and multiple-family dwellings used by households at the beginning and at the end of the family life-cycles.

The vertical dimension also divides into four status echelons. The top-ranked type A tracts (Zones 1A, 2A, 3A, 4A) contain mainly white-collar workers who have good educations, live in the highest priced housing and earn the highest incomes. At the other extreme, the type D tracts spread across the bottom of the community space and contain the fewest white-collar workers, poorly educated adults, cheap housing units and low incomes. Within the framework of a community space thus defined, the question was asked whether destinations for a set of movers in the community space could be predicted on the basis of the location of their origin zone, as well as whether origins could be predicted for movers into a specific zone.

Turning first to the social status stratification of the community space, if the volume of movement, say, from tracts of type A to those of type B depended solely on the fraction of all recorded moves starting in echelon A (i.e. 0.239) and the fraction ending in B(0.444), then of the total of 1 196 moves 127 should be from tracts of type A to those of type B ($0.239 \times 0.444 \times 1196 = 127$). But several factors, especially tastes and status aspirations, meant that only

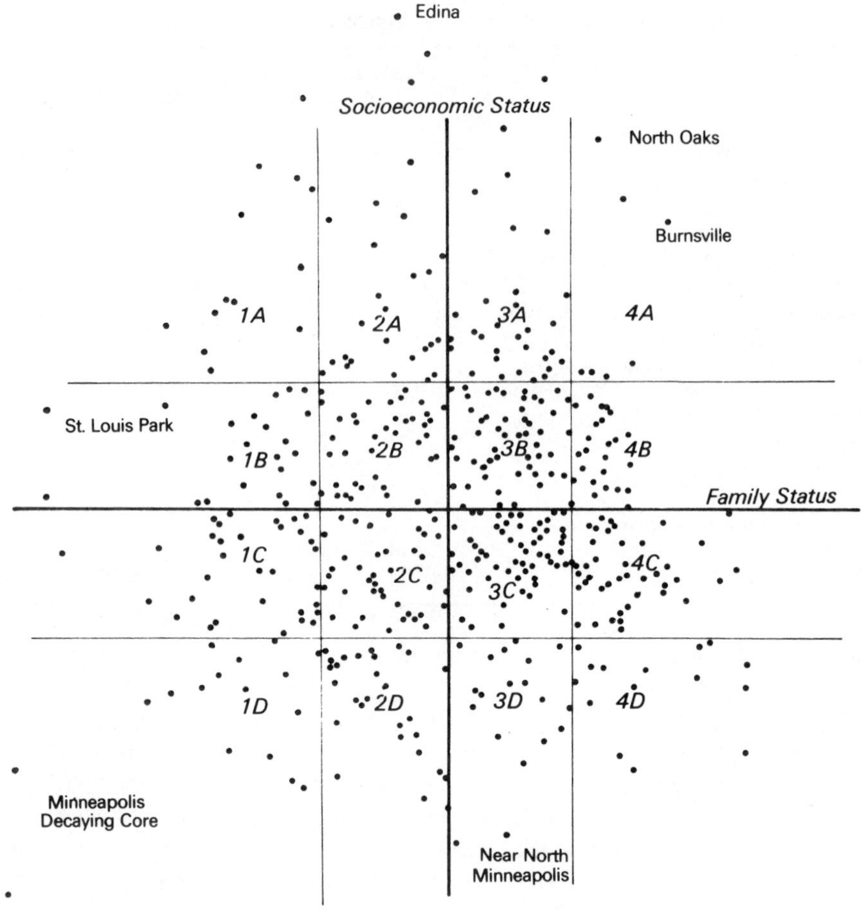

FIGURE 5.4 Minneapolis area 1970 census tracts located in a community space. (Reproduced by permission of Earl A. Nordstrand, 1973, p. 72)

109 households abandoned tracts of type A for lower status tracts of type B. In all pairings of social status types, movers show a strong tendency to stay in the same status echelon (Table 5.2).

Examining the same moves in terms of their tendency to stay within or leave behind tracts of approximately the same family status, we see a clear tendency to stay in the same tract or same type of tract, with the notable exception of extra moves from 1 to 2, from 3 to 4 and from 4 to 3 (Table 5.3). A large but unknown fraction of these results depends on three simple facts: most moves are short and house-related; most tracts resemble their neighbours; and most tracts are so internally heterogeneous that they can satisfy a wide variety of housing needs over small areas. These facts also help account for the detailed move patterns among the sixteen zones in the community space when Table 5.2 is expanded (Table 5.4). Each cell of Table 5.4 is an entry in a sub-matrix

Table 5.2 Moves between social status echelons in the Minneapolis area, 1970–71

From tract type	To	Actual moves A	B	C	D	Total	Fraction
A (high class)		124	109	41	12	286	0.239
B		118	293	80	26	517	0.432
C		29	93	120	33	275	0.230
D (low class)		16	36	26	40	118	0.099
Total		287	531	267	111	1 196	
Fraction		0.240	0.444	0.223	0.093		1.000

From tract type	To	Actual moves minus expected moves A	B	C	D
A (high class)		55	−18[a]	−23	−15
B		− 6	64	−35	−26
C		−37	−29	59	7
D (low class)		−12	−17	0	29

[a]0.239 × 0.444 × 1 196 = 127 expected moves. Actual moves (109) minus expected (127) equals −18.

Reproduced by permission of Earl A. Nordstrand.

Table 5.3 Moves between family status echelons in the Minneapolis area, 1970–71

From tract type	To	Actual moves 1	2	3	4	Total	Fraction
1 (small households, multiple housing)		165	95	53	26	339	0.283
2		91	155	99	38	383	0.320
3		50	69	147	69	335	0.280
4 (large families, single houses)		16	14	45	64	139	0.116
Total		322	333	344	197	1,196	
Fraction		0.269	0.278	0.288	0.165		1.000

From tract type	To	Actual moves minus expected moves 1	2	3	4
1 (small households, multiple housing)		74	1	−44	−30
2		−12	49	−11	−25
3		−40	−24	51	14
4 (large families, single houses)		−21	−25	5	41

Reproduced by permission of Earl A. Nordstrand.

TABLE 5.4 Minneapolis area sample moves in community space

From To	1A	2A	3A	4A	1B	2B	3B	4B	1C	2C	3C	4C	1D	2D	3D	4D	Origins per group
1A	15	8	3	0	15	9	4	0	3	2	1	0	6	1	1	0	68
2A	7	29	12	2	9	7	9	2	4	7	8	2	2	0	1	0	101
3A	4	7	27	3	7	12	17	17	5	2	2	5	0	1	0	0	109
4A	0	1	2	4	0	1	0	0	0	0	0	0	0	0	0	0	8
1B	9	12	8	0	32	18	12	9	4	1	1	1	4	0	0	0	111
2B	7	21	18	0	22	57	20	8	8	7	5	6	6	5	1	0	191
3B	2	6	21	3	13	12	39	20	5	8	8	5	3	3	1	0	149
4B	0	0	11	0	2	3	6	20	0	3	12	6	2	1	0	0	66
1C	3	3	3	1	10	8	10	5	26	5	4	7	8	3	3	0	99
2C	2	1	4	0	9	4	10	4	4	8	4	6	5	1	1	0	63
3C	2	1	3	0	3	4	7	7	1	2	11	6	2	3	1	0	53
4C	5	1	0	0	2	0	4	6	2	0	8	26	3	2	0	1	60
1D	1	7	0	1	9	7	2	1	4	4	1	1	16	7	0	0	61
2D	0	0	1	0	4	2	1	4	0	1	3	3	2	5	1	1	28
3D	0	3	3	0	1	0	2	1	2	1	2	1	0	4	3	1	24
4D	0	0	0	0	0	1	1	0	0	1	1	1	0	0	0	0	5
Destinations per group	57	100	116	14	138	145	144	104	68	52	71	76	59	36	13	3	1 196

Reproduced by permission of Earl A. Nordstrand, 1973, p. 93.

describing how movers within or between social status echelons simultaneously moved in terms of tract familism scores. Of the 1 196 movers, 531 stayed in the same family status milieu, 380 moved toward greater familism (larger, younger families, lower residential densities, more single-family houses) and only 285 moved into tracts of less familism (e.g. from type 4 to 3, or from type 3 to 2 or 1). Of the moves to areas of high average social status, such as B to A or D to B, every cell in Table 5.5 also shows more moves to higher than to lower family status. For example, of the 93 households moving up from tracts of type C to those of type B, 27 entered tracts of the same family status, 44 had higher familism and 22 had lower. Of the moves downward to tracts of lower social status undoubtedly including many inward toward the city core, half the classes (B to C, B to D and C to D) indicate simultaneous large-scale movement to tracts of lower familism.

TABLE 5.5 Moves toward tracts of greater familism (above diagonal) and lower familism (below) by social status of origins and destinations in a Minneapolis sample, 1970–71

	Actual moves			
From status level	A	B	C	D
A (high)	21 \ 28	29 \ 41	11 \ 18	3 \ 3
B	26 \ 41	58 \ 87	36 \ 19	15 \ 1
C	11 \ 11	22 \ 44	17 \ 32	15 \ 7
D (low)	3 \ 9	7 \ 16	5 \ 13	6 \ 10

Reproduced by permission of Earl A. Nordstrand (see Table 5.4).

In conclusion, the Minneapolis data confirm that for this large urban area most moves are short, whether measured in physical space (Figure 5.2) or in a two-dimensional community space (Figure 5.3). There is a clear tendency to move within tracts of the same status, with some gradual shifting into higher status areas. There is somewhat less of a tendency to stay in the same familism milieu, with many movers shifting into tracts of higher familism. The sample of movers excludes households without private phone service, a majority of which are probably poor, and households with unlisted numbers.

A similar study in smaller Cedar Rapids examined moves among four zones or subdivisions of the community space:

I. Middle-class households, moderate familism.
II. Upper middle class, late life-cycle.
III. Lower economic status, rented duplexes.
IV. Lower economic status, multi-family units.

The search process showed no directional or sectoral bias in physical space, but there were differences in the spatial characteristics of the search according to location and zone type. If the origin is taken as the reference node, then moves from suburban areas emphasized search in the origin area and in the direction of the C.B.D. Moves from the inner city showed no directional or sectoral bias. Movers from Zones I and III showed the widest range of search behaviour, while those from Zones II and IV searched within a restricted range (Brown and Holmes, 1970).

In Toronto, search patterns were studied with the aid of three indices (Barrett, 1973). The *temporal intensity* of a household's search for housing equals the number of houses examined divided by the time spent searching. Scores from a sample of movers within that urban area showed low intensity with few houses searched in a short time, and a random spatial distribution of the houses. Households searching only one house tended to be in central-city 'sellers' market' areas. As the number of units inspected increases, their distribution edges toward the suburbs.

The *spatial intensity* of a household's search pattern equals the mean distance to all searched units from the mean centre of their distribution. Over 92 per cent. of the households had search radii of three miles or less, compared to an urban area radius of thirteen miles. Those of below-average and lowest socioeconomic status concentrated in the search class confined to one mile or less.

Dividing the index of temporal intensity by that of spatial intensity yields an index of *concentration of search*. High values indicate casual and erratic search and tend to be assigned to central-city searchers. Low values indicating intensive and thorough search behaviour are common in new subdivisions.

THE DECISION TO MOVE

A household's decision to seek a new dwelling begins by comparing its *needs* with what its current housing offers (a) internally, (b) in the neighbourhood and (c) in its relative location within the urban area. If there is a large negative discrepancy between the housing it has and what it needs, then stress develops. Beyond an endurance threshold characteristic to each household, given its tastes, resources and outlays for housing vis-à-vis other consumption items, stress produces strain leading to a decision either to move or to absorb the strain in situ, which if unsuccessful leads to a delayed decision to move. A decision to absorb the strain and remain at the old location may be later revoked when conditions change. Objectionable environmental changes may include encroaching blight, neighbourhood turnover that is interpreted as lowering its average social class, environmental degradation or reduction in neighbourhood accessibility to important destinations. Housing needs may change following changes in occupation, position, income, family size, job location, marital status or life-cycle stage, leading again to a decision whether to move or to absorb the strain.

In the migration context, stress arises from the disparity between the collective housing needs of the household and the offering of the house, the neighbourhood and its situation within the household movement pattern. The effect of stress depends on the intensity of the resulting strain, which depends in turn on how the stress interrupts household equilibrium and how the household responds to the interruption. Strain can be reduced or maintained at tolerable levels by adjusting needs, by restructuring the environment to satisfy household needs better or by relocating to another house (Brown and Longbrake, 1970; Brown and Moore, 1970).

Another way to unravel the complexity surrounding the decision to move is for a household to consider the present and discounted future :(a) the benefits of living in a different house; (b) the costs of moving to a different house; (c) the benefits of staying in the same house; and (d) the costs of staying in the same house. The difference between (a) and (b) yields the household's perception of the net benefit of moving, which on balance should trigger a decision to move if it exceeds the difference between (c) and (d), the net benefit of staying in the same house. Move costs may be too high when compared with benefits from eliminating a small degree of dissatisfaction. The move effort is usually lower for renters than owners, irrespective of age or income. The effort is higher with duration of residence, which is correlated with the age of the household head. Finally, the strength of social networks curtails some moves, although in general it contributes little in prohibiting household mobility (Moore, 1972). Moreover, the net benefits of moving versus staying, to be logical and consistent, must be reckoned in terms of other household purchases compared to their costs. Additional net outlays for housing means resources unavailable for other goods and services.

Since most households are neither perfectly logical nor consistent, the sheer complexity of major decisions, plus the fact that consumption decisions are usually made sequentially rather than simultaneously, produces haphazard consumption patterns revealing non-transitive preferences. Moreover, tastes may change during the search as households discover in an immediate, tangible way what the housing market can offer, leading some households to place too high a value on the immediate and future benefits of a move, while underestimating the direct costs and opportunity costs of a higher housing outlay, thus setting the stage for later regret. Such an outcome often follows a selection made under stress in anticipation of an inter-urban move. Another household of similar means and housing needs, but with more experience and greater skill in coolly appraising both costs and benefits, might make a different choice.

Sometimes families are forced to move by events outside their control, such as eviction for conversion of rental property or demolition of a building (Table 5.6). (Eviction accounted for 12 per cent. of a sample of 313 recently moved households in Christchurch, New Zealand—see Clark, 1970.) The voluntary moves, forming the dominant proportion, are stimulated by dissatisfaction related to household size, dwelling space and household requirements. In one nationwide study in the United States, the main reason given for intra-urban moves was the need for more space (Butler and coauthors, 1969). In the Toronto

TABLE 5.6 Sample moves in Baltimore in the early 1950s

Free choice moves		61%
Forced moves		39%
Involuntary moves: (evictions, dwelling destruction, severe income losses)	23%	
Inter-city migration	8%	
Previous dwelling occupied temporarily	4%	
Newly married	3%	
Others (mainly recently divorced)	1%	
100% equals 444		

Source. Why Families Move, Rossi, P. H., 1955. (Reproduced by permission of Macmillan Publishing Co. Inc., New York.).

study of 380 households which moved in the early 1970s, 121 (32 per cent.) wanted to own a house, whereas 112 (30 per cent.) reported that their previous accommodation was too small: the third largest response to the question 'Why did you move from your previous address?' was 'I didn't like the area' (40 replies—11 per cent.). Whether examining overall responses or the order in which the replies were given, changes in attitude accounted for the greatest number of responses (Table 5.7).

Table 5.7 Reasons intra-urban movers left previous residence in Toronto in the early 1970s

Reason	First reason	%	Second reason	%	Third reason	%	Total	%
Forced	32	8	17	10	1	4	50	9
Change in space requirements	108	28	41	24	3	12	152	26
Locational consideration	52	14	50	29	12	46	114	20
Attitude change	188	50	65	38	10	38	263	45
Total	380	100	173	100	26	100	579	100

Reproduced by permission of the Department of Geography, Atkinson College, York University, from F. A. Barrett, 1973, Geographical Monographs no. 1, p. 97.

Other studies focus not on the space need itself but on the bases for changing space needs. For example, of the eight or nine moves a household might make in its lifetime, only about five are related to changes in the life-cycle (Table 5.8). Within a moderately growing city, over 50 per cent. of intra-urban moves are tied to changes in the life-cycle (Simmons, 1968).

For every class of intra-urban moves, in one national study the proportion of families gaining rooms with a move was higher than of those increasing in

TABLE 5.8 Moves during the life-cycle

Age	Stage	Moves
0	Birth	
	Child	1
10		
	Adolescent	
20	Maturity	1
	Marriage	1
30	Children	1
40		
	Children mature	
50		
60		1
	Retirement	
70		
	Death	
80		

Reproduced with permission, from the *Geographical Review*, vol. **58**, 1968, p. 630, copyrighted by the American Geographical Society.

size. Rather than resulting from tenure change, the explanation lies in the normal lag between changes in household size, and (a) changes in the amount of living space obtained and (b) adjustments in the household's economic level (Butler and coauthors, 1969).

Moves are most likely in the early phases of a family's history—first upon marriage and then as children arrive and housing needs change markedly. The years when children are in school, when careers are consolidating, and when job security and income levels reach a relative plateau, are years of high stability. When children leave home and retirement nears, some households reduce their housing space.

A small fraction of movers dislike their former area because of dirt, poor upkeep or nearby noxious facilities. The Toronto study revealed that complaints can arise from changes in the social composition of a neighbourhood or from a change in household expectations about neighbourhood character, but these are relatively unimportant as move motivators (Table 5.9). In the United States study, the effect of minorities entering a neighbourhood is less to push majority households out than to divert prospective majority newcomers from entering. Apparently, the dwelling unit itself produces more dissatisfaction than does the milieu or access to friends, work, schools or other facilities (Butler and coauthors, 1969). Lower classes seem to show a greater need to retain proximity to friends, although this result may come indirectly from their difficulty in making long moves. The only case in which accessibility was reported as a significant element in the decision to move was for persons living more than 40 minutes from work (Simmons, 1968). On the other hand, accessibility might have been one important constraint for many movers, but once obtained was taken for granted.

TABLE 5.9 The role of complaints in the decision to move in Baltimore (1950s) and Toronto (1970s)

Type of Complaint	Baltimore	Toronto
Space	45%	26%
Neighbourhood	14%	18%
Cost	12%	7%
	71% (924)	51% (197)
Other	29%	49%
	100%	100%
	$N = 1\ 300$	$N = 380$

Reproduced by permission of the Department of Geography, Atkinson College, York University, from F. A. Barrett, 1973, Geographical Monographs No. 1, p. 98.

If households are not pushed into moving by unsatisfactory housing, neighbourhood or location, or by movement to a new stage in the family life-cycle, they may be pulled into better housing by their aspirations for any of the following (Moore, 1972):

1. Material consumption outside the home, enjoying material benefits of urban society with an in-town apartment or town house.
2. Family-oriented material consumption at home, with maximum yard and dwelling space.
3. Social prestige, with a house and neighbourhood selection that corresponds to one's job or community position.
4. Community involvement, with neighbourhood and house selected for the social milieu or life-style accompanying it.

THE RELOCATION PROCESS

The household relocation process moves systematically through three stages: establishing *criteria* for a different house, the *search* procedure during which criteria may change and, finally, *selection*. The criteria established by a household before the search range from objective, easily articulated items such as price, the number of bedrooms or amount of yard space, through equally objective but harder to measure items such as ages and social class of neighbours, to hard to articulate but nonetheless important matters of taste such as architectural styles inside and out and how the neighbours decorate and landscape their properties. These latter items seldom appear in a criteria list, but emerge with veto force when a household confronts an available house and must decide whether or not to take it. Establishing criteria therefore involves an initial stage in which measurable objectives are spelled out and ranked, followed by a subsequent subjective stage when latent criteria are invoked in response to specific houses. A household usually can easily decide that it dislikes the kitchen, or the arrangement of the rooms, or the neighbourhood, but may be unable to specify exactly what it seeks.

Households repeatedly report that space needs and neighbourhood character top their lists of criteria (Brown and Moore, 1970; Butler and coauthors, 1969). Since most households lack the resources to gain everything they want in a house, they end up weighing the available options and trading-off desirable but less important items to gain the more important ones. During the search, if several vacancies satisfy the aspiration criteria, then the household begins to define secondary or subsidiary aspiration criteria. The longer the time allotted for the search, the more explicit become the secondary criteria. Finally, choice among equivalent options is made according to cost (Table 5.10).

TABLE 5.10 Reasons reported for selecting new residence; Toronto sample, 1970s

Reasons	Frequency	Percentage
Best value for money	188	23.9
House style	136	17.3
Met space requirements	108	13.7
Liked the area	94	11.9
Convenient location	52	6.6
Same schools for the children	33	4.2
Neighbourhood amenities	32	4.1
Well maintained	29	3.7
Wanted a backyard	21	2.7
Close to work	21	2.7
Good investment	20	2.5
Wanted a new home	16	2.0
Wanted to be closer to family	11	1.4
A windfall	9	1.1
Wanted an older home	6	0.8
More economical to maintain	4	0.5
Desperate	3	0.4
Children welcomed	2	0.3
Wanted a separate driveway	1	0.1
Wanted a swimming pool	1	0.1
Impulse	0	0.0

Reproduced by permission of the Department of Geography, Atkinson College, York University, from F. A. Barrett, 1973, Geographical Monographs No. 1, p. 100.

The actual search takes place within a geographical search space, a sub-set of the household's larger awareness space. The household's search space has a social, economic and spatial character, as defined by the primary then secondary aspiration criteria. The awareness space includes places learned of directly through day-to-day activity in the city, plus locations learned indirectly through mass media or the experience of acquaintances.

The awareness space has a set of locations or nodes with information about them diminishing in distance decay-fashion away from the household's home, except for extensions along major transport arteries. The four important information sources during the housing search include mass media, especially newspapers and television, real estate agents, sign displays at the available sites or elsewhere, and personal contacts (Table 5.11). The Baltimore study in the unusually tight housing market of the early 1950s found personal contact to be the second most frequently used source after newspapers, but it was most effective. Almost 50 per cent. of all housing units studied had been obtained through personal contact. The proportion of advertising effort devoted to each medium by the owner of the vacancy depends on his evaluation of the likelihood of success compared to the cost in money, effort and time remaining until the vacancy must be filled (Rossi, 1955).

TABLE 5.11 Information sources used in looking for a house

Source	Initial use	Subsequent use	Total
Newspaper	104	35	163
Real estate agents	117	145	262
Sign on property	16	115	131
Personal search or contact			
Driving	71	126	197
Friend	28	52	80
Walking	8	69	77
Relative	11	37	48
Friend in real estate	25	4	29
Fellow employee	0	15	15
Total	380	622	1 002

Reproduced by permission of the Department of Geography, Atkinson College, York University, from F. A. Barrett, 1973, Geographical Monographs No. 1, 105.

In small towns and cities, the searcher can learn about and examine all vacancies. In larger urban areas, vacancies develop faster than they can be identified and evaluated. Each household searching for housing decides how much time to spend on each information source, each of which has its own special biases in terms of the houses and neighbourhoods described. The sources are also biased in the clientele they reach. Personal contact is used more frequently by lower-income or central-city households, whereas real estate agents are especially useful to upper-income households. Newspaper selectivity is often spatial, with houses listed by area. Real estate agents select by price and size, using criteria supplied by searchers. Vacancy information supplied by personal contacts will be biased by the tastes of friends and associates.

Within the confines of its search space, the household samples and uses available information, defining a behaviour path as it searches. The choice of information sources and the intensity with which each is sampled depends on:

1. Subjective probability of finding a suitable vacancy by using a certain information source at a certain level of intensity.
2. Perceived effort involved in using it at that level.
3. Amount of time remaining before a choice must be made.

When time begins to run out, additional sources are used and all may be employed more intensively (Brown and Moore, 1970).

The search space is likely to be revised as the searching household gains experience in the urban area during the search. Accurate information about places in and outside the original awareness space adds and deletes places in the search space. When time starts to run out, the search strategy must change to ensure that a house will be found; otherwise the household must reverse its decision to move.

Alternative strategies include continuing existing behaviour, assuming that it will succeed; redefining aspirations by either adjusting in situ or relaxing some search criteria; increasing the intensity of the search; and widening the search space. As time runs out, strain increases, judgement is impaired, criteria for evaluating vacancies are reduced, perception of 'acceptability' becomes ill-defined and a hasty decision is likely. Under these circumstances, the customary strategy is to redefine aspirations.

The first part of the search tends to be space-covering and generally sectoral for those in suburban areas. The second part is space-organizing, with the search concentrating in a small area where a satisfactory vacancy is likely to be found. In Barrett's (1973) Toronto sample, the large number of houses not seriously considered yet located in familiar areas suggests that familiarity yields unpredictable results. Yet familiarity with places, especially when based on experience, can act as a subconscious selection mechanism, though the selection can be positive or negative depending on what the household knows of the places.

In large, single-centred urban areas, residents build up and retain a narrow, wedge-shaped image of their city, sharply in focus for places close to home and within the home sector, and blurry or blank for distant places. During the search, the criteria variables and the associated ranges of acceptable values allow the household to reject most vacancies from serious consideration. For many households, the residence chosen was the only one seriously considered or even visited, perhaps revealing the screening of possible vacancies in the examination of newspaper and real estate listings, but also reflecting the uncertainty of the conservative household, taking an acceptable vacancy instead of pushing on to find an even better outcome. The greater the time pressure, the greater the likelihood of choosing the first acceptable vacancy. In one nationwide survey, 60 per cent. of all groups never *seriously* considered more than one unit (Butler and coauthors, 1969). A majority of the households said they looked at most units that would suit them. Households apparently define their needs about as narrowly as the market will permit.

The best predictors of *where* and *what* families move to are income and race. Poorer and non-white households tend, more than others, to move shorter distances, locate in the central city, rent apartments, have fewer rooms and either pay lower rents or own cheaper houses. The worst predictors of movement parameters are age of household head, attitudinal indices of familism, style of consumerism, urban versus suburban orientation, social mobility commitment and the household's attitude about the importance of neighbourhood for social mobility. Yet age and attitude remain important for predicting *why* families move.

The tendency of movers to choose nearby destinations may come from deliberate attempts to maintain geographical familiarity, social contacts and institutional links, or to maintain access to the city as a whole while adjusting housing size or tenure. The decline in the number of destinations with distance, though, suggests that short moves may also reflect imperfections in the housing market, especially since location is relatively unimportant and nearby alternatives are more likely to be evaluated than distant ones. Among the Toronto sample, the average move length was 3.4 miles, the median lay between 2.0 and 2.9 miles, and the modal distance was 0.5 miles. Central city moves were shorter than suburban, and there was a clear tendency for outward movement. Three times as many interviewees wanted to move further from than closer to the C.B.D. The number wanting to move from apartments to single family units was greater than the number wanting the reverse (Barrett, 1973).

In several Minneapolis migration samples for different decades, the 1920s, the 1940s and the 1960s, distributions of the move angles formed by the line drawn from the origin to the C.B.D. and from the origin to the destination approached U-shapes (Figure 5.5). Evidently, during these periods, when downtown orientation was strong households tended to move outward from

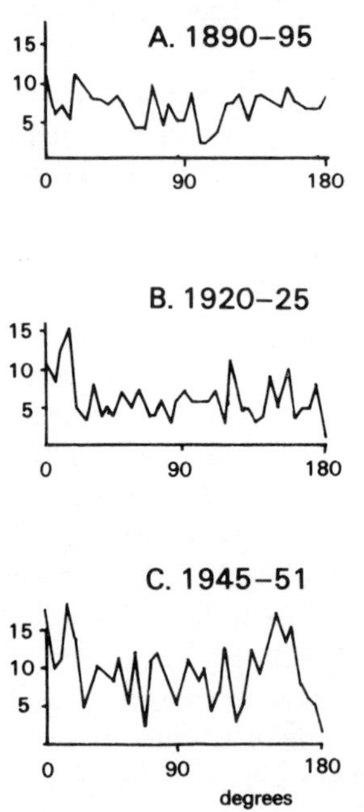

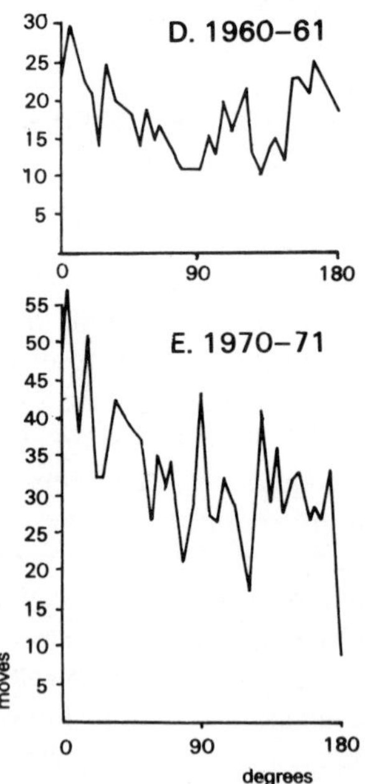

FIGURE 5.5 Distribution of move angles for five Minneapolis area intra-urban migration samples. (Reproduced by permission of Earl A. Nordstrand, 1973, p. 87)

the C.B.D., or inward rather than laterally. Moreover, when people moved outward, they did so gradually in short moves, but moving inward they tended to make radical revisions in their pattern of housing consumption (Adams, 1969).

IMPERFECTIONS IN LOCAL HOUSING MARKETS

The demand side of the housing market is represented by households of various sizes, tastes and levels of prosperity. It resembles the demand side of the market for other commodities. In contrast, the share of the housing stock supplied to the market at any time has three major peculiarities:

1. Most housing units reach the market only when their occupants decide to move. This emphasis on used rather than new housing means the housing market is largely divorced from the housing production industry.
2. Most housing units cannot be purchased separately from their neighbourhood setting or their relative location because they usually are permanently attached to sites.
3. Finally, standardization of housing in the United States and Canada is so rare that units are unique, making comparisons difficult for units of different prices at different locations.

As a consequence of sporadic supply, the complexity of the product and the uniqueness of each housing unit, local housing markets operate quite imperfectly. In-migrants are steered into certain neighbourhoods and away from others. In a Minneapolis study of the previous addresses of the purchasers of new houses, 36 per cent. of those sampled in the higher-income south-west suburbs came from out-of-town, compared to only 9 per cent. of the buyers of identical new houses in the northern working-class and middle-class suburbs (Adams, 1973). Over time, these trends become self-reinforcing. Areas that attract and retain high income newcomers develop reputations attractive to subsequent high income newcomers. Certain real estate firms begin specializing in meeting the needs of the newly arriving business executive or professional person. The firms focus their efforts on a few areas, promoting their qualities while simultaneously diverting attention away from others.

Migrants into an urban area, especially those with high incomes, tend to cluster in areas of new construction. Their high incomes correspond to the typically high prices of new houses. The choice of new rather than used higher priced housing minimizes uncertainty about the neighbourhood future because of the tendency for new construction to occur in areas of previous success (Wyatt and Winger, 1971).

The essential feature of the housing stock in every urban area is its heterogeneity, yet this creates problems for the migrant arriving from another area. Local residents moving within the area know something about the specific community and neighbourhood factors they feel might have a bearing on the range and character of services that will accompany the selection of a specific housing unit. In contrast, the newcomer is restricted to the knowledge of basic characteristics acquired from visual inspection, plus stereotypic neighbourhood information supplied by real estate agents, business associates, plus any friends or relatives. The characteristics of a house itself—its heating system, air conditioning, size, design features, and so forth—are easily examined, and newly constructed units often appear to the newcomer more attractive, less risky and easier to finance than a comparably priced used house. Reliable data on neighbourhood and community factors—the quality of schools and shopping facilities or the degree of neighbourhood stability—are harder to acquire. These items may be as important to the newly arriving household as the housing unit itself, but they usually remain matters about which it has little specific knowledge as it makes its decision about whether to buy. Moreover, in contrast to the comparative advantages a new housing unit often offers over a used house, the standing stock of housing units usually provides comparative advantages in neighbourhood and community services, making the newcomer's choice even harder. On balance, 61 per cent. of the migrants into American metropolitan areas go directly to the suburbs, except for non-whites, 90 per cent. of whom settle in the central city (Butler and coauthors, 1969).

Corrective moves

We can distinguish between 'total displacement migrations', that completely displace a household's daily and weekly reciprocal movement patterns, and 'partial displacement migrations', that displace only part of the everyday reciprocal movements of migrating households. A household transferred to another city makes a total displacement move, and usually uses somewhat inadequate secondhand information from colleagues, advertising media or real estate brokers; a household that moves down the block to a larger house makes a partial displacement move, and can use more reliable firsthand information. Moreover, a household that plans to make a partial displacement move usually has more time for information-gathering and leisurely decision-making. In contrast, an out-of-town household often must search, assemble information and make a housing selection in a matter of days. The choice of a general area and the specific location within it are more likely to be satisfactory with total displacement moves, but dissatisfaction with house or immediate neighbourhood may require a partial displacement move within a short time after a household enters a new area.

In a Minneapolis study, 79 per cent. of 159 old residents of that area who moved during the 1960–70 study period made no subsequent move, but 50 per cent. of the new arrivals moved again the first year and 61 per cent. within three years (Adams and coauthors, 1973). Real estate agents often dismiss large portions of a metropolitan region as unsuitable for the new arrival executive group which makes up the largest proportion of inter-city migrants in the Minneapolis area. The initial dependence of this group on institutional and often self-serving sources of advice lends further support to the argument that follow-up moves are the result of more complete information on the part of the mover, and the ability to choose areas more in line with personal tastes and means. Perhaps follow-up moves are only a conservative indication of the need for adjustment. The pressures of moving, changing schools and arranging financial transactions may limit the number of subsequent moves. Further research on new migrant residential satisfaction would do much to develop this idea. More efficient collection and dissemination of information about housing needs and housing opportunities would enable new arrival households to satisfy their needs more economically and efficiently, and would drastically reduce the volume of fruitless intra-urban migration.

There appears to be a close correlation between the quality of information available to prospective home buyers and their subsequent satisfaction with the choices they have made. Those that use inadequate information sources are more likely to be dissatisfied with their residence because it fails to provide what was implied by initial perceptions. Thus; another move is highly probable.

Vacancy chains

Another view of the housing market examines the creation of housing vacancies and transmission of vacancy chains. Mobile families moving through a geographically fixed, local housing stock is the conventional view of the housing process. Yet the view is complicated by the special preferences of many families. Some couples will move to a larger apartment or to a house when their first child is born, yet others will stay in a small apartment. Some households will translate a job promotion and salary raise into a fancier house, while others will increase outlays for entertainment, clothing or cars. A widow or widower may or may not choose to vacate a large empty house when left to live in it alone.

A complementary view of the local housing process traces the flow of vacancies. Vacancies are created when a new housing unit is built, when an existing unit is subdivided, when a family dies or when a household leaves the old market. When a vacancy at address A is filled by a family moving in from B, the vacancy is transmitted from A to the family's previous address B. The two addresses, A and B, form the first link in the vacancy chain. Address B is vacant until a family moves in from address C. Addresses B and C form the second link in the chain, and so on. The vacancy chain grows outward from the original vacancy, link by link, until the chain ends. A vacancy chain ends when a housing until is demolished, consolidated into another unit, stands permanently vacant or leaves the local housing market area. The length of a vacancy chain, measured by the number of links, determines the amount of local impact created by a new housing unit. If a chain has seven links, seven households were able to acquire housing more suitable to their circumstances at a given time than what they previously occupied.

The location of the links in the chain and the location of the vacancy chain end reveal the extent to which housing construction and other vacancy-creating activities at one location affect housing opportunities for people elsewhere in the local housing market.

In a Minneapolis area study, 303 public housing vacancy chains had an

TABLE 5.12 Vacancy chain lengths for selected public and private housing projects opened for occupancy from 1969 to 1971

Project	Chains	Average length	Chains traced to valid ends	Average length
Public housing for the elderly—St. Paul				
Project A	50	1.6	18	1.9
Project B	47	1.9	29	2.1
Public housing for the elderly—Minneapolis				
Project A	72	1.7	22	2.0
Project B	88	1.6	34	2.0
Project C	46	1.4	13	1.5
Private housing: identical houses at different locations[a]				
Project A	25	2.1	25	2.1
Project B	25	2.1	25	2.1
Other private housing				
Project A—Singles	15	2.5	8	2.9
Project B—Fourplexes	28	2.1	25	2.2
Project C—Townhouses	22	1.6	10	2.0
All public housing	303	1.6	116	2.0
All private housing	115	2.1	93	2.2

[a]Only four of fifty chains reach invalid ends because of incorrect information or non-cooperation. Average lengths are unaffected.
Source. Adams and coauthors, 1973, p. 7.

average length of only 1.6 links. The 116 chains traced to valid ends (demolition, permanent vacancy, incorporation into another unit or move to another city) averaged only 2.0 links (Table 5.12). Vacancy chains from public projects ended in the vicinity of the project. Most chains ended before they could spread much throughout the city and suburbs. The chains were short because the first link, along with most subsequent links, involved the elderly poor and other poor, who are people at or near the bottom of the socioeconomic ladder. Except for public housing units, the units typically used by the poor all along the vacancy chains in the private sector are small apartments, sometimes only one room, of poor quality, rapidly approaching the end of their useful life in the filter-down process and often ready for removal and replacement.

When the elderly poor move into public high-rise apartments, the vacated housing is unattractive to families who can afford better housing. Presumably, there are few families who are worse off financially than the elderly poor who qualify for public-assisted housing. There are few people, therefore, who could 'move up' to the newly evacuated housing. Thus, when new housing is built explicitly for the elderly poor, or other poor for that matter, vacancy chains are short because there is little chance for much household adjustment up to better housing except for the persons who get the new units, unless new housing

TABLE 5.13 Mean length of vacancy chains beginning with owner-occupied and renter-occupied homes for which information is complete

Owner-occupied housing		Renter-occupied housing	
Value	Average chain length	Monthly Rent	Average chain length
Under $15 000	2.2	Under $100	1.7
$15 000–$19 000	2.6	$100–$124	1.9
$20 000–$24 999	3.0	$125–$149	2.0
$25 000–$34 999	3.8	$150–$199	2.7
$35 000 and more	3.3	$200 and more	3.2

Source. Lansing, Clifton and Morgan, 1969, pp. 17, 115.

is built in volumes large enough to cause major price declines. The major consequence when new units are built is that the average quality of housing occupied by the elderly poor rises dramatically.

In contrast to the low-rent, public high-rise projects, the new higher-priced single-family houses and townhouses serve quite a separate portion of the housing market. When expensive housing is built, it is usually occupied either by newcomers to the area, thereby transmitting the vacancy outside the region, or it is occupied by a family that is upgrading its housing consumption. As the vacancy created by an expensive house trickles down, it has much farther to go than does the vacancy from the public units, so observed vacancy chains should be much longer. Lansing, Clifton and Morgan (1969), in studying 3 545 vacancy chains, found that the more expensive the new house, the longer is the average vacancy chain (Table 5.13). Thus, many people can improve their housing indirectly as a result of the construction of a new expensive housing unit, whereas the principal consequence of constructing a new low-priced unit is that the average quality of housing is raised at the tail-end of the housing cycle.

CONCLUSIONS

On the supply side of the housing market, the product differs sharply from all other consumer goods. Some commodities, like crude oil or wheat, move from production areas to markets through international trading. Others move from producer to consumer through national (cars, clothes) or local markets (bread, milk). In the case of the used housing market, there is a market but no market-place: the buyer moves to the product. As a result of product immobility and product heterogeneity, a prospective buyer is constrained by time and distance to examine only a few of the units available, and only a portion of the available stock enters the supply considered by a searching household. That portion is usually located within a limited part or sector of the urban area. Since for a buyer, or group of similar buyers, the housing supply often becomes sector-specific, oversupply in one sector can coexist with undersupply in another.

Upper-income groups, despite the pronounced sectoral bias in their move behaviour, display relatively little directional or distance bias in their *search* for housing, perhaps because they are better equipped to acquire and assimilate more information on available vacancies. Lower-income groups, facing a much longer menu of choices but perhaps lacking the skills or professional assistance needed to acquire and collate market information, show extreme biases in distance and direction so that vacancies are sought and found only nearby in the home sector. In real estate sales, as in other business, the talented and aggressive personnel move to locales where rewards are highest. Those who can handle demanding and discriminating buyers and sellers are usually more eager to sell houses for \$60000 than for \$16000. Thus, the poor expect and get relatively less help from agents than they need in finding a suitable house and in arranging the financing.

When the poor are also non-white or some other disadvantaged minority group, the migration obstacles promoting short moves get augmented through active discrimination by members of the majority in majority neighbourhoods, and by the migrant's reluctance to be a pioneer since it means leaving behind a comfortable presence of friends, relatives and minority neighbours.

The current chaos of an imperfect real estate market might disappear if larger marketing organizations did a better job of matching up buyer needs with available housing units. A. Richard Immel (1974) outlined a current proposal for reorganizing the housing market for inter-city as well as intra-urban migrants:

> A homeowner is transferred to another city. But instead of calling up his local real estate agent, his Sears store handles the deal in one package: sale of his house, arrangements to purchase a new one through the real estate department in a Sears store somewhere else, escrow services, title search, home insurance, perhaps a mortgage and even some furnishings that will probably be needed in the new house. Besides the convenience of one-stop shopping, the homeowner will pay no more and possibly less than he would have if separate firms had handled each part of the deal.

Current planning emphasizes the increasingly lucrative corporate–personnel transfer market for real estate, but once large marketing networks are installed they could work just as well for the intra-urban mover, providing a large package of more satisfactory services at a significantly lower cost.

The question raised at the outset was whether by knowing the characteristics of a mover and his origins, we can predict his destination, or vice versa. The findings that were presented come from a relatively short period of research, and encompass a restricted set of social characteristics of households and physical characteristics of housing. The regularities observed to date will change over time as the number of household heads increases relative to the total population, and as the household formation rate rises—both trends indicated by recent United States census figures. Who moves and where they go will also be affected by the location and type of newly constructed units, for example single-family detached houses versus apartment houses, town-houses and condominiums. Yet as parts of newly built-up areas age and change their residential composition, they will generate significantly different origin and destination fields.

Intra-urban mobility decisions are constrained by financial institutions, and to a lesser extent by planners. At any instant, there are more households in the market uncommitted to move but desiring to do so than there are those committed to move. Hence, mobility decisions and their consequences remain especially vulnerable to particular public and private influences on the variables affecting the decision to move.

REFERENCES

Adams, J. S. (1969). 'Directional bias in intra-urban migration'. *Economic Geography*, **45**, 302–323.

Adams, J. S. (1970). 'Residential structure of midwestern cities'. *Annals, Association of American Geographers*, **60**, 37–62.

Adams, J. S. (1973). *New Homes, Vacancy Chains, and Housing Submarkets in the Twin City Area*, Center for Urban and Regional Affairs, University of Minnesota, Minneapolis.

Adams, J. S., Caruso, D. J., Nordstrand, E. A., and Palm, R. (1973). 'Intraurban migration. Commentary'. *Annals, Association of American Geographers*, **63**, 152–155.

Barrett, Frank A. (1973). *Residential Search Behavior: A Study of Intra-urban Relocation in Toronto*, Geographical Monographs No. 1, York University, Atkinson College, Toronto.

Bell, W. (1958). 'Social choice, life styles and suburban residence'. In W. Dobriner (Ed.), *The Suburban Community*, George Putnam, New York, pp. 225–247.

Berry, B. J. L., and Rees, P. H. (1969). 'The factorial ecology of Calcutta'. *American Journal of Sociology*, **74**, 445–491.

Brown, L. A. (1971). 'Intra-urban migrant lifelines: a spatial view'. *Demography*, **8**, 103–122.

Brown, L. A., and Holmes, J. (1970). *Search Behavior in an Intra-urban Migration Context: A Spatial Perspective*, Discussion Paper No. 13, Department of Geography, Ohio State University.

Brown, L. A., and Longbrake, D. (1970). 'Migration flows in intra-urban space: place utility considerations'. *Annals, Association of American Geographers*, **60**, 368–384.

Brown, L. A., and Moore, E. G. (1970). 'Intra-urban migration: an actor oriented framework' *Geografiska Annaler*, **52B**, 1–13.

Butler, Edgar W., Chapin, F. Stuart Jr., Hemmens, G. C., Kaiser, E. J., Stegman, M. A., and Weiss, S. F. (1969). *Moving Behavior and Residential Choice: A National Survey*, National Cooperative Highway Research Program Report No. 81, Highway Research Board, Washington.

Clark, W. A. V. (1970). 'Measurement and explanation in intra-urban residential mobility'. *Tijdschrift voor Economische–Sociale Geografie*, **61**, 49–57.

Clark, W. A. V. (1972). 'Behaviour and the constraints of spatial structure'. *New Zealand Geographer*, **28**, 171–180.

Greer-Wootten, Bryn, and Gilmour, G. M., (1972). 'Distance and directional bias in migration patterns in depreciating metropolitan areas'. *Geographical Analysis*, **4**, 92–97.

Haggerty, Lee J. (1971). 'Another look at the Burgess hypothesis: time as an important variable'. *American Journal of Sociology*, **76**, 1084–1093.

Herbert, D. T. (1973a). 'The residential mobility process: some empirical observations'. *Area*, **5**, 44–48.

Herbert, D. T. (1973b). 'Residential mobility and preference: a study of Swansea'. In B. D. Clark and M. B. Gleave (Eds.), *Social Patterns in Cities*, Special Publication No. 5, Institute of British Geographers, London, pp. 103–121.

Immel, A. Richard. (1974). 'Real estate brokers increasingly abandon independent status'. *New York Times*, 23, July, 1974, 1ff.

Johnston, R. J. (1969a). 'Population movements and metropolitan expansion: London, 1960–61'. *Transactions, Institute of British Geographers*, **46**, 69–91.

Johnston R. J. (1969b). 'Processes of change in the high status residential areas of Christchurch, 1951–64'. *New Zealand Geographer*, **25**, 1–15.

Johnston, R. J. (1969c). 'Some tests of a model of intra-urban population mobility: Melbourne, Australia'. *Urban Studies*, **6**, 34–47.

Lansing, J. B., Clifton, C. V., and Morgan, J. N. (1969). *New Homes and Poor People: A Study of Chains of Moves*, Institute for Social Research, University of Michigan, Ann Arbor.

Moore, Eric G. (1972). *Residential Mobility in the City*, Commission on College Geography Resource Paper No. 13, Association of American Geographers, Washington, D. C.

Morgan, Barrie S. (1973). 'Why families move: a re-examination'. *Professional Geographer*, **25**, 124–129.

Nordstrand, Earl Alan (1973). *Relationships Between Intraurban Migration and Urban Residential Social Structure*, M. A. Thesis, University of Minnesota, Minneapolis.

Rossi, P. H. (1955). *Why Families Move*, The Free Press, Glencoe, Illinois.

Sanders, Ralph A. (1974). *Bilevel Effects in Urban Residential Ecology*. Ph.D. Dissertation, Department of Geography, University of Minnesota, Minneapolis.

Simmons, J. W. (1968). 'Changing residence in the city: a review of intra-urban mobility'. *Geographical Review*, **58**, 621–651.

Wyatt, G. L., and Winger, A. R. (1971). 'Residential construction, mover origin, and urban form'. *Regional Studies*, **6**, 95–99.

Chapter 6

Residential Area Characteristics: Research Methods for Identifying Urban Sub-areas–Social Area Analysis and Factorial Ecology

R. J. Johnston

The preceding chapters have discussed the mechanisms by which people and households either choose or are allocated to residential areas within a city, a series of individual and corporate decisions which collectively produce the urban mosaic. If these mechanisms were deterministic, a clearly segmented map would ensue. Unfortunately for the analyst, this simple situation does not exist; although neighbourhood differences can be observed in most cities, so too can overlaps and deviant cases. Thus, the study of social areas, both as descriptive mapping and as preparation for predictive analyses, requires a methodology which will unravel the complexities of spatial differentiation between and within districts. The present chapter reviews those methodologies which have been, and are still being, used.

Many reasons can be proposed for the failure of location/allocation mechanisms to produce patterns of complete separation of various socioeconomic, demographic and housing groups. The first rests on their lack of deterministic power; because some residents, at least, have a degree of freedom of choice of where to live, there is a possibility either of 'irrational' behaviour or of individuals basing their location decisions on attitudes and values which are not consonant with those of the social group(s) to which they belong. Secondly, the various mechanisms are not independent, but they may vary in their relative effect. Nor are the various groupings within society independent; most people are members of several (socioeconomic, demographic, ethnic, life-style, etc.) and may differ as to which group's norms they rate most highly when choosing where to live. Thirdly, and following from this, the social groups which we identify rarely have precise boundaries. In residential choices, there are some groups with clearly defined limits, as in societies where there is a maximum income above which no householder will be allotted a publicly-owned or -financed home. But most group boundaries are ill-defined, resulting in overlapping residential patterns—as noted in Chicago (Duncan, 1956;

Duncan and Duncan, 1955). Finally, individuals, households, areas, cities themselves—all are continually changing, the first two in their characteristics and attitudes, the second two in their attributes and forms. Change may be sudden, but is usually slow, in which case observation at one time may view different areas at different states and rates of change.

All of these factors suggest that the residential mosaic of a city, especially one with considerable freedom of choice for at least some individuals and reliant on market operations for its form, will be far from clear-cut in its patterns. This is why methodologies are needed for its description and analysis and why it is a challenging field for researchers. The problem is invariably compounded, however, by the data which are available for such investigation, and since in this, as in many large-scale research areas, methodology is so dependent on data, discussion of information sources is a prerequisite for this chapter.

THE DATA OF URBAN SUB-AREAL STUDY

The average town, let alone a city, is too large for researchers with relatively limited resources to allow collection of specific data for a study of the residential mosaic. There are, of course, exceptions to this, the classic being Charles Booth's mammoth survey of London at the end of the nineteenth century (Booth, 1889–1902; Pfautz, 1967). Others have sampled households, perhaps as part of a data collection exercise by or for a planning agency (Forrest and Tan, 1971), many of whom have developed massive data banks to support their operations. Data on individual properties may be obtained from such sources as property tax rolls in several countries (Davies, Giggs and Herbert, 1968; Forrest, 1968), but these deal only with 'impersonal' measures. If the researcher is unable to design and conduct his own surveys, he must rely on those operated by others. He then confronts the confidentiality problem; many such sources are made available only when they are irrelevant to living persons, as with the release of British census enumerators' books a century after their collection (Lawton, 1955). Thus it is that research in urban historical geography has been based on some of the most detailed data (Doucet, 1972; Goheen, 1970; Ward, 1969), though the advantages that these bring are often counterbalanced by the tedium involved in their collection.

Most students of the residential mosaic who are interested in its general patterning rely, often exclusively, on decennial and quinquennial censuses for their data. They are thus dependent on the policy of the collecting bodies—invariably government departments—regarding the nature and quality of those data. Two major aspects of this reliance, which very much influence the methodology applied, concern the questions asked, plus the variables tabulated from them, and the areas for which tabulations are produced.

Censuses are objective counts, their origins being in tax-gathering exercises (Glass, 1973). They aim to record the number of people in a place at a given moment, but they also collect information on resident and dwelling characteristics which are relevant to their sponsor, to bodies allied with this sponsor (such as local governments) and perhaps also to other bodies who can influence the census-takers in their choice of questions. A census questionnaire must be simple and easy to answer, as well as easy to administer, requirements which are increasing in importance with the trend towards self-enumeration. Questions must be straightforward, perhaps requiring only a multiple-choice answer. They can record income and occupation, which are 'objective indices', but not socio-economic status, which involves attitudes; age and household structure can be recorded, but not life-style or activity patterns. Thus, the researcher is constrained to variables which can be construed as indices of the constructs he investigates. Often the data provide poor surrogates, because what he considers to be necessary questions are not asked. Many census authorities have been wary of asking for information on 'touchy' subjects; income has been one of these and religion another (not asked in Britain since 1851, for example). In addition, information is rarely collected which is relevant to studies of housing markets.

Censuses are confidential documents; their publications refer to population aggregates only. As well as national totals, almost all publish at least some tabulations by areal subdividisons. The constitution of these reflects two constraints: the responsibility of the census to provide information for sub-national territories, such as local government areas, and ease of administration. The latter concerns the actual census-taking. Most censuses employ enumerators, who distribute and collect the questionnaires in a defined area, demarcated for logistic convenience. Such enumerators', or collectors', districts form the basic building blocks. Data are too numerous to be published at this level, though they can usually be purchased, often in machine-readable form.

Together, these two constraints produce the basic areal mesh of census districts. This is hierarchical, since the enumerators' districts must have common boundaries with local government areas. (The hierarchical structure may be a severe constraint if there are overlapping independent areas—such as political constituencies and local governments—for which data must be provided.) The value of such data varies from place to place, from census to census. Often the design of enumerators' districts pays no heed to the social pattern on the ground, producing a set of areas whose analysis suggests spatial heterogeneity, perhaps only as a result of boundary locations. Census authorities vary in the extent to which they work with local interests to produce a 'relevant' set of areas. The United States censuses are exemplary in this way, for they have designed special areas, at all scales, such as census tracts, urbanized areas and standard metropolitan statistical areas, to assist users of their material in the portrayal of spatial realities. (Of course, these spatial realities change, and often the areas lag behind in accommodating these changes; see Berry, Goheen and Goldstein, 1968, and Guest and Zuiches, 1972. They sometimes lag in the information they tabulate; there are several large ethnic groups in Toronto, for example, for which no detailed areal breakdown is provided.) By way of contrast, the British census has traditionally offered much less to the researcher (see Hall and coauthors, 1973). A final parameter of a census of relevance here is its representativeness. Some censuses ask all of their questions of every household and resident (e.g. Australia and New Zealand); others ask a basic set of questions of all, but a more detailed set of only a sample (such as the 10 per cent. which is the basis of many detailed tabulations in the British census); some collect information from all, but then only tabulate it for a sample. Often such samples are so small that their standard errors are very large for small-area data, with consequent confounding effects on areal analyses.

Most research on urban residential mosaics is, and must be, based on census material, therefore. In this way, its philosophy, its methodology and its results are all subject to external decisions concerning the nature and the quality of the data. Since such research concerns areal characteristics—amalgamations of individuals—the pattern of such areas, their size, shape and relevance to other features (and the variance of all of these) all very much affect the input–output matrix of such investigations. It is in this light that their procedures and findings must be assessed.

SOCIAL AREA ANALYSIS

Early studies of social patterns within cities were limited by both data paucity and technical ability to handle the available information. Thus Burgess' pioneer studies of Chicago in the 1920s were based on single-variable maps (see Burgess and Bogue, 1967, p. 6) and verbal comparisons of maps and 'gradients' (Burgess, 1927). By the 1940s, the more detailed census tract data available in the United States were being employed in relatively sophisticated mapping of 'natural areas' (Hatt, 1946), an exercise which was the prelude to the development of a 'census-tract-based methodology'.

The 'theory'

The breakthrough was made by three interrelated groups of researchers at universities in the three main cities—Los Angeles, San Francisco, Seattle—on the United States' West Coast. Characteristics of all three included a concern for theory, rather than description as a prelude to practice which typified the Chicago approach; a focus on *areas* as aggregates of individuals, rather than on individuals within areas; and the development of multivariate analyses.

The initial statement, a monograph (Shevky and Williams, 1949), was an empirical presentation of census tract differences in the metropolitan area of Los Angeles. Three indices of tract characteristics were derived: social rank, urbanization and segregation. Reviewers pointed out the lack of any theoretical rationale for the selection of these three—the work was judged a novel method for using census tract data to display areal differentiation in selected population and dwelling characteristics.

Following the Los Angeles study, the methods were refined for a similar investigation of San Francisco (Bell, 1953), after which the Los Angeles data were reworked. In 1955, the basic statement on the method was published

(Shevky and Bell, 1955). In this, social area analysis is presented as part of an apparently deductive model of social change, based on a concept of increasing scale or interdependence (Wilson and Wilson, 1945), on Colin Clark's (1940) observations concerning the division of labour in a society and on Louis Wirth's (1938) classic deductions of the relationships between population concentration and social forms. (Note, however, a later admission by Bell and Moskos (1964), that the theory was an *ex post facto* rationalization of the earlier empirical work.)

Shevky and Bell's model (Figure 6.1) is based on three postulated major trends of industrial societies: changes in the range and intensity of relations, differentiation of function and complexity of organization. Operational measures of these trends are then listed—for the first, changing intersectoral division of labour; for the second, the declining role of the household as an economic unit; and for the third, greater population mobility and concentration. From these are derived the three basic constructs of increasing scale: social rank, urbanization and segregation. (These were Shevky's terms; as made clear in an appendix, Bell preferred economic status, family status and ethnic status.) A range of possible variables indexing these constructs was provided, from which seven were selected—three each for the first two and one for the third. (The third index for social rank—rent—was later omitted because of the influence of rent controls.) Choice of these variables has been criticized (e.g. by Udry, 1964, who claims that the trends Shevky and Bell describe were not typical of the United States over previous decades). Further, as will be suggested in a later section, selection of the variables to represent urbanization provided a set poorly related either to the general trends or to the sample statistics.

Several strong attacks were launched by reviewers against this theory and its application. Shevky and Bell (1955, p. 20) had defined social areas as 'containing persons with similar social positions in the larger society', but, as Hawley and Duncan (1957) argued in the most detailed critique, there is no way of relating social differentiation, which is a product of increasing scale, with spatial differentiation at the census tract level. Shevky and Bell (1955, p. 20) may argue that:

> The social area ... is not bounded by the geographical frame of reference as is the natural area, nor by implications concerning the degree of interaction between persons in the local community as is the subculture. We do claim, however, that the social area generally contains persons having the same level of living, the same way of life, and the same ethnic background; and we hypothesize that persons living in a particular type of social area would systematically differ with respect to characteristic attitudes and behaviours from persons living in another type of social area.

Their methods might, within the bounds of census tract data (on which Hawley and Duncan are sceptical, although Duncan—Duncan and Duncan, 1955—was using them for somewhat similar descriptive purposes at the same time),

Postulates concerning industrial society (aspects of increasing scale) (1)	Statistics of of trends (2)	Changes in the structure of a given social system (3)	Constructs) (4)	Sample statistics related to the constructs) (5)	Derived measures (from column 5) (6)	
Change in the range and intensity of relations →	Changing distribution of skills: → Lessening importance of manual productive operations; growing importance of clerical, supervisory, management operations	Changes in the arrangement of occupations based on function →	Social rank (economic status) →	Years of schooling → Employment status Class of worker Major occupation group Value of home Rent by dwelling unit Plumbing and repair Persons per room Heating and refrigeration	Occupation Schooling Rent	Index I
Differentiation of function →	Changing structure of productive activity: → Lessening importance of primary production growing importance of relations centred in cities; lessening importance of the household as an economic unit	Changes in the ways of living; movement of women into urban occupations; spread of alternative family patterns →	Urbanization (family status) →	Age and sex Owner or tenant → House structure House structure Persons in household	Fertility Women at work Single-family dwelling units	Index II
Complexity of organization →	Changing composition of population: → increasing movement; alterations in age and sex distribution; increasing diversity	Redistribution in space; changes in the proportion of supporting and dependent population; isolation and segregation of groups →	Segregation (ethnic status) →	Race and nativity → Country of birth Citizenship	Racial and national groups in relative isolation	Index III

FIGURE 6.1 The Shevky-Bell theory of increasing scale and it's relationship to index construction (Reprinted with permission of Stanford University Press, from *Social Area Analysis: Theory, Illustrative Application and Computational Procedures* by Eshref Shevky and Wendell Bell, 1955, Figure IV, p. 26)

show differences between the residents of different areas, and their field studies may indicate the hypothesized attitude and behaviour differences (Bell, 1969; Bell and Boat, 1957; Bell and Force, 1956a, 1956b, 1957; but see Palm, 1973a), but nowhere do they suggest the mechanisms by which the different groups are propelled to, or choose, their allotted social areas. As Jones (1969, pp. 18–21) has observed, Shevky and Bell's model is better suited to inter-urban studies, of places at different levels of increasing scale, than to intra-urban investigation. It has been left to later theorists (reviewed in preceding chapters of this book) to suggest the relevance of Shevky and Bell's indices, if not their theory, to intra-urban areal differentiation.

While other scholars have been reviewing, testing and sophisticating Shevky and Bell's methods, McElrath (1965, 1968) has revised the theory. He replaces the master trends by two major interrelated processes of social change, industrialization and urbanization (Johnston, 1973a). The former produces the changing intersectoral and interpersonal divisions of labour covered by the social rank and urbanization constructs; the latter produces population aggregation (migrant status) and a greater spatial hinterland for metropolitan growth which brings visible minorities to the cities (ethnic status).

The method

Social areas are defined according to the three-dimensional space of the Shevky–Bell model. For each dimension, a standardized index ranging from zero to one hundred is defined as an unweighted average of similar standardized scores for each of the relevant variables. The standardized score for a tract on a variable is

$$S_t = X(r_t - 0) \tag{6.1}$$

where 0 = the lowest value of the variable over all census tracts
r_t = the variable for tract t
X = 100 divided by the range for the variable
S_t = the score for tract t

Each variable set (in all cases a vector of ratios, e.g. the proportion of the population aged 25 and over who had no more than eight years' schooling) is ordered so that within any one construct, a high value on one variable has the same status connotation as a high variable on another. The final index is simply

$$I_t = \Sigma S_t / n \tag{6.2}$$

where S_t = the score as defined in equation (6.1)
n = the number of variables forming the index
I_t = the index for tract t

In the Los Angeles study, eighteen social area types were defined. The social rank and urbanization indices for the universe of tracts were plotted against each other. The social rank indices were then trichotomized, using the thirds of the range of values as the inner boundaries; and the urbanization indices

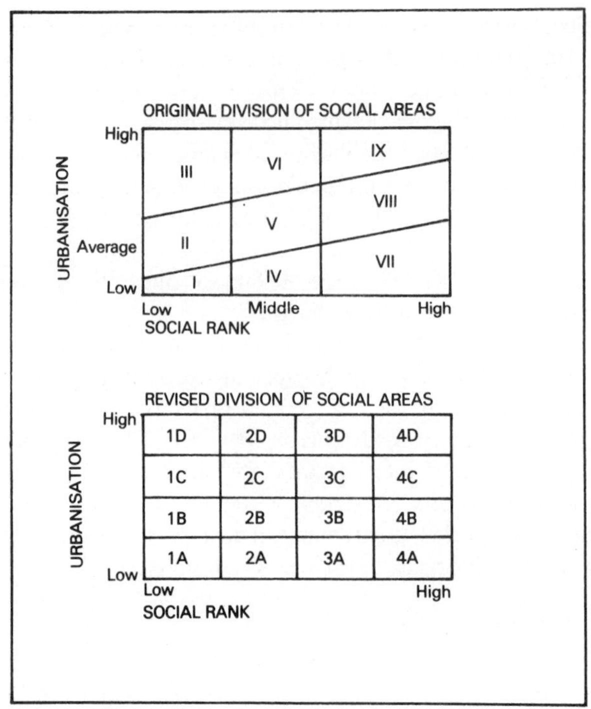

FIGURE 6.2 The Social Area Classification Schemes (Reprinted with permission of Stanford University Press, from *Social Area Analysis: Theory, Illustrative Application and Computational Procedures* by Eshref Shevky and Wendell Bell, 1955, Table II. I, p. 4)

were trichotomized using the area within $\pm$ 2 standard errors of the regression line of social rank on urbanization to define the average, with high and low beyond these. The resulting nine-cell social space (Figure 6.2) was further dichotomized into areas of high and low indices of segregation. For the 1955 monograph, the procedure was simplified, replacing the regression approach—variable between cities in its slope, and also (not noted by Shevky and Bell) in whether urbanization or social rank is used as the independent variable—by a standardized fourfold division of each variable, using index values of 25, 50 and 75 as the boundaries. The resulting sixteen cells (Figure 6.2) are further subdivided into low and high segregation tracts, with the percentage of the total population of the relevant urban area in the designated ethnic groups as the dividing line: thirty-two cells ensue as the major social areas.

The procedure adopted by Shevky and Bell as a standard, and presumably generally applicable, method is not problem-free. As Bell notes in his factor analyses of the same data sets, the constructs are related, especially social rank and segregation. If these relationships vary, by time and place, comparative study of social areas defined by the standard diagram will be impeded (as it will also by the use of local averages, especially in the segregation index). Such problems are likely to be especially acute in applying the method in other societies, as Herbert (1967) discovered in his work on Newcastle-under-Lyme. (Extra problems may have been introduced there by the use of only one urban unit of a larger conurbation.) Within the monograph, however, the use of only Los Angeles and San Francisco as examples, especially the latter, restricts the recognition of these possible problems; there is no reference, either, to Bell's (1955) factor analyses, which suggests that the manuscript for the monograph was completed several years before its publication. Discussion concentrates on the social space, on its constituent variables and on relationships with others, notably referring to age and sex composition. The social areas of San Francisco are mapped, but this pattern is covered in only ten lines of the 68-page text.

Use, developments, critiques

Perhaps because of the initial debate on its value, the Shevky-Bell methodology has not been widely used. In the United States, several 'disciples', notably Greer and McElrath, employed the procedures (see the list in Bell, 1969), but Timms' (1971, pp. 150–151) listing shows only seven social area analyses conducted in other countries (a later addition is Parkes, 1972). In part, this represents a time-and-space lag in diffusion, but more importantly it reflects the later availability of census tract or equivalent data in other countries, which availability coincided with the rapid worldwide spread of high-speed computer hardware plus the software for the factorial ecology method discussed in the next section.

As already noted, one of the initial criticisms of Shevky and Bell's methodology was its 'theoretical' base, the imposition of the three-dimensional social area framework. Yet parallel to their work, Tryon's (1955) cluster analysis of the San Francisco tract data produced an empirical set of dimensions very similar to Shevky and Bell's. This may be taken as indicative of the validity of the latter's procedure, irrespective of its relationship to their general theory, but it may be interpreted more sceptically as showing that both studies—separately or in consultation—exhausted the main possibilities of the available census data.

The Seattle group of researchers, headed by Schmid, initially followed a different line, being more concerned with the interrelationships among a wider set of variables over the universe of census tracts, and with changes over time, than in the characteristics of areas *per se* (Schmid, 1950; Schmid, MacConnell and van Arsdol, 1958). In this, their work was closer to the Michigan–Chicago-based investigations of intra-urban spatial differentiation, although the latter used a simpler, statistically less-demanding index (Duncan and Duncan, 1955). But the Seattle group were attracted to social area analysis, both for the particular purpose of Schmid's (1960) crime area study and 'to determine by empirical research whether or not Shevky's scheme might possess distinctive features as well as indicate a compelling persistence and a pragmatic value' (van Arsdol,

Camilleri and Schmid, 1962, p. 10). This was done by replicating Bell's factor analyses (see below), on a sample of ten medium-sized cities. The aims of these analyses were (a) to see whether the three Shevky-Bell dimensions were separate indices of areal differences and (b) to see whether the individual variables were closely related to the relevant dimension of the theory. Bell's (1955) work provided strong support for the dimensional model; the Seattle workers discovered some variations which were explicable in terms of the different social environments of the sample cities (van Arsdol, Camilleri and Schmid, 1958a, 1958b). However, they then argued (van Arsdol, Camilleri and Schmid, 1961, p. 27) that 'Despite the theoretical difficulties, the case for social area analysis would be strengthened if it could be shown that empirical advantages are obtained by combining the six traditional census tract measures into composite indexes and types', which they investigated by relating both the indices and their constituent variables to measures of spatial stability and age structure. The variables performed better than the indices; the pragmatic value of the latter was disclaimed, despite contrary arguments that high-level generalizations are not meant to predict specific patterns (van Arsdol, Camilleri and Schmid, 1962; Bell and Greer, 1962).

FACTORIAL ECOLOGY

As a research procedure, social area analysis has virtually disappeared. In large part, it has been made redundant by technological advances, which have brought with them a greater concern for inductive theory, based on empirical results, as opposed to deductive formulations (though the pedigree of social area analysis as a deductive theory remains in doubt). Social area analysis has received a fairly detailed review here, however, both because it has provided the general framework within which most recent studies of intra-urban residential mosaics have been set and because the later, factor analysis-based studies of its dimensions heralded the application of that body of techniques to social area investigations.

Factorial ecology described

The term factorial ecology was coined by Sweetser (1965a, 1965b) 'as a model for ecological structure, . . . the method par excellence for comparing cross-nationally (and intra-nationally) the ecological differentiation of residential areas in urban and metropolitan communities' (Sweetser, 1965a, p. 219). He was not the first to use this method, Bell (1955) having preceded him by at least a decade, followed by the van Arsdol and coauthors' studies, by Anderson and Bean's (1961) Toledo investigation, and by Schmid (1960), Gittus (1964) and Jones (1965), among others. Sweetser's term was rapidly adopted by other researchers, most notably at the University of Chicago's Center for Urban Studies, as collective description of all studies applying the techniques of factor analysis to the study of areal differentiation. It thus can be applied to any spatial scale and any set of characteristics, not exclusively to intra-urban population and housing patterns, but it is commonly applied only to studies of the type discussed here.

A more detailed definition of factorial ecology than given by Sweetser is provided by Berry (1971). The term ecology, he claims, indicates that the research focus is a system of component parts (census tracts or their equivalents) which interact among themselves and with their environment. Interest is in the variance between the components only; variability within tracts is ignored. Factorial ecology asks (Berry, 1971, p. 215): '"How does the system cohere and pattern?" The answer is sought by trying to identify repetitive sequences of spatial variation present in many observable attributes of areas'. Factor analysis methods are used in the answer.

The methods of factorial ecology have been applied widely in the last decade to cities in every continent (Rees, 1972, gives perhaps the most comprehensive, recent catalogue). As with many innovations, it developed something of a bandwagon effect, with many somewhat 'unthinking' replications applied to whatever data were available. Not surprisingly, this flood of studies has been followed by retrenchment and rethinking. Nevertheless, factorial ecology demonstrably offers a widely accepted approach to identification of underlying determinants of intra-urban residential patterns, as well as providing series of indices of value for further study of ecologies; hence its preeminence in this chapter.

The procedures of factorial ecology

The set of procedures and operations which comprise a factorial ecology is outlined in Figure 6.3; Table 6.1 and Figures 6.4 to 6.6 provide an example of these, for the Whangarei (population 34 029) urban area, New Zealand, in 1971. Some of the stages are standard parts of the process and are indicated thus in the diagram; others are only included where either necessary or desired.

The first stage, assembly of the data matrix, is straightforward, although, as indicated later, some technical and interpretative problems may arise from the selection of variables. In the Whangarei example, eight variables were selected—four ($X_1 - X_4$) representing the Shevky–Bell family status construct, three (X_5–X_7) representing economic status and one (X_8) for ethnic status. According to Bell's (1955) hypothesis, these should cluster on three separate dimensions in a factor or component solution. Stage Ia, data transformation, is not always employed. Since principal components and factor analyses usually operate on matrices of product moment correlations, the data should meet the requirements of those correlations, especially those relating to *linearity* of relationships (Poole and O'Farrell, 1971, succinctly list these; some are not relevant if description is the aim of the analysis, as against inference to a population from a sample). With the Whangarei data, inspection of frequency distributions (Figure 6.4) indicated positive skewness for variables X_3, X_7 and X_8, and these were transformed to base ten logarithms, giving approximate normal

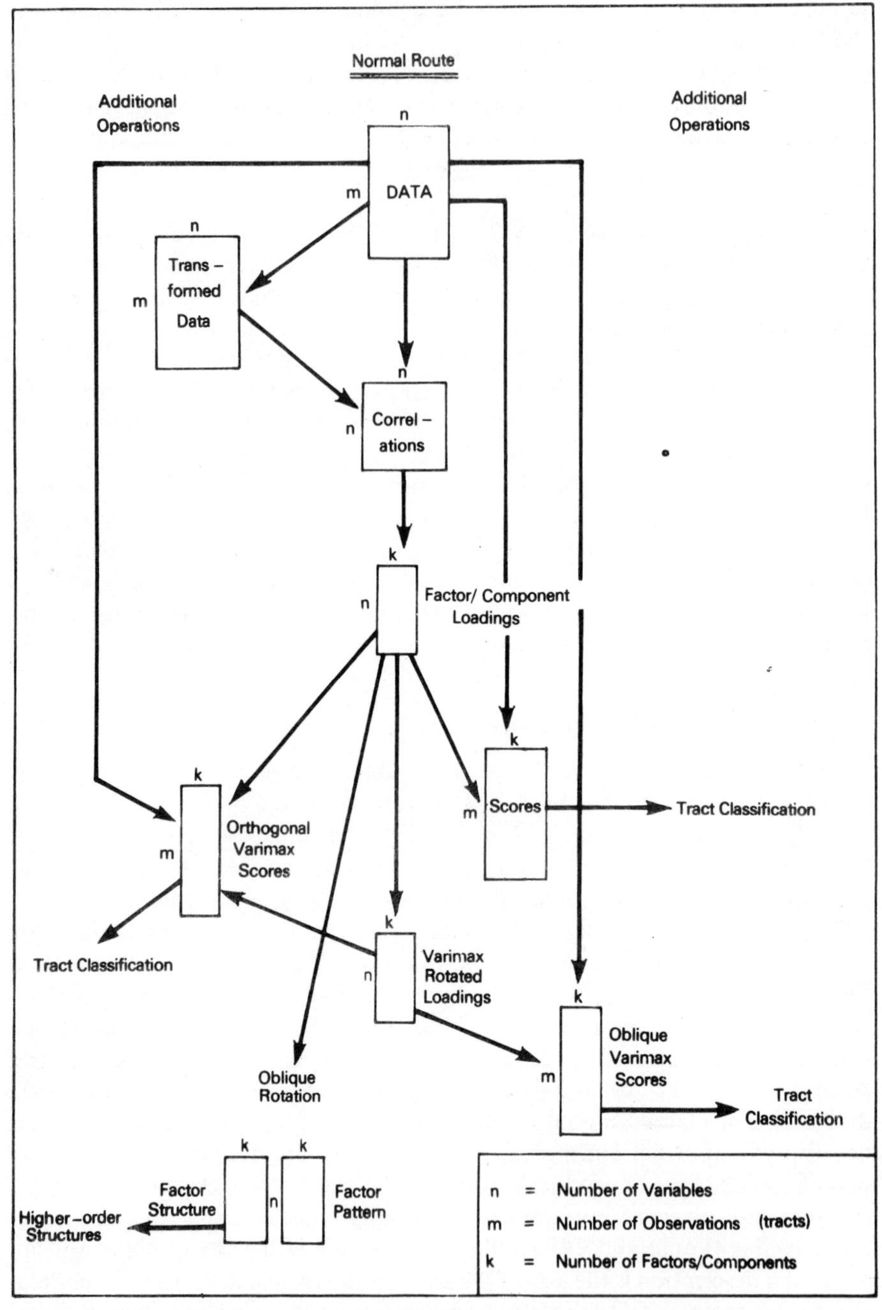

FIGURE 6.3 Flow diagram of the procedures involved in the factorial ecology method

TABLE 6.1 Whangarei, New Zealand, 1971 A Factorial Ecology

Variables
X_1 Proportion of those aged 16 + not married
X_2 Proportion of households that are one-family households
X_3 Proportion of dwellings that are flats
X_4 Proportion of dwellings that are rented
X_5 Proportion of male workers in professional/managerial occupations
X_6 Proportion of male workers earning $6 000 + per annum
X_7 Proportion of male workers with a university degree
X_8 Proportion of population who are Maori

A. Original data

District	X_1	X_2	X_3	X_4	X_5	X_6	X_7	X_8
1	0.18	.79	.07	.14	.17	.07	.04	.12
2	0.12	.83	.05	.15	.10	.04	.02	.12
3	.17	.72	.11	.24	.19	.15	.06	.03
4	.23	.67	.13	.54	.08	.02	.02	.39
5	.21	.76	.04	.16	.16	.02	.02	.03
6	.20	.66	.16	.32	.14	.05	.03	.07
7	.20	.59	.16	.26	.14	.06	.03	.03
8	.29	.55	.32	.37	.21	.11	.07	.04
9	.24	.66	.16	.27	.12	.06	.02	.08
10	.33	.59	.21	.35	.21	.04	.02	.12
11	.40	.48	.34	.64	.13	.06	.06	.09
12	.18	.69	.08	.21	.21	.07	.01	.09
13	.31	.70	.23	.35	.16	.08	.09	.15
14	.16	.83	.03	.17	.15	.08	.04	.06
15	.16	.78	.06	.24	.06	.02	.01	.23
16	.20	.73	.08	.21	.08	.04	.01	.11
17	.17	.81	.03	.13	.16	.08	.02	.09
18	.08	.84	.01	.08	.19	.07	.07	.04
19	.16	.74	.00	.67	.06	.00	.00	.68
20	.16	.80	.02	.09	.14	.06	.06	.12
21	.17	.74	.00	.13	.13	.06	.06	.13
22	.20	.77	.00	.19	.08	.03	.03	.20

B. Product moment correlations

	X_1	X_2	X_3	X_4	X_5	X_6	X_7	X_8
X_1	1.00							
X_2	−0.84	1.00						
X_3	0.57	−.61	1.00					
X_4	0.60	−.66	.15	1.00				
X_5	0.01	−.09	.36	−.34	1.00			
X_6	0.04	−.10	.40	−.26	.77	1.00		
X_7	0.29	−.22	.61	−.30	.67	.71	1.00	
X_8	0.02	.15	−.42	.45	−.75	−.64	−.67	1.00

C. Unrotated component solution

Variable	Component I	Component II	Component III	Communality
X_1	.36	.85	−.06	.87
X_2	−.41	−.85	−.07	.90
X_3	.73	.44	−.37	.85
X_4	.19	.88	.36	.93
X_5	.82	−.33	.32	.88
X_6	.82	−.26	−.35	.86
X_7	.89	−.10	−.19	.84
X_8	−.81	.33	.06	.77
Eigenvalues	3.67	2.70	0.53	
Cumulative % of variance	45.88	79.66	86.33	

D. Unrotated component scores

District	Component I	Component II	Component III	District	Component I	Component II	Component III
1	0.29	−0.73	−0.14	12	0.39	−0.33	1.03
2	−0.62	−0.79	−1.24	13	0.81	0.70	−0.13
3	1.50	−0.79	1.67	14	0.28	−1.04	0.27
4	−0.88	1.42	−0.36	15	−1.30	0.04	−1.38
5	0.12	−0.49	−0.90	16	−0.59	0.14	−1.40
6	0.30	0.32	0.46	17	0.09	−1.01	0.57
7	0.78	0.28	−0.44	18	0.38	−1.88	0.48
8	1.85	0.72	1.24	19	−2.85	0.89	2.76
9	0.20	0.43	−0.55	20	−0.19	−0.91	−0.39
10	0.22	1.39	−0.85	21	−0.14	−0.57	−0.41
11	0.89	2.61	0.23	22	−1.50	−0.38	0.42

E. Varimax—rotated component solution

Variable	Component I	Component II	Component III
X_1	−0.01	.87	−.33
X_2	−.10	−.91	.24
X_3	.30	.49	−.73
X_4	−.27	.87	.31
X_5	.93	−.04	−.11
X_6	.92	.03	−.09
X_7	.68	.06	−.60
X_8	−.76	.14	.43
Sum of squared component loadings	2.93	2.60	1.37
Trace (%)	34.12	69.12	86.25

F. Varimax—rotated component scores

District	Oblique I	Oblique II	Oblique III	Orthogonal I	Orthogonal II	Orthogonal III
1	0.41	−0.60	−0.76	0.42	−0.66	−0.20
2	−0.41	−0.99	1.53	−0.82	−1.18	−0.67
3	1.54	−0.20	−3.41	2.27	0.00	0.74
4	−1.10	1.04	2.04	−1.37	1.04	−0.00
5	0.16	−0.47	−0.93	−0.15	−0.66	−0.78
6	0.14	0.37	−1.60	−0.07	0.25	−0.58
7	0.55	0.48	−3.24	0.35	0.32	−0.80
8	1.44	1.32	−5.80	1.86	1.40	0.05
9	0.03	0.44	−1.40	−0.23	0.31	−0.62
10	−0.21	1.33	−2.21	−0.67	1.14	−0.97
11	0.13	2.74	−4.28	−0.02	2.70	−0.51
12	0.47	−0.14	−0.31	0.91	0.03	0.71
13	0.50	0.90	−3.31	0.38	0.80	−0.59
14	0.50	−0.87	−0.22	0.70	−0.84	0.19
15	−1.18	−0.44	3.37	−1.73	−0.59	0.52
16	−0.62	−0.13	0.81	−1.18	−0.36	−0.91
17	0.36	−0.90	0.70	0.68	−0.79	0.54
18	0.79	−1.63	0.08	1.16	−1.56	−1.40
19	−2.39	0.08	1.91	−1.41	0.88	3.73
20	0.03	−0.93	0.81	−0.03	−0.99	−0.15
21	−0.00	−0.60	0.43	−0.11	−0.67	−0.22
22	−1.12	−0.80	5.81	−0.93	−0.58	1.16

G. Inter-component correlations

	I	II	III		I	II	III
I	1.00	0.03	−0.86	I	1.00	−0.03	0.00
II	0.03	1.00	−0.41	II	−0.03	1.00	0.00
III	−0.86	−0.41	1.00	III	0.00	0.00	1.00

H. Direct oblimin rotation

Variable	Factor structure I	Factor structure II	Factor structure III	Factor pattern I	Factor pattern II	Factor pattern III
X_1	.02	.82	−.60	−.05	.71	−.46
X_2	−.10	−.86	.57	−.10	−.81	.35
X_3	.39	.36	−.91	.03	.17	−.86
X_4	−.35	.93	.04	−.04	.98	.24
X_5	.94	−.20	−.40	.97	.01	.05
X_6	.92	−.12	−.41	.97	.09	.07
X_7	.77	−.10	−.78	.46	−.14	−.60
X_8	−.82	.30	.58	−.60	.26	.36

I. Inter-component correlations

	I	II	III
I	1.00	−.20	−.47
II	−.20	1.00	−.22
III	−.47	−.22	1.00

distributions. Each vector of the data matrix was then standardized to Z-deviate form where

$$Z_{ij} = \frac{X_{ij} - \bar{X}_i}{S_i} \tag{6.3}$$

where X_{ij} = the value of variable i in district j
$\bar{X}_i$ = the mean for variable i
S_i = the standard deviation for variable i
Z_{ij} = the Z-deviate of variable i in district j

The matrix of intercorrelations gives a general impression of the strength of intervariable relationships and the degree of independence between clusters of variables. For Whangarei, variables X_1–X_4 apparently form one cluster and variables X_5–X_7 another, with X_8 related to variables of both clusters, but especially the latter. Such visual interpretation is difficult, however, especially where many variables are used: hence the next stage.

There is a great variety of ways to factor a data matrix. The two main alternatives differ in their treatment of the communalities, the entries on the major diagonal of the correlation matrix. Principal components analysis uses unities as communality estimates, making it a closed model which accepts that all of the variance among the variables can be accounted for endogenously. Factor analysis, on the other hand, accepts that there are exogenous variables influencing those in the matrix; it isolates only the common variance. To do this, its communalities are estimates of that common variance. This is frequently done by entering in the main diagonal the squared multiple correlation between the relevant variable and all others.

Once the communality estimate has been determined, factoring of the correlation matrix proceeds. The common methods produce an iterative set of hybrid, orthogonal variables, with each successive hybrid (factor or component) accounting for a smaller proportion of the variance. In components analysis, the total possible number of hybrids is the number of variables in the original matrix (except in cases where there are fewer observations than variables, in which case the number of observations determines the maximum). Factor analysis will produce fewer factors than variables, because of the reduced communalities. In both cases, however, it is usual to extract fewer components or factors than variables, since the aim is to represent the major common patterns and to ignore the minor elements. Determining the number of components or factors to extract involves subjective judgement, though a variety of

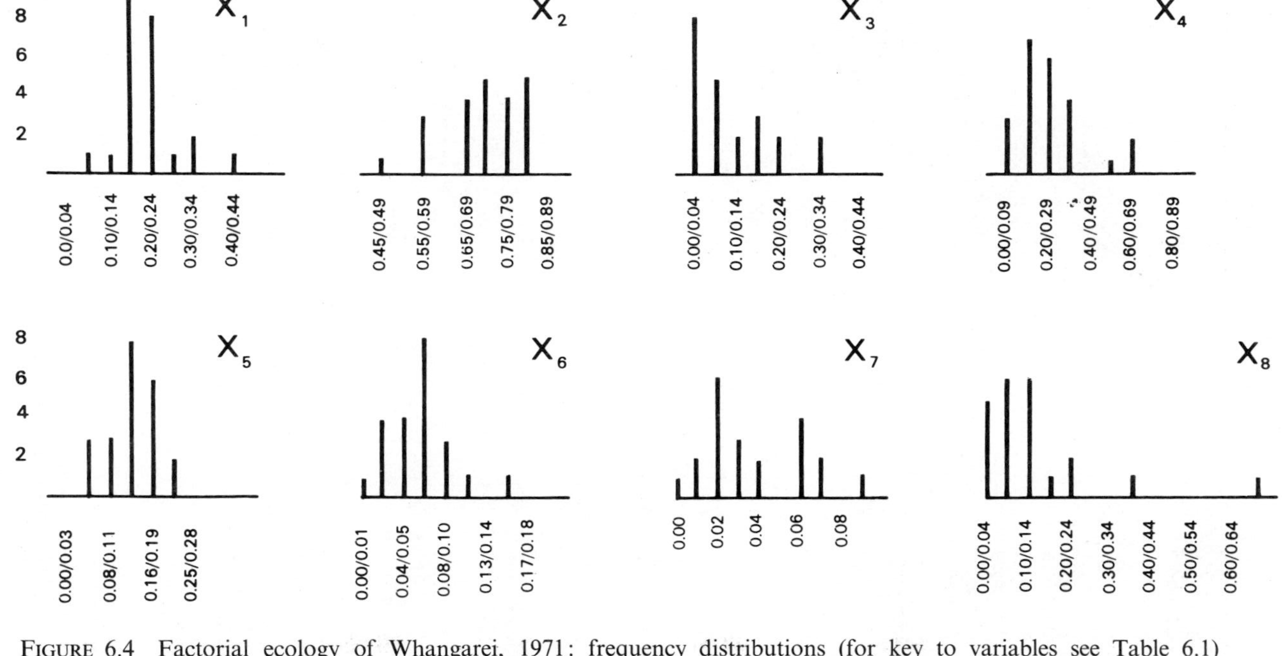

FIGURE 6.4 Factorial ecology of Whangarei, 1971: frequency distributions (for key to variables see Table 6.1)

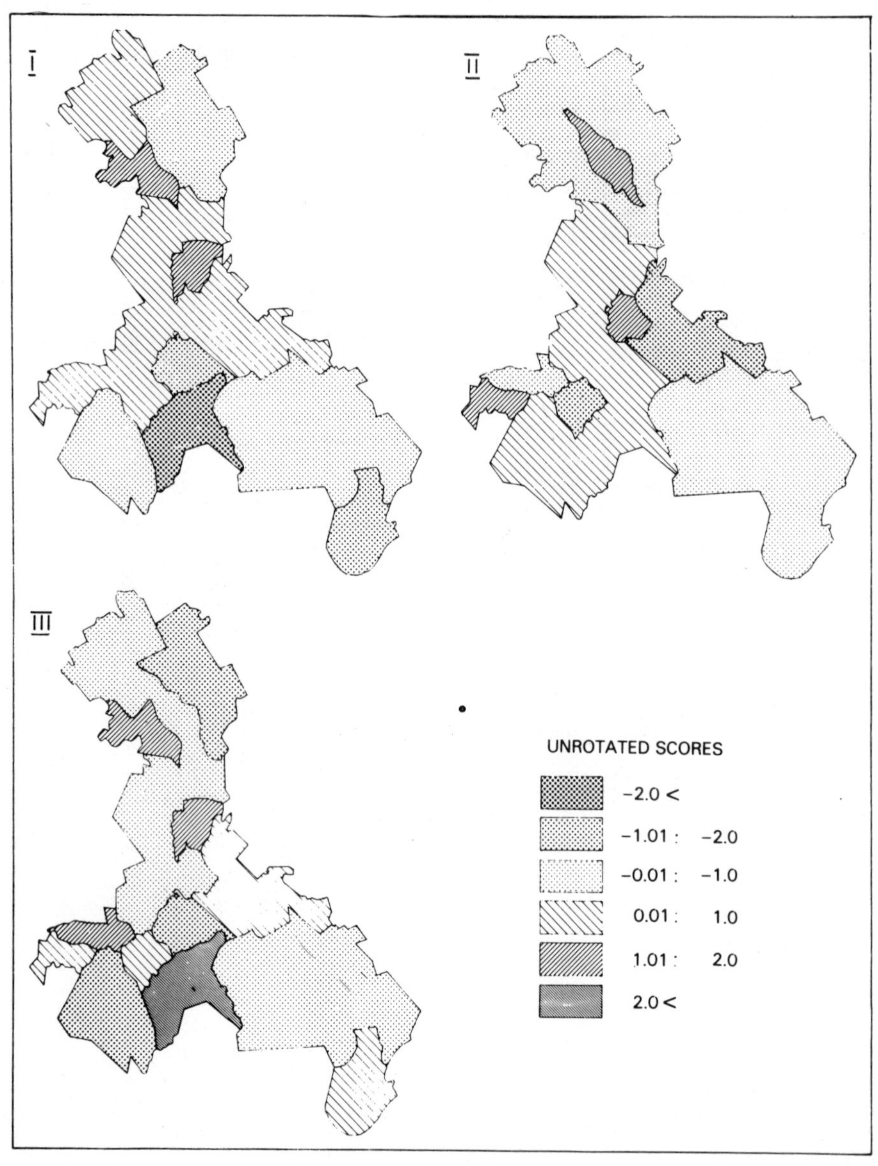

FIGURE 6.5A Factorial ecology of Whangarei, 1971; unrotated component scores (I socioeconomic status dimension, II family status, III unnamed)

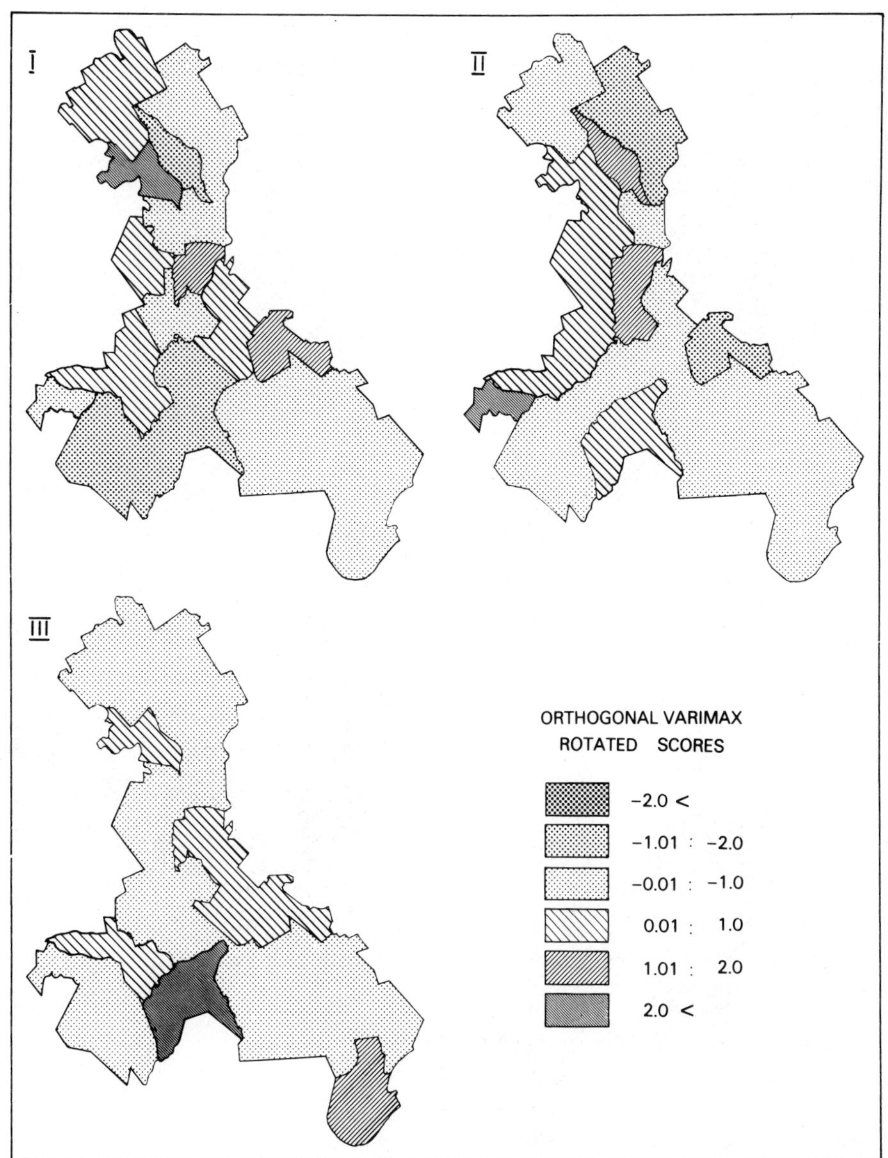

FIGURE 6.5B Factorial ecology of Whangarei, 1971: orthogonal rotated component scores (I socioeconomic status, II family status, III flats and highly educated persons)

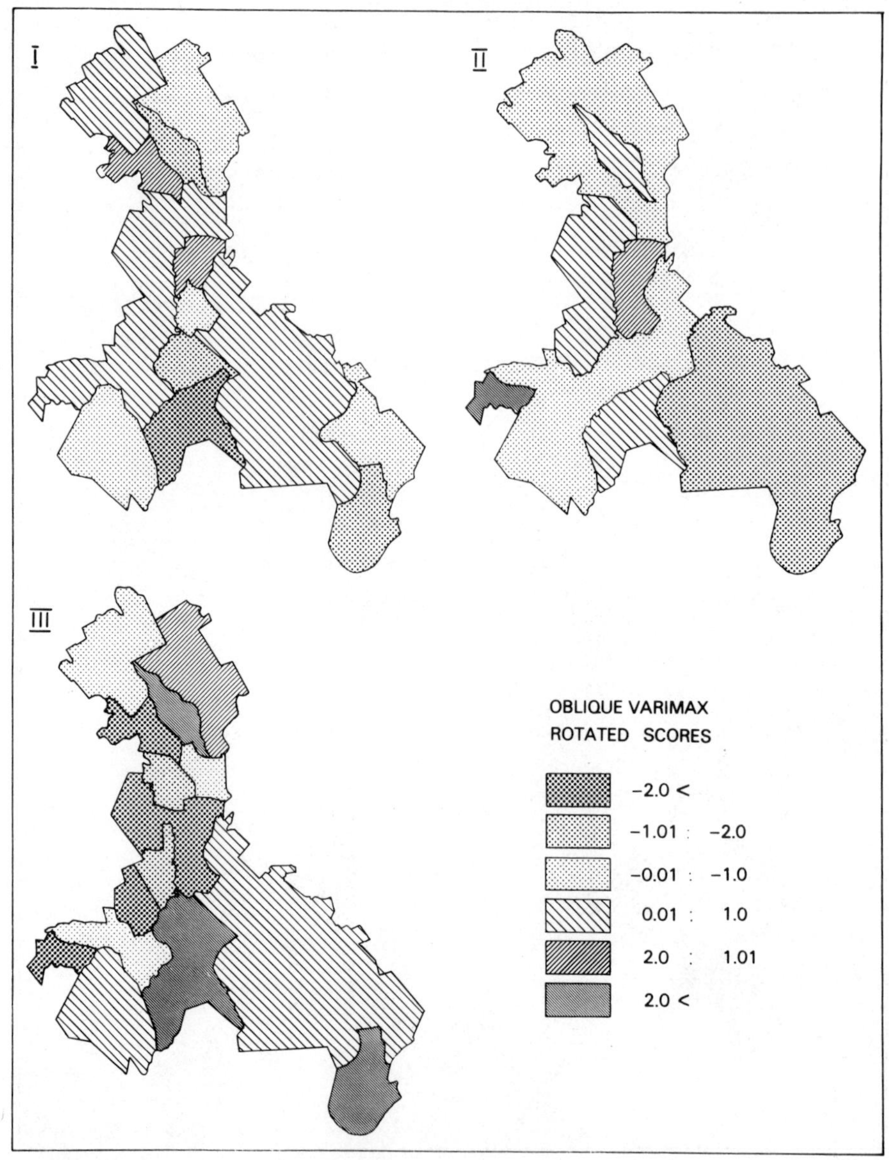

FIGURE 6.5C Factorial ecology of Whangarei, 1971: oblique rotated component scores (key as for Figure 6.5B)

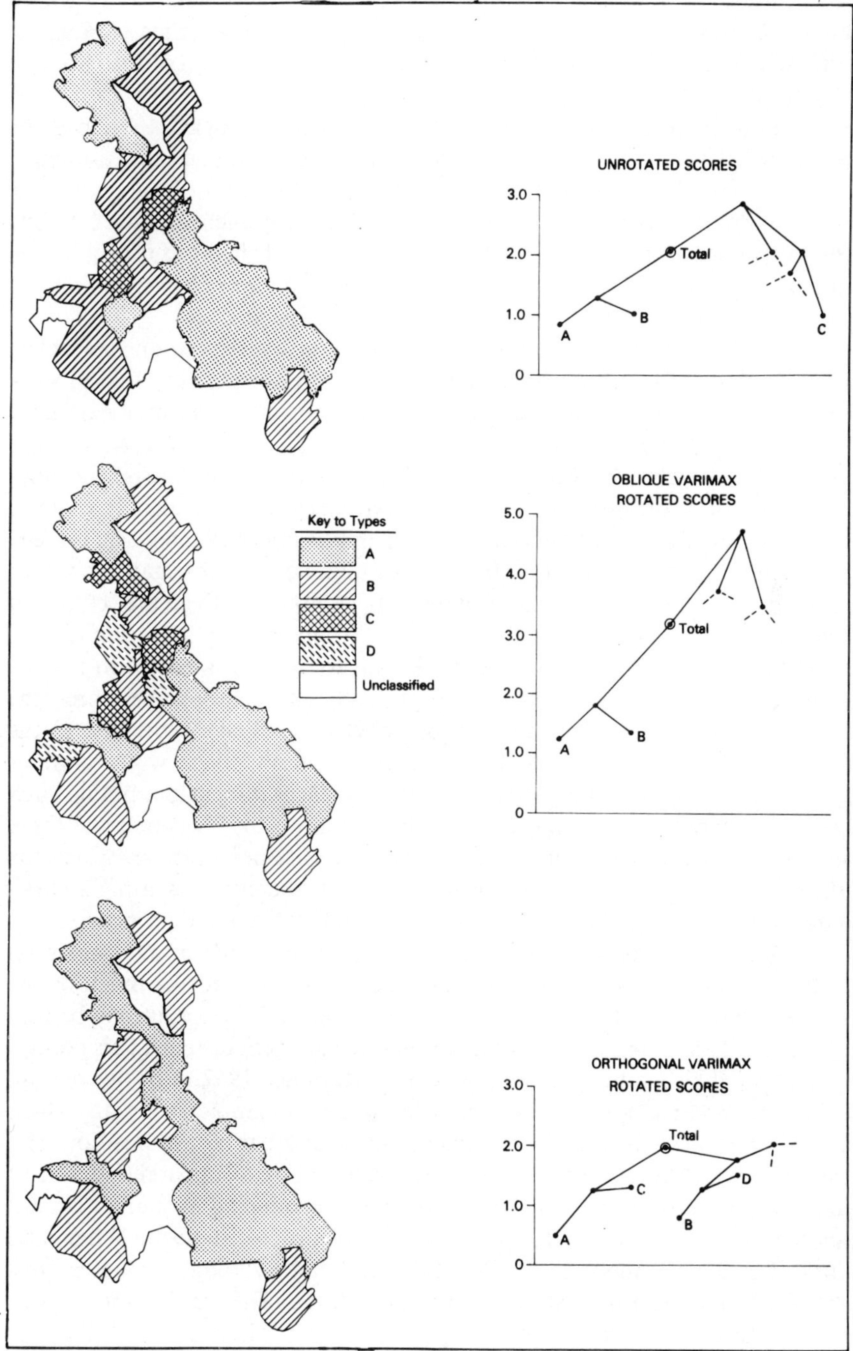

FIGURE 6.6 Factorial ecology of Whangarei, 1971: graphs show the average intra-group distance at various stages of the classification procedure

rule-of-thumb methods has been advanced (Davies and Barrow, 1973). A common method is to extract only those with eigenvalues, sums of squared loadings, exceeding 1.0, which account for a greater proportion of the variance than does one of the original variables.

Both models are frequently employed in factorial ecologies, though there has been little discussion of the relevance of the various communality estimates (Tarrant, 1974). A components approach was used with the Whangarei data and three dimensions were extracted; the third has an eigenvalue of 0.53 but was used (a) because the Shevky–Bell theory suggested the need for three and (b) because after rotation (see below) the summed squared factor loadings all exceeded 1.0.

The aim of this part of the analysis is to reduce the overlap among variables, which are different measures of some more general concepts. The hybrid variables are interpreted by their loading vectors, their correlations with the original variables. Thus, the first Whangarei component (Table 6.1C) suggests, through high positive correlations with variables X_5, X_6 and X_7, that areas with high proportions of professional and managerial male workers also have high proportions of high income earners and of university graduates. Such areas tend also to have low proportions of Maoris, suggested by the negative correlations with X_8, and high proportions of flats (X_3). (Note that these are ecological correlations—see Alker, 1969; Robinson, 1950—indicating characteristics of areas, but not implying that, for example, university graduates live in flats or that no Maoris earn more than \$6 000 annually.) In general, therefore, this first component suggests the validity of Shevky and Bell's economic status dimension. The correlations with the second, notably those with variables X_1, X_2 and X_4, are very suggestive of the family status dimension, but no such easy interpretation can be made of the third component. Together the three components account for over 86 per cent. of the variance in the distributions of the eight variables over the twenty-two districts, thereby presenting a parsimonious description of the patterns displayed in the original data matrix.

The usual methods of component and factor extraction are variance-maximizing; they locate the hybrid variables in order to account for as much of the variance as possible. Thus in the n-dimensional variable space, it may be that components/factors bisect two or more separate variable clusters. (This point is best illustrated by geometrical analogies, as in Rummel, 1967.) For this reason, the pioneer factor analysts introduced the notion of simple structure, which involved rotation of the factor/component axes to another best-fit position. The most common of these, the Varimax procedure, aims to maximize the fit of hybrid variables to original variable clusters, by producing as many loadings as close to either ± 1.0 or 0.0 Application of this procedure to the Whangarei matrix (Table 6.1E) more clearly identified the first two components as, respectively, economic/ethnic status and family status. The third stands out as intermediate to these two, emphasizing that the areal distribution of flats and university-educated persons tended to be relatively independent of the two main dimensions, with a slight negative relationship between these two distributions and that of Maori persons. (Note that the relative importance of the components, indicated by the eigenvalues and the summed squared loadings, is usually of little relevance to the interpretation, since it is largely a function of the number of variables selected to represent each major social area concept.)

Components analysis may be likened to a process of superimposing sets of maps portraying the distributions of different variables over a common set of areas and attempting to isolate shared patterns. Having identified these shared patterns from the various loading vectors, the computation of component scores produces composite maps, standardized values for the observations on the hybrid variables. In the case of the unrotated solution, these are obtained by summing the products of the original standardized variables and the component loadings (weighted by the reciprocal of the eigenvalue). The result is a vector of scores, which has the attributes of a normal curve, on which the observations are scaled according to their rating on the hybrid variable. In Whangarei, therefore, the district with the highest positive score on component I (8) can be interpreted as that with the highest economic status, whereas district 19, with the largest negative score, has the lowest such status. (Note that if a factor analysis is used, scores can only be estimated, because the correlation matrix factored did not use all of the information in the original data matrix but only the common variance.)

Component scores may also be estimated after the rotation procedure. Two approaches are available. Using the same formula as in the unrotated case produces score vectors which are non-orthogonal, the scores being crude weighted indices of the original values. The alternative formula retains the orthogonal independence of the score vectors (see Table 6.1G). In many examples in the literature, the approach which has been taken is not stated. Parkes (1973), however, has compared them in a study of Newcastle, N.S.W., arguing that the correlated vectors provide a clearer classification of suburban types. The argument is that, although the 'pure' dimensions of the residential mosaic may be independent, additive components, any one set of sub-areas may be far from independent in their scores on these 'pure' constructs. Thus, in Whangarei, the oblique or correlated rotated component scores indicate a very strong correlation between the third dimension and the first, and a lesser one between two and three; the latter is clearly a composite map, intermediate to the independent first two components.

The component scores can be used as mappable data, providing representations of areal differences on these components of the residential mosaic (Figures 6.5A, B, C). They can also be used as input to classification procedures, producing groups or types of social areas. Such exercises are particularly valuable in analyses using very large numbers of observations and for general multivariate regional delimitations, but they involve many decisions. A wide array of classificatory procedures is available (see Johnston, 1968, 1970; Spence and Taylor, 1970; and chapter 5 in this book by Adams and Gilder), involving considerable analyst choice and judgement. One method—intercolumnar correlation analysis (McQuitty and Clark, 1968)—has been applied to distance matrices derived, using Pythagoras' theorem, from the three matrices of component scores obtained in the Whangarei analyses. The resulting groups are shown in Figure 6.6, three maps which are in a sense composites of the relevant series in Figures 6.5A, B, C.

A final stage, or an alternative to the Varimax rotation, is to obtain an oblique rotation of the factor or component loading matrix. This removes the orthogonality constraint and allows the identification of separate yet related clusters of variables which underlie the residential mosaic. As shown in Bell's (1955) original use of the method, related dimensions are very likely and, indeed, arguments are frequently advanced that the orthogonality constraint is unrealistic—that it is unlikely that dimensions of the mosaic are independent. Few oblique rotations have been undertaken, however, largely because of the absence of easily available computer programs—that most generally used (developed by Jenrich and Harman) requires analyst decisions which can only be intuitively made. Where oblique rotations have been conducted, they either have not been fully interpreted (van Arsdol, Camilleri and Schmid, 1958a, 1958b) or have been accepted as little different from an orthogonal solution (Carey and Hughes, 1972). Only Timms (1970, 1971) has used multiple-group factor analysis, which is a hypothesis-testing device producing factors which may be either oblique or orthogonal, and only Davies and his associates (Davies and Barrow, 1973; Davies and Lewis, 1973) have used oblique solutions as the input to higher-order factor analyses, which suggest hierarchical or nested factor structures of dimensions and sub-dimensions.

As the orthogonality criterion introduces an unnecessary constraint on the researcher's ability to identify the proper structure of the underlying dimensions of residential differentiation, a strong argument can be made for using oblique rotation procedures, either the inductive ones such as Davies uses or the multiple group procedures espoused by Timms. An orthogonal result would then be a special case of the more general oblique. Unfortunately, application of oblique methods involves more analyst decision and experimentation.

The Jenrich–Harman method was applied to the Whangarei matrix and, with a delta value of 0.0, produced the results given in Table 6.1H. The factor structure matrix, depicting the correlations between variables and components, emphasizes, more clearly than the Varimax solution, the interrelationships among the three dimensions. Variables 2, 3, 7 and 8, in particular, have considerable correlations with more than one of the dimensions, clearly stressing that, in this urban area at least, socioeconomic, family and ethnic status do not produce independent processes leading to spatial differentiation, at the given areal scale, of residences.

The findings

Variants of the factorial ecology method have been applied to many cities since the mid-1960s. The rapidity of antibandwagon developments in modern social science means that criticisms, both general and specific, have appeared already, although the first major geographical studies were not published until 1969. Nevertheless, the method is still being widely applied, being the basis, for example, of major urban studies presently being conducted by the Association of American Geographers. No detailed review of the completed studies is to be presented here, along with a complete bibliography, since such a task has recently been undertaken by Rees (1970, 1971, 1972; see also Berry and Rees, 1969). Instead, the major findings are outlined, as an introduction to a critique of the approach.

By far the major finding, common to a majority of studies, irrespective of the location and cultural context of the relevant city, is the generality of Shevky and Bell's three-dimensional model of the bases to residential area differentiation. This must, in part, reflect the data used, the variables collected by census authorities and made available for small areas, and the inference that Shevky and Bell derived their theory concurrently with their experimentation with census data. Yet, within this constraint, there can be no doubt that socio-economic status, family status/life-cycle and ethnic status are consistently major determinants of where people live, irrespective of the degree of institutional intrusions to the processes of residential location.

The factorial ecology methods, and the computer hardware and software on which they rely, allow researchers to employ a larger number of variables than was available to Shevky and Bell, and to Schmid and his coworkers. Not surprisingly, extra variables tend, at least partly, to confuse the basic three-dimensional pattern. Often these do not deny the Shevky–Bell theory, but rather add to it, developing aspects which were either overlooked by those authors in their search for high-level generalizations or were not relevant to their data sets and study areas. Examples of such findings are the following.

1. Identification of dimensions whose main loadings are with variables representing aspects of population mobility. In their model, Shevky and Bell placed demographic urbanization—the spatial concentration of people—within the ethnic status dimension; McElrath (1965), however, recognized the need for a separate construct representing the intra-urban location of recent immigrants, from whatever origin, a construct which has been identified in studies including variables indexing movement into the city during a recent period (e.g. Schmid and Tagashira, 1965). Shevky and Bell also presented only static analyses of individual cities, not identifying the intra-urban mobility characteristics (often related to other population and dwelling variables) of areas of recent residential development and/or redevelopment (e.g. Murdie, 1969; Schmid and Tagashira, 1965).
2. Identification of clusters of dimensions rather than the single dimension postulated by Shevky and Bell. For example, those authors derived a single index of ethnic status composed of the residential distributions of several minority groups. Factorial ecologists have often placed each group as a separate variable, with several ethnic status dimensions emerging rather than one (e.g. Murdie, 1969). Each is a reflection of similar social tendencies, which produce 'segregation', but indicates that such groups are often as

spatially separate from each other as they are from their host society. (Indeed, if intra-cultural data were available by island of origin among Cook Islanders in Auckland, for example, or village/district of origin among Italians in many cities of the 'New World', analyses would undoubtedly derive further 'clusters within clusters'.)

Similar clusters of dimensions have been obtained for the other Shevky–Bell axes. Indeed the first factorial ecology of a wider range of variables (Anderson and Bean, 1961) isolated two family status dimensions, one with loadings on life-style variables (dwelling type, dwelling tenure, marital status, etc.) and the other on family composition variables (fertility, working females). This indicates that areas of familism are differentiable according to their age structure (often also identified when age variables are employed; see Johnston, 1973b), as well as showing that high fertility—and the associated proportion of women working—is a feature of certain family life-style areas only. The latter feature is becoming more significant with the trend to concentration of child-bearing into but a few years of the average woman's fertile life (Willmott, 1969), perhaps indicating that the fertility variable is no longer particularly valid as a general index of life-style. Finally, one of Parkes' (1973) analyses of data for Newcastle, N.S.W., suggested a division of the socioeconomic status dimension into 'wealth' and 'occupational status'.

3. Identification of specialized areas, usually as a consequence of heteroscedastic correlations (Johnston, 1971a). Examples of this include Schmid and Tagashira's (1965) 'Skid Row' dimension for Seattle. All Skid Row areas are very low on both socioeconomic and family status, but since the converse does not hold (all low socioeconomic status and all low family status areas are not Skid Rows) a separate dimension representing such specialized areas may emerge from the analysis (see also Johnston, 1973b). Indeed, I have argued that ethnic status may properly be related to this type of sub-dimension (Johnston, 1971a), as Berry and Rees (1969, p. 468) also hint. My suggestion is that the larger the minority group relative to a city's population, the more closely socioeconomic and ethnic status dimensions will be related.

With the above caveats, which are relatively minor in the total set of factorial ecology results, the basic conclusion to be derived from this burgeoning literature is the general applicability of Shevky and Bell's model, at least within the constraints of most census data sets. (See, however, the criticisms of Meyer, 1971, and Palm and Caruso, 1972, which are discussed below.) There are patterns to which the model is not directly applicable, in cities with no obvious ethnic minorities, for example, and in cities set in very different socioeconomic/cultural environments (with consequent differences in the census variables provided). Among the latter, the limited range of studies (e.g. Abu-Lughod, 1969; Berry and Spodek, 1971; Curson, 1973; Schwirian and Smith, 1971; Timms, 1970, 1971) suggests a sequence of dimensional states in non-socialist cities whose progress follows that of 'modernization':

(a) Pre-industrial, in which the only dimension is communal, usually reflecting areal and perhaps tribal origin of groups.
(b) Transitional, in which the communal division becomes associated with occupational divisions and eventually gives way to a socioeconomic status dimension.
(c) 'Modernizing', in which life-style choice becomes increasingly divorced from socioeconomic status.
(d) Industrial, with the full Shevky–Bell range of dimensions.
(e) Post-industrial.

Analyses of change

The residential pattern of a city is not a constant, therefore, and the long-term changes in its structure, just identified, are not the only alterations which are in progress. In most cities, certainly in those of the 'developed' world, population movement is considerable. The personnel of areas changes—sometimes rapidly, often rather slowly. The fabric changes also; new buildings are added, others are removed, while a third category have their characteristics markedly changed. A factorial ecology of one data set, referring to one census, thus provides but a single snapshot of the ongoing readjustment of urban form, function and population. Indeed, because areas may be changing at different rates and in different ways, the single snapshot may produce results which are not typical of the system at other times, or in its long-term, almost certainly only partial, equilibrium.

The need is for studies of systems at more than one date and for studies of changes between dates. Unfortunately, these are few and are difficult because of data (both variables and areas) incompatibilities between censuses, which may be taken a decade or more apart—and therefore may miss important, short-term changes. Nevertheless, several attempts at spatiotemporal factorial ecologies have been made, using one of two basic methods. In the first, separate factorial ecologies for the various dates are compared, either by visual interpretation (e.g. Hunter, 1971; Timms, 1971), or by the use of correlation-type methods such as congruence coefficients (Haynes, 1971) and Veldman's (1967) RELATE procedure (Johnston, 1973b). In the other, variables measuring the changes between two dates in each of a set of variables, over a constant set of areas, are constructed and the resulting matrix submitted to factorial ecology procedures (Murdie, 1969; Brown and Horton, 1970; Johnston, 1973c). From both, the findings suggest:

1. Considerable stability in the basic dimensions of the residential structure.
2. Variations which parallel the basic dimensions, in that variables which cluster together on the same component in a 'static' analysis tend to cluster similarly in a 'dynamic' analysis.
3. Generally little change between two dates in the characteristics of most areas (see also Tryon, 1967), with the main exceptions being areas of rapid change in their ethnic status.

FACTORIAL ECOLOGY—A CRITIQUE

Widespread continuing use of the factorial ecology method indicates its acceptance for studies of intra-urban residential differentiation. At the descriptive level it provides, within the constraints of variables and areas, suggestions of the basic patterns of differentiation and maps of these. Such output can be used to test general hypotheses concerning social areas and to generate further hypotheses concerning the mechanisms producing the patterns, concerning the place-to-place variations in patterns and concerning the processes of 'neighbourhood' change. Further analytical work can make use of various pieces of output, in particular the component or factor score matrices, which can be employed in analyses of spatial form (see chapter 7), as the bases for sampling frameworks in the mould of social area analysis (see Herbert and Evans, 1974) and as independent variables for a wide variety of ecological regression analyses, as illustrated in volume two of this book.

A methodology of such potential power requires careful appreciation in order that these latent qualities may be realized. The analyst must choose from a number of basic techniques, must select an appropriate path through the methodological procedures and must make a number of subjective judgements (for example, in the classification procedure; see Johnston, 1968). Interpretation of the output, notably of the 'meaning' of the factors/components which is basic to the whole procedure, also involves personal assessments. Development of a detailed appreciation of the methodology, which may lead to its modification or extension, is necessary, and the remainder of this chapter essays an introduction to such a task.

Variables and interrelationships

A basic element of factorial ecology is the correlation matrix, on which the remaining procedures operate. As a consequence, the method must be based on variable interrelationships that meet the criteria of the general linear model. (More particularly, those criteria relevant to the descriptive use of linear correlation methods should be met, since only rarely are factorial ecologies used inferentially, using sample data to generalize to a population. It may be argued that a data set—even if based on a complete census and not on a sample count—is a sample, both temporally and for one set of areas out of an infinite possible range, but this has never been advanced. See, however, Meyer, 1972, and Court, 1972.) The particular criteria (Poole and O'Farrell, 1971) are that the relationship between the two variables is linear, that the variance be homoscedastic (equal variance in one variable at all levels of the other) and that the residuals be serially independent (not related to one of the two variables). Further, less important criteria require normally distributed variables, no measurement error and that the errors (the 'unexplained' variation) have a mean of zero.

Correlation coefficients are interpreted as the square root of the proportion of the standardized variation in one variable which can be accounted for, statistically, by the variation in another. Component factor loadings are interpreted similarly, as the square roots of the proportion of standardized variation in a variable which can be accounted for by the hybrid variable (the component or factor). One consequence of this is that such correlations are often not as substantive as their numerical size would indicate; a correlation coefficient or a component loading of ± 0.6 indicates only 36 per cent. agreement in the bivariate distributions of the two items being related. There is thus a danger of overinterpretation, of identifying, for example, a component by two variables which are themselves but slightly related. Thus, in a study of Melbourne in 1966, one component of six extracted from a matrix of twenty-eight variables had the following loadings exceeding ± 0.70: per cent. Greek-born, $+0.72$; per cent. Italian-born, $+0.73$; per cent. United Kingdom-born, -0.79; per cent. non-Australian-born, $+0.71$; per cent. non-British nationality, $+0.87$. Interpretation of this, in the usual manner, suggested an ethnic status dimension to that city's residential mosaic, a bipolar map which at one extreme had large clusters of persons born in Great Britain and Ireland and at the other immigrants from Greece and Italy. But, in fact, the original correlation between the Greek and Italian variables was only 0.42; their residential distributions over the given set of areas were more different than similar.

Analysis of these problems of substantive interpretation of factorial ecology outputs is given in Meyer's (1971) study of black residential areas in Detroit and Memphis. He points out that the hybrid variables, Varimax-rotated factors in his case, are but 'averages' of the original variables which lie in their sector of the geometric variable space, averages which may be based on a considerable scatter. The smaller the correlations on which the factoring procedure is based, the greater is the likelihood of substantial overinterpretation, even despite apparently high loadings. This suggests caution in interpretation, especially if the results are to be used in later analyses. As Meyer points out, to say that residential differentiation in black residential areas largely produces two statistically unrelated dimensions—socioeconomic and family status—is a valid high-level generalization. But it does not imply either that particular variables are completely accounted for by only one of these dimensions or that, within any one of them, relationships among the constituent variables are complete (e.g. that within the socioeconomic status domain levels of family income and median educational attainment display a one-to-one correspondence, in their standardized form).

Part of this problem of overinterpretation is, perhaps, mainly a problem of imprecise goals. Does the analyst wish to make a high-level generalization or a more detailed statement about areal covariations? In part, too, it may be technically derived, as a result of the use of orthogonal rotation methods and of failure to approximate simple structure (the ideal situation when all loadings are either ± 1.0 or ± 0.0). Nevertheless, there is clearly a cautionary moral in Meyer's work.

The overinterpretation problem extends into other elements of a factorial ecology, notably those involving the derivation or approximation of component/factor scores. As scores are obtained by multiplying the original standardized values for each variable by the standardized loadings, where the component/factor solution does not approach simple structure, it may be that the same result, a score value, can be derived from many combinations of high and low values for individual variables. (Horn, 1973, demonstrated this by reworking data in King's 1969 text on statistical methods.) Thus, in a study of Katmandu, Joshi (1972) observed that, although his loadings matrix clearly identified, *inter alia*, a socioeconomic status dimension, the spatial pattern of the scores on this in no way correlated with his field knowledge of the city's social areas. The reason was, apparently, that the dimension had a number of relatively small loadings on variables other than those used to name it; in total, because of the large number of variables in the study, these 'smaller' variables were having more influence on the pattern of scores than were the main ones by which the dimension was identified.

Given the importance of the scores matrices to geographical factorial ecologies, and especially their potential as independent variables in other ecological analyses, the problems raised here may be serious ones. Joshi (1972) suggests their circumvention by removal of the troublesome smaller loadings before computing scores, but this involves a degree of analyst judgement which may prove tricky. Alternatively, the analyst may attempt to move closer to simple structure by the removal of variables from his analysis, perhaps after a series of tests for the general stability of the results (Schmid and Tagashira, 1965). Rees (1974) suggests that scores should not be computed but that separate indices of the relevant dimension be obtained by returning to the original values for the prototype variables—those with the highest loadings. Perhaps in many cases the problem arises from the overcatholic selection of variables, and more careful and limited selection may reduce the difficulties.

Selection of variables may contribute to overinterpretation in another way. Because areas differ in their numbers of residents or dwellings, the variables are often expressed either as ratios or as percentages of the area's total. In the latter case, this can fabricate high correlations and lead to spurious dimensions, if a closed system is generated. To take an extreme example, over any set of areas the variables percentage of an area's population male and percentage of an area's population female must be completely, and negatively, correlated, since the two categories exhaust the total population. Because of this correlation of -1.0, a component or factor analysis will almost certainly produce a bipolar male–female dimension. Of itself, this could be disregarded, but because the two variables are likely to be correlated with others their dimension will distort the variable space and result in a spurious result. Of course, these two variables are never both included in an analysis, but larger closed systems spread over several categories of a fixed total often are (e.g. age, occupation, race and birthplace groups); these, too, will distort the results, in a less obvious and therefore potentially more confusing way. More careful variable selection can overcome this problem. Alternatively, one of the available methods of orthogonalizing such variables should be employed (Dent and Sakoda, 1973; Gorsuch, 1973).

Although methods can be found to avoid these overinterpretation problems, it may be that some of the questions raised are fundamental to certain aspects of factorial ecologies and their use. For example, in his study of attitudes to education in Sunderland, which used the results of a factorial ecology as the sampling frame, Robson (1969) discovered that attitudes differed in one of his study areas from those in others which were outwardly very similar in their characteristics. In this case, the difference was in a variable (neighbourhood integration) which could not be included in the factorial ecology. But it could have resulted from differences concealed by the high-level generalization employed; this suggests the use of other indices than the scores, either replacing or paralleling them.

Socioeconomic status is generally considered to be a composite of income, education and occupation, but these three attributes are usually not completely correlated at either the individual or the areal scale. Thus, for metropolitan Toronto in 1961, it was possible to suggest a single major dimension of socioeconomic status, using education, income and occupation variables (Table 6.2), on which only the 'lower white-collar' occupations did not have a large loading. Multiple regression analyses, however, using each of the six variables as the dependent in turn, accounted for 50 to 94 per cent. of the relevant variation (see Table 6.2; the regression equations are not shown since, because of multi-

TABLE 6.2 The socioeconomic status dimension: Toronto, 1961

A. Unrotated principal component loadings

Variable	Component I	II	Communality
X_1 Per cent. with university education	0.90	0.30	0.91
X_2 Per cent. males, professional managerial	0.96	0.19	0.96
X_3 Per cent. males, sales/clerical	0.55	−0.79	0.93
X_4 Per cent. males, labourers	−0.82	0.42	0.85
X_5 Per cent. males, craftsmen	−0.91	−0.20	0.86
X_6 Average male income	0.91	0.16	0.85
Percentage variance	72.8	16.5	

B. Regresson analyses

Dependent variable	Independents	R^2
X_1	X_2, X_3, X_4, X_5, X_6	0.92
X_2	X_1, X_3, X_4, X_5, X_6	0.97
X_3	X_1, X_2, X_4, X_5, X_6	0.71
X_4	X_1, X_2, X_3, X_5, X_6	0.84
X_5	X_1, X_2, X_3, X_4, X_6	0.92
X_6	X_1, X_2, X_3, X_4, X_5	0.93

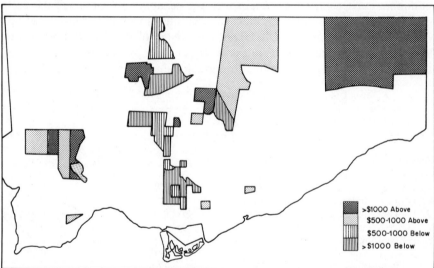

FIGURE 6.7 Socioeconomic status in metropolitan Toronto, 1961. Top, scores on the principal component; bottom, residuals from regression of median income on the other five variables (for key see Table 6.2)

collinearity, the *b*-coefficients are not interpretable). The residuals from these regressions identify areas which deviate from the general pattern of socioeconomic status, deviations which may be as important in analyses using the factorial ecology results—either as sample frame or as independent variables—as the scores on the general dimension. In Figure 6.7, for example, the map of scores on the first component, representing general socioeconomic status, is contrasted with the major absolute residuals from a regression in which the variable X_6 (median income) was the dependent and the other five the independents. Among the positive residuals, the most apparent cluster of 'nouveaux riches' is in the western borough of Etobicoke, whereas the major cluster of negative residuals is in and around the area of the Annex, a popular residential area for professionals such as academics.

In the study of the dimensions of change in a residential mosaic, the structuring of the variables can lead to overinterpretation as the chosen indices tend to 'make change happen'. In both Murdie's (1969) analysis of Toronto, 1951–1961, and Brown and Horton's (1971) study of Chicago, 1950–1960, the variables measured the change in a characteristic between the two dates as a proportion of the value at the first. (Murdie standardized these ratios, by dividing them by the city-wide rate of change for that characteristic.) Fed into a correlation routine, each of these change variables is given equal weight, irrespective of any differences in the rate of change; the result may be some spurious findings (Johnston, 1973c). Alternative methodologies, which do not 'make change happen', have been suggested (Haynes, 1971; Johnston, 1973c); as yet, sufficient data have not been made available to allow use of three-mode factor analysis in this context (Cant, 1971).

Two researchers (Palm and Caruso, 1972) have suggested an overinterpretation problem which involves sins of omission rather than comission. Their claim is that analysts tend to interpret factors/components through a few major loadings only, disregarding the smaller loadings. Comparison of socioeconomic and family status dimensions for ten medium-sized United States cities indicated relatively low congruence levels, especially on the latter dimension, suggesting important differences between places in their ecological structures. In most cases, however, the differences were in the patterns of minor loadings rather than those loadings on the variables characteristically used to identify and nominate the dimension. At the level of high-order generalizations, therefore, the usual factor-labelling procedures and conclusions of inter-city similarity are valid; at a more detailed level, providing a less simplistic statement and suggesting residential choice processes, there is strong support for their argument made in statements such as (Palm and Caruso, 1972, p. 131): 'The blanket appellation of the education–occupation–income factor as "socio-economic status" belies the great variety of associated attributes'.

Areas

An argument frequently raised against factorial ecologies, and other classification exercises based on correlation methods, is that they involve circular reasoning—that their aim is to group like areas, which are such because they are subdivided into smaller units (see Harvey, 1969, for example, but also Gould, 1970). This is but a part of a larger problem of an inability to define, operationally at least, the geographical individual, which is the observation unit in a factorial ecology. The set of areas employed—usually census tracts—is but a single sample of the very large number of ways that an area can be subdivided (or a set of individuals aggregated with a contiguity constraint). Presumably, this difficulty could be countered by the development of sampling distributions against which to compare results. Tests could also be made of the stability of results over different sets of areas. Unfortunately, as pointed out earlier, census tracts can only be aggregated in most cases, not disaggregated and then reconstituted. Hence, such tests could only be made at different spatial scales, raising the intriguing question as to whether any variations between scales represent the operation of scale-specific processes or are merely artifacts of the data set. Research aimed at searching for possible scale processes is a clear need for factorial ecology research (see Bourne, 1970). Davies and Barrow (1973) have attempted this by comparing towns of different sizes, but, if census tracts are designed on uniform criteria to meet logistic needs, they may well differ in relative size between places and so confound interpretations.

Other problems arise from the mis-match between census tracts and social distributions. This may introduce spurious internal heterogeneity to areas because of unfortunate boundary locations, but more importantly it could bias the correlations on which the factorial ecology is based. For example, Figure 6.8 shows in the left-hand graph the values for four neighbourhoods on two variables, between which there is a zero correlation. In the right-hand graph those four neighbourhoods have been divided into census tracts: neighbourhoods A and B by far the larger and are divided into five and four tracts respectively; the smaller neighbourhoods C and D occupy only one tract each. The correlation in the second case is approximately 0.6.

Again, ideally this problem should be soluble by using a set of areas whose boundaries conform to those of the city's social divisions. In practice, however, blurred social boundaries or transition zones are probably the rule rather than the exception. Any attempt to study neighbourhoods, which are presumed

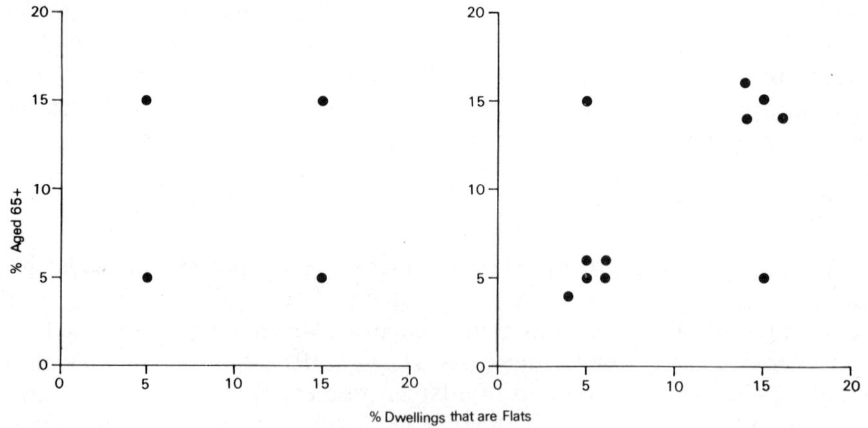

FIGURE 6.8 The autocorrelation problem (see text)

to be areas with identity, rather than artificial units such as census tracts, is probably doomed to failure. Furthermore, a set of neighbourhoods defined on one criterion—income, say—may not be the same as that based on another—perhaps family structure. Which would be used? Multivariate studies would seem to be ruled out by approaches such as these.

The problem being discussed is an example of the general problem facing many geographical analyses—that of spatial autocorrelation. This was first identified by Galton (see Berry, 1972, 1973), who noted that if a trait (such as economic development) is diffused out from a certain pole, the various observations at different locations are not independent of each other, since their values in the economic development variable are a function, partly at least, of their location relative to the pole. Correlation methods are based on an assumption of independent observations. Thus, when a neighbourhood is divided into census tracts, those tracts are not independent observations. An insuperable obstacle appears to exist: to reconstitute the tracts into 'neighbourhoods' is, as I have already argued, a very difficult, if not impossible, task, and a major function of factorial ecology is, through the classification procedures, to suggest an approximation of those neighbourhoods. Factorial ecology is, it seems, unable to do what it sets out to do, because this must be done first in order for its methods to be valid! But an alternative argument can be raised. If the eleven census tracts in the right-hand graph of Figure 6.8 are of equal population size, then surely the resulting correlation of 0.6 is a more relevant one than the zero recorded for the four neighbourhoods. The latter value indicates that there is no relationship in the proportions of older people and of flats among the four areas; the former correlation suggests that, for most old people, where they live probably contains a high proportion of flats.

Moving away from the questions of autocorrelation and of modifiable units, one final problem concerning the stability of the results of factorial ecologies relates to their relevance to different groups and areas within the city. Do different, clearly identifiable groups within an urban population structure their residential mosaic in the same way? Are different major areas of a city similarly structured? The first question is most easily answered for groups which are almost completely segregated from others, such as in the black residential areas in the United States. For these, Meyer's (1970, p. 197) investigations suggest the general relevance of the commonly observed socioeconomic status and family status dimensions, but other studies (Johnston, 1971b, p. 268; Roseman, Christian and Bullamore, 1972) indicate less agreement between the black residential mosaic and the white. With other groups, such tests are difficult to perform, not only because of data problems but also because, as they are not completely segregated, to separate out the group is to remove its members from the environment in which they interact, to greater or lesser degree. As to different areas of the city, comparisons of analyses of the entire Chicago metropolitan area with separate studies of the central city and of the suburbs indicated considerable congruence, with the main differences resulting from the concentration of certain groups in one area, such as the blacks in the central city (Rees, 1970). In somewhat more detail, Sweetser (1969) compared the factorial structures of zones and sectors of both Boston and Helsinki with those for the entire metropolis, finding that only in the inner-city zones was there any marked difference from the general pattern, suggesting to him greater inter-tract differentiation in the urban core than in the suburbs. These zones and sectors, and to a slightly lesser extent the city–suburban distinction, are as arbitrarily defined as their constituent tracts. More realistic is Robson's (1969) separation of public and private sector housing areas in Sunderland. Unfortunately, however, he only analysed differences in the correlation matrices and did not proceed to separate component analyses.

And methods

Factor analysis is a collective term for a range of slightly different techniques, but researchers conducting factorial ecologies have been conservative in their choice from this range (perhaps because only a few are available in computer program packages). Experimentation has been proposed, however (see Hunter, 1972), and Berry (1971) has suggested a typology of possible approaches from which informed selection may be made. Each variant of factor analysis has a unique algebra and, unless there is simple structure in the data set, each must produce unique results (compare the many programs given in Horst, 1965). Thus, Rees (1972, p. 291) has emphasized the clear differences between two studies of Montreal's 1961 urban mosaic, one of which (Greer-Wootten, 1972) used image–factor analysis whereas the other (an unpublished University of Chicago paper) employed principal axis factor analysis. (There is a third study of the same city—Haynes, 1971.)

Factor and components analysis need not operate on a correlation matrix; various methods—such as direct factor analysis (Berry, 1967)—operate on the raw data; others use alternative matrices of agreement, such as those of crossproducts and of covariances. The last two have advantages over the correlation matrix, because they use more of the information in the original data. Product–moment correlations are based on data standardized to Z-deviates; they index similarity in relative profile shape only. The covariance between two variables is the average product of deviations from the relevant means:

$$\mathrm{COV}_{xy} = [\Sigma\,(x_i - \bar{x})\,(y_i - \bar{y})]/n \qquad (6.4)$$

where x_i, y_i = the values for x and y in tract i
$\bar{x}, \bar{y}$ = the means of x and y
n = the number of observations (less one when x and y are the same variable)

Study of the covariances, therefore, looks at absolute deviations from the means. The cross-product between two variables is their average product:

$$\mathrm{CP}_{xy} = (\Sigma\, x_i y_i)/n \qquad (6.5)$$

Notation is as before. It studies profile height as well as profile shape.

The potential value of components analyses of cross-products and covariance matrices has been suggested recently (Johnston, 1973d). A drawback of factorial ecologies using correlation matrices is that they must ignore intra-tract variation. Theoretically, if segregation is complete, and is captured by the tract boundaries, percentage values for each variable should be close to either 100 or zero. But whether this is so is not captured in the analysis, an omission which is especially significant, both in comparative studies (between places and between dates) and in investigations which use the output of factorial ecologies as independent variables. Studies of cross-products matrices provide intensity indices, those of covariance matrices focus on absolute variation and those of correlation matrices look at relative shape. All three may be relevant to a particular investigation.

Covariance and cross-products components analyses are useful either as alternatives or as complements to correlation-based factorial ecologies. They have their drawbacks, however, particularly in the derivation of component scores, which could be dominated by variables with the highest absolute values. But in these, and in correlation-based analyses, other approaches are possible. The main focus of factorial ecologies is the areas (the composite maps which can be derived), and for this it may be better to use a Q-mode approach, which transposes the usual data matrix, using the areas as the variables. This procedure leads more directly to a classification of observations, with each variable given equal weight. Such weighting is often unjustified, as variables are selected in unequal numbers to represent the expected dimensions, usually derived from social area analysis; a prior R-mode analysis removes inter-variable redundancy and provides equally weighted constructs. Where a single dimension is investigated (Johnston, 1973b; Jones, 1969), a Q-mode approach may be feasible and the results from several separate analyses may be combined for a total classification.

Factor and components analyses are one group of procedures in a wide range of multivariate scaling procedures (Shepard, Romney and Nerlove, 1972), many of which may prove useful for the study of social areas. To date, only one alternative has been tried, the Guttmann–Lingoes smallest space algorithm, which operates on distance matrices such as those produced in the classic studies of residential differentiation in Chicago (Duncan and Duncan, 1955). The procedure is akin to factor/components analyses in reducing the matrix to a smaller number of orthogonal dimensions, aiming to maintain the rank ordering of distances in the original matrix in a derived matrix of inter-point distances calculated from the new set of orthogonal dimensions (Golledge and Rushton, 1972; Guttmann, 1968; Lingoes, 1973). It can be used in either R- or Q-mode and has been successfully applied in a study of ethnic segregation in three Israeli cities (Klaff, 1973); one of its advantages over correlation-based factorial ecologies is that it can use percentage data which form closed-number systems.

CONCLUSIONS

Unravelling the complexity of the urban residential mosaic is clearly a major research task. Its multivariate causes, ongoing processes and static and dynamic patterns demand comprehensive data, referring to relevant variables and areas, and a technical arsenal for their analysis and interpretation. At present, the factorial ecology method is the most favoured, which accounts for its primacy within the present chapter. As it is presently practised, the method is not ideal for the test set, yet it appears to promise greater sophistication as it embraces a wider range of multidimensional scaling algorithms.

Perhaps more concern should be expressed about the nature of the material fed into factorial ecologies than with the method itself. On the surface, replication to various cities suggests clear basic dimensions to intra-urban spatial differentiation, yet much of this common structure may be an artifact of the data which censuses collect. Palm (1973a), for example, has shown that the social areas of Minneapolis, as defined by a factorial ecology, are not communities of common interests, as indicated in their reading patterns of journalistic material; nor are they clearly defined functional regions, as indexed by telephone call volumes (Palm, 1973b). Smith (1973), too, has suggested the need for a much broader data base than presently employed if factorial ecologies are to be of value in uncovering spatial patterns of welfare and 'illfare' within cities. In part, however, it may be that the variables Smith considers indices of pathologies are, in part, consequences of the social environmental variations defined by the factorial ecologies, and should therefore be analysed in a more obvious causal modelling program (as is demonstrated in several of the chapters in the second volume of this book). For all its disadvantages of omission and commission, therefore, the factorial ecology method has a clear lead at present in the search for ways to describe intra-urban environments and to uncover resulting man–environment interactions.

REFERENCES

Abu-Lughod, J. L. (1969). 'Testing the theory of social area analysis: the ecology of Cairo, Egypt'. *American Sociological Review*, **34**, 198–212.

Alker, H. R. (1969). 'A typology of ecological fallacies'. In M. Dogan and S. Rokkan (Eds.), *Quantitative Ecological Analysis in the Social Sciences*, The M.I.T. Press, Cambridge, Massachusetts, pp. 69–86'.

Anderson, T. W., and Bean, L. L. (1961). 'The Shevky–Bell social areas: confirmation of results and a reinterpretation'. *Social Forces*, **40**, 119–124.

Van Arsdol, M. D., Camilleri, S. F., and Schmid, C. F. (1958a). 'An application of the Shevky social area indexes to a model of urban society'. *Social Forces*, **37**, 26–32.

van Arsdol, M. D., Camilleri, S. F., and Schmid, C. F. (1958b). 'The generality of urban social area indexes'. *American Sociological Review*, **23**, 277–284.

van Arsdol, M. D., Camilleri, S. F., and Schmid, C. F. (1961). 'An investigation of the utility of urban typology'. *Pacific Sociological Review*, **4**, 2632.

van Arsdol, M. D., Camilleri, S. F., and Schmid, C. F. (1962). 'Further comments on the utility of urban typology'. *Pacific Sociological Review*, **5**, 9–12.

Bell, W. (1953). 'The social areas of the San Francisco Bay region'. *American Sociological Review*, **18**, 39–47.

Bell, W. (1955). 'Economic, family, and ethnic status: an empirical test'. *American Sociological Review*, **20**, 45–52.

Bell, W. (1969). 'Urban neighborhoods and individual behavior'. In P. Meadows and E. H. Mizruchi (Eds.), *Urbanism, Urbanization, and Change: Comparative Perspectives*, Addison-Wesley, Reading, Massachusetts, pp. 120–146.

Bell, W., and Boat, M. D. (1957). 'Urban neighborhoods and informal social relations'. *American Journal of Sociology*, **62**, 391–398.

Bell, W., and Force, M. T. (1956a). 'Urban neighborhood types and participation in formal associations'. *American Sociological Review*, **21**, 25–34.

Bell, W., and Force, M. T. (1956b). 'Social structure and participation in different types of formal association'. *Social Forces*, **34**, 345–350.

Bell, W., and Force, M. T. (1957). 'Religious preference, familism and the class structure'. *Midwest Sociologist*, **19**, 79–86.

Bell, W., and Greer, S. (1962). 'Social area analysis and its critics'. *Pacific Sociological Review*, **5**, 3–9.

Bell, W., and Moskos, C. C. (1964). 'A comment on Udry's "Increasing scale and spatial differentiation"'. *Social Forces*, **42**, 414–417.

Berry, B. J. L. (1967). 'Grouping and regionalizing: an approach to the problem using multivariate analysis'. In W. L. Garrison and D. F. Marble (Eds.), *Quantitative Geography*, Studies in Geography No. 17, Northwestern University, Evanston, Illinois, pp. 219–251.

Berry, B. J. L. (Ed.) (1971). 'Comparative factorial ecology'. *Economic Geography*, **47**, Part 2.

Berry, B. J. L. (1972). 'Problems of data organization and analytical methods in geography'. *Journal, American Statistical Association*, **66**, 510–522.

Berry, B. J. L. (1973). 'A paradigm for modern geography'. In R. J. Chorley (Ed.), *Directions in Geography*, Methuen, London, pp. 3–21.

Berry, B. J. L., Goheen, P. G., and Goldstein, H. (1968). *Metropolitan Area Definition*, United States Bureau of the Census, Washington, D.C.

Berry, B. J. L., and Rees, P. H. (1969). 'The factorial ecology of Calcutta'. *American Journal of Sociology*, **74**, 445–491.

Berry, B. J. L., and Spodek, H. (1971). 'Comparative ecologies of large Indian cities'. *Economic Geography*, **47**, 266–285.

Booth, C. (1889–1902). *Life and Labour of the People of London* (17 volumes). Macmillan, London.

Bourne, L. S. (1970). *Dimensions of Metropolitan Land Use: Cross-sectional Structure and Stability*, Research Paper No. 31, Centre for Urban and Community Studies, University of Toronto, Toronto.

Brown, L. A., and Horton, F. E. (1971). 'Social area change: an empirical study'. *Urban Studies*, **7**, 271–288.

Burgess, E. W. (1927). 'The determination of gradients in the growth of the city'. *Publications of the American Sociological Society*, **21**, 178–184.

Burgess, E. W., and Bogue, D. J. (1967). *Contributions to Urban Sociology*, University of Chicago Press, Chicago.

Cant, R. G. (1971). 'Changes in the location of manufacturing in New Zealand 1957–68: an application of three-mode factor analysis'. *New Zealand Geographer*, **27**, 38–55.

Carey, G. W., and Hughes, J. W. (1972). 'Factorial ecologies: oblique and orthogonal solutions. A case study of the New York SMSA'. *Environment and Planning*, **4**, 147–162.

Clark, C. (1940). *The Conditions of Economic Progress*, Macmillan, London.

Court, A. (1972). 'All statistical populations are estimated from samples'. *The Professional Geographer*, **24**, 160–161.

Curson, P. H. (1973). 'A factorial ecology of Avarua, Cook Islands'. *Pacific Viewpoint*, **14**, 23–37.

Davies, W. K. D., and Barrow, G. (1973). 'Factorial ecology of three prairie cities'. *The Canadian Geographer*, **17**, 327–353.

Davies, W. K. D., Giggs, J. A., and Herbert, D. T. (1968). 'Directories, rate books, and the commercial structure of towns'. *Geography*, **53**, 41–54.

Davies, W. K. D., and Lewis, G. J. (1973). 'The urban dimensions of Leicester'. *Institute of British Geographers, Special Publication*, **5**, 71–85.

Dent, O. F., and Sakoda, J. M. (1973). *Potential Sources of Spuriousness in Factorial Ecology Studies*. Institute of British Geographers, Quantitative Methods Study Group, Pre-circulated Papers, Birmingham Conference.

Dogan, M., and Rokkan, S. (Eds.) (1969). *Quantitative Ecological Analysis in the Social Sciences*, The M.I.T. Press, Cambridge, Massachusetts.

Doucet, M. J. (1972). *Nineteenth Century Population Mobility: Some Preliminary Comments*, Discussion Paper No. 4, Department of Geography, York University, Toronto.

Duncan, B. (1956). 'Factors in work-residence separation: wage and salary workers, Chicago, 1951'. *American Sociological Review*, **21**, 48–56.

Duncan, O. D., and Duncan, B. (1955). 'Occupational stratification and residential distribution'. *American Journal of Sociology*, **50**, 493–503.

Forrest, J. (1968). 'An approach to the analysis of subareas in Timaru'. *New Zealand Geographer*, **24**, 195–201.

Forrest, J., and Tan, M. (1971). Residential Location and Place of Work in a New Zealand City. *Proceedings, Sixth New Zealand Geography Conference*, pp. 51–57.

Gittus, E. (1964). 'The structure of urban areas'. *Town Planning Review*, **35**, 5–20.

Glass, D. V. (1973). *Numbering the People*, D. C. Heath, Farnborough.

Goheen, P. G. (1970). *Victorian Toronto 1850–1900*, Research Paper No. 127, Department of Geography, University of Chicago, Chicago.

Colledge, R. G., and Rushton, G. (1972). *Multidimensional Scaling: Review and Geographical Applications*, Commission on College Geography, Association of American Geographers, Washington.

Gorsuch, R. L. (1973). 'Data analysis of correlated independent variables'. *Multivariate Behavioral Research*, **8**, 89–107.

Gould, P. R. (1970). 'Is statistix inferens the geographical name for a wild goose?' *Economic Geography*, **46**, 439–448.

Greer-Wootten, B. (1972). 'Changing social areas and the intra-urban migration process'. *Review de Géographie de Montreal*, **26**, 271–292.

Guest, A., and Zuiches, J. (1972). 'Another look at residential turnover in urban neighborhoods'. *American Journal of Sociology*, **77**, 457–471.

Guttmann, L. (1968). 'A general nonmetric technique for finding the smallest co-ordinate space for a configuration of points'. *Psychometrika*, **33**, 469–506.

Hall, P., Thomas, R., Gracey, H., and Drewett, J. R. (1973). *The Containment of Urban England* (2 volumes). George Allen and Unwin, London.

Harvey, D. W. (1969). *Explanation in Geography*, Edward Arnold, London.

Hatt, P. K. (1946). 'The concept of natural area'. *American Sociological Review*, **11**, 423–427.

Hawley, A. H., and Duncan, O. D. (1957). 'Social area analysis: a critical appraisal'. *Land Economics*, **33**, 227–245.

Haynes, K. E. (1971). 'Spatial change in urban structure: alternative approaches to ecological dynamics'. *Economic Geography*, **47**, 324–335.

Herbert, D. T. (1967). 'Social area analysis: a British study'. *Urban Studies*, **4**, 41–60.

Herbert, D. T., and Evans, D. J. (1974). 'Urban sub-areas as sampling frameworks for social survey. *Town Planning Review*, **45**, 171–188.

Horn, C. J. (1973). *Factor Scores and Geographical Research*, Institute of British Geographers, Quantitative Methods Study Group, Pre-circulated Papers, Birmingham Conference.

Horst, P. (1965). *Factor Analysis of Data Matrices*, Holt, Rinehart and Winston, New York.

Hunter, A. A. (1971). 'The ecology of Chicago: persistence and change 1930–1960'. *American Journal of Sociology*, **77**, 425–444.

Hunter, A. A. (1972). 'Factorial ecology: a critique and some suggestions'. *Demography*, **9**, 107–118.

Johnston, R. J. (1968). 'Choice in classification: the subjectivity of objective methods'. *Annals, Association of American Geographers*, **58**, 575–589.

Johnston, R. J. (1970). 'Grouping and regionalizing: some methodological and technical observations'. *Economic Geography*, **46**, 293–305.

Johnston, R. J. (1971a). 'Some limitations of factorial ecologies and social area analysis'. *Economic Geography*, **47**, 314–323.

Johnston, R. J. (1971b). *Urban Residential Patterns: An Introductory Review*, G. Bell, London.

Johnston, R. J. (Ed.) (1973a). *Urbanisation in New Zealand: Geographical Essays*, Reed, Wellington.

Johnston, R. J. (1973b). 'The factorial ecology of major New Zealand urban areas: a comparative study'. *Institute of British Geographers, Special Publication*, **5**, 143–168.

Johnston, R. J. (1973c). 'Social area change in Melbourne, 1961–1966'. *Australian Geographical Studies*, **11**, 79–98.

Johnston, R. J. (1973d). 'Possible extensions to the factorial ecology method: a note'. *Environment and Planning*, **5**, 719–734.

Jones, F. L. (1965). 'A social profile of Canberra, 1961'. *Australian and New Zealand Journal of Sociology*, **1**, 107–120.

Jones, F. L. (1969). *Dimensions of Urban Social Structure*, Australian National University Press, Canberra.

Joshi, T. (1972). 'Towards computing factor scores'. *International Geography*, **2**, 906–908.

King L. J. (1969). *Statistical Analysis in Geography*, Prentice-Hall, Englewood Cliffs, New Jersey.

Klaff, V. Z. (1973). 'Ethnic segregation in urban Israel'. *Demography*, **10**, 161–184.

Lawton, R. (1955). 'The population of Liverpool in the mid-nineteenth century'. *Transactions, Lancashire and Cheshire Historical Society*, **107**, 189–200.

Lingoes, J. C. (1973). *The Guttmann–Lingoes Nonparametric Program Series*, Mathesis Press, Ann Arbor, Michigan.

McElrath, D. C. (1965). 'Urban differentiation: problems and prospects'. *Law and Contemporary Problems*, **30**, 103–110.

McElrath, D. C. (1968). 'Societal scale and social differentiation: Accra, Ghana'. *The New Urbanization*, St Martin's Press, New York. pp. 33–52.

McQuitty, L. L., and Clark, J. A. (1968). 'Clusters from iterative, intercolumnar correlational analysis'. *Educational and Psychological Measurement*, **28**, 211–238.

Meyer, D. R. (1970). *Spatial Variation of Black Urban Households*, Research Paper No. 129, Department of Geography, University of Chicago, Chicago.

Meyer, D. R. (1971). 'Factor analysis versus correlation analysis: are substantive interpretations congruent?'. *Economic Geography*, **47**, 336–343.

Meyer, D. R. (1972). 'Geographical population data: statistical description not statistical inference'. *The Professional Geographer*, **24**, 26–28.

Murdie, R. A. (1969). *Factorial Ecology of Metropolitan Toronto, 1951–1961*, Research Paper No. 116, Department of Geography, University of Chicago, Chicago.

Palm, R. (1973a). 'Factorial ecology and the community of outlook'. *Annals, Association of American Geographers*, **63**, 341–346.

Palm, R. (1973b). 'The telephone and the organization of urban space'. *Proceedings, Association of American Geographers*, **5**, 207–210.

Palm, R., and Caruso, D. (1972). 'Labelling in factorial ecology'. *Annals, Association of American Geographers*, **62**, 122–133.

Parkes, D. N. (1972). 'A classical social area analysis: Newcastle and some comparisons'. *The Australian Geographer*, **11**, 555–578.

Parkes, D. N. (1973). 'Formal factors in the social geography of an Australian industrial city'. *Australian Geographical Studies*, **11**, 171–200.

Pfautz, H. W. (1967). *Charles Booth on the City*, University of Chicago Press, Chicago.

Poole, M. A., and O'Farrell, P. N. (1971). 'The assumptions of the linear regression model'. *Transactions, Institute of British Geographers*, **52**, 145–158.

Rees, P. H. (1970). 'Concepts of social space'. In B. J. L. Berry and F. E. Horton (Eds.), *Geographical Perspectives on Urban Systems*, Prentice-Hall, Englewood Clifis, New Jersey, pp. 306–394.

Rees, P. H. (1971). 'Factorial ecology: an extended definition, survey, and critique'. *Economic Geography*, **47**, 220–233.

Rees, P. H. (1972). 'Problems of classifying sub-areas within cities'. In B. J. L. Berry, (Ed.), *City Classification Handbook*, John Wiley, New York, pp. 265–330.

Rees. P. H. (1974). *Residential Patterns in American Cities*, Research Paper No. 162, Department of Geography, University of Chicago, Chicago.

Robinson, W. S. (1950). 'Ecological correlations and the behavior of individuals'. *American Sociological Review*, **15**, 351–357.

Robson, B. T. (1969). *Urban Analysis*, Cambridge University Press, Cambridge.

Roseman, C. C., Christian, C. M., and Bullamore, H. W. (1972). 'Factorial ecologies of urban black communities'. In H. M. Rose (Ed.), *Geography of the Ghetto*, Northern Illinois University Press, De Kalb, Illinois, pp. 239–256.

Rummel, R. J. (1967). 'Understanding factor analysis'. *Journal of Conflict Resolution*, **40**, 440–480.

Schmid, C. F. (1950). 'Generalizations concerning the ecology of the American city'. *American Sociological Review*, **15**, 264–281.

Schmid, C. F. (1960). 'Urban crime areas'. *American Sociological Review*, **25**, 527–542 and 655–678.

Schmid, C. F., MacConnell, E. H., and van Arsdol. M. D. (1958). 'The ecology of the American city: further comparison and validation of generalizations'. *American Sociological Review*, **23**, 392–401.

Schmid, C. F., and Tagashira, K. (1965). 'Ecological and demographic indices: a methodological analysis'. *Demography*, **1**, 194–211.

Schwirian, K. P., and Smith, R. K. (1971). *Primacy, Modernization, and Urban Structure: The Ecology of Puerto Rico Cities*, Unpublished Paper, Department of Sociology, Ohio State University, Columbus, Ohio.

Shevky, E., and Bell, W. (1955). *Social Area Analysis: Theory, Illustrative Application and Computational Procedure*, Stanford University Press, Stanford, California.

Shevky, E., and Williams, M. (1949). *The Social Areas of Los Angeles*, University of California Press, Los Angeles.

Shepard, R. N., Romney, K., and Nerlove, S. B. (1972). *Multidimensional Scaling*, Seminar Press, New York.

Smith, D. M. (1973). *The Geography of Social Well-being in the United States*, McGraw-Hill, New York.

Spence, N. A., and Taylor, P. J. (1970). 'Quantitative methods in regional taxonomy'. *Progress in Geography*, **2**, 1–64.

Sweetser, F. L. (1965a). 'Factorial ecology: Helsinki, 1960'. *Demography*, **2**, 372–385.

Sweetser, F. L. (1965b). 'Factor structure as ecological structure in Helsinki and Boston'. *Acta Sociologica*, **8**, 205–225.

Sweetser, F. L. (1969). 'Ecological factors in metropolitan zones and sectors'. In M. Dogan and S. Rokkan (Eds.), *Quantitative Ecological Analysis in the Social Sciences*, The M.I.T. Press, Cambridge, Massachusetts, pp. 413–456.

Tarrant, J. R. (1974). *The identification and interpretation of principal components*, Monash University Publications in Geography No. 5, Monash University, Clayton, Victoria.

Timms, D. W. G. (1970). 'Modernisation and the factorial ecology of the Cook Islands, Brisbane and Auckland', *Australian and New Zealand Journal of Sociology*, **6**, 139–149.

Timms, D. W. G. (1971). *The Urban Mosaic*, Cambridge University Press, Cambridge.
Tryon, R. C. (1955). *Identification of Social Areas by Cluster Analysis*, University of California Press, Berkeley, California.
Tryon, R. C. (1967). 'Predicting group differences in cluster analysis: the social area problem'. *Multivariate Behavioral Research*, **2**, 453–475.
Udry, J. R. (1964). 'Increasing scale and spatial differentiation: new tests of two theories from Shevky and Bell'. *Social Forces*, **42**, 404–413.
Veldman, D. J. (1967). *Fortran Programming for the Behavioral Sciences*, Holt, Rinehart and Winston, New York.
Ward, D. (1969). 'The internal spatial structure of immigrant residential districts in the late nineteenth century'. *Geographical Analysis*, **1**, 327–353.
Willmott, P. (1969). 'Some social trends'. *Urban Studies*, **6**, 286–308.
Wilson, G., and Wilson, M. (1945). *The Analysis of Social Change*, Cambridge University Press, Cambridge.
Wirth, L. (1938). 'Urbanism as a way of life'. *American Journal of Sociology*, **44**, 1–24.

Chapter 7

Spatial Form in the Residential Mosaic

R. A. Murdie

During the past half-century much of the discussion and analytical work concerning the spatial form of residential areas within cities has centred on the zonal, sectoral and, to a somewhat lesser extent, multiple nuclei models of urban structure and growth. Until recently, however, debate concerning the adequacy of these models or hypotheses has been based primarily on a subjective interpretation of mapped patterns. It is only within the last fifteen years that more rigorous attempts have been made to evaluate the relative utility of the models in describing the social geography of the city. The ultimate goal, as expressed over twenty years ago by Bogue (1953), is to design a statistical or mathematical model 'which measures how much of a total distributional pattern is explained by each of these hypotheses alone and how much all three fail to explain when used in conjunction with each other' (Bogue, 1953, p. 14).

There are, of course, other approaches to the study of urban form which do not depend on evaluating the adequacy of the classical models (see, for example, the conceptual overview by Foley, 1964, and the research papers in Bourne, MacKinnon and Simmons, 1973). Nonetheless, the spatial form of residential patterns within cities, as derived from social area analyses and factorial ecologies, has been analysed primarily in the context of the three classical models. Indeed, efforts to develop more precise evaluations of these spatial models have paralleled development of the research strategies in social area analysis and factorial ecology, which are outlined in the preceding chapter. This essay builds on the previous chapter by focusing more directly on *spatial form* in the residential mosaic. Major emphasis is placed on recent work and the relative success of these studies in modelling the spatial form of urban residential areas.

A necessary prerequisite for this discussion is a review of the zonal, sectoral and multiple nuclei models of urban structure and growth. The review is relatively brief because the bases of the classical models, their underlying assumptions, and the major criticisms and reappraisals by the original authors have been discussed at length in the literature and are well known (recent reviews include Herbert, 1972; Johnston, 1971; Robson, 1969; Timms, 1971).

THE CLASSICAL MODELS

Generalized statements concerning the spatial structure and development of urban areas can be traced back to the city plans of Plato and Aristotle (Firey, 1947, p. 9), but the zonal, sectoral and multiple nuclei models are creations of the present century. All three were first published between 1924 and 1945, a point which is of considerable importance in evaluating their present-day relevance.

The zonal model

Although there were antecedents, such as Engels' description of social class zonation in Manchester (as reported in Berry, 1973; Harvey, 1972; Schnore, 1965) and Booth's monumental social survey of London (Pfautz, 1967), the zonal or concentric model of residential structure and growth is usually attributed to Ernest W. Burgess, a University of Chicago sociologist. Details of the model were first presented to a meeting of the American Sociological Society in 1923 and published a year later (Burgess, 1924). The article was republished the following year in the now-famous collection of essays entitled *The City* and elaborated in two subsequent papers (Burgess, 1927, 1929).

Burgess was particularly fascinated with social pathology and crime. He taught courses on these subjects at the University of Chicago and, in the decade prior to 1925, got his students to map the spatial distribution of juvenile delinquency, patrons of the public dance halls and various other social indicators for which data were available for Chicago (Burgess and Bogue, 1964, pp. 5–6). Although not specifically stated by Burgess, it is reasonable to hypothesize that the zonal model was a logical outcome of a detailed examination and synthesis of these maps.

The model was formulated in terms of urban growth as well as functional zonation. In Burgess's words (1924, p. 88):

> The typical processes of the expansion of the city can best be illustrated, perhaps, by a series of concentric circles, which may be numbered to designate both the successive zones of urban extension and the types of areas differentiated in the process of expansion.

The circles are five in number: (1) the central business district, (2) the zone in transition, (3) the zone of workingmen's homes, (4) an exclusive residential zone and (5) the commuters' zone (Figure 7.1). A more complete description of the zones is given in Burgess (1929), but confusion still exists over their meaning (Johnston, 1971, pp. 67–68). Although they were initially conceived primarily in terms of socioeconomic status differentials, variables relating to life-style and family status were subsequently used by Burgess and his students to test the model (Burgess, 1927, for example). Another point of confusion relates to the definition of the zones. They were first defined by Burgess (1924) as discrete zones with sharp breaks, but later evaluated by the same author

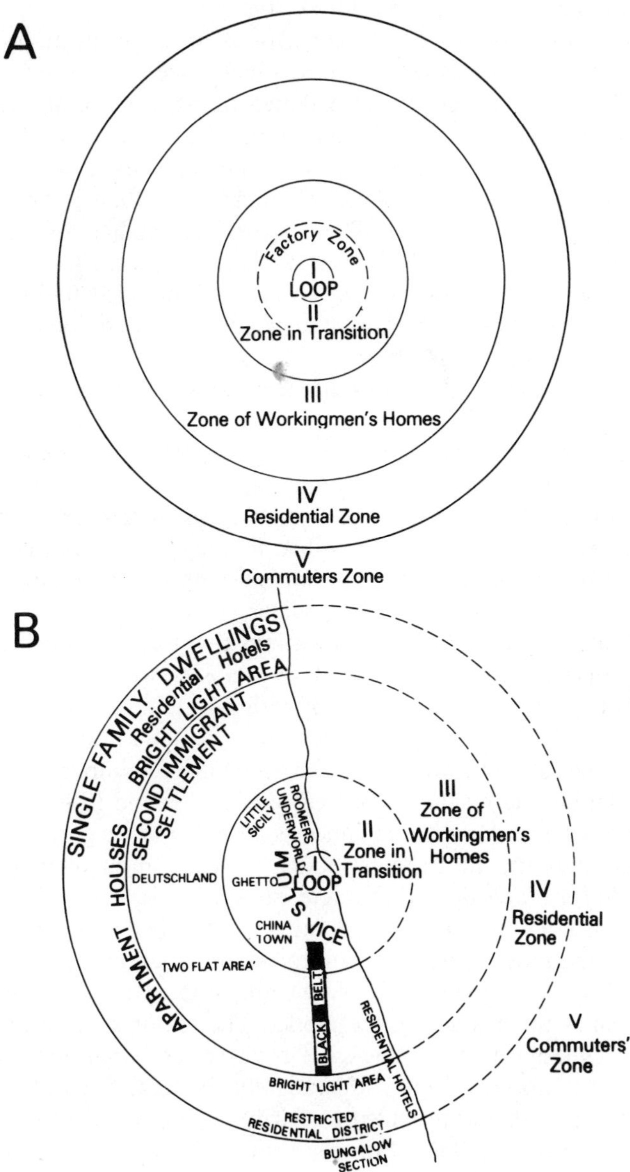

FIGURE 7.1 E. W. Burgess's zonal model: A. the idealized pattern, B. application to Chicago. (Reproduced by permission of the University of Chicago Press, from R. E. Park, E. W. Burgess and R. D. McKenzie, *The City*, 1925, charts I and II)

(Burgess, 1927) using a rather crude gradient analysis with data aggregated into one-mile zones encircling the centre of the city.

Expansion of the city is viewed primarily as an invasion and succession process with inner zones expanding into outer zones as the city grows in areal extent. The model is deterministic, therefore, but Burgess also recognized that it is an ideal concept and deviations should be expected (Burgess, 1924). Evidence of these deviations can be seen in his application of the model to Chicago—residential hotels along Lake Michigan, a 'black belt' and nucleated ethnic communities (Figure 7.1). These spatial anomalies and subsequent descriptive accounts (Burgess, 1929) indicate that the zones, especially the zone in transition and the commuters' zone, were not intended to be viewed as homogeneous areas. Indeed, the commuters' zone was described as the most heterogeneous in the Chicago region.

In the following decade, numerous attempts, mostly descriptive, were made to apply the zonal model to cities in the United States and elsewhere (see Quinn, 1940a, for a review). Although Burgess (1927) suggested the use of more rigorous techniques for evaluating the model, few made use of these. In Burgess's words (1927, p. 184): 'The further steps in the study are to plot frequency curves and to derive, if possible, mathematical formulas for these gradients in urban organization and growth.' Also during this period the model was severely attacked by critics such as Davie (1938) and Alihan (1938). The basis of these attacks related to: (a) indications that the spatial distribution of residential patterns did not correspond very closely with the ideal scheme; (b) evidence of a considerable amount of within-zone heterogeneity, not only in the zone of transition and the commuters' zone, as acknowledged by Burgess, but in other zones as well; (c) a failure to recognize the importance of heavy industry in shaping the residential structure of cities; and (d) confusion concerning zones as natural areas and zones as abstractions (e.g. was it intended that *one* zonal pattern, the Burgess model, with its unique configuration of five zones, held for *all* residential characteristics?). These criticisms are enumerated by Quinn (1940b), who also identified a number of requirements for testing the model, most of which relate to obtaining an extensive knowledge of the structure and growth of the city being studied rather than detailing specific guidelines for evaluating the model. The major specific requirement suggested by Quinn was that time–cost zones rather than zones based on simple linear distance be used. Unfortunately, Burgess did not respond to these criticisms and, therefore, failed to clarify the ambiguities and omissions of the original model. In fact, Burgess published only two articles on this topic after 1930, a general discussion of urban research needs (Burgess, 1953) and a useful historical review of research in urban sociology at the University of Chicago (Burgess and Bogue, 1964).

Burgess developed his model using data from Chicago and, in the main, intended that its application be limited to the commercial and industrial cities of North America. However, he never fully indicated the specific conditions under which the model might be expected to apply. It remained for Quinn

(1950) and, more recently, Schnore (1965) to enumerate these in detail. In sum, these conditions or assumptions suggest that the zonal model may not be applicable to non-industrial cities and cities of relatively small size. Indeed, it is assumed that the model is most applicable to large, rapidly growing cities with a heterogeneous population which have developed under a free enterprise system and are supported by a commercial-industrial economic base. Furthermore, the model may be time-dependent and only applicable to these cities at a particular stage in their technological development.

Concerning non-industrialized cities, the data which are available seem to indicate that the upper classes in these cities occupy land at the centre of the city and the lower classes at the periphery, a reversal of the Burgess model (Schnore, 1965; Sjoberg, 1960; Timms, 1971). In a broader context, Schnore (1965) has suggested the possibility of a general evolutionary theory of spatial form with the residential structure of cities in the same stage of technological development displaying broad similarities in spatial form. For example, the available evidence suggests that the spatial form of present-day non-industrialized cities parallels the distribution of residential patterns in North American cities prior to the transportation innovations and industrialization of the late nineteenth and early twentieth centuries.

The sectoral model

Despite the descriptive evaluations and criticisms of the zonal model during the 1920s and 1930s, Homer Hoyt (1939) was the only person to present a clear alternative to the Burgess hypothesis during this period. It may be hypothesized that this was partially due to his consideration of a large number of American cities, rather than a single urban area. Hoyt is a land economist and, at the time of this study, was engaged by the United States Federal Housing Administration to classify areas in American cities according to their mortgage lending risk. The specific goal of the Federal Housing Administration was to protect its insured mortgage loans by identifying those areas where the expectation of defaults in mortgage payments would be relatively low.

Hoyt was aware of Burgess's earlier study and there are some who view his model as an extension and modification of the zonal hypothesis (Johnston, 1971, p. 79). Indeed, Hoyt presents a careful review of the Burgess model before discussing his own study and concludes that 'the concentric circle theory of land use, while convenient as a starting hypothesis for a pattern of land uses, is subject to modification' (Hoyt, 1939, p. 23). The analysis begins with an examination of eight housing characteristics, mapped by block, for 142 United States cities of varying size, location, age and rate of growth. These data, which were obtained from the real property surveys of 1934 to 1936, include information on average rentals, age of structures, owner occupancy, condition of structures, existence of bath and heating facilities, race and crowding. Initial comparison of the data using map overlays indicates considerable coincidence amongst variables, thus suggesting a single pattern measuring poor housing conditions.

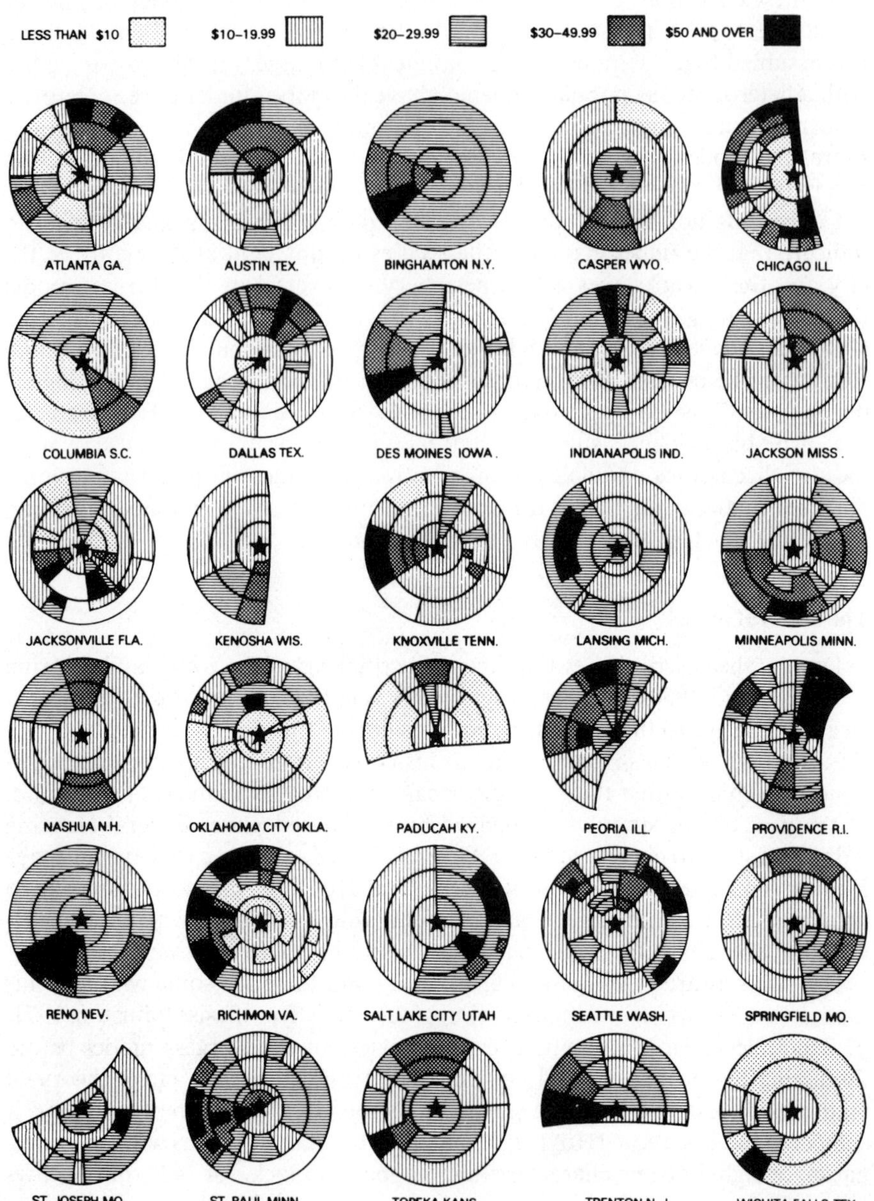

FIGURE 7.2 Hoyt's descriptive maps on which his sectoral model was based. (from: Hoyt, 1939)

One variable, average rent, is then selected to represent this pattern in a subsequent study of the spatial form of residential areas in each of the 142 cities.

From this study, Hoyt concludes that while the specific pattern of rental areas within individual cities is somewhat unique there are generalizations which extend to all United States cities. Inspection of the maps led to the following generalizations (Hoyt, 1939, p. 76):

> ... rent areas in American cities tend to conform to a pattern of sectors rather than of concentric circles. The higher rent areas of a city tend to be located in one or more sectors of the city. There is a gradation of rentals downwards from these high rental areas in all directions. Intermediate rental areas, or those ranking next to the highest rental areas, adjoin the high rent area on one or more sides, and tend to be located in the same sectors as the high rental areas. Low rent areas occupy other entire sectors of the city from the center to the periphery. On the outer edge of some of the high rent areas are intermediate rental areas .... There is an upward gradation of rents in the one or more sectors in which the highest rental area is located but there are also low rent sectors in which there is no increase in rents as one goes from the center to the periphery of the city.

The schematic maps of rental patterns which Hoyt (1939) drafted for a set of thirty United States cities illustrate most of these generalizations. In almost all of the cities socioeconomic status varies according to sectors, but within-sector variations are limited primarily to the larger cities such as Atlanta, Minneapolis and Seattle, which are highly differentiated and incorporate areas which are representative of almost all of the rental categories (Figure 7.2).

A second major section of the study concerns the movement of rental areas in American cities. Hoyt is quite specific about the need for such a study (Hoyt, 1939, pp. 77–78):

> If the concentric circle theory of the location of rent areas be accepted literally, all points on the periphery of the city are of equal importance as high rent areas, and no detailed examination of any city would be necessary. Since the high rent areas are located in the periphery of only one or more sectors, however, and are not distributed along the entire outer circumference of the city, it is necessary to ascertain for each city the location of the high rent sector. Therefore, the forces that determine which of the many sectors of the city will become the high rent sector are of vital importance to the analyst of city growth.

Evidence for the analysis was obtained by asking long-term residents of a number of cities to draw a line around the blocks which were highest rental in 1900 and 1915. Despite the subjectivity of this procedure, the results generally verified the intuitive impressions derived from supplementary material such as photographic and historical records and, combined with the 1936 real property inventory, gave data for three points in time. Analysis of the resulting maps (Figure 7.3) indicated that high rent areas move outwards through time within

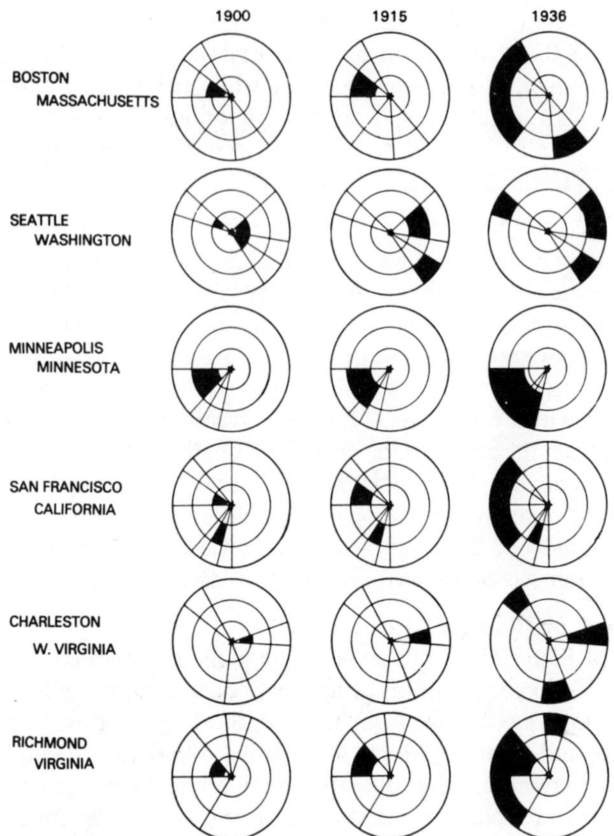

FIGURE 7.3 The sectoral movement of fashionable residential areas. (From Hoyt, 1939)

specific sectors of a city. The process is viewed in the context of filtering (see chapter 4) whereby middle and upper-middle income families move into houses left vacant by high income families as the latter move towards the periphery of the city.

Finally, Hoyt enumerates a number of factors or 'forces' which he views as important in determining the origin of high rental sectors and the direction of their movement. In brief, high rent areas are attracted along major transportation lines towards open country, high ground, waterfronts which are not used for industry and the homes of community leaders (for a more detailed discussion, see Hoyt, 1939, pp. 117–119). Since the sectors are uniquely defined for each city, these are the guidelines which were important to the Federal Housing Administration for identifying areas of favourable mortgage investment in individual cities.

Rodwin (1950a) recognized two major weaknesses in Hoyt's analysis. The first relates to oversimplification and is based on an evaluation of the forces identified by Hoyt as important in determining the pattern and movement of high rental districts, using Boston as a case study. Of particular concern was Hoyt's rather vague definitions of sector, of intermediate rental groups and of leaders of society or community leaders. As a prescription, Rodwin offered a slightly more precise definition of sector, a more refined view of class structure, and recognition that the desire by low and middle income families for an improved physical environment, both natural and man-made, may be as important as the attraction to homes of community leaders in accounting for the retention of high rental sectors in cities.

The second weakness of the Hoyt study concerns what Rodwin termed 'the somewhat narrow perspective and problem which guided the inquiry' (Rodwin, 1950a, p. 312). Rather than focusing exclusively on the adequacy of the model in accounting for regularities in the spatial pattern of residential areas, this discussion relates more specifically to its normative value and provoked a subsequent exchange between Rodwin (1950b) and Hoyt (1950) on the desirability of public intervention in urban development.

Aside from this response, Hoyt published two additional reappraisals of sector hypothesis: the first is a review of recent changes in urban structure and growth which may necessitate modifications of the classical models (Hoyt, 1964) and the second is a confirmation of the earlier study using income data (Hoyt, 1966).

The multiple nuclei model

Unlike the zonal and sectoral hypotheses, both of which assume a single centre, the multiple nuclei model postulates a set of nuclei about which urban activities cluster (Harris and Ullman, 1945). The number and type of nuclei vary from one city to another but usually give rise to wholesale and light manufacturing, heavy industrial, residential suburban and central business districts, as well as more specialized areas which may be unique to industrial cities. The development of separate nuclei are explained by four major factors: (a) some activities require specialized locational facilities such as the waterfront or a rail connection; (b) certain activities, such as those engaged in the garment industry, obtain mutual benefit from clustering together; (c) other activities, such as industries and high class residential, are repulsive to each other; and (d) certain activities, particularly those requiring large amounts of storage space, are unable to afford a central location. Concerning residential areas, it is suggested that (Harris and Ullman, 1945, p. 16):

> In general, high class districts are likely to be on well-drained, high land and away from nuisances such as noise, odors, smoke and rail road lines. Low class districts are likely to arise near factories and railroad districts, wherever located in the city.

And regarding ethnic groups, in particular (Harris and Ullman, 1945, p. 16):

> Residential neighborhoods have some measure of cohesiveness. Extreme

cases are the ethnically segregated groups, which cluster together although including members in many economic groups; Harlem is an example.

The multiple nuclei model is an attempt to develop a generalization about city structure and growth which is more closely related to reality than the zonal and sectoral models. Indeed, Harris and Ullman argue that the ecological patterns of cities are sufficiently variable and complex that they cannot be completely accounted for by a single model. Instead, they suggest that the spatial form of most cities may be best described by some combination of the three models—zonal, sectoral and multiple nuclei. It is towards efforts to evaluate the spatial form of residential areas in terms of a combination of the models that we now turn.

EMPIRICAL TESTS OF THE MODELS

As early as the turn of this century, it was recognized that more than one spatial model might be needed to describe the essentials of urban structure and growth (Hurd, 1903). Hurd's contribution was acknowledged enthusiastically by Hoyt (1939, 1950), but it is mainly during the past twenty-five years that the spatial form of residential areas within cities has been evaluated simultaneously in terms of more than one model of urban structure and growth.

A social values approach

One of the first evaluations of both the zonal and sectoral models was based on a strong condemnation of their deterministic assumptions. In his study of Boston, Firey (1947, pp. 84–85) acknowledged the presence of 'vague concentric and sectoral patterns', but was much more impressed by variations within sectors and zones and concluded that 'land use is apparently too variable to be conceived of in terms of two-dimensional cartographic generalizations'. His evaluation of the mapped patterns of a set of socioeconomic data reflects this position (Firey, 1947, p. 83):

> In the light of these findings it is reasonable to conclude that neither of the idealized descriptive schemes satisfactorily explains the distribution of working class families. To be sure, sectors and rings can be formed in the land use maps that we have just examined; they are just tangible enough to lend a superficial plausibility to descriptive 'cartographic' theories. But closer analysis reveals that such theories account for only a part of the phenomenon which they are supposed to explain. The remaining portion lies wholly outside the scope of these theories.

Firey gives no indication, however, of how much variation remains unexplained. Instead, he demonstrates by detailed analysis how the use of areas such as Beacon Hill, the Common and the Italian North End—the unexplained residuals—can be accounted for in terms of the values which become attached to a place. In conclusion, he argues for the incorporation of the cultural factor into ecological theory, but his conceptual procedure for doing so has been heavily attacked (Rodwin, 1950a) and has not been operationalized.

At a somewhat later date, Firey's general proposition concerning the importance of social values was verified by Jones (1960) for Belfast. Following a detailed examination of Belfast's physical and social development, Jones evaluated the adequacy of the zonal and sectoral models in describing the city's social geography and found them wanting (Jones, 1960, pp. 273–274):

> ... the exceptions are too big to contemplate, and the idealized patterns, whether concentric, zonal or sector, fall to the ground both as a description of Belfast and as a suggestion for the possible explanation of the pattern. There are elements in the sector theory to which we will return, but for the moment, sectors and zones must be set aside as *complete* answers.

Instead, Jones found that social values were operative and important in the social differentiation of Befast within the first century of the city's development and have continued their importance since then. Jones further argued that social values are invested in land outside of the present bounds of urban areas, well in advance of the movement of residential areas to the periphery and beyond. Residential sectors, if they are present (and they are to some extent in Belfast), are shaped by the values attached to the areas into which they are moving.

Thus, both Firey and Jones conclude that the zonal and sectoral models do not provide an adequate description and understanding of the social geography of Boston and Belfast. Both argue that exceptions to the generalized models are so numerous that the spatial patterns of residential structure and growth can only be adequately accounted for by the cultural values which are attached to particular parts of the city.

Subsequent studies, especially by Mann (1965) for Northern England and McGee (1969) for New Zealand, have used schematic diagrams to depict the residential structure of cities in these areas. The outcome, in each case, is a stylized representation in which the Burgess and Hoyt models are modified to accommodate cultural values and public intervention in the housing market which are specific to the two areas.

The 'social values' and related studies are particularly useful in focusing attention on the importance of factors which may account for deviations from the hypothesized zonal and sectoral patterns. But aside from qualitative judgements such as 'vague concentric and sectoral patterns' (Firey, 1947, pp. 84–85) or 'sectors and zones must be set aside as *complete* answers' (Jones, 1960, p. 274), none answer the question which Bogue (1953) posed over two decades ago. That is, how much of the spatial variation in residential patterns can be accounted for by each of the classical models and how much remains unexplained? In attempting to provide a more precise answer to this question, researchers have recently turned to the use of statistical and mathematical techniques.

Analysis of variance

The spatial pattern of residential areas within cities was first investigated through the use of an analysis of variance design by Anderson and Egeland (1961). Although there are previous examples of the use of this technique in spatial analysis, especially of geological data (Krumbein, 1955), this is the first published record in the urban literature.

The essentials of the Anderson and Egeland study, as well as seven related studies which have appeared since 1961, are summarized in Table 7.1. The unifying feature of these studies is their use of two-way analysis of variance for identifying the relative significance of the zonal, sectoral and, in some instances, multiple nuclei models in describing spatial patterns of urban residential structure. Beyond that, the studies differ in terms of the cities which are investigated (most are single-city studies), the variables used, the specifics of the research design and the details of the findings—although the overall results are similar.

The objective of a two-way analysis of variance in this context is to determine whether a spatial pattern of residential differentiation varies according to zones, sectors and, depending on the research design, the interaction between zones and sectors. The pattern can be any mapped distribution relating to residential structure, such as (a) census or other variables describing some aspect or residential differentiation, (b) social area indices and (c) the scores from factorial ecologies (see chapter 6). Of the studies summarized in Table 7.1, social area indices have been used most frequently (Anderson and Egeland, 1961; McElrath, 1962; McElrath and Barkey, 1964; Timms, 1971), although there are examples of the use of individual variables (Johnston, 1969; Timms, 1971) and factor scores (Murdie, 1969; Rees, 1970).

The first step in the analysis is the identification of a grid of zones and sectors which can be superimposed on the spatial pattern to be investigated. Despite earlier suggestions that zones be modified to take into account travel times (Quinn, 1940b) and that sectors straddle major transportation routes (Hoyt, 1939), most of the empirical studies which are referenced in Table 7.1 have used a rather arbitrary geometric grid. Exceptions include McElrath (1962), Johnston (1969) and Timms (1971), all of whom altered the definition of sectors and/or zones to conform more closely with reality. Murdie's (1969) study of Toronto, on the other hand, is typical of the norm. A grid of six zones and six sectors was identified, using the peak land value intersection (PVI) as a reference point (Figure 7.4). Zones were marked off in two mile bands encircling the PVI and sectors were placed 30 degrees apart through the 180 degrees lying above a horizontal baseline extending through the PVI.

The second, and somewhat related step, is the selection of observations for analysis. These have usually been some form of census unit—often a census tract. Some studies have used a sample of tracts, whereas others have employed all inhabited tracts within the city. Anderson and Egeland (1961), for example, selected four sectors out of the twelve defined for each city and, within each sector, chose four census tracts at approximately equal intervals outwards from the centre of the city—or one observation per cell. One of the implications of this design is that the variation which is not explained by zonal and sectoral

TABLE 7.1 Analysis of variance studies of spatial patterns within cities

Author (date)	City	Variables	Research design	Major findings
Anderson and Egeland (1961)	Four medium-sized United States cities with roughly circular shape—Akron, Dayton, Indianapolis, Syracuse	Two social area indices—social rank and urbanization	Selected four sectors out of twelve defined for each city and, within each sector, chose four tracts at approximately equal intervals outwards from the centre—sixteen tracts for each city with one observation per cell	Social rank—primarily sectoral except for Indianapolis (the largest city) which displayed a secondary distance pattern Urbanization—zonal for all cities
McElrath, (1962)	Rome	Two social area indices—social rank and urbanization; slightly altered to account for differences between censuses	All census districts (tracts) contiguous to three major transportation lines and their projections—three concentric zones with each zone differentiated by administrative boundaries	Social rank and urbanization are both zonal and sectoral; social rank is highest in the city centre
McElrath and Barkey (1964)	Chicago	The social area indices and their constituent measures	Ten zones and ten equally spaced sectors; approximately one tract per cell for a sample of sixty-eight	Urbanization—zonal Social rank—zonal Ethnicity (segregation)—slightly sectoral

Table 7.1 *(Continued)*

Author (date)	City	Variables	Research design	Major findings
Johnston (1969)	Melbourne	Forty-seven census measures: socioeconomic status (11) family status (6) minority groups (16) demographic (8) dwelling type and occupancy (6) —no information on income, occupation or completed education	Four zones and three sectors altered to adhere more closely to reality—stratified random sample of collectors' districts	Socioeconomic status—9 variables sectoral 5 variables zonal Family status—6 variables zonal 1 variable sectoral Minority groups—10 variables zonal 10 variables sectoral Demographic—5 variables zonal 4 variables sectoral Dwelling type and occupancy—no significant zonal or sectoral effects
Murdie (1969)	Metropolitan Toronto	Factor scores from analysis of census data for 1951, 1961 and 1951–61	Six zones and six equally spaced sectors; all inhabited tracts	Economic status (1951 and 1961)—primarily sectoral Family status (1951 and 1961 —primarily zonal Ethnic status (1951)—both sectoral and zonal Italian ethnic status (1961)—more sectoral than zonal Jewish ethnic status (1961)—primarily sectoral
Rees (1970)	Chicago	Factor scores for socioeconomic status and family status	six zones and five equally spaced sectors; included 222 community areas and outlying municipalities	Socioeconomic status—both zonal and sectoral Family status—zones more important than sectors

Timms (1971)	Brisbane, Australia	The social area indices; also examined four variables for two English cities, Luton and Derby: rateable value, electoral stability, adult criminality, mental illness	Six zones and nine sectors, the latter defined along arterial roads; included 108 collectors' districts or two for each cell	Urbanization—between zone variation predominates Social rank—between sector variation predominates Ethnicity—between zone variation predominates—all indices show both zonal and sectoral patterns and, in each case, the interaction effect is also significant
Schwirian (1972)	Comparative study of eleven Canadian metropolitan areas	Social rank, infertility, women in the labour force, multiple dwellings, language (surrogate for ethnicity)	Same as Anderson and Egeland (1961)	Social rank—distributed primarily by sector in all but two cases Infertility—highly variable Women in the labour force—highly variable Multiple dwellings—primarily zonal Language—considerable variation between cities

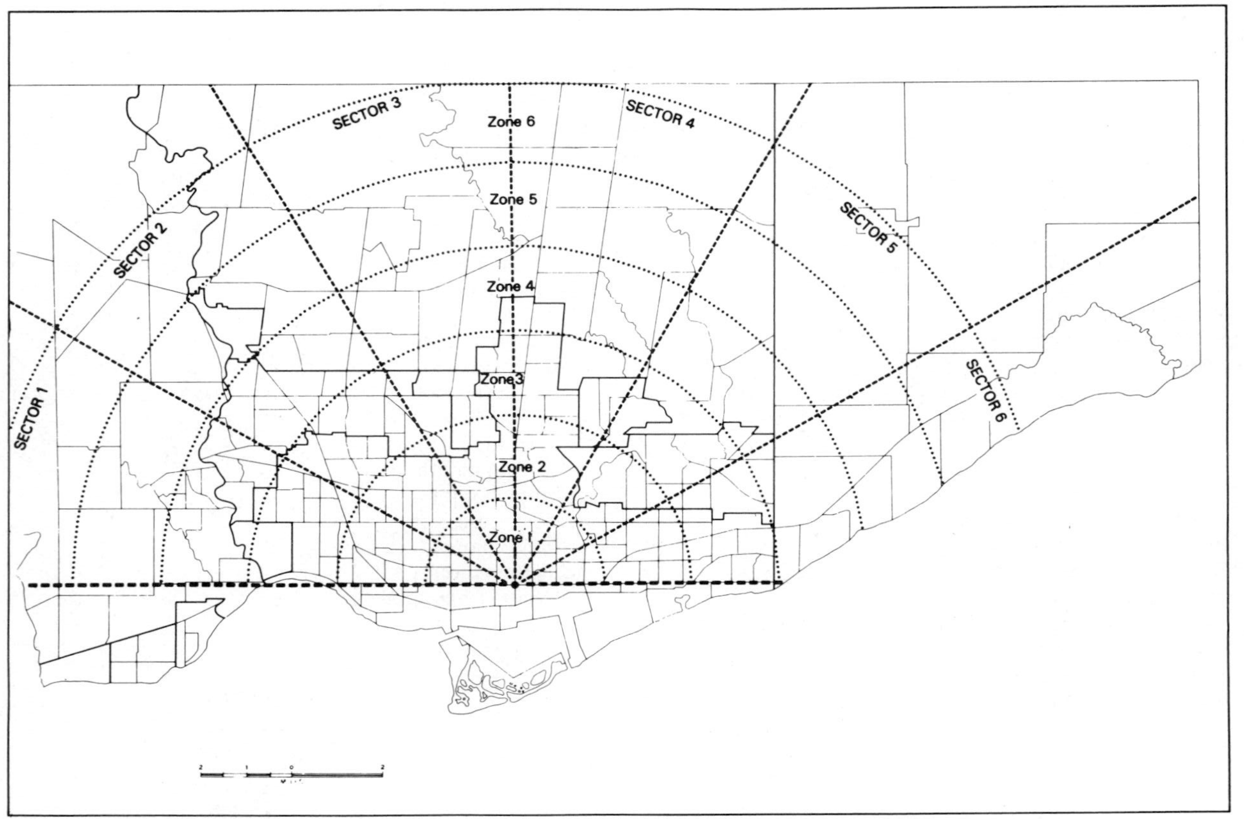

FIGURE 7.4 The definition of zones and sectors for metropolitan Toronto. (From Murdie, 1969)

differences is not broken down into its interaction and error components (both of which are described below). The result is a study which is usually relatively easy to interpret, but which does not incorporate most of the complexities of the spatial pattern being investigated. In contrast to the Anderson and Egeland study, Murdie (1969) used all the inhabited census tracts in Toronto lying north of the horizontal baseline (Figure 7.4). Tracts were assigned to cells according to the approximate centre of population of each tracts. In this design, there are at least two observations in most of the cells, with the result that interaction and error or within-cell components are separated out and must be considered in the interpretation.

One of the advantages of two-way analysis of variance is that several hypotheses can be tested independently in the same analysis. Using Figure 7.4 as an example, the following hypotheses are relevant (Murdie, 1969, pp. 154–155):

1. The hypothesis that column or sectoral means are equal. This hypothesis implies that residential patterns in Metropolitan Toronto do not vary according to the *sectors* which are defined in Figure 7.4.
2. The hypothesis that row or zonal means are equal. This hypothesis implies that residential patterns in Metropolitan Toronto do not vary according to the *zones* which are defined in Figure 7.4.

These hypotheses are generally referred to as the *main effects* of the two independent variables—sectors and zones in this case. When there is more than one observation or census tract in each grid cell, the *interaction effect* must also be considered. The result is a third hypothesis which concerns the effect of sectors and zones acting jointly:

3. The hypothesis that the interaction between sectors and zones is zero. The implication of this hypothesis in the present context is not entirely clear, although Figures 7.5 and 7.6 provide some clues.

One way of expressing the interaction problem using a grid of sectors and zones is as follows: do zonal differences have the same effect on a variable in one sector as they have in other sectors (Hagood and Price, 1952, p. 399)? Consider Figures 7.5 and 7.6. In the former, socioeconomic status varies by sector and by zones within sectors (as hypothesized by Hoyt, 1939, at least for sectors of high socioeconomic status). A closer inspection also shows that zonal differences have the same effect on socioeconomic status in all three sectors (i.e. socioeconomic status increases in a linear fashion outwards from the city centre. This pattern is further illustrated in the accompanying graph, where it will be noticed that the 'lines' representing the relationship between socioeconomic status and distance from the city centre for each sector are almost parallel to each other. Parallel or near-parallel lines in this type of graph are characteristic of non-significant interaction. In fact, there is almost no interaction between sectors and zones in this hypothetical example (Johnston, 1970, p. 364).

Now, contrast Figure 7.5 with Figure 7.6. The latter is a simplified representation of Toronto's socioeconomic status in 1951, using the grid of sectors and

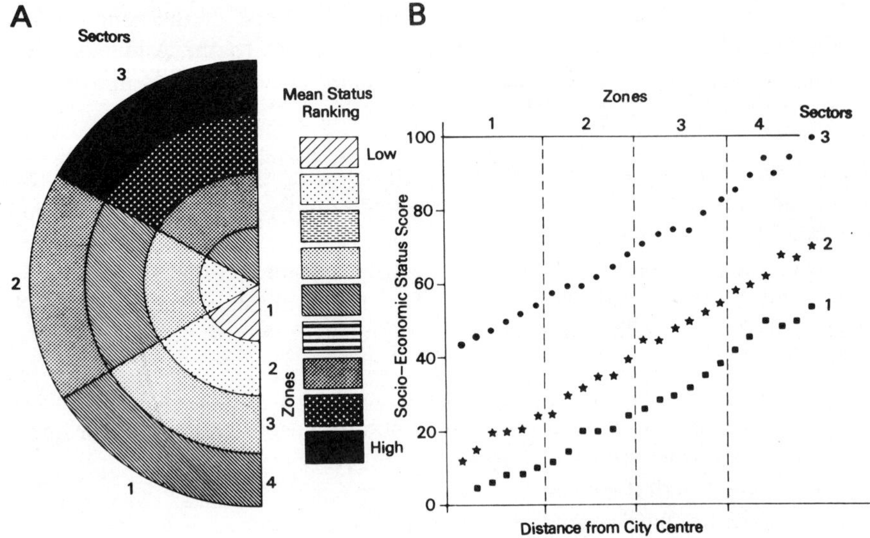

FIGURE 7.5 The residential structure of a hypothetical city according to the Burgess and Hoyt models: A. the zonal and sectoral pattern, B. the relationship between socio-economic status and distance from the city centre. (Reproduced by permission of R. J. Johnston, 1970, Figure 1)

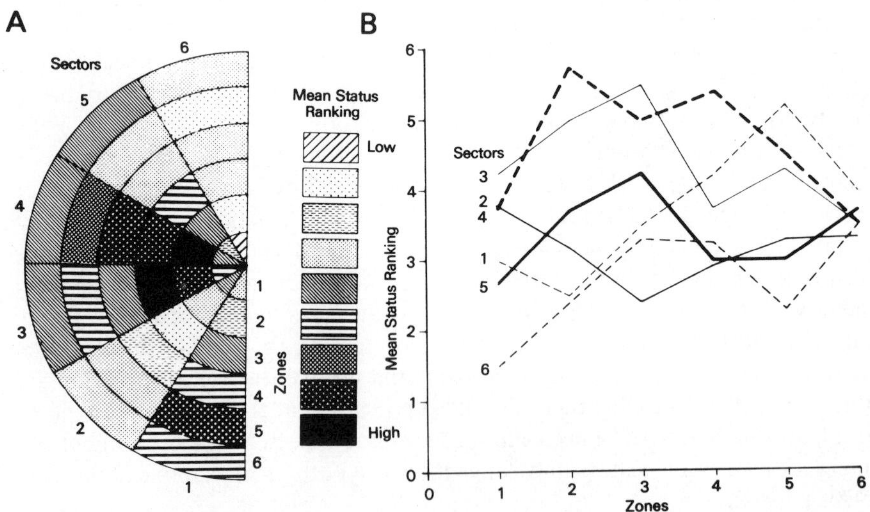

FIGURE 7.6 The residential pattern of metropolitan Toronto: economic status, 1951. A. the zonal and sectoral pattern, B. zonal profiles along sectors. (Reproduced by permission of R. J. Johnston, 1970, Figure 2)

zones from Figure 7.4. In this example, zonal differences clearly vary from one sector to another. The lines representing each sector are, for the most part, nowhere near parallel to each other and the result is a significant amount of interaction between sectors and zones (Johnston, 1970, p. 365).

In statistical terms, interaction represents the between-cell variation, which is not explained by the two main effects, namely sectors and zones. But how should a statistically significant interaction effect be interpreted in the context of spatial analysis? Aside from Murdie (1969), this question has been largely ignored, possibly because some researchers (Anderson and Egeland, 1961; Schwirian, 1972) have used a research design which does not isolate the interaction effect, whereas others have found a non-significant interaction between sectors and zones (McElrath, 1962; Rees, 1970). Murdie (1969) hypothesized that interaction could be interpreted as an indication of the presence of localized groupings within the city, in a form somewhat analogous to the multiple nuclei concept of urban structure and growth. In order to make this association between social groupings and interaction, however, the grid cells contributing to the interaction effect must be clearly identified.

To test each of the three hypotheses, a variance or F-ratio is calculated as follows. (This discussion is based on Murdie's 1969, p. 155, description of the procedure as it relates to sectors and zones.) Firstly, the total sum of squares (sum of squared deviations of a set of values from their mean) is parcelled into four components: between-sector, between-zone, sector × zone (interaction) and within-cell. A mean square value or variance estimate is then obtained by dividing each sum of squares by an appropriate number of degrees of freedom. Finally, the between-sector, between-zone and interaction F-ratios are calculated by dividing the within-cell variance estimate into the variance estimate for each of these effects. (We ignore here the question of whether the interaction variance, if it proves to be statistically significant, should be used as the denominator for calculating the between-sector and between-zone F-ratios.) The calculated F is then compared with F at a particular level of statistical significance. If the calculated F exceeds F for the selected level of significance, the null hypothesis or the hypothesis that the sectoral or zonal means are equal is rejected.

The typical output from a two-way analysis of variance is illustrated in Table 7.2 for socioeconomic status in Toronto in 1951. In this example, since the F-ratio for the between-sector variation exceeds F at the 0.01 significance level, the hypothesis that the sectoral means are equal is rejected and the conclusion is that socioeconomic status varies significantly by sector in Toronto.

The findings from the various analyses which have been conducted to date are shown in the right-hand column of Table 7.1. Although there are variations from city to city, the evidence suggests that socioeconomic status is distributed predominantly by sectors and family status by zones. Thus, preliminary observation of a limited number of cities, using the analysis of variance technique, indicates that the Hoyt and Burgess models each describe a different aspect of the social geography of modern industrial cities.

TABLE 7.2 Analysis of variance for socioeconomic status classified by sectors and zones in Metropolitan Toronto, 1951

Source of variation	Sum of squares	Degrees of freedom	Estimate of variance	F	$F_{0.05}$	$F_{0.01}$	Est ω_r^2
Total	1 477 602	210					
Sectors	292 923	5	58 584	11.9	2.27	3.13	0.18
Zones	20 028	5	4 006	0.8	2.27	3.13	0.00
Interaction	310 528	25	12 021	2.4	1.58	1.90	0.15
Within-cells	864 115	175	4 938				

Source. Murdie, 1969, p. 159.

Although the overall results are important, they are also subject to qualification. For example, important secondary effects are present in some of the cities whereby the zonal effect for socioeconomic status is significant or approaches significance, and the same is true of the sectoral effect for family status. Concerning the zonal effect for socioeconomic status, the evidence derived from inspecting individual cell means and analysing the zonal variations individually by sector (Johnston, 1970) suggests that the highest status groups live in the middle zones of the city, rather than at the centre or the periphery (Johnston, 1969; Timms, 1971). In the case of Rome (McElrath, 1962), however, socioeconomic status is highest at the centre of the city, as might be expected in a city which is somewhat less industrialized than the North American cities, whose spatial patterns have been examined using analysis of variance.

Additional evidence from the studies which are referenced in Table 7.1 suggests that the spatial patterning of other factors of residential differentiation cannot be generalized to the same extent as socioeconomic status and family status. Ethnicity is an example. In Toronto, for instance, Murdie (1969) found that in 1951 ethnicity was distributed by both sectors and zones with a highly significant interaction effect. Further investigation of this pattern led to the conclusion that 85 per cent. of the interaction effect could be attributed to two cells which overlap with the immigrant reception area in Toronto. In a 1961 analysis for the same city, two ethnic factors were identified, Italian and Jewish, with both distributed predominantly by sectors. During a decade characterized by a large influx of European immigrants, these two large and highly segregated non-Anglo Saxon ethnic groups had moved outwards in distinct but almost parallel directions from the reception area. Analyses of the spatial patterning of minority groups in some of the other cities listed in Table 7.1 have resulted in conflicting findings, although the predominant pattern appears to be sectoral.

One of the characteristics of the studies described above is the relatively large number of statistically significant relationships. In Murdie's (1969) study of social structure and change in Toronto, for example, forty-two out of fifty-four possible relationships were found to be significant at a probability equal to or less than 0.01. These results highlight a fundamental problem concerning the use of the *F*-ratio or any other measure of statistical significance —the ease of achieving a statistically significant relationship when a study is based on a large number of observational units. The *F*-ratio is also deficient in another sense. It does not directly measure the relative proportion of variation in a spatial pattern which can be attributed to the zonal, sectoral and multiple nuclei models of urban structure and growth. There is a need, therefore, to measure the strength of an association as well as its existence.

Murdie (1969) did this rather arbitrarily by comparing the relative size of the *F*-ratios for zonal and sectoral effects. In this way, variables or factors were allocated to one of five categories ranging from primarily sectoral to primarily zonal (Table 7.1 and Murdie, 1969, pp. 164–165). A more appropriate way of assessing the relative importance of zonal, sectoral and interaction effects is to calculate the proportion of the total sums of squares which each accounts for (Schwirian, 1972) or to use a more refined measure such as the intra-class correlation or the so-called (Guilford and Fruchter, 1973) general index of relationship, ω^2 (omega, squared). In order to illustrate that a statistically significant relationship need not indicate a strong association between two variables, ω^2 is used to calculate comparable coefficients for the data in Table 7.2. The results indicate that only about 18 per cent. of the total variation is accounted for by the sectoral effect, a negligible amount by the zonal effect and about 15 per cent. by the interaction between sectors and zones. The remaining 65 per cent. may be attributed to within-cell variation.

While these results suggest that well over half of the total variation remains unexplained (the within-cell variation), it must be pointed out that the amount of unexplained variation is partially dependent on differences in research design. For example, Schwirian (1972), using a design similar to Anderson and Egeland (1961) with only one census tract in each grid cell, found that 62.8 per cent. of the variation in Toronto's social status pattern in 1961 could be accounted for by sectoral differentiation and 11.2 per cent. by zones, leaving only 16 per cent. of the variation unexplained. It is therefore difficult (if not impossible) to compare percentage explanations between studies unless these studies use the same research design, including similar variables of residential differentiation, spatial units of analysis and grid overlays. Even more important, it is difficult to answer in absolute terms Bogue's (1953) question concerning the relative amount of spatial variation accounted for by each of the classical models. The effects of decisions such as the selection of spatial units of analysis and the number and arrangement of sectors and zones are too variable to permit a definitive answer to this question.

Aside from the inability of the analysis of variance tests to detail precisely the adequacy of the classical models in describing the social geography of the city, other criticisms, many of which have been mentioned above, are summarized by Johnston (1971, pp. 332–340) and Schwirian (1972, pp. 155–156). These include (a) the arbitrary definition of zones and sectors, (b) little consideration of potentially important zonal variations within separate sectors and of the form of zonal gradients, (c) no consideration of the possible interrelationships between factors or social area indices and (d) restriction of most of the studies to individual cities, thereby limiting broader generalizations.

Notwithstanding these criticisms, the limited number of studies which have been undertaken using the analysis of variance technique suggest that at a fairly high level of generalization there may be considerable order to the social structure and spatial patterning of residential areas within cities. This theme will be considered in more detail below, but, before doing so, we review two other techniques which have been used recently in an attempt to model the spatial pattern of residential areas within cities.

A data-smoothing technique

A smoothing or filtering procedure for evaluating the importance of the three classical models has been developed by Haynes (1971), using a set of factor score maps which describe the ecological structure of Montreal in 1951 and 1961 as data input. It proceeds as follows. Firstly, by means of a series of 'grouping algorithms' (one each for sectors, zones and nucleations), three sets of 'new average scores' are calculated for each map. These are then correlated with the original scores in an attempt to isolate the importance of each model in describing the spatial distribution of the residential patterns. In the case of sectors, the following algorithm is used for calculating the new average scores. Firstly, for each spatial unit of analysis (census tract or aggregates of tracts), the sum of all factor scores within ± 15 degrees of a line extending from the Central Business District to the tract centroid is derived. This sum is then divided by the number of scores within each 30-degree sector in order to obtain an average score for every spatial unit. Calculations for the zonal algorithm are undertaken in much the same way, except that the 30-degree sectors are replaced by one-mile zones. In the case of the nucleated algorithm, two figures are calculated for each spatial unit: (a) the differences in factor score values between that unit and every other unit of analysis and (b) the corresponding distances between these units. The two figures are then multiplied together, and the results summed and divided by the total number of scores minus one, in order to obtain an average score for each unit of analysis.

The results from the Montreal study generally correspond with those obtained from the analysis of variance procedure as applied to cities such as Toronto (Murdie, 1969). For example, in the case of the 1961 socioeconomic status pattern, the original scores exhibit a correlation of 0.782 with the sectoral scores and 0.413 with the zonal scores. For family status in 1961, the reverse is true, with coefficients of 0.423 and 0.889 between the original scores and scores from the sectoral and zonal algorithms respectively. In each example, the difference between pairs of coefficients is statistically significant. Of perhaps more significance, however, is the importance of the nucleated scores for all patterns of residential differentiation except family status. In part, these results may reflect the fact that nucleated patterns are not explicitly tested in the analysis of variance methodology. It is also suggested by Haynes (1971) that the patterns from previous studies which were considered indeterminate between sectors and zones may, in fact, be primarily nucleated.

The importance of this study is its attempt to develop an objective test of all three spatial models of urban structure and growth. Like many of the analysis of variance studies, it suffers from arbitrary definitions of sectors and zones and, in this case, nucleations. In an attempt to counteract this problem, Haynes employed sectors of 10 degrees as well as 30 degrees and found very similar results. As a further evaluation of the invariance of the results, the analysis could be extended to incorporate a number of different parameters of the spatial filters in a series of independent tests.

The possibility also exists of extending the analysis to a multiple correlation and regression framework, in an attempt to answer more precisely Bogue's (1953) question about the relative importance of the three spatial models when considered simultaneously in accounting for spatial variation in residential patterns. There are problems with the procedure, however, including the potentially high degree of interdependence among two or more of the zonal, sectoral and nucleated scores—the independent variables in such a study.

Fourier analysis

In a study of the spatial distribution of selected population characteristics for Baltimore, Hawkes (1973) uses two models simultaneously—the polynomial and Fourier series—to evaluate the relative importance of the zonal and sectoral hypotheses of urban structure and growth. Initially, locational coordinates were assigned to each census tract and the tracts were identified according to (a) their distance (d) from the city centre and (b) their angular direction (θ) about a straight line extending due east of the city centre. A mathematical model of the spatial patterning of urban residential characteristics was derived by first considering distance and direction independently and then combining the two explanatory variables into a single equation.

The simplest way of modelling the relationship between a characteristic of residential differentiation and distance from the city centre is the linear regression equation:

$$f(d) = a + b(d) \tag{7.1}$$

where d is the distance from the city centre. This basic equation can be modified to take into account more complex relationships, by transforming variables and/or adding more terms and thereby deriving a second- or even higher-order two-dimensional polynomial equation. Variations in gross population density, for example, which increase to a peak just outside the city centre and then decrease towards the periphery, are often best described by a second-order polynomial or quadratic equation with density transformed to natural logarithms:

$$\ln D_d = \ln D_0 - b_1(d) + b_2(d^2) \tag{7.2}$$

where

D_d = the gross population density at some distance (d) from the centre of the city
D_o = the gross population density at the city centre
d = the distance from the city centre
$\ln$ = the natural logarithm

Although more terms could be added to the equation or additional transformations undertaken, Hawkes indicates that there is no theoretical rationale for doing so. Consequently, the subsequent empirical work is limited to linear and quadratic expressions.

The relationship between a characteristic of residential differentiation and direction about the city centre is considerably more difficult to model. Hawkes accomplishes this by using the Fourier series of sine and cosine terms. Fourier series is most useful for modelling spatial patterns which are characterized by periodicities or oscillations such as alternating sectors of high and low socioeconomic status about the city centre. In its mathematical form, the periodic function $g(\theta)$ can be represented as:

$$g(\theta) = a_{0/2} + \sum_{n=1}^{\infty} (a_n \cos_n \theta + b_n \sin_n \theta) \tag{7.3}$$

In order to fit the function to empirical data, some limit, L, is chosen for the summation and the coefficients are estimated by regression techniques. The limit, L, is generally analogous to the use of $2L + 1$ sectors. Thus, if L is set equal to three, it is assumed that the characteristic under consideration is differentiated by seven sectors about the city centre.

The next task is the merging of the distance and direction effects into one equation. Firstly, consider the linear regression model, $f(d) = a + b(d)$, where a represents the value of a particular characteristic at the centre of the city and b is the slope of the regression line. Now consider the effect of direction on the parameters a and b. Direction has no meaning in the case of a, but the slope of the line, as measured by b, does vary with direction. Therefore, $g(\theta)$ may be substituted for b and the resulting equation accounts for the combined effects of distance and direction:

$$h(d,\theta) = c + d\left[a_{0/2} + \sum_{n=1}^{L} (a_n \cos_n \theta + b_n \sin_n \theta)\right] \tag{7.4}$$

This equation can be modified to accommodate a second- or even higher-order polynomial expression by adding more terms.

The usual criterion for evaluating the success of a simple regression model in accounting for variations in the dependent variable is the coefficient of determination (R^2). Complications arise in the present example, however, for there may be two sources of variation—systematic and random. In order to test for the systematic variation of the errors or residuals, a measure of autocorrelation must be calculated; Hawkes uses Geary's (1954) contiguity ratio (c). If there is very little contiguity among the residuals (value for c approaches 1), it may be assumed that the model has explained most of the variation in the dependent variable. Conversely, if there is a high degree of contiguity (value for c approaches zero), it may be concluded that the model has not been very effective in explaining the spatial variations which exist. The results from the analysis may be conceptualized in terms of four possible outcomes (Hawkes, 1967, pp. 39–40 and p. 78):

1. $R^2 = 0$, $C_r < 1$
   The model explains none of the variation, but the residuals are systematic in space. In other words, there is spatially systematic variation but the model failed to account for it.
2. $R^2 = 0$, $C_r = 1$
   The model explains none of the variation and the variation is not systematic in space. No model of spatial variation would explain the distribution.
3. $R^2 > 0$, $C_r < 1$
   The model explains some variation, but the residuals are still systematic, so the model has not adequately accounted for the spatial distribution of the observations (unless $R^2 = 1$).
4. $R^2 > 0$, $C_r = 1$
   The model explains some of the variation and the variation which is systematic has been adequately accounted for. To account for more of the variation it would be necessary to use variables other than measures of location.

In these outcomes:

$R^2 = 0$ indicates that R^2 (the coefficient of determination) is not statistically significant.

$R^2 > 0$ indicates that R^2 (the coefficient of determination) is statistically significant.

$C_r = 1$ implies no statistically significant contiguity effect for the residual values.

$C_r < 1$ implies a statistically significant contiguity effect for the residual values.

Outcome 4 is ideal, outcome 1 is a disaster, outcome 3 falls between outcome 1 and 4 and outcome 2 is trivial in the sense that the spatial pattern is random.

In the original study (Hawkes, 1967), the model was applied to census tract data for Baltimore in 1960. The variables included measures of education, age, race, labour force participation and occupation. In a subsequent summary paper (Hawkes, 1973), percentage of adults 25 years of age and older who are high school graduates is used as an illustration of the technique. A contiguity

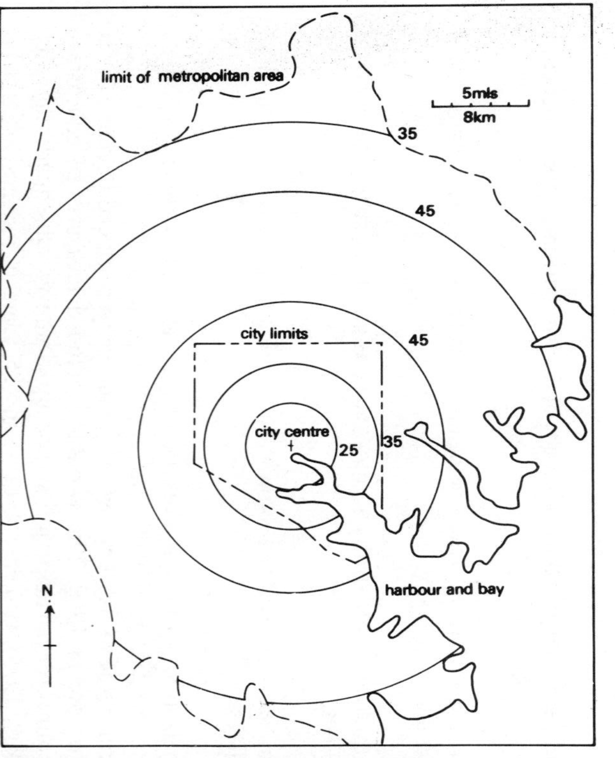

FIGURE 7.7 Percentage of persons in Baltimore who are high school graduates, estimates using a quadratic distance equation. (Reproduced by permission of the University of Chicago Press, from R. K. Hawkes, 'Spatial Patterning of Urban Population Characteristics', *American Journal of Sociology*, **78**, (1973), Figure 1)

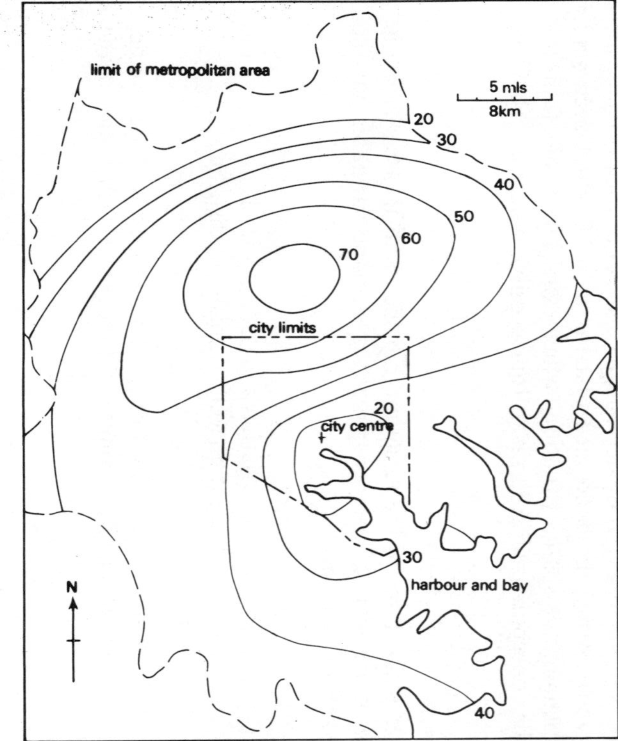

FIGURE 7.8 Percentage of persons in Baltimore who are high school graduates, estimates using both distance and direction (Reproduced by permission of the University of Chicago Press, from R. K. Hawkes, 'Spatial Patterning of Urban Population Characteristics', *American Journal of Sociology*, **78**, (1973), Figure 2)

ratio of 0.222 for the original variable indicates that the percentages of high school graduates are distributed in a spatially systematic pattern. In general terms, it may be said that about 22 per cent. of the variation in this variable is randomly distributed and not capable of statistical explanation. Using distance alone and a quadratic equation, about 33 per cent. of the total spatial variation was explained.

A spatial surface for this equation was generated (Figure 7.7). As expected, using the quadratic expression, the percentage of high school graduates is lowest at the city centre, increases in all directions to a maximum about 11 miles from the centre and then decreases towards the periphery. A contiguity ratio of 0.33 for the residual values indicates that a considerable amount of the systematic variation has not been accounted for. Nevertheless, when distance was combined with direction in a single equation, the explanation increased to 69.3 per cent. of the total variation.

The spatial surface for this latter equation is a more complex pattern than the one generated using distance alone (Figure 7.8). To the east, in a sector of low socioeconomic status, the percentage of high school graduates never exceeds 20 to 30 per cent. and there is very little variability within the sector. To the north, however, the percentage of high school graduates reaches a peak of more than 70 per cent. about 10 miles from the city centre and then declines rapidly towards the periphery. Clearly, then, the percentage of high school graduates varies according to *both* distance and direction. These results also correspond closely with Hoyt's (1939) initial hypothesis and with the findings from a number of the empirical studies which are summarized in Table 7.1 (Johnston, 1969; Rees, 1970; Timms, 1971).

But distance and direction (as measured in Hawkes's study) do not account for all of the systematic variation in the percentage of high school graduates. The contiguity ratio for the residuals from this analysis is 0.663, indicating that additional systematic variation remains to be explained. A summary measure of the adequacy of the model in accounting for the systematic variation may be obtained by relating the proportion of total variation explained (0.693) to the proportion of total variation which is systematic rather than random (0.778). The result indicates that 0.891 of the spatially systematic variation has been explained by a model incorporating both distance and direction. What about the unexplained variation? Presumably much of this is nucleated and could be accounted for by adding additional terms to the equation, but the result would be horrendously complicated and extremely difficult to interpret, especially in terms of sectors and zones. In this context, Haynes's (1971) simpler measure of nucleation has considerably more appeal.

Of the other variables used in the Baltimore analysis, those relating to socioeconomic status and race were the least randomly distributed. These are also the characteristics whose variance was most adequately described by the model. In contrast, the age variables (under fourteen, fourteen to twenty-four, and twenty-four and over) displayed relatively little systematic variation—less than one-third—and were least well accounted for by the model. In general, the results for most variables correspond to outcome (3), indicating that the model explains some of the variation but that additional systematic variation remains to be accounted for.

Because the study is restricted to one city at one point in time, it is difficult to derive generalizations from it about the spatial patterning of residential characteristics. Most of the socioeconomic characteristics, for example, '. . . vary by distance and direction' but '. . . in different ways' (Hawkes, 1967, p. 116). With respect to the variables which are usually associated with family status (especially persons under fourteen and female labour force participation), it is rather surprising that these variables do not display a more systematic pattern and are not better accounted for by the model. It may be that they are distributed in a complex non-linear form outwards from the city centre, thereby producing interaction effects similar of those found in some of the studies using two-way analysis of variance (Table 7.1).

Alternative methodologies: a brief evaluation

The mathematical model which has been described above differs from the analysis of variance and data-smoothing procedures in several important ways; each has advantages and disadvantages. Firstly, the mathematical model assumes a continuous surface rather than discrete zones and sectors. Unlike the variance procedure, it searches out its own sectors (although the number of sectors must be specified) in an attempt to maximize statistical explanation. This means, of course, that the form of the sectors cannot be specified *a priori* to coincide with the city's transportation network or some other aspect of urban development as advocated by Hoyt (1939) and subsequent researchers (Johnston, 1971; Timms, 1971). This is also true of the data-smoothing technique.

Both the analysis of variance and Fourier procedures are characterized by the difficulty of modelling complex zonal variations, and neither accounts directly for multiple nuclei variations. In the analysis of variance procedure, zonal variations which are not the same in all directions often result in a large interaction effect which, in some instances (Murdie, 1969), has been interpreted as an indication of local groupings or multiple nuclei. An advantage of the analysis of variance procedure is that zonal variations can be analysed separately for each sector using a one-way analysis of variance test. In the case of a mathematical model incorporating polynomial and Fourier series, more terms can be added in an attempt to capture additional complexities in the spatial pattern. By doing so, however, the model may become virtually uninterpretable.

Despite these qualifications, the model developed by Hawkes has some advantages over the other two procedures. The specific distinction between systematic and random variance, for example, is an important conceptual refinement. Also, the model provides a somewhat more direct answer to Bogue's (1953) question concerning the relative amount of spatial variation of specific variables or indices which can be accounted for by the classical models of urban structure and growth.

It also needs to be pointed out that these are not the only techniques which have been developed to test the classical spatial models. For example, the Duncans (Duncan and Duncan, 1955) and others (Davies, 1964; Uyeki, 1964) have used a simple index of centralization to test the zonal differentiation of occupation groups for cities as a whole and for sectors within cities. Results from these studies indicate a general decentralization of higher status groups and centralization of lower status groups, but with considerable variation from this pattern within certain sectors.

As part of their work on the residential structure of Chicago, the Duncans also developed an index of sector concentration which measures the extent to which an occupation group is concentrated in particular sectors. The results from this study are not referenced in their published work, but Davies (1964) reports that zones and sectors were of equal importance in describing the spatial differentiation of occupation groups in Chicago. This finding corresponds with that obtained by Rees (1970) for the same city some time later, using a different methodology and a more recent set of data (see Table 7.1). In his own study of two South African cities, however, Davies (1964) found that sector concentration, especially of the high and low status groups, was of more importance than zonal concentration, thereby confirming the results from most studies which have evaluated the spatial distribution of socioeconomic status patterns (see Table 7.1).

Although not without problems, measures such as the indices of centralization and sector concentration have the advantage of relative simplicity of calculation and ease of interpretation. To date, they have been used exclusively for studies of occupation groups, but they could be employed to examine the spatial distribution of any residential pattern. In their attempts to develop more sophisticated methodologies, recent analysts appear to have overlooked this simple but potentially useful set of measures for evaluating spatial form in the residential mosaic.

SYNTHESIS

Factorial ecologies of a relatively large number of industrialized cities indicate that urban sub-areas can be differentiated according to three basic constructs: socioeconomic status, family status and ethnicity (see chapter 6). The details vary from city to city depending, among other things, on the data input, but the broad generalizations seem to hold for most cities which have been studied in the 'developed' world. In the main, it appears that the three dimensions are conceptually independent—if not completely independent in a statistical sense. And even in the statistical context, what published studies are available indicate that a factor analysis of the correlations between oblique dimensions usually results in the three general constructs with very little, if any, correlation between them (Davies and Barrow, 1973; Davies and Lewis, 1973; also confirmed by Murdie for Toronto in an unpublished study).

Are these structural dimensions related in any way to spatial form in the

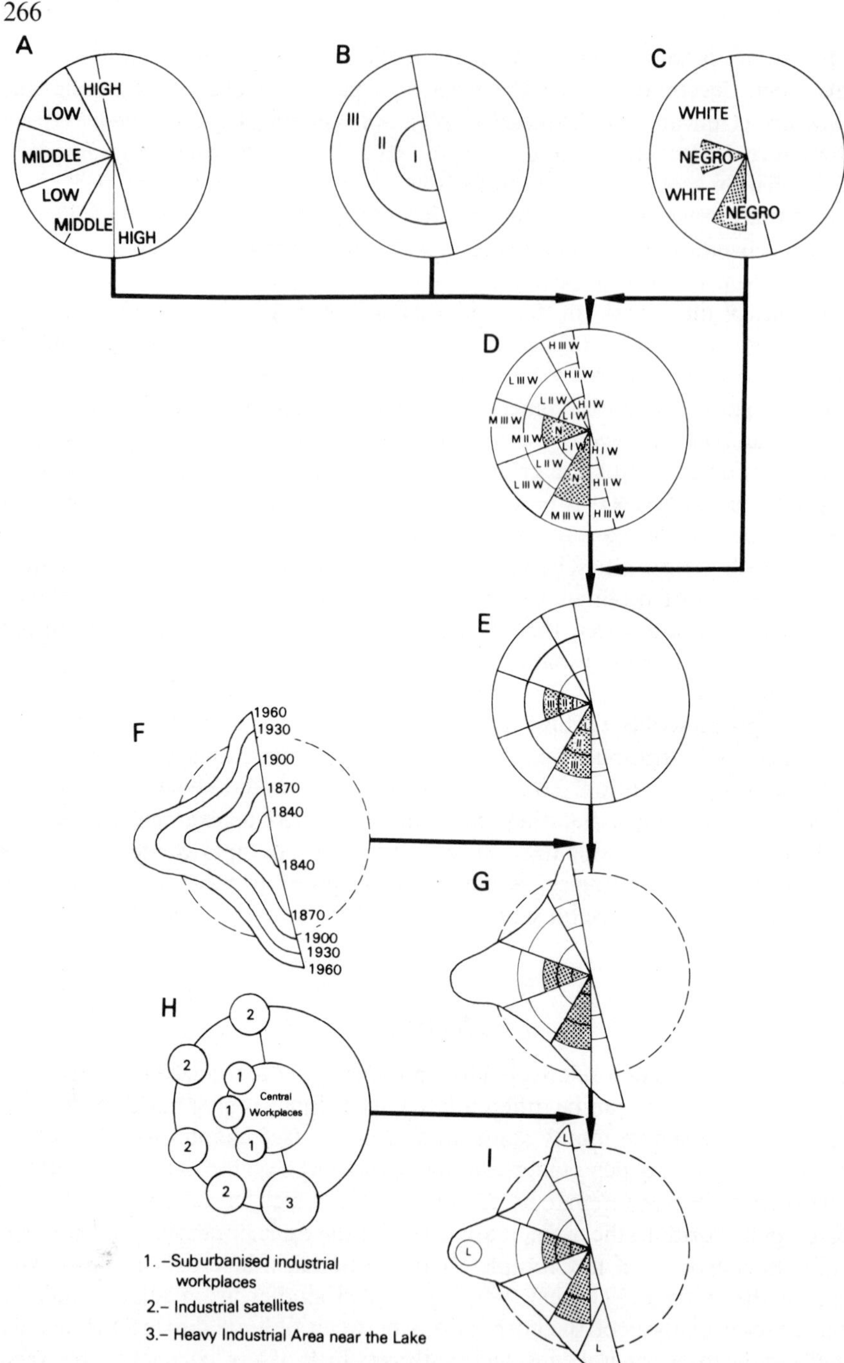

FIGURE 7.9 An integrated spatial model of the metropolis. (Reproduced by permission of the University of Chicago Press, from B. J. L. Berry and P. H. Rees, 'The factorial ecology of Calcutta', *American Journal of Sociology*, **74** (1969), Figure 13)

residential mosaic? Results from the limited set of studies which are available and have been reviewed in this chapter indicate that at a highly generalized level the social area–factorial ecology constructs can be merged with the classical models of urban structure and growth to form a relatively complete view of urban social structure. The essentials of the argument have been summarized by Berry and Rees (1969), using Chicago as an example, and their diagram (Figure 7.9) forms the basis of the subsequent discussion. (Visual inspection of the mapped patterns from a number of social areas or factorial ecology studies which have not been reviewed in this chapter—e.g. Davies and Barrow, 1973; Janson, 1971; Salins, 1971–substantiate the generalizations presented below.)

Although some of the results are ambiguous or even contradictory, the general evidence suggests that (a) socioeconomic status is arranged primarily by sectors (Figure 7.9A), (b) family status is distributed principally by zones (Figure 7.9B) and (c) minority groups are arranged in nuclei or segregated areas (Figure 7.9C). When these dimensions are statistically independent (which occurs by definition in the case of an orthogonal rotation of the factor loading matrix), they may be superimposed on each other to form relatively homogeneous communities (Figure 7.9D). The result is an idealized representation which can be altered in a number of ways of provide a closer approximation of the real world.

What are these distortions? Three specific variations are detailed in Figure 7.9. Firstly, the segregated areas show the entire range of family status characteristics, but in a compressed form. Therefore, the zonal variation in family status differs by direction about the city centre (Figure 7.9E). A second distortion results from variations in the growth of the city (Figure 7.9F), the effect of which is to accentuate zonal variations within sectors by the creation of a star-shaped city (Figure 7.9G). And thirdly, the decentralization of industry (Figure 7.9H) results in the formation of areas of relatively low socioeconomic status about some of these industrial nodes at the periphery of the city (Figure 7.9I).

Johnston (1971) agrees that the Berry and Rees model is an excellent synthesis of spatial form in the residential mosaic at one point in time, but argues that '. . . a complete model requires incorporation of the known processes operating to produce neighbourhood change, with the consequent patterns, as well as some of the findings . . . which disagree with the generally held views . . . ' (Johnston, 1971, p. 348). The latter include (a) the zonal variation of socioeconomic status within sectors (Rees, 1970, p. 374, postulates a direct relationship between this secondary effect and city size) and (b) complex interrelationships between the main dimensions of social structure which may be masked by the use of standard correlation procedures and orthogonal factor rotations.

Spatial patterns of neighbourhood change have not been highlighted in this review, partially because the patterns are complex and, for the few studies which are available, generalizations have been derived primarily from a visual inspection of the mapped patterns rather than a more objective analysis. The studies are of two types: (a) those which compare the mapped patterns from two or more cross-sectional studies for the same city and (b) those which directly analyse a set of change measures and map the results.

Results from the first group of studies suggest that, at least for a ten-year period (most often 1950–60), the spatial patterning of socioeconomic status is the most stable of the three social area constructs and ethnicity patterns are the most likely to change, predominantly in a sectoral direction (Greer-Wootten, 1972; Johnston, 1973; Murdie, 1969). Studies over a longer period of time have often been thwarted by a lack of data for urban sub-areas, although there are notable exceptions. These include Goheen's (1970) detailed analysis of Toronto's changing social geography in the second half of the nineteenth century, Guest's (1974) evaluation of Schnore's (1965) evolutionary hypothesis for American metropolitan areas, Hunter's (1974) classification of Chicago's community areas according to changes during the period, 1930–60, and a detailed evaluation by Richardson, Vipond and Furbey (1974) of the sector model using property value data for Edinburgh at yearly intervals from 1910 to 1971.

Findings from the studies which have analysed longitudinal data are more difficult to summarize. Firstly, in contrast to the cross-sectional studies, the structural dimensions which have been derived from these analyses are usually more complex and not as directly related to the social area constructs. The percentage of variance explained is relatively low and the dimensions are often not easily interpreted (Brown and Horton, 1971; Greer-Wootten, 1972; Hunter, 1971; Johnston, 1973; Murdie, 1969). Notwithstanding these limitations, some generalizations are possible. Most of the studies have identified a factor which indicates increasing socioeconomic status at the periphery, at least one other dimension related to life-cycle changes, and one or more dimensions incorporating changes in ethnicity. With the exception of ethnic changes, zonal patterns characterize most of the factors, although the overall spatial distributions are much more random than those from the cross-sectional analyses.

Hopefully, as longer series of comparable data for urban sub-areas become available, more specific generalizations concerning changes in the spatial form of the residential mosaic will be possible. In the meantime, however, a number of methodological issues need to be solved, not the least of which is a careful evaluation of the relative merits of various measures of change.

CONCLUSIONS

This chapter has focused on the classical models of urban structure and growth and recent attempts, using statistical and mathematical techniques, to evaluate the adequacy of these hypotheses for describing the social geography of the city. The overriding question concerns the proportion of variation, especially non-random variation, which can be attributed to each model. But it has proven difficult, even with the aid of relatively sophisticated statistical and mathematical techniques, to obtain a precise answer to this question. The incorporation of polynomials and Fourier series into a single mathematical model has clarified the problem, but, unfortunately, the application of this model has been limited to a single city. Comparative studies applying the same or similar procedures to other cities are needed before the technique can be fully evaluated.

These problems notwithstanding, the evidence which is available suggests that at a high level of generalization the zonal, sectoral and multiple nuclei models are complementary, with each describing a specific aspect of spatial form in the residential mosaic. Whether the specific details of the models are relevant today is probably not very important. After all, these details relate to cities of the 1920s and 1930s—not the 1970s. Conditions have changed dramatically since the early part of this century and the spatial organization of residential areas within cities has changed accordingly. Decentralization of commercial and industrial activities has resulted in a multi-nucleated metropolis rather than a single-centred city. Increased participation by all levels of government in the housing market has resulted in a mixture of housing types from the centre to the periphery of the city, often intermingled with each other. It is perhaps too early to measure the full impact of these and other factors on the spatial form of the residential mosaic, but it seems evident that the classical models—especially the zonal and sectoral hypotheses—may be too simplistic to capture all, or even a large proportion, of the spatial variation of residential areas within industrialized cities of the 1970s. Indeed, the spatial patterning of residential areas is probably becoming more random and less systematic, so that variables such as government policies, cultural values and political clout will be of considerable importance in explaining the residual values.

The models are descriptive, somewhat deterministic and macro in scale. They have proved useful as an organizing framework for a generalized descriptive model of the social geography of the city, but, in the main, they do not say very much about process in contemporary urban society—nor should they be expected to. The processes which account for spatial variation in the residential mosaic are complex and result from the cumulative summation of a host of individual decisions—both by the producers and consumers of housing (see chapters 2, 3 and 6). As Robson (1969) and Harvey (1970, 1973) have pointed out, there is need for a much greater integration between analyses of social processes and spatial form. We not only need to identify generalizations in spatial form but also to search for the factors which produce that form. Progress will probably be slow, however, for as Harvey (1970, 1973) has suggested, working at the interface between spatial form and social processes is a challenging but difficult task.

REFERENCES

Alihan, M. A. (1938). *Social Ecology: A Critical Analysis*, Columbia University Press, New York.

Anderson, T. R., and Egeland, J. A. (1961), 'Spatial aspects of social area analysis'. *American Sociological Review*, **26**, 392–398.

Berry, B. J. L. (1973). *The Human Consequences of Urbanisation*, Macmillan, London.

Berry, B. J. L., and Rees, P. H. (1969). 'The factorial ecology of Calcutta'. *American Journal of Sociology*, **74**, 445–491.

Bogue, D. J. (Ed.) (1953). *Needed Urban and Metropolitan Research*, Scripps Foundation, Oxford, Ohio.

Bourne, L. S., MacKinnon, R. D., and Simmons, J. W. (Eds.) (1973). *The Form of Cities in Central Canada: Selected Papers*, University of Toronto Press, Toronto.

Brown, L. A., and Horton, F. E. (1971). 'Social area change: an empirical analysis'. *Urban Studies*, **7**, 271–288.

Burgess, E. W. (1924). 'The growth of the city: an introduction to a research project'. *Publications of the American Sociological Society*, **18**, 85–97. Also in R. E. Park, E. W. Burgess and R. D. McKenzie. (1925), *The City*, University of Chicago Press, Chicago, pp. 47–62.

Burgess, E. W. (1927). 'The determination of gradients in the growth of the city'. *Publications of the American Sociological Society*, **21**, 178–184.

Burgess, E. W. (1929). 'Urban areas'. In T. V. Smith and L. D. White (Eds.), *Chicago: An Experiment in Social Science Research*, University of Chicago Press, Chicago, pp. 114–123.

Burgess, E. W. (1953). 'The ecology and social psychology of the city'. In D. J. Bogue (Ed.), *Needed Urban and Metropolitan Research*, Scripps Foundation, Oxford, Ohio, pp. 80–84.

Burgess, E. W., and Bogue, D. J. (1964). *Contributions to Urban Sociology*, University of Chicago Press, Chicago.

Davie, M. R. (1938). 'The pattern of urban growth'. In G. P. Murdoch (Ed.), *Studies in the Science of Society*, Yale University Press, New Haven, Connecticut, pp. 131–161.

Davies, R. J. (1964). 'Social distance and the distribution of occupational categories in Johannesburg and Pretoria'. *South African Geographical Journal*, **46**, 24–39.

Davies, W. K. D., and Barrow, G. T. (1973). 'A comparative factorial ecology of three Canadian prairie cities'. *The Canadian Geographer*, **17**, 327–353.

Davies, W. K. D., and Lewis, G. J. (1973). 'The urban dimensions of Leicester, England'. *Institute of British Geographers, Special Publication*, **5**, 71–85.

Duncan, O. D., and Duncan, B. (1955). 'Residential distribution and occupational stratification'. *American Journal of Sociology*, **60**, 493–503.

Firey, W. (1947). *Land Use in Central Boston*, Harvard University Press, Cambridge, Massachusetts.

Foley, D. L. (1964). 'An approach to metropolitan spatial structure'. In M. M. Webber and coauthors, *Explanations into Urban Structure*, University of Pennsylvania Press, Philadelphia, Pennsylvania, pp. 21–78.

Geary, R. C. (1954). 'The contiguity ratio and statistical mapping'. *The Incorporated Statistician*, **5**, 115–141.

Goheen, P. G. (1970). *Victorian Toronto, 1850–1900: Pattern and Process of Growth*, Research Paper No. 127, Department of Geography, University of Chicago, Chicago.

Greer-Wootten, B. (1972). 'Changing social areas and the intra-urban migration process'. *Revue de Géographie de Montreal*, **26**, 271–292.

Guest, A. M. (1974). 'Neighbourhood life cycles and social status'. *Economic Geography*, **50**, 228–243.

Guilford, J. P., and Fruchter, B. (1973). *Fundamental Statistics in Psychology and Education*, McGraw-Hill, New York.

Hagood, M. J., and Price, D. O. (1952). *Statistics for Sociologists*, Holt, New York.

Harris, C. D., and Ullman, E. L. (1945). 'The nature of cities'. *Annals of the American Academy of Political and Social Science*, **242**, 7–17.

Harvey, D. (1970). 'Social processes and spatial form: an analysis of the conceptual problems of urban planning'. *Papers of the Regional Science Association*, **25**, 47–69.

Harvey, D. (1972). 'Revolutionary and counter-revolutionary theory in geography and the problem of ghetto formation'. in H. M. Rose (Ed.), *Geography of the Ghetto: Perceptions, Problems and Alternatives*, Northern Illinois University, De Kalb, Illinois.

Harvey, D. (1973). *Social Justice and the City*, Edward Arnold, London.

Hawkes, R. K. (1967). *A Model of the Spatial Distribution of Urban Residential Area Characteristics*, Unpublished Ph.D. dissertation, Johns Hopkins University, Baltimore.

Hawkes, R. K. (1973). 'Spatial patterning of urban population characteristics'. *American Journal of Sociology*, **78**, 1216–1235.

Haynes, K. E. (1971). 'Spatial change in urban structure: alternative approaches to ecological dynamics'. In B. J. L. Berry (Ed.), 'Comparative factorial ecology'. *Economic Geography*, **47**, 324–335.

Herbert, D. T. (1972). *Urban Geography: A Social Perspective*, Praeger, New York.

Hoyt, H. (1939). *The Structure and Growth of Residential Neighborhoods in American Cities*, Federal Housing Administration, Washington.

Hoyt, H. (1950). 'Residential sectors revisited'. *The Appraisal Journal*, **27**, 445–450.

Hoyt, H. (1964). 'Recent distortions of the classical models of urban structure'. *Land Economics*, **40**, 199–212.

Hoyt, H. (1966). 'Where the rich and the poor people live'. *Technical Bulletin* No. 55, Urban Land Institute, Washington, D. C.

Hunter, A. (1971). 'The ecology of Chicago: persistence and change, 1930–1960'. *American Journal of Sociology*, **77**, 425–444.

Hunter, A. (1974). 'Community change: a stochastic analysis of Chicago's local communities, 1930–1960'. *American Journal of Sociology*, **79**, 923–947.

Hurd, R. M. (1903). *Principles of City Land Values*, The Record and the Guide, New York

Janson, C-G. (1971). 'A preliminary report on Swedish urban spatial structure'. In B. J. L. Berry (Ed.), 'Comparative factorial ecology'. *Economic Geography*, **47**, 249–257.

Johnston, R. J. (1969). 'Zonal and sectoral patterns in Melbourne's residential structure: 1961'. *Land Economics*, **45**, 463–467.

Johnston, R. J. (1970). 'On spatial patterns in the residential structure of cities'. *The Canadian Geographer*, **14**, 361–367.

Johnston, R. J. (1971). *Urban Residential Patterns: An Introductory Review*, G. Bell, London.

Johnston, R. J. (1973). 'Social area change in Melbourne, 1961–1966'. *Australian Geographical Studies*, **11**, 79–98.

Jones, E. (1960). *The Social Geography of Belfast*, Oxford University Press, Oxford.

Krumbein, W. C. (1955). 'Statistical analysis of facies maps'. *Journal of Geology*, **63**, 453–470.

McElrath, D. C. (1962). 'The social areas of Rome: a comparative analysis'. *American Sociological Review*, **27**, 376–391.

McElrath, D. C., and Barkey, J. W. (1964). *Social and Physical Space: Models of Metropolitan Differentiation*, Unpublished paper, Northwestern University, Evanston, Illinois.

McGee, T. G. (1969). 'The social ecology of New Zealand cities: a preliminary investigation'. In J. Forster (Ed.), *Social Process in New Zealand*, Longman Paul, Auckland, pp. 144–183.

Mann, P. H. (1965). *An Approach to Urban Sociology*, Routledge and Kegan Paul, London.

Murdie, R. A. (1969). *Factorial Ecology of Metropolitan Toronto, 1951–1961: An Essay on the Social Geography of the City*, Research Paper No. 116, Department of Geography, University of Chicago, Chicago.

Park, R. E., Burgess, E. W., and McKenzie, R. D. (1925). *The City*. University of Chicago Press, Chicago.

Pfautz, H. W. (1967). *Charles Booth on the City*, University of Chicago Press, Chicago.

Quinn, J. A. (1940a). 'Topical summary of current literature on human ecology'. *American Journal of Sociology*, **46**, 191–226.

Quinn, J. A. (1940b). 'The Burgess zonal hypothesis and its critics'. *American Sociological Review*, **5**, 210–218.

Quinn, J. A. (1950). *Human Ecology*, Prentice-Hall, Englewood Cliffs, New Jersey.

Rees, P. H. (1970). 'Concepts of social space'. In B. J. L. Berry and F. E. Horton (Eds.), *Geographic Perspective on Urban Systems*, Prentice-Hall, Englewood Cliffs. New Jersey, pp. 306–394.

Richardson, H. W., Vipond, J., and Furbey, R. A. (1974). 'Dynamic tests of Hoyt's spatial model'. *Town Planning Review*, **45**, 401–414.

Robson, B. T. (1969). *Urban Analysis*, Cambridge University Press, Cambridge.

Rodwin, L. (1950a). 'The theory of residential growth and structure'. *The Appraisal Journal*, **27**, 295–317.

Rodwin, L. (1950b). 'Rejoinder to Dr. Firey and Dr. Hoyt'. *The Appraisal Journal*, **27**, 454–457.

Salins, P. D. (1971). 'Household location patterns in American metropolitan areas'. In B. J. L. Berry (Ed.), 'Comparative factorial ecology'. *Economic Geography*, **47**, 234–248.

Schnore, L. F. (1965). 'On the spatial structure of cities in the two Americas'. In P. M. Hauser and L. F. Schnore (Eds.). *The Study of Urbanization*, John Wiley, New York, pp. 347–398.

Schwirian, K. P. (1972). 'Analytical convergence in ecological research: factorial analysis, gradient, and sector models'. In D. C. Sweet (Ed.), *Models of Urban Structure*, Heath, Lexington, Massachusetts, pp. 135–158.

Sjoberg, G. (1960). *The Preindustrial City: Past and Present*, The Free Press, New York,

Sweet, D. C. (Ed.) (1972). *Models of Urban Structure*, D. C. Heath, Lexington, Massachusetts.

Timms, D. (1971). *The Urban Mosaic: Towards a Theory of Residential Differentiation*, Cambridge University Press, Cambridge.

Uyeki, E. S. (1964). 'Residential distribution and stratification, 1950–1960'. *American Journal of Sociology*, **69**, 491–498.

Index

(Compiled by Ann P. Barham)
Note: Page numbers in italics refer to maps and diagrams

Acculturation, 43
Ageing of buildings, 135, 137
Algiers
  ethnic residential segregation, 46
America (*see also* Canada; United States)
  Black Power movement, 50
  ethnic residential segregation, 47, 48, 67, 69–73
  middle and upper class housing, 87
  personal space, 102
  public housing and ethnic groups, 60
America, colonial
  occupational housing structure, 83
Analysis of variance, 247–58, 264
Apartheid, 26
Apartments, 100, 105
Asian in-migrants
  attitudes to housing, 60
  segregation in Glasgow, 49, 60, 67, *68*
Assimilation of ethnic groups, 33, 41, 43–4, 57–74, 161
  resistance to, 60–61, 73
Attack functions of ethnic clusters, 49–50
Auckland, New Zealand
  Pacific Islander segregation, 44, 49
Australia (*see also* names of individual cities, e.g. Melbourne)
  changes in housing supply, *116*
  indices of residential dissimilarity, 20
  peripheral ethnic clusters, 59
Autocorrelation, 227, 260–61
Avoidance functions of ethnic clusters, 46–8

Baltimore, Md.
  analysis of spatial form, 259, 261–4
  housing sub-markets, 119, 120, *121*
  intra-urban migration, 178, 180, 182
Banks and banking, 96–7
Barbon, Nicholas, 84, 96
Behaviour
  relation to residential area, 21
Behavioural approach to housing markets, 130–31, 132
Behavioural assimilation, 43
Belfast, N. Ireland
  ethnic residential segregation, 45, 50
  religious residential differentiation, 20, 26, 67, 73
  role of social values in residential differentiation, 247
Benefits of intra-urban migration, 177
Biological analogies, 27–8
Birmingham, England
  council housing, 60, 95, 98, 99
Black Power movement, 50
Boston, Mass.
  role of social values in residential differtiation, 246–7
Brisbane, Australia
  analysis of spatial form, 251
  indices of residential dissimilarity, 20, 21
Britain (*see also* names of individual cities, e.g. London)
  council housing and ethnic in-migrants, 47, 59–60
  ethnic conflict, 50
  ethnic residential segregation, 46–7, 49, 52–3
  housing classes, 35
  housing policy, 35, 60, 96, 98–9
  New Towns, 101–2
  post-war reconstruction, 101–2, 103
  private house-building, 96, 98–9
  private housing finance, 96–7
  residential mobility, 160
  vacancy chains, 142, 143
Building and loan associations, 96–7

Building cycles, 136, 161
Building societies, 96–7

Canada (*see also* names of individual cities, e.g. Toronto)
 analysis of urban spatial form, 251
 changes of housing supply, *116*
 housing statistics, 115
Cartographic display of ethnic group distributions, 58, *62–3*, *65*, *68–72*
Cedar Rapids, Iowa
 intra-urban migration, 175
Census data, 13–14, 194–6, 225–7, 230, 248–53
Centralization, index of, 265
Chain migration, 35
 relation to ethnic residential segregation, 48
Charter group, 42–3
Chicago, Ill.
 analysis of spatial form, 249, 250
 ethnic residential segregation, 41, 49, 56, 61, 66
 house values, 126, 127
 indices of residential dissimilarity, 21
 rebuilding, 91
 spatial pattern changes, 268
 spatial pattern of crime, 238
 zonal model, 239, 240
Chicago School, 27–8
Children
 neighbourhood influence on socialization, 24
Christchurch, New Zealand
 vacancy chains, 144
City size
 relation to social problems, 2
Classification of social areas, 199–200
Classification of urban sub-communities, *see* Social area analysis
Cleveland, Ohio
 ethnic residential segregation, 56
Colony, ethnic
 operation, 57, 62–4
Columbus, Ohio
 vacancy chains, 144
Communities, 14, 23
Community space, 162–3
 movement within, 167–8, *169*, 171–6
 subdivision of, 170–71
Commuting, 90
Concentric model of residential structure, *see* Zonal model of residential structure
Concentric rings of house-building, 161
Concentric spatial pattern of ethnic groups, 61, 64, 67
Conflict, ethnic, 45, 49–50
Construction industry
 instability, 136
Contiguity ratio, 260–63
Core, *see* Inner city
Correlation coefficient
 overinterpretation, 221
Correlation matrix in factorial ecology
 assemby, 203, 208, 220
 factoring, 208, 214–6
Cosa Nostra in American cities, 48
Cost of residential movement, 165, 177
Covariance analysis, 228–9
Crime
 in ethnic clusters, 47–8
 spatial pattern in Chicago, 238
Cross-products components analysis, 228–9
Culture, ethnic
 preservation, 48–9

Data set in segregation analysis, 52
Data smoothing techniques, 258–9, 264
Data sources, 13, 194–6, 225–7, 230, 248–53
Data sub-set in segregation analysis, 52–3
Decision making
 in housing provision, 130–31, 132
 in intra-urban migration, 30–36, 176–80
Defensive functions of ethnic clusters, 45–6
Discrimination in housing markets, 146–7
Distance from city centre
 relation to residential differentiation, 253–4, 259–60
Dutch
 in Kalamazoo, 62–4

Ecology, urban, 27–8
Economic classes
 housing provision contrasts, 85–90
Economic competition
 role in residential differentiation, 27–8
Economic market housing provision, 98, 99–100
Economic standards for housing provision, 85–90
Edinburgh, Scotland
 sectoral spatial model, 268
Employers
 housing provision by, 83

Employment
  proximity to housing, 86
Enclave, Jewish
  in American cities, 64–6
Enclave-ghetto, 57, 64–74
England (*see also* names of individual cities, e.g. London)
  working class housing, 86
Entrepreneurs, ethnic, 47
Enumeration district, 195
Estate agents
  role in housing markets, 10–11, 185, 186
Ethclass segregation, 55–6, 66, 73
Ethnic group
  assimilation, 33, 41, 43–4, 57–74, 161
  definition, 41–3
  housing market discrimination, 146–7
  in-migration
    spatial outcomes, 56–74
  social stratification, 55–6
Ethnic homogeneity
  desirable levels, 54–5, 74
Ethnic identity
  preservation, 48–9
Ethnic institutions, 44, 46
Ethnic residential segregation, 9–10, 20–21, 26, 41–79, 100, 163
  analysis
    scale problems, 52–3
  attack functions, 49–50
  avoidance functions, 46–8
  cartographic record, 58, *62–3*, *65*, *68–72*
  clusters-within-clusters, 217–8
  defensive functions, 45–6
  definitions, 51–2
  housing fabric effects, 58–61
  policy approach, 74–6
  preservation functions, 48–9
  social and ethnic causes, 56
  spatial patterns, 57–74, 256, *266*, 267
  voluntary, 66, 67, 74
Ethnic status
  influence on residential location, 217
Europe
  middle and upper class housing, 87, 108
  personal space, 102
  post-war housing policy, 103–4
  working class housing, 86
Externalities, 6–9, 145–6

Factor analysis, 208, 228–9
Factorial ecology, 13–14, 202–30, 265–8
  areas used, 225–7
  overinterpretation problems, 221–5
  procedures, 203–16, 228–9
  results, 216–9
  spatiotemporal, 219
Family life-cycle
  influence on residential location, 217
  relation to intra-urban migration, 31–2, 168, 171–6, 178
Family status
  zonal spatial variation, 250, 255, *266*, 267
Filtering in housing markets, 138, 140–41, 244
  relation to vacancy chains, 143–4
Financial institutions
  behaviour in housing sub-markets, 119, 120, *121*
  role in urban morphological development, 10, 11, 96–7, 163
Fourier analysis, 259–64

Garden City, Long Island, 93
Garden City movement, 91, 92–3
Gatekeepers, *see* Urban gatekeepers
Gentrification, 11
Germany
  small holdings round cities, 108
  suburbanization, 95
Ghetto (*see also* Enclave-ghetto), 57
  as guerilla warfare base, 50
  Jewish, 45, 46, 48–9, 83
  security of, 47
Glasgow, Scotland
  Asian segregation, 49, 60, 67, *68*
  public housing, 32
  vacancy chains, 144
Government
  role in housing markets, 10, 11, 35
  role in housing provision, 83, 89–90, 92–5, 98–9, 100–109
Grand Rapids, Michigan
  ethnic enclave-ghetto, 69–73
Grid pattern in analysis of variance studies, 248, *252*
Guerilla warfare
  urban, 46, 50

Hampstead Garden Suburb, 93
Health hazards of high housing densities, 86, 88
High-rise construction, 148
Homestead Act, 88–9
Homogeneity, ethnic, 53–5, 74
House-building trade (*see also* Housing construction), 84

House prices
changes, *117*, 140–41
effect on vacancy chains, 189
spatial variability, 125–8
Household characteristics
use in sub-market identification, 121, *122*
Household location, *see* Housing markets; Migration, intra-urban; Residential location choice
Housewives
neighbourhood influence on social interaction, 25–6
Housing
alternative study methods, 111–2
as social problem, 144–9
attitudes to, 148
competition for, 6
properties, 114–5, 116–7
Housing characteristics
spatial pattern, 241
Housing classes, 35
Housing construction, 136–8
high-rise revolution, 148
multiplier effects, 141–4
Housing demand, 123
Housing densities
concentric ring pattern, 161–2
Housing expenditure
income elasticities, 124
Housing markets (*see also* Residential location choice), 10–12, 58–61, 111–50
definition, 113–4
discrimination, 61, 146–7
failures and imperfections, 144–9, 185–91
operation, 123–31
behavioural studies, 130–31, 132
instabilities, 136
micro-economic models, 123–8
urban development models, 128–30
structural adjustments, 133–5
Housing policies
conflict with social attitudes, 148–9
Housing provision
by economic unit, 83, 87
historical development, 82–109
welfare concept, 87–8
Housing services
components, 112–3
Housing space, 162
Housing stock
changes, 131, 133–4
characteristics
influence on house prices, 125–7
use in sub-market identification, 121, *122*
definition, 112
national statistics, 115
Housing stress, 176–7
Housing sub-markets
delineation, 116–22
effect of new construction, 136–7
Housing supply, 111–50
changes, *116*, 133–8
impact of social attitudes, 147–9
problems, 145–6
Housing units, 82
Howard, Ebenezer, 90–91
Huddersfield, England
Asian population, 53

Immigrants
spatial segregation, *see* Ethnic residential segregation
Income
relation to length of intra-urban migration, 166
Index construction in social area analysis, 197, 198, 199–200
Index of centralization, 265
Index of residential dissimilarity, 20–21
Index of sector concentration, 265
Index of segregation, 52, 53
Industrialization
effect on housing provision, 85–8
Inequalities, 6, 8
in housing supply, 145–6
Information on housing opportunities, 34–5, 181–3, 185–7
In-migrants
residential clustering, 185–7
In-migrants, ethnic, *see* Ethnic groups; Ethnic residential segregation
Inner city
enclave-ghetto development, 66–7, 68–9
housing for ethnic in-migrants, 59, 100
overcrowding, 93–6
residential mobility rates, 164–5
Institutions (*see also* Estate agents; Ethnic institutions; Financial institutions; Government; Welfare institutions)
influence on city form, 81–109
Interaction effect in analysis of variance, 253–5
International variations in housing, 114, 115
Inter-urban migration, *see* Migration, inter-urban

Intra-urban migration, *see* Migration, intra-urban
Invasion, ethnic
  resistance to, 44
Ireland, *see* Northern Ireland
Irish clusters in England and America, 50
Italians
  in America, 48
  in Toronto, 256
  in Wellington, New Zealand, 48, 64
Italy
  medieval city republics, 83

Jewish enclaves in American cities, 64–6
Jewish ghetto, 45, 46, 48–9, 83
Jews
  in Toronto, 256
  in 'Yankee City', 44

Kalamazoo, Mich.
  Dutch households, 62–4

Land costs, 94–6, 98, 99, 104–5, *117*
Land uses
  spatial separation, 2–3
Leeds, England,
  house values, 127
Letchworth Garden City, England, 93
Llandudno, Wales
  early development, 30
London, England
  council housing, 92, 93, 95, 99
  economic and physical growth, 84
  ethnic residential segregation, 53, 56, 61
  house values, 127
  inter-war private house-building, 98–9
  middle and upper class housing, 87
  philanthropic housing, 89, 97
  slum clearance, 89
  vacancy chains, 144

Maps of ethnic group distribution, 58, *62–3*, *65*, *68–72*
Measurement of segregation, 52–3
Medieval housing, 83, 87
Melbourne, Australia
  analysis of spatial form, 250
  factorial ecology, 221
Mental maps of social areas, 8, 13
Micro-economic models of housing markets, 123–8
Middle and upper class housing, 86–7, 88, 108
Migration, inter-urban, 13, 185–7, 217
Migration, intra-urban (*see also* Residential location choice), 12–13, 159–91
  decision making, 176–80
  distance moved, 166–9, 183–4
  origins and destinations, 165–70, 171–6
  processes involved, 180–85
  reasons for, 176–80
  relation to residential structure, 160–64, 217
  sectoral pattern, 160–61, 164, 168
Minneapolis, Minn.
  housing markets, 136, *137*
  in-migrants, 185, 186
  intra-urban migration, 12, *167*, *169*, 170–76, 183–5
  vacancy chains, 187–8
Minority groups
  spatial segregation (*see also* Ethnic groups; Ethnic residential segregation), 9–10, 163
Models of urban community, 19–20
Models of urban spatial form, 237–69
Montreal, Quebec
  analysis of spatial form, 258–9
Mosque
  welfare functions, 47
Multiple nuclei model of residential structure, 245–6, 258–9
Neighbourhood
  change, 267–8
  characteristics
    as cause of migration, 177–9, 181
    influence on house prices, 125–7
    use in sub-market identification, 121, *122*
  homogeneity, 162
  identity development, 33
  life-cycles, 137–8, 139
  social influence, 23–7, 33–4
  status
    spatial pattern, 162–3
New Deal, 100–101
New Haven, Conn.
  house values, 127
  vacancy chains, 144
New York, N.Y.
  government role in housing provision, 89–90
  inter-war apartment housing, 100
  vacancy chains, 144
New Zealand
  changes in housing supply, *116*
  ethnic residential segregation, 44, 48, 49

Newburyport, Mass.
ethnic institutions, 44
Non-industrialized cities
spatial form, 241
Northern Ireland
council housing and Catholics, 60
ethnic residential segregation, 45–6, 50, 59

Objective approach to residential differentiation, 22–3
Occupational categories
residential differentiation, 21
Occupational housing provision, 83, 87
Old people
residential concentration and social interaction, 24–5
Opportunities
neighbourhood influence, 26–7
Organic city evolution, 82
Overcrowding, 108–9
Owner occupiers, 113, 189

Pacific Islanders
segregation of in Auckland, 44, 49
Pakistanis
segregation of in Britain, 49
Paris, France
public housing, 95
transport problems, 94
Partial displacement migration, 186–7
Peripheral sites
low cost, 94–6, 98–100
Personal contact
role in residential location choice, 35, 182
Personal space, 88, 90, 102, 108–9
Philanthropic housing, 92, 97
Physical form of cities, 81
Planning legislation, 11
Policies towards ethnic residential segregation, 74–6
Polish ethnic clusters
resistance to black invasion, 73
Political housing districts
medieval, 83
Political representation of ethnic groups, 49–50
Population concentration
relation to social problems, 1–2
Population growth
influence on housing, 84–5, 86
Population mobility, *see* Migration
Preservation functions of ethnic clusters, 48–9
Principal components analysis, 206–8, *210–13*, 214–6
Property values, 8, 10–11, *117*, 125–8, 140–41, 189
Public housing, 11, 89–90, 92–5, 98–9, 103, 106–8
and ethnic groups, 59–60
construction
effect on vacancy chains, 187–9
influence on residential mobility, 159–60, 163
stigmatization of, 32

Reading, England
house values, 127
Real estate agents, *see* Estate agents
Regression analysis, 259–61
Religious residential differentiation, 20, 26, 45–6, 50, 59
Rent
influence on residential differentiation, 27
Rental areas
sectoral spatial pattern, *242*, 243–4
Rental housing
development of need for, 84
Research design in urban spatial analysis, 257
Residential alternatives
information on, 34–5
Residential development, 130–31, 132
Residential differentiation, 19–37
analysis and description, 13–14, 193–230
factorial ecology, 202–30
social area analysis, 13–14, 29–30, 196–202
use of census data, 194–6, 225–7, 230
dynamic equilibrium, 12, 36
effects, 23–7
explanations, 27–36, 196–202
classical urban ecology approach, 27–8
social area analysis approach, 13–14, 29–30, 196–202
social values approach, 28, 246–7
urban gatekeeper approach, 30–36
factors influencing, 5–15
measurement, 20–22
models, 237–69
objective and subjective approaches, 22–3
processes involved, 30–36
temporal pattern, 219

validity of popular images, 19–20
Residential dissimilarity, index of, 20–21
Residential location choice (*see also* Housing markets; Migration, intra-urban)
constraints, 145
economic criteria, 10–12, 34–6, 58–9
impact of housing supply changes, 141–4
importance of for ethnic groups, 75
influence of accessibility, 32, 34
physical criteria, 31
social criteria, 6–10, 32–4
Residential mixing, 51
Residential mobility (*see also* Migration), 159–91
rates of, 164–5, *166*
relation of family structure, 31–2
role in social mobility, 32–3
Residential opportunities
access to, 35
Residential search behaviour, 181–4
Residential structure
impact of high-rise revolution, 148
relation to intra-urban migration, 160–64
Ring-and-sector residential structure, 160–64
Riverside, Ill., 93
Roman Catholics
distribution in N. Ireland, 59, 67, 73
Rome, Italy
analysis of spatial form, 249, 256

St. Louis, Mo.
house values, 126
resistance to Negro assimilation, 60–61
Scale, spatial, 14, 52–3, 226
Scotland (*see also* Edinburgh; Glasgow)
working class housing, 86
Sector concentration, index of, 265
Sectoral mobility patterns, 160–61, 164, 168
Sectoral model of residential structure, 241–5
evaluation, 246–69
limitations, 244–5
Sectoral spatial pattern of ethnic groups, 61, 64, 67, 69–73, 163, 256, 268
Security
relation to ethnic homogeneity, 45–6
Segregation, *see* Ethnic residential segregation
Segregation, index of, 52, 53
Shape of city
effect on residential structure and migration, 163
Size of city
effect on migration patterns, 163, 168, 170
Skid Row, 218
Slum clearance, 89–90, 94, 101
Social advancement, 7
Social area analysis, 13–14, 29–30, 196–202, 265–8
Social area indices
use in analysis of variance studies, 248, 249, 251
Social attitudes
influence on housing supply, 147–9
relation to residential area, 21
Social class
contribution to ethnic segregation, 56
influence on intra-urban migration, 166–8
Social classes
conflict between, 6–8
Social distance
correlation with ethnic residential segregation, 44
Social environment
competition for, 6–8, 32–4
Social groups
imprecise boundaries, 193–4
Social interaction
relation to ethnic homogeneity, 74
relation to spatial proximity, 7, 23–7, 33–4
Social mobility
role of residential mobility, 32–3
Social problems, 1–4, 19, 21
Social space, 162
Social status
relation to intra-urban migration, 171–6
Social stratification of ethnic groups, 55–6
Social structure, 162
Social values
role in residential differentiation, 28, 246–7
Social welfare housing provision, 98–9
Socio-economic status
in factorial ecology, 223–5
influence on residential location, 217
sectoral spatial variation, 243–4, 249–51, 255–6, *266*, 267, 268
Space problem in cities, 90–96
Space requirements as cause of migration, 177, 178, 180–81
Spatial allocation of households
models, of, 128–9

Spatial differentation, *see* Residential differentation
Spatial form, urban, *see* Urban spatial form models
Spatial outcomes of ethnic in-migration, 56–74
Statistical and mathematical techniques
  use in explaining spatial form, 247–65
Status
  competition for, 7
Stigmatization of public housing, 32
Street-car
  role in urban morphological development, 93
Structural assimilation, 43
Subjective approach to residential differentiation, 22–3
Substitution
  housing sub-markets, 116–7
Suburb
  original meaning, 83
Suburban estates, 32
Suburbanization, 87, 88, 91, 92, 93–6, 98–100, 102, 139
Suburbs
  residential mobility rates, 165
  security in, 45–6
Swansea, Wales
  residential mobility, 160
Sweden
  housing statistics, 115
Synagogue
  in 'Yankee City', 44

Techniques in urban analysis, 193–230, 247–65
Telephone directories
  use in migration studies, 170
Territoriality, 9, 26–7, 45–50
Tipping-point, 54
Toronto, Ontario
  analysis of spatial form, 248, 250, *252*, 253–7
  ethnic residential segregation, 56
  housing sub-market changes, 133, 135
  intra-urban migration, 176, 178, 179, 180, 183, 184
  19th century social geography, 268
  socio-economic status, 223–5
  vacancy chains, 143, 144
Total displacement migration, 186
Transportation
  influence on housing, 90, 93, 94, 95, 96, 98, 100, 103–4, 105, 136

Ulster, *see* Northern Ireland
United Kingdom (*see also* names of individual cities, e.g. London)
  house price changes, *117*
  housing statistics, 115
United States (*see also* names of individual cities, e.g. Chicago)
  analyses of urban spatial form, 249
  census areas, 195
  changes in housing supply, *116*
  economic market housing provision, 98, 99–100
  ethnic residential segregation, 56
  housing market discrimination, 147
  housing statistics, 115
  indices of residential dissimilarity, 20–21
  inter-war housing policy, 100–101
  intra-urban migration, 166–7
  post-war apartment housing, 105
  post-war housing policy, 104–6
  private housing finance, 96–7
  public housing, 32, 106, 107–8
  residential mobility rates, 164, *166*
  sectoral rental patterns, *242*, 243–4
  vacancy chains, 144
  working class housing, 86
United States Federal Home Loan Bank System, 100
United States Federal Housing Administration, 101, 241, 244
United States Reconstruction Finance Corporation, 101
Urban development cycles, 135–8
Urban development models, 128–30
Urban gatekeepers, 35
Urban growth
  containment of, 101–2, 103–4
Urban social problems, 1–4, 21
Urban spatial form
  analysis and description, 13–14, 29–30, 193–230
  as cause of social problems, 2–3
  factors influencing, 5–15
Urban spatial form models, 237–69
  empirical testing, 246–65
    by analysis of variance, 247–58, 264
    by data smoothing, 258–9, 264
    by Fourier analysis, 259–64
  integration with social area-factorial eco-

logy constructs, 265–8
multiple nuclei, 245–6
sectoral, 241–5
zonal, 238–41

Vacancy chains, 141–4, 187–9
relation to filtering, 143–4
Variable selection
in factorial ecology, 203, 220, 222
in social area analysis, 197
Variation
systematic and random, 260–61, 263–4
Varimax procedure, 206–7, *211–3*, 214–6
Venice, Italy
Jewish ghetto, 83
Violence in ethnic clusters, 49–50
Voluntary segregation, 66, 67, 74

Walled cities, 94
Warsaw Ghetto, 46
Welfare concept of housing provision, 87–8, 98–9
Welfare institutions, 47
Wellington, New Zealand
ethnic residential segregation, 48, 64
Welwyn Garden City, England, 93
West Indian in-migrants
attitudes to council housing, 60
segregation of in England, 46–7, 56
Whangarei, New Zealand
factorial ecology, 203–16
Winnipeg, Manitoba
ethnic residential segregation, 44, *65*, 66
Working class housing, 85–6, 88–90, 92–103

'Yankee City', 44

Zonal model of residential structure, 238–41
evaluation, 246–69
limitations, 240–41